FOOTBALL
FANS
GUIDE

The ultimate football travel book

FOOTBALL
FANS
GUIDE

The ultimate football travel book

Mark Bisson

FOOTBALL FANS GUIDE
The ultimate football travel book

© 2007 Mark Bisson
Mark Bisson has asserted his rights in accordance with the Copyright, Designs and Patents Act 1988 to be identified as the author of this work.

Published By:
Pitch Publishing (Brighton) Ltd
A2 Yeoman Gate
Yeoman Way
Worthing
BN13 3QZ
Email: info@pitchpublishing.co.uk
Web: www.pitchpublishing.co.uk

First published 2007

A catalogue record for this book is available from the British Library.

10-digit ISBN: 1905411073
13-digit ISBN: 978-1905411078

Images Action Images: Cover; Wembley Stadium: P36-39

Design & layout: Swallow Company

Printed and bound in Great Britain by Cromwell Press

Contents

Setting out   8

In this section you'll find vital information to help plan your away trip; including how to avoid the tailbacks and delays, and how to save money on petrol, rail fares and flights.

Pitstops   14

Ensure you arrive refreshed and relaxed for the match by using our detailed guide to find the best pubs, cafés, hotels and supermarkets close to the major motorways - plus where you can find the best service areas across the UK.

City guides   22

Here you'll find extended guides to London, Birmingham, Manchester, Newcastle, Liverpool, Nottingham, Bristol, Southampton and Brighton, detailing hotels, restaurants, bars, pubs, clubs and other entertainment.

Head office   36

If you're heading to the new national stadium, then check out our in-depth detailed guide to Wembley Stadium, its facilities and what's on offer in the surrounding area.

Club-by-club guides   40

92 comprehensively researched guides to every Premiership and Football League club. Listed alphabetically, you'll find all the details about the stadiums, plus information on the surrounding area: parking, pubs, restaurants, hotels and what else is on offer locally.

What's the number one club in England?

Accrington Stanley, no doubt about it.

Our A-to-Y club guide begins on page 40.

Acknowledgements

Richard Walker for an excellent editing job; Jon Vallance for his assistance in supplying various data and stats; Bill and Jan Swallow for the design and proof reading; Paul at Pitch for his invaluable assistance; Lucy Cotton at Wembley; Steve Tinniswood for his northern insights; press officers at many Premiership and Football League clubs (too many to mention but all a great help); and Paul Wootton for his knowledge of the bar scene nationwide.

introduction

WE'VE ALL HAD THOSE TERRIBLE AWAY TRIPS. YOU KNOW, THE ONE WHERE you're stuck in a tailback miles from the ground as the clock ticks ever closer to three o'clock; or so delayed by 'essential engineering works' that you miss your connection.

The game is already ten minutes old by the time your train pulls in; or you can hear the teams running out as your frantic hunt for the only parking space in a three-mile radius finally ends.

Even then the nightmare's not over: the heavens open and unleash a downpour... and nobody told you it would be uncovered seating in the away end.

The journey home's not much better: after eventually getting away from the crowds all you find is overpriced stale leftovers at some dreary roadside services for tea... and (of course) to top it all off your team are awful and get stuffed.

Help is at hand: while The Football Fans' Guide can't guarantee a successful away record over the course of the season, it does have all the information you need to make your trip a success off the pitch... and more importantly save you a small fortune along the way.

Comprehensively researched, there's all the details you'd expect for every Premiership and Football League club, their grounds and how to find them - but there's also information on the surrounding area: the decent pubs, restaurants and hotels, where's good to park and (if you're planning a weekend) what else our football towns and cities have to offer.

The Football Fans' Guide also has two added bonus sections, which will really help cut costs:

Setting Out has vital information on planning your journey. Car drivers can learn to avoid the tailbacks, save at the pump and ensure they arrive in time for kick-off. Train travellers can avoid high prices and potential delays - but also slash their rail fares week after week. And whatever your team's position in the league, anyone can become a high flier with our guide to UK domestic budget flights.

And the Pit Stops section will ensure you arrive at the game refreshed and (hopefully) relaxed. Detailing the best of the UK's service areas, and some of the worst, in order to avoid them, Pit Stops also lists a plethora of alternative refreshment stops, just a few minutes from the UK's major motorways. Including a number of pubs, cafés, hotels and supermarkets - each listed by motorway - to help you avoid the potential expensive service stations.

Whatever the new season brings (promotion, relegation, mid-table mediocrity, pleasure, pain) make sure your travel choices are champion throughout the campaign... and if you are one of the lucky ones whose season ends in success, our guide to the new Wembley is on page 36.

Setting out

Hit the road

If you're embarking on an away trip, there's nothing up more frustrating than ending up bumper to bumper in a jam for half an hour. Check out these useful websites and phone numbers to help you avoid the traffic blackspots and improve journey times.

Automobile Association (www.theaa.com)
AA Roadwatch offers live traffic reports for motorways and A-roads wherever you are. Call the AA's traffic and weather information line on 09003 401 100 or 401 100 from your mobile. You can also set up SMS traffic alerts on your mobile. AA Roadwatch will monitor your route and tell you about delays before you leave.

On the website, you can also plan quickest routes and search for AA-inspected pubs and restaurants. Breakdown cover (existing members): 08705 444 444

RAC (www.rac.co.uk)
The RAC offers similar services. Its route planner preferences allow you to plan the shortest (by mileage), fastest (by road type) and also how much you want to use motorways. You can get the Routeplanner and Mileage Calculator on your desktop with the RAC Widget. The website also offers live traffic news by region, so you can find out about the latest incidents or roadworks before you set off.

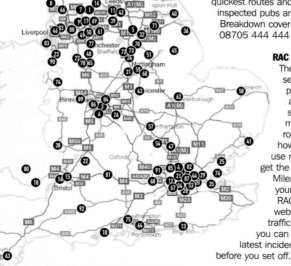

JOURNEY-PLANNING

Numbers refer to clubs in alphabetical order. See individual entries.

RAC Customer services (08705 722 722)

	Birmingham	Brighton	Bristol	Cardiff	Carlisle	Hereford	Hull	Leeds	Lincoln	Liverpool	Manchester	Middlesbrough	Newcastle	Northampton	Norwich	Nottingham	Oxford	Peterborough	Plymouth	Portsmouth	Preston	Sheffield	Shrewsbury	Southampton	Stoke-on-Trent
Brighton	171																								
Bristol	90	169																							
Cardiff	109	202	44																						
Carlisle	199	376	281	300																					
Hereford	59	189	54	59	250																				
Hull	139	258	230	250	170	198																			
Leeds	120	262	211	230	123	179	59																		
Lincoln	98	216	185	205	182	154	44	74																	
Liverpool	101	278	182	202	126	151	128	74	139																
Manchester	89	266	171	190	120	139	97	44	85	34															
Middlesbrough	176	318	267	286	95	235	89	64	122	145	114														
Newcastle	207	349	298	317	60	266	142	95	154	176	145	39													
Northampton	56	133	115	162	249	111	152	136	94	151	139	189	220												
Norwich	160	168	233	266	282	215	147	174	103	240	185	223	254	118											
Nottingham	51	193	142	161	189	110	93	77	39	112	71	130	161	64	119										
Oxford	68	109	73	107	274	81	190	174	132	176	164	227	258	44	146	102									
Peterborough	86	158	173	193	229	142	110	121	51	159	132	170	201	45	78	58	86								
Plymouth	205	218	124	153	397	169	346	334	301	298	287	382	413	257	364	257	196	288							
Portsmouth	154	53	125	158	360	152	276	260	215	262	250	313	344	130	204	188	85	157	172						
Preston	110	287	191	211	89	160	122	69	134	36	35	103	139	159	235	121	184	180	306	270					
Sheffield	91	233	182	201	161	150	66	38	47	79	39	100	131	104	148	45	142	93	297	228	73				
Shrewsbury	48	226	130	111	181	52	162	119	124	65	71	190	221	98	203	87	123	129	245	209	92	88			
Southampton	135	66	106	140	342	133	258	241	199	243	232	294	325	111	204	169	67	157	152	20	252	209	191		
Stoke-on-Trent	48	226	130	150	156	99	129	93	91	57	46	164	195	98	172	54	123	99	245	209	66	50	38	191	
LONDON	121	54	120	153	314	136	186	201	143	216	204	254	285	68	118	129	56	86	241	75	225	169	163	77	161

Setting out

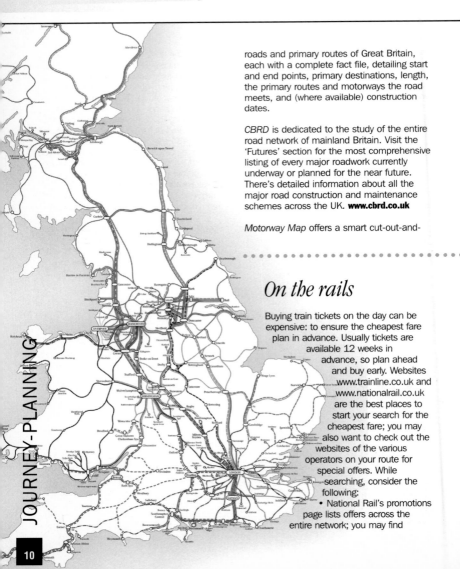

roads and primary routes of Great Britain, each with a complete fact file, detailing start and end points, primary destinations, length, the primary routes and motorways the road meets, and (where available) construction dates.

CBRD is dedicated to the study of the entire road network of mainland Britain. Visit the 'Futures' section for the most comprehensive listing of every major roadwork currently underway or planned for the near future. There's detailed information about all the major road construction and maintenance schemes across the UK. **www.cbrd.co.uk**

Motorway Map offers a smart cut-out-and-

On the rails

Buying train tickets on the day can be expensive: to ensure the cheapest fare plan in advance. Usually tickets are available 12 weeks in advance, so plan ahead and buy early. Websites www.trainline.co.uk and www.nationalrail.co.uk are the best places to start your search for the cheapest fare; you may also want to check out the websites of the various operators on your route for special offers. While searching, consider the following:
• National Rail's promotions page lists offers across the entire network; you may find

keep map of England, Scotland and Wales, turned into a handy London Underground-style graphic. **www.motorwaymap.co.uk**

Transport Direct offers information for door-to-door travel for public transport and car journeys. It provides easy-to-use information to help you plan your journeys effectively and efficiently. **www.transportdirect.info**

The Highways Agency, which is responsible for managing, maintaining and improving the strategic road network in England, has a useful site if you want to find out more about a particular roadwork project. *For live traffic 24hr updates call 08700 660 115* **www.highways.gov.uk**

If you don't fancy the drive, check out the *National Express* site for coachcards and low-cost fares. Book and pay online and print your ticket. **www.nationalexpress.com** *or 08705 80 80 80*

PLUSBUS is a bus ticket that you buy with your train ticket. It gives unlimited bus travel around town, at the start, finish or both ends of your train journey. With a valid ticket you can make as many journeys as you like on all participating bus operators' services. It's now available for over 200 towns. You can change between train and bus services at more than 270 selected train stations. For more info on the schemes that operate visit **www.plusbus.info**

splitting your journey to take advantage of offers along the way saves a fortune. Check www.moneysavingexpert.com travel section for more info on where to split your journey.

- Consider a railcard if you're under 26, a senior citizen or travelling with children. You may find railcards can even pay for themselves on one or two journeys. Check out www.railcard.co.uk.
- If you're travelling during peak time, only pay for the portion of your journey that is during peak time.
- Check out www.megatrain.com. It's mainly cut-price bus travel on offer, but if you book early enough you can get inter-city train (or bus) tickets here from a few pounds.

National Rail's website also has details on engineering works and any possible delays – plus live arrival and departure boards. (For details on using London Underground check out our London Guide on page 32).

UK train operators

Arriva Trains (regional routes in Wales) **www.arrivatrainswales.co.uk** / Sales: 08709 000 773

Central Trains (regional routes in Midlands) **www.centraltrains.co.uk** / Sales: 0870 609 60 60

First Great Western (S & W England, Cotswolds and Sth Wales) **www.firstgreatwestern.co.uk** / Sales: 08457 000 125

Gatwick Express (only non-stop London Vic - Gatwick service) **www.gatwickexpress.com** / Sales: 0845 850 15 30

Heathrow Connect (direct access to Heathrow from stations incl Hayes, Southall, Hanwell, West Ealing, Ealing Broadway and Paddington. **www.heathrowconnect.com** / 0845 678 6975

Hull Trains (Hull - London King's Cross services).

Setting out

On the rails

www.hulltrains.co.uk / 08450 710222

Merseyrail (Liverpool and Merseyside)
www.merseyrail.org / 0151 702 2071

Northern Rail (north of England)
www.northernrail.org / 0845 00 00 125

Silverlink (Northampton/Milton Keynes/Watford areas - London Euston) **www.silverlink-trains.com** / Sales: 08705 125 240

South West Trains (London Waterloo - south coast & south west) **www.southwesttrains.co.uk** / Sales : 0845 6000 650

Transpennine Express www.tpexpress.co.uk / Sales: 0845 678 6974

Chiltern Railways M40 corridor between London and Birmingham, Aylesbury, Stratford **www.chilternrailways.co.uk** / Sales: 08456 005 165

First Capital Connect (connecting Brighton, Bedford, Peterborough, Cambridge and King's

JOURNEY-PLANNING

NEWCASTLE 🛪
🛪 DURHAM TEES VALLEY

BLACKPOOL 🛪
🛪 LEEDS BRADFORD
DONCASTER SHEFFIELD
🛪 🛪 HUMBERSIDE
🛪 MANCHESTER
LIVERPOOL

NORWICH 🛪
🛪 EAST MIDLANDS
🛪 BIRMINGHAM
COVENTRY 🛪
LUTON 🛪 🛪 STANSTED
CARDIFF
🛪 LONDON CITY
🛪 BRISTOL HEATHROW 🛪 🛪
🛪 GATWICK
🛪 SOUTHAMPTON
🛪 EXETER BOURNEMOUTH

Jetting to the footie

Airport sites: general
www.airportguides.co.uk Directions to and details of 70+ airports in UK and Ireland. Useful links.
www.airport-maps.co.uk One-stop resource incl flight booking details and rail connections.
www.uk-airport-news.info Daily airport updates; includes parking and hotels.
www.a2btravel.com Parking, hotels and directions including public transport.
www.airport-hotels-guide.co.uk Hotel price comparisons.
www.1stairportparking.co.uk Parking price comparisons.
Airport sites: specific
London
Gatwick www.gatwickairport.com
Heathrow www.heathrowairport.com
City www.londoncityairport.com
Stansted www.stanstedairport.com
Luton www.london-luton.co.uk
Midlands
Birmingham www.bhx.co.uk
Coventry www.coventryairport.co.uk
East Midlands www.eastmidlandsairport.com

Lynn via London) **www.firstcapitalconnect.co.uk** / 0845 026 4700

GNER (from London to north east and Scotland) **www.gner.co.uk** Sales : 08457 225 225

Heathrow Express (From London Paddington every 15 mins) **www.heathrowexpress.com** Telesales: 0845 600 15 15

Midland Mainline (M1 corridor from Sth Yorkshire to St Pancras) **www.midlandmainline.com** / Sales: 08457 125 678

One (London Liverpool St to E of England) **www.onerailway.com** / Telesales: 0845 600 7245

Southeastern **www.southeasternrailway.co.uk** 0845 000 2222

Southern (Sth London plus central London - Sussex/Kent coast) **www.southernrailway.com** Sales : 08451 27 29 20

Virgin Trains (W Coast main line & routes radiating from Birm) **www.virgintrains.co.uk** / Sales: 08457 222 333; enqs: 0870 010 1127

Norwich www.norwichinternational.com
North
Blackpool www.blackpoolinternational.com
Doncaster Finningley www.robinhoodairport.com
Humberside www.humberside-airport.co.uk
Leeds/Bradford www.lbia.co.uk
Sheffield www.sheffieldcityairport.com
Durham www.durhamteesvalleyairport.com
Liverpool John Lennon www.liverpoolairport.com
Manchester www.manchesterairport.co.uk
Newcastle www.newcastleairport.com
South
Bournemouth www.flybournemouth.com
Bristol www.bristolairport.co.uk
Plymouth www.plymouthairport.com
Exeter www.exeter-airport.co.uk
Southampton www.southamptonairport.com
Wales
Cardiff www.cwlfly.com

Low-cost airline sites
▓ **Bmibaby** Flights between Manchester and Newquay, E Mid and Edinburgh, Glasgow. **www.bmibaby.com** / 0871 224 0224
▓ **EasyJet** Stansted - Newcastle; Newcastle - Bristol. **www.easyjet.com** / 0905 821 0905
▓ **Flybe** Big coverage: Exeter, Manchester, Newcastle, Leeds/Bradford, Norwich, Southampton, Liverpool. **www.flybe.com** / 0871 522 6100
▓ **Jet2** Includes Gatwick - Newcastle. **www.jet2.com** / 0871 226 1737
▓ **Ryanair** Stansted - Newquay and Stansted - Blackpool. **www.ryanair.com** / 0871 246 0000

▓ **British Airways** Gatwick - Newquay/Manchester; Heathrow - Manchester/Newcastle. Not cheap but reduce pain by booking early. **www.britishairways.com** / 0870 850 9850

General public transport sites

www.tfl.gov.uk Transport for London's guide to getting around the capital using all modes of public transport. **www.traveline.org.uk** Quote... UK's No.1 website for impartial information on planning your journey, by bus, coach or train... or any combination of the three... unquote / 0871 200 22 33

Pit stops / services

If you're burning up the tarmac to reach a far-flung destination, there's nothing more galling than stopping off at a motorway service station only to find that everything's ludicrously overpriced, and coffee goes by the name skinny latte. Shelling out for an over-packaged poor quality sandwich, posh coffee, substandard service and expensive petrol hikes up the cost of your round trip - especially when all you really want is a decent sandwich, sausage roll or cup of tea.

Three motorway service operators dominate the industry - Moto, Welcome Break and Roadchef. Moto is the biggest, running over forty service areas, while the other two each operate about thirty. In recent years, they've pumped millions into revamping and expanding the facilities and food they offer. There's no doubt these motorway service providers are upping their game – but it is a slow process. You can visit their respective websites to find out more.

Moto, for instance, promises 'a wide choice of products and services, great value for money'. You can sample the delights of Burger King and Marks & Spencer outlets at some of the stop-offs. The websites of Welcome Break and Roadchef list their facilities in a similar way. But the reality is that most services operated by this gang of three remain a drain on finances and are best avoided. A bit of judicious planning can help slash costs for food and fuel stops over the course of the season. However, if you do prefer the hassle-free approach of the motorway service station, the Football Fans' Guide recommends the following:

1 / M1: Newport Pagnell
Operated by Welcome Break, between junctions 14 and 15
The M1 has plenty of service areas, and the

Numbers refer to pitstops on this and following pages.

two operated by Welcome Break – Newport Pagnell and Leicester Forest East at junction 21a (although this is to be demolished to make way for road improvements) – are the best of the bunch. The two Welcome Break areas are pretty similar in layout and the facilities offered. Both are clean & comfortable and in addition to the standard restaurant, there are fast-food joints in the shape of KFC and Burger King – but be aware that they often close before 9pm on Saturday nights.

Northampton services at junction 15a isn't far behind these two: it's modern, well appointed and boosts an M&S Food store, standard restaurant and a Wimpy. It's also worth noting all three include a mobile phone accessories shop – just in case you've forgotten your in-car charger and are low on battery.

2 / M6: Tebay Services
Operated by Westmorland, between junctions 38 and 39
Tebay is the undoubted champion of service stations. This independently run service station is as good as it gets with its genuine home-cooked meals – but the fact is unless you're playing Carlisle United or an exile north of the border it's unlikely you'll be stopping here. Facilities include shop, café, fuel, toilets and an excellent farm shop. It's the best motorway services anywhere thanks to its individual style, clean facilities, and good and reasonably priced food.

3 / M6(T): Norton Canes
Operated by Roadchef, between junctions T6 and T7
Whether you use the M6 toll road is open for debate. It can often wipe a fair few minutes off of your total journey, but there are many factors to consider: time of day, amount of traffic, road closures, accidents. One of the plus points is the services on the toll road. Bright, new, modern and never overly busy; facilities include Costa Coffee, toilets, Wimpy, Premier Travel Inn, BP petrol.

4 / A1(M): Peterborough
Operated by Extra, at junction 17
Another tidy independent outlet, Extra at Peterborough wins the plaudits for its well-equipped and clean facilities, range of reasonably priced fast food outlets – and also the stress-relieving massage chairs.

5 / M5: Strensham
Operated by Roadchef, between junctions 7 and 8
Facilities include Wimpy, shop, restaurant, toilets, shower, Costa Coffee. Users recommend it for "fantastic value kids' meals" in main restaurant and good customer service.

6 / M40: Oxford
Operated by Welcome Break, at junction 8A
Although named Oxford, this one's a bit of a way from the city. Nonetheless it's a pleasant setting, with a nice water feature at the front. This pit stop is especially pleasant on sunny days, because of its outdoor seating. Facilities include a Welcome Break restaurant; KFC and Burger King, both reasonably priced; BP Fuel, internet café, shop, toilets and shower. The Welcome Break services up the M40 aren't bad either.

 Star choice   Recommended

BREAK-TAKING

And those to avoid...

If you're desperate for a 'comfort break' they might prove unavoidable – but unless they get their act together fast, these areas don't offer much more than a pot to... you get the gist.

Birchanger Green
Operated by Welcome Break, at junction 8 of M11
Well known for poorly maintained facilities, stinky toilets and pricey food.

Bolton West
Operated by First Motorway Services, between junctions 6 and 7 of M61
They might know how to provide decent facilities at the Reebok Stadium a few miles down the motorway, but it's hard to find anyone with a kind word to say about these services. Dilapidated facilities, dirty toilets and poor customer service are among criticisms.

And more of the same – poor facilities and pricey food – is at Charnock Richard, Sandbach and Donington Park.

Get off the beaten track

If you have the time and the inclination, the Football Fans' Guide recommends that you avoid the overpriced service stations and head to one of the supermarkets, where you'll find more choice and better value – and often just a few minutes from the motorway. If you don't pack your own sarnies, the cafés at supermarkets are the best option to keep matchday costs down. And there are plenty more fantastic refreshment stops and cheap petrol stations within minutes of motorway junctions. Here are a few tips on where to find the best and most convenient cheaper choices.

Supermarket sweep

All the major supermarkets have store locators on their websites allowing you to quickly locate stores near to the motorway network. You can search by post code, town as well as type of store, but unfortunately not by motorway – so you'll need to select a mid-point on your journey in advance... or you can beat a path to some of the supermarket outlets found just minutes from major motorways by checking out these stores specially selected by the Football Fans' Guide.

Remember, 24-hour stores usually close at 10pm on Saturday evenings because of Sunday trading laws, while the evening closing times of cafés may vary.

7 / M1: Tesco: Garforth, Aberford Road Directions: Exit junction 47 and head about one mile along the A642 (Aberford Rd)

8 / M1: Sainsbury's: Loughborough, Greenclose Lane Directions: Exit junction 23, head to Loughborough on A512 for a couple of miles until you get to Greenclose Lane. Also has inhouse bakery.

9 / M1: Sainsbury's: Grove Farm Triangle, Fosse Park, Leicester Directions: Exit junction 21, and follow Fosse Park signs.

10 / M1: Asda: Milton Keynes, Bletcham Way Directions: Exit at junction 13 on the A421 and follow signs to Bletchley - not far from MK Dons - for a couple of miles until you get to Bletcham Way and Denbigh Roundabout. Has inhouse bakery.

 Open 24hrs fuel deli toilets  cashpoint café

24 ⊕ ⊙ ⊙ ⊙ ⊙ **11 / M3: Tesco: Sandhurst Extra, The Meadows, Marshall Road** Directions: Exit junction 4 and head north on A321 towards Blackwater. Come off this road at roundabout, taking third exit up Tank Road with Tesco on your left.

24 ⊕ ⊙ ⊙ ⊙ ⊙ **12 / M3: Morrisons: Thornycroft Industrial Estate, Worting Road, Basingstoke** Directions: Exit junction 6 heading along A30 (Ringway S) for a mile or so and then the A340 until you reach Worting Road. It's got a pie shop!

⊕ ⊙ ⊙ ⊙ **13 / M4: Tesco: Osterley Park, Syon Lane, Isleworth** Directions: Exit at junction 2 onto A4 south for one mile, then turn right onto B454 (Syon Lane).

⊕ ⊙ ⊙ ⊙ ⊙ **14 / M4: Asda: Telford Drive, Slough** Directions: Exit junction 6 heading along A355 towards Beaconsfield, take first left at roundabout onto Cippenham Lane. Telford Drive is fourth left. Fresh pizza counter.

⊙ ⊙ ⊙ **15 / M5: Morrisons: Glevum Shopping Centre, Heron Way, Abbeydale** Directions: Exit junction 11a and follow the A417 then A38 (Eastern Ave) towards Gloucester for just over a mile, left onto Painswick Rd for 600m and left onto Heron Way, following the road round another 600m. Fresh pizzas *and* pie counter.

⊕ ⊙ ⊙ ⊙ **16 / M5: Tesco: Clevedon, Kenn Road** Directions: Exit junction 20 and you'll find it heading south on B3133 Kenn Road.

⊕ ⊙ ⊙ ⊙ ⊙ **17 / M5: Sainsbury's, Alphington Road, Alphington, Exeter** Directions: At the end of the motorway (J31), take the A30 for a mile then take A377 (Alphington Road) until you hit the store.

24 ⊕ ⊙ ⊙ ⊙ ⊙ **18 / M32: Tesco: Bristol East Extra, Eastgate Road** Directions: If you're coming into Bristol, nip off the M32 at junction 2 and take exit onto Eastgate Road and then first left at roundabout to find the store.

24 ⊕ ⊙ ⊙ ⊙ ⊙ **19 / M6: Tesco: Leyland Extra, Town gate** Directions: Exit junction 28, go left along B5256, south onto B5264 to meet B5248 where store is at junction.

⊕ ⊙ ⊙ **20 / M6: Asda: Queensway, Stafford** Directions: Exit junction 14 and take A5013 (Eccleshall Road) as far as the A34, following this around Guildhall Shopping Centre until you get to the store.

⊕ ⊙ ⊙ ⊙ **21 / M25: Tesco: Leatherhead, Oxshott Road** Directions: Exit junction 9 and head onto B2430 (Kingston Road) for just over half a mile until it becomes Oxshott Road.

⊕ ⊙ ⊙ ⊙ **22 / M25: Sainsbury's: The Causeway, Staines** Has hot food counter and bakery. Directions: Exit junction 13 onto A30 (Staines Bypass), then go right at the roundabout following the A308 until you hit another roundabout. Turn right onto The Causeway where you'll find the store a few yards away.

⊕ ⊙ ⊙ ⊙ **23 / M25: Morrisons: Southbury Road, Enfield** Offers pizzas, pies and a bakery. Directions: Exit junction 25 and get onto A10 (Great Cambridge Road) heading south of M25 until you hit Southbury Road, then follow signs.

24 ⊕ ⊙ ⊙ ⊙ ⊙ **24 / M25: Tesco: Lakeside Extra, Cygnet View, Lakeside Estate, West Thurrock** Directions: Exit junction 31 and get onto A1306 heading east

BREAK-TAKING

of the M25. The supermarket is just over 400 yards off the motorway.

24 ⭐ 🅿️ 🅿️ 🅿️ 🅿️ **25 / M40: Tesco: Bicester Pingle Drive** Directions: Exit junction 9 and head into Bicester on A41 for two miles. Over the first roundabout; Tesco is off the second.

24 ⭐ 🅿️ 🅿️ 🅿️ **26 / M40: Sainsbury's: Shires Retail Park, Tachbrook Park Drive, Warwick** Bakery and hot food counter in lieu of café. Directions: Exit junction 13 and head towards Leamington Spa on the A452 Banbury Rd for 1.5 miles. Store on Europa Way roundabout.

24 ⭐ 🅿️ 🅿️ 🅿️ **27 / M42: Tesco: Solihull Extra, Stratford Road, Shirley** Directions: Exit junction 4, head north on A34 to Shirley. Take first right onto local roads and then third exit at roundabout onto local road to store.

24 ⭐ 🅿️ 🅿️ 🅿️ 🅿️ **28 / M42: Sainsbury's: Bonehill Road, Tamworth** Also offers bakery & hot food counter. Directions: Exit junction 10 following the A5 for a couple of miles, then turn right following signs for A51 for a few hundred metres to the store.

24 ⭐ 🅿️ 🅿️ 🅿️ 🅿️ **29 / A1(M): Tesco: Newton Aycliffe, Greenwell Rd** Directions: Exit junction 59, north on A167, left on to B4463, right into Newton Aycliffe and left on to Greenwell Road.

24 ⭐ 🅿️ 🅿️ 🅿️ 🅿️ **30 / A1(M): Asda: Metro Centre, Gibside Way, Gateshead** Directions: After end of A1 (M) continue onto A1 north, then turn right onto Hollingside Road (A69) and follow signs for the Metro Centre or store.

Other handy websites to check before setting out

If neither supermarkets nor services are your cup of tea then these websites are worth a look. Perhaps you crave a traditional British breakfast at an independent greasy spoon; or you want to stop off for a typical English pub lunch. Listing the best pit-stops close to the motorway, these sites include the best caffs, diners, restaurants and pubs.

NeartheMotorway.co.uk

This is an incredibly useful online resource to plan your pit-stops. Here you can find cheap accommodation, wonderful eating places and other amenities close to all the motorways.

For instance, if you fancy breaking up your journey with a relaxing pub meal far from the madding crowds at motorway services, this is the place to find a decent public house. You can run a quick search to find accommodation, shops and retail park, takeaway and fast-food outlets, petrol stations and supermarkets, but also pubs and bars. It tells you how far these facilities are from motorway junctions and includes brief descriptions. It's also worth noting that Greene King, Old English Inns and New Bridge Inns have registered all their pubs with accommodation.

Offmotorway.com

A travel directory for motorists looking to find accommodation, food, meeting places and other services located close by to the UK's major motorways. Including stop-overs, short breaks and holiday offers. You can pick a motorway and click on all the junctions to see what's nearby. Directions and phone numbers

are listed. It's another invaluable online tool for football fans.

Transportcafe.co.uk

The A & B roads list of lorry parks, transport caffs and truckstops. They may not be for everyone but, when you consider that even the hungriest of lorry drivers isn't easily ripped off, you generally get more for your buck at these stop-offs than regular motorway service stations. That's not to say that you can't get wholesome meals either. In fact, many caffs will offer a decent range of hot and cold food at cheap rates. This website offers useful directions and delivers lots of detail on the facilities at different stops. Comments from drivers offer added value.

FILLING UP

Petrolprices.com
If you want to save at the pump then this is the site for you. Aimed at motorists looking to save on petrol and diesel across the UK, petrolprices.com lists fuel prices for almost ten thousand petrol stations throughout Britain. Free of charge, the site allows you to search for the cheapest petrol in your area in double quick time. And you can see the petrol stations plotted on an easy to navigate map. Daily updates ensure the data is accurate. Once signed up, you will have 20 petrol price searches to use each week. All you need to do is insert a postcode to find the lowest petrol price in your area. You can also receive

regular email alerts to notify you when the prices change. Petrolprices.com also offers fuel saving tips to help you get more miles per gallon, information on car parking, and restrictions and fines. There's a guide to fuel tax along with facts and figures about the UK's largest fuel companies. For devoted football fans planning to clock up the miles during the season, this site can save you a significant wedge on fuel.

OVERNIGHT PIT-STOPS:
Hotels close to motorways

M6/M56: Quality Hotel, Langham Road, Bowdon, Altrincham
Good for Greater Manchester clubs and Manchester International Airport. This AA 3-star hotel is a good value option. Directions: Exit junction 20 of M6 onto M56, then get off at junction 7 onto A556 (Chester Road) and go over one roundabout before turning right onto Bow Green Road heading into Bowdon where you need to hang a right onto Langham Road. The hotel is a few hundred metres away. *0161 928 7121*

M25: Custom House Hotel, 272-283 Victoria Dock Road, London Docklands
Offering comfortable accommodation and varied choice of restaurants, the hotel is well placed for east and south London football clubs. Docklands Light Railway (DLR) stops at Custom House for ExCeL, providing quick access to the centre of London. London City

Pit stops / hotels

Airport is adjacent to the hotel.
Directions: From the M25 north, exit junction 27 and follow the M11 towards London City going off at junction 4 onto the A406 (towards Ilford, Barking and Excel). Then follow the A1020 in the direction of City Airport/ExCeL. Pass Gallions roundabout, the Docklands Campus and the Regatta Centre and follow signs to Custom House/Canning Town. *020 7474 0011*
www.customhouse-hotel.co.uk

M4/M1/M25: The Fox and Goose Hotel, Hanger Lane, Ealing, west London
The new Wembley Stadium is only two miles from here and the West End a tube ride away. Situated on the A406 North Circular, the hotel is within easy reach of the motorway network. Accommodation is at the cheaper end and you'll find excellent home-cooked snacks or full restaurant meals on offer all day.
Directions: From start of M4, head north on A406 for a couple of miles until you reach Hanger Lane. Or head south from M1 on A406 for about four miles to get to hotel. *020 8998 5864* www.fullershotels.com

M3: The Ely, London Road (A30), Blackwater, Camberley in Surrey
A traditional English country pub with beamed ceilings, cask conditioned ales and friendly home from home atmosphere. Directions: Exit junction 4A onto the A327 (Minley Road) until you reach the A30. Turn right at the roundabout and the hotel is on your left. *01252 860 444* www.theely.com

M40: Tree Hotel, 63 Church Way, Iffley Village, Oxford
Pleasant spot to get a tasty meal and a good

kip before tackling a long journey north or to the south west. It's only two miles from the city centre. Directions: Exit junction 8 and take the A40 to Oxford. Turn left at the Headington Roundabout towards Cowley and head to the Littlemore Roundabout, then turn right towards Iffley. Continue to traffic lights at the bottom of the hill, then turn left after the lights on Iffley Turn. After the mini roundabout, the hotel is on the left. *01865 775974*
www.treehotel.co.uk

A14: Sleep Inn Cambridge, Cambridge Services, Boxworth
Well-equipped budget accommodation for fans visiting clubs in the area, ideally placed for onward journeys up north or west. Directions: Exit junction 28 of A14 into services, six miles north of Cambridge. *01954 268 400*

M1: Swan Revived Hotel, High Street, Newport Pagnell, Buckinghamshire
Situated just two miles from junction 14 of the M1 and five miles from central Milton Keynes, this is a good overnight stopover in a value-for-money hotel. Directions: Exit junction 14 along A509 into Newport Pagnell town centre. *01908 610565*
www.swanrevived.co.uk

M27: The Red Lion Hotel, East Street, Fareham, Hampshire
You'll get a warm welcome at this hotel situated in a beautiful Grade II listed building, originally an old coaching inn. Good place to break up your journey between any of the south coast clubs. Directions: From M27 J11, take A32 signposted Gosport. At first interchange avoid flyover and take third exit

from roundabout into East Street. Hotel is on your left. *01329 822 640*
www.theredlion-hotel.co.uk

M4: Quality Hotel, Merthyr Road, Tongwynlais, Cardiff

This hotel makes a good base for Cardiff City and Swansea City just down the road. Also a good location to explore city centre sights. Directions: Exit junction 32 and take the A4054 (Merthyr Road) going away from Cardiff and look out for the hotel. *029 20 529988* www.quality-hotel-cardiff.com

M5: Laburnum House Lodge Hotel, Sloway Lane, West Huntspill, Somerset

Affordable accommodation in a converted farmhouse situated between the seaside town of Burnham-On-Sea and the historic market town (and port) of Bridgwater. Directions: Exit junction 22, then take the A38 towards Bridgwater. Drive through Highbridge to the "Crossways" public house and turn right into Church Road. Continue on for approx. 80 yards and turn left into Sloway Lane where you'll find the hotel. *01278 781830* www.laburnumhh.co.uk

M42: Drayton Court Hotel, 65 Coleshill Street, Fazeley, Tamworth

If you're heading north or south of Birmingham on a long return trip, this is a good place to pitch up for a night and easily accessible from M42 and M6 Toll. Directions: From the north on the M42, exit junction 10 and take the A5 to Tamworth, stay in the left hand lane, take the first exit onto the B5404 to Fazeley. On approach to Fazeley, at the large island, turn left and the hotel is just past the shops on the left-hand side. *01827*

285805 www.draytoncourthotel.co.uk

M6: Best Western Tillington Hall Hotel, Eccleshall Road, Stafford

Good location to rest your weary head and with decent facilities including a restaurant. Directions: Exit junction 14 Stafford north, then take A5013 to Stafford, signposted Eccleshall Road. Ignore A34 to Stafford and A5013 to Eccleshall. Hotel is a few hundred metres off the motorway *01785 253531* www.bw-tillingtonhall.co.uk

M62: Best Western Pennine Manor Hotel, Nettleton Hill Road, Scapegoat Hill, Huddersfield

Located on the edge of the Pennines with panoramic views over the Yorkshire countryside, it's a decent place to break up a road trip between north east clubs and the south. Directions: Exit junction 24, follow A640 to Rochdale, turn left after The Commercial Pub then follow signs to hotel. *01484 642368* www.bw-penninemanor.co.uk

A1(M): Aston Hotel, Coatham Munderville, Darlington

Comfortable and decently priced accommodation two minutes from motorway and 15 minutes from Durham Tees Valley International airport. Directions: Exit junction 59 and join A167 in the direction of Durham/Newton Aycliffe. Take first left (about 200 metres) and turn into Newton Park. The hotel is straight ahead.
01325 329600
www.astonhoteldarlington.co.uk

Birmingham

Introduction

The country's second city can provide the perfect weekend base for matches in the Midlands, or as an overnight stop off on the way to and from some of those longer-haul away trips. The city centre has plenty to offer, with the redeveloped Bull Ring Shopping Centre and Broad Street area along the waterfront – while if curry's your thing then you won't be disappointed if you disappear into the Balti Triangle...

drink!

Broad Street is fine if you don't mind dodging bouncers on the doors of chain bars but an exception is The Brasshouse - one of the best traditional boozers here and a decent place for a civilised drink.

If Broad Street isn't to your taste, stroll down to Brindleyplace. Birmingham's regenerated waterfront has a buzzing barscene and there are plenty of good watering holes to choose from. The Slug and Lettuce here is much more refined than the average pub with this name. It's well worth a pre-match visit. Several hours

A The Brasshouse B Brindleyplace/City Inn C Sobar D Barton's Arms E The Wellington F Mr Egg G The Zinc Bar & Grill H Al Frash, Sparkbrook, Balsall Heath, and Moseley I Chung Ying Cantonese J Novotel K Jurys Inn L Travelodge M Premier Travel Inn N Etap Hotel O Comfort Inn P Copthorne Hotel Q Macdonald Burlington Hotel

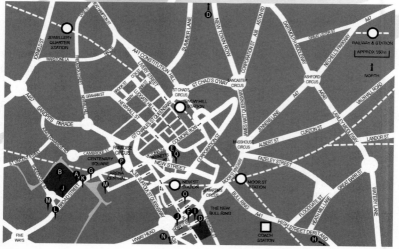

RIGHT IN THE MIDDLE OF IT ALL

later consider Sobar in The Arcadian Centre on Hurst Street, Chinatown. It's taken the city's bar culture to a new level; the food includes tasty noodle dishes. Real ale fans should head elsewhere, possibly to the impressive The Bartons Arms on High Street, Aston, within walking distance of Villa Park. Original architecture, huge ale-range and top-notch Thai food. The Wellington on Bennetts Hill, near New St and Snow Hill stations, was CAMRA pub of the year in 05 and 06. You can see why.

eat!

Mr Egg on Hurst St is a Brummie institution. It's a cheap and cheerful place for a fry-up. Brindleyplace is a relaxed canalside environment with no end of choice. Consider choosing Cielo for Italian or the Handmade Burger Co for... One of FFG's favourites is Zinc Bar & Grill at Regency Wharf, off Broad Street - well-priced food and great music.
Balti The Sparkbrook, Balsall Heath and Moseley areas of south Birmingham is known as the Balti Triangle. We like Al Frash Balti on Ladypool Road, Sparkbrook.
Chinatown by the Hippodrome Theatre is noodles-deep in excellent restaurants. Try Chung Ying Cantonese (16-18 Wrottesley St) or Chung Ying Garden (17 Thorp St).

sleep!

Want a budget-priced buzz? In the heart of things are Novotel (0121 643 2000), Jurys Inn (0121 606 9000) and Travelodge (0870 191 1564) and a clutch of Premier Travel Inns. Etap Hotel on Great Colmore Street offers rooms from £35 (0121 622 7575). And it's only five minutes from New Street station. Even closer to the station is Comfort Inn (0121 643 1134). If you want to escape the hustle and bustle, stay at City Inn on Brunswick Sq, Brindleyplace, a pleasant canalside retreat (0121 643 1003). If you're off to Villa or St Andrews, try the Campanile, Aston Locks, near the nightlife. (0121 3593 330).

enjoy!

Appliance of science
The Thinktank museum of science is three miles from M6 J6, includes a changing programme of exhibitions and events. Loads for kids.
www.thinktank.ac / 0121 202 2222

Entertaining nights
Birmingham Academy near New Street station attracts big rock and pop names: *www.birmingham-academy.co.uk*. And talking of big, the NEC Arena and National Indoor Arena are down the road: visit *www.necgroup.co.uk*. If you need cheering up try stand-up comedy at Jongleurs, Quayside Tower, Broad Street.

getting around!!

Air: There are frequent rail and bus services to the airport eight miles east of the city.
Train: *www.networkwestmidlands.com* or Centro on 0121 200 2787 for details - either will also tell you about the Midland Metro tram system operating between Wolverhampton, Wednesbury, West Bromwich and Birmingham with park & ride sites at four stations. The light rail network is expanding, which will make it easier to get to and from the centre to St Andrews and Villa Park. For timetables and fares call Centro or the site above.
Bus: For info on Travel West Midlands timetables and prices, *www.travelwm.co.uk* or 0870 608 2 608.

FFG STAR CHOICES

PUB GRUB
Bartons Arms

BEST BOOZER
The Wellington

HEAD REST
Campanile Hotel

Liverpool

Introduction

The city that gave us The Beatles, Rooney and Gerrard also comes up trumps if you're looking to extend your stay in the north west. The 2008 Capital of Culture – with a £920m city centre facelift – ticks all the boxes when it comes to pubs, clubs, bars, restaurants, entertainment… and culture. If you get the chance check out the city's waterfront: it's particularly stunning at night – but you need to cross the Mersey for the ultimate view.

drink!

If you're coming into Lime Street Station, try The Crown for cheap food and beers or The Vines, better known as 'The Big House' and one of a number of wonderful Victorian boozers in the centre - including Thomas Rigby's on Dale Street, known for its excellent range of cask ales and quality pub grub. Concert Square and Mathew Street are packed with pubs and bars bustling with revellers at the weekends.

You'll find more bars, restaurants and clubs at the waterfront Albert Dock complex - an

A The Crown/The Vine B Thomas Rigby's C Mathew Street D Albert Dock/Hotel Ibis/The Tate E The Living Room/Mosquito/The Mandarin F Heebie Jeebies/Chinatown/Sapporo G Me Mam's Kitchen/Travelodge (Old Haymarket) H St John's Shopping Centre I Travelodge (Vernon Street) J 62 Castle Street K Everton FC L Liverpool FC

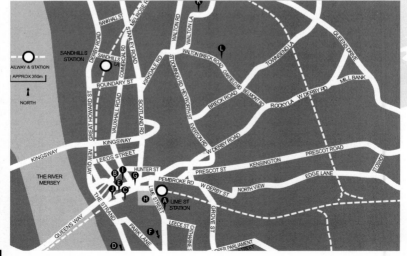

TICKING ALL THE BOXES

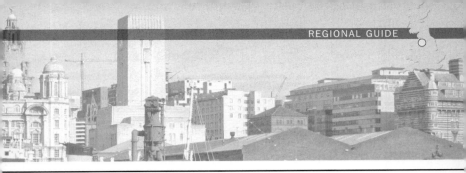

area popular with football stars and local celebs. Check out the funky Baby Blue in The Vaults at Edward Pavilion or The Pan American Club at Britannia Pavilion, a fancy bar-restaurant regularly hosting live music. In the city centre, Victoria Street is home to some groovy late-night bars including FFG favourite The Living Room and Mosquito. Heebie Jeebies is a top live music venue on Seel Street where you can drink and dance into the small hours.

eat!

Me Mam's Kitchen in the Old Haymarket is a terrific caff serving a mean Full English - great if you're staying at the Travelodge two doors down. If you simply hanker for a quick butty or pasty, sandwich shops in the city centre are plentiful. St John's shopping centre has a large food court including McDonald's, Subway and KFC. The Mandarin on Victoria Street is one of the best Chineses around. Chinatown, based around Berry Street, is lined with plenty of other oriental food options. For good Japanese, head to Sapporo Teppanyaki Restaurant Sushi & Noodle Bar on Duke Street, East Village.

sleep!

No shortage of affordable accommodation. A good budget stop is the Litherland Park B&B, at Litherland Park, 15 minutes by car from the centre (0151 928 1085). Travelodge on Old Haymarket is 10 mins' walk from Lime Street - and two miles from the city's Premiership clubs (0870 191 1656). Other budget hotels in the centre include Hotel Ibis at Wapping (0151 706 9800) and Premier Travel Inn on Vernon Street (0870 238 3323). 62 Castle Street is a centrally located boutique hotel offering rooms with all mod-cons (0151 702 7898).

enjoy!

Cavern Club legends

The Beatles Story within Liverpool's Albert Dock takes you on an atmospheric journey into the life, times, culture and music of John, Paul, George and Ringo. While the Cavern Club on Mathew Street is a 'must-see' for Beatles fans. *0151 709 1963 / www.beatlesstory.com*

Artistic impressions

At Tate Liverpool, you can view selections from the national collection of international modern art alongside creative and diverse temporary exhibitions. *www.tate.org.uk/liverpool* Tel: 0151 702 7400

getting around!

Air: Liverpool John Lennon is eight miles from centre. Merseytravel operates a regular low-cost bus service into the city seven days a week.

Train: The Merseyrail network is the biggest outside London and provides a fast and inexpensive way of getting around. For times and routes, Travelwise 0870 608 2608.

Bus: Merseytravel provides good bus services - and you can use the Night Bus network to get about if you're out till late. There are discount smart cards to help you get the most out of your day out or mini break in the city, combining travel discounts and FREE entry offers to attractions such as The Beatles Story and Cavern Club. Call Travelwise on 0870 608 2 608 or visit www.merseytravel.gov.uk

FFG STAR CHOICES

PUB GRUB
Thomas Rigby's

BEST BOOZER
The Vines

HEAD REST
Hotel Ibis

Newcastle

Introduction

If you're heading to one of the north east's football teams – and fancy extending your stay then stop off at the region's party capital. There is plenty on offer during the daytime: with excellent shops and plenty of leisure opportunities. Fun and frolics are on offer from about 6pm onwards on any weekend evening as Newcastle's flesh-flashing glitterati come out to play... (even in the depths of winter warm clothing is very much optional in Newcastle with both the men and ladies).

drink!

The Bigg Market is where the boisterous gather at weekends. It has about 20 pubs and bars. Fine if you want to crawl around some tacky bars but best avoided otherwise. The Bee Hive, a cosy corner pub showing big screen sports, is among the better hostelries. It's best to head to the more fashionable Jesmond area. Osborne Road's bars are good for a crawl. Osbornes is one of the largest and best - ideal for groups of fans. The Carriage is perfect for a Newcastle Brown Ale and pub meal - a train carriage at one end is now an Indian restaurant.

A Bigg Market B The Beehive C The Quayside D Apartment E Blake's Coffee House F The Gate G Eldon Square H Newgate Shopping Centre I Panis J Charlies K Fujiyama L Express Holiday Inn M The Jurys Inn N Newcastle United FC.

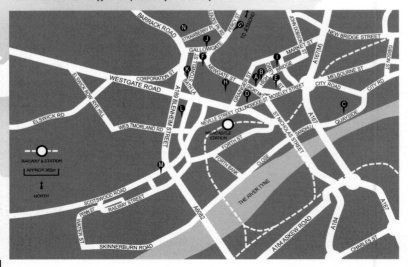

COATS ARE FOR WIMPS

26

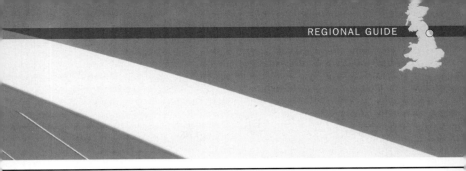

Another top spot for drinking is the Quayside, which is littered with a variety of watering holes: Slug and Lettuce to Pitcher and Piano. The Crown Posada on The Side is one of the oldest pubs in town, it's full of Victorian charm and serves fantastic ales. On the bar scene, Mr Lynch on Archbold Terrace (next to Jesmond Metro) is an FFG favourite. Great place for drinks and food (check out the Northumbrian Steak Sarnie), plus live music and comedy. For a more luxurious bar experience, head to Apartment on Collingwood Street.

eat!

There are pavement cafés, fast food joints and pie shops galore in the centre. If you're after a cheap snack Munchies takeaway chain is recommended. Blake's Coffee House on Grey Street is good for breakfast and sandwiches. Alternatively, eat cheaply in Newcastle shopping mall, Eldon Square or The Gate on Newgate Street. Panis, an Italian on Highbridge Street, is fine for a pre- or post-match sandwich or pasta. Head to the Stowell Street area for the best Chineses. Charlies on Gallowgate serves a wonderful all-you-can-eat buffet for about £6. Fujiyama, a Japanese teppan-yaki restaurant on Bath Lane, has long tables suitable for large groups and for Indian, try the legendary Curry Capital (also known as Rupali) in the Bigg Market, FFG's pick of the city's curry houses.

sleep!

Express by Holiday Inn off Waterloo Street (0870 428 1488) is very central; while The Jurys Inn (0191 201 4400) with a good bar and restaurant is another good base – and often has special rates. But the hotels on Osborne Road in Jesmond - a mile from the centre - are a better base due to the area's lively restaurant/bar scene. The street is packed with good accommodation for fans wanting to be right on top of the vibrant nightlife. Try the friendly Jesmond (0191 281 5377), Carlton (0191 281 3361) or New Kent (0191 281 7711).

enjoy!
Music to your ears

Catch a concert at The Sage Gateshead, the north east's pioneering music venue. You can see everything from indie rock and dance to folk and classical music. *www.thesagegateshead.org / 0191 443 4666*

Dynamic art

BALTIC Centre for Contemporary Art on South Shore Road, Gateshead, is well worth checking out for its ambitious programme of exhibitions and events. *www.balticmill.com / 0191 478 1810*

getting around!

Air: The airport is linked via Metro to Central Station (20 mins). For train times, 08457 48 49 50 or *www.nationalrail.co.uk*. By car: about 15 minutes.
Metro: The Metro links NewcastleGateshead with the rest of Tyne and Wear. You can buy your ticket at any Metro station. A Metro DaySaver gives all day unlimited travel. Traveline: 0870 608 2 608.
Bus: Frequent & plentiful: discount tickets include a Day Rover for unlimited travel by any public transport in Tyne & Wear.

FFG STAR CHOICES

PUB GRUB
The Carriage

BEST BOOZER
The Crown Posada

HEAD REST
New Kent Hotel

Nottingham

Introduction

With a central location and bohemian city centre Nottingham is the ideal stop-off on those long journeys up and down the country – it's also perfect if your team is in action in the city or elsewhere in the East Midlands. There's plenty on offer during the day, while Nottingham's huge student population brings the place alive at night.

drink!

Nottingham has a dizzying array of pubs and bars. South Bank Bar on Bridgford Road is one of the city's top sports bars and close to both County and Forest. FFG recommends The Stratford Haven on Stratford Road for its real ales. One of the city's most famous pubs is Ye Olde Trip to Jerusalem on Brewhouse Yard underneath Nottingham Castle, reputed to be England's oldest inn. Excellent ales on tap and delicious grub. Plenty of drinking establishments in town: Old Market Square is home to the big chain pubs and party bars. Just up the road

A South Bank Bar B Stratford Haven C Ye Olde Trip to Jerusalem D Chapel Bar E Waterfront F The Brass Monkey G Jongleurs H The Cornerhouse I Café Hockley J Brown Betty's K Chino Latino / Memsaab L La Vecchia Romagna / Strathdon Hotel M Premier Travel Inn N The Britannia O Best Western Westminster P Comfort Inn Q Nottingham Forest FC R Notts County FC

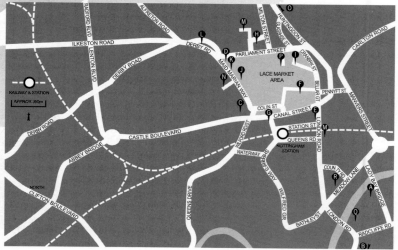

LIVELY CITY AND AN IDEAL STOP-OFF

is Chapel Bar with its assorted restaurant-bars. Derby Road and Canning Circus is an up-and-coming area for night-time revelry thanks to its eclectic mix of independent pubs, bars and restaurants. It's about 10 minutes from Old Market Square. The Waterfront (near Canal Street) is popular, especially in the summer due to its abundance of outdoor seating. Over in Hockley & The Lace Market, you'll find stylish bars - the FFG recommends Brass Monkey for its classy cocktail action. Cabaret and Jongleurs host comedy nights. Foreman Street has The Cornerhouse, with cinema and rooftop terrace bar.

eat!

Snack bars and sandwich shops are ubiquitous. Two fine places for cheap English brekkies are Café Hockley on Heathcoat Street and Brown Betty's on St James Street. The Cornerhouse includes Nandos, Pizza Hut, Subway, TGI Fridays, Wagamama and Bella Italia. Something different? Five minutes' walk from Old Market Square is pan-Asian Chino Latino. The FFG's pick of the best Indians is MemSaab on Maid Marian Way. For an authentic Italian, check out family-run La Vecchia Romagna on Derby Road.

sleep!

Budget options include the Premier Travel Inns on London Road, near the station (0870 990 6574). The Britannia Nottingham Hotel on St James Street is inexpensive (0115 988 4000), while Best Western Westminster Hotel on Mansfield Road is reasonable and within walking distance of the centre (0115 955 5000). Another is the Strathdon Hotel on Derby Road (0115 941 8501), close to the Rock City nightclub and bus station. If you want to be in the heart of the lively Lace Market, go to the

Comfort Inn on George Street, although you'll pay a little more (0115 947 5641).

enjoy!

Who are you calling a cave dweller?
Trek 10 minutes from the city centre to reach Nottingham Castle on Friar Lane, off Maid Marian Way. It houses collections of armour and interactive displays. You can also tour man-made caves and tunnels. www.nottinghamcity.gov.uk / 0115 915 3700

Join the merry men
The legend of Medieval England's most famous outlaw and his merry men is brought to life at 'Tales of Robin Hood' - two minutes walk from the castle. www.robinhood.uk.com / 0115 948 3284

getting around!

Air: East Midlands Airport is 13 miles out. Take the Skylink bus to the centre. Or a £26 cab. Book at the airport's taxi office. Checker Cars: 01332 814000.

Tram: the Nottingham Express Transit (NET) network is fast, efficient and modern. All day 'tram only' tickets are available at about £2.50 per adult. And with a CityRider ticket you can travel cheaply all day on NET trams and NCT buses. Call 0115 942 7777 or go to *www.thetram.net*

Bus: The city is well served by buses. You can buy a Kangaroo card, which allows all-day use. Contact Traveline for info on routes and discounts on 0870 608 2608, or via *www.traveline.org.uk*.

**FFG
STAR CHOICES**

PUB GRUB
Ye Olde Trip to Jerusalem

BEST BOOZER
The Stratford Haven

HEAD REST
Britannia Nottingham Hotel

Manchester

Introduction

Manchester - with excellent transport links and thousands of hotel rooms - provides the perfect weekend base not just for a visit to one of the Greater Manchester clubs, but for any of those in the north west. The city centre is great fun during the day, with its glut of nice eateries and a wealth of free attractions. As night-time approaches, Deansgate and the Locks are one of the many places where you can relax away the evening.

drink!

The trendy barscenes of Deansgate and Deansgate Locks are popular with people who are over 25, footballers or beautiful. Yards away from the Locks in Great Bridgewater St is The Britons Protection, a perfect trad boozer, or you could try the lively Lass O'Gowrie at 36 Charles St. Promoted as "the perfect village inn for Manchester", it knocks socks off its rivals. It has a microbrewery on site, a cheerful pub atmosphere and good value homemade pies. If you're a student at heart try Oxford Road for a host of welcoming pubs and clubs.

A Premier Travel Inn B Jurys Inn C Novatel Hotel D Jarvis Hotel E Midland Hotel F Radisson Hotel G Lowry Hotel H The Golden Rice Bowl
I Buffet City J Café Roma K Cloud 23 L Peverill on the Peak M Britons Protector N Lass O'Gowrie O Museum of Science & Industry

RIGHT UP YOUR STREET

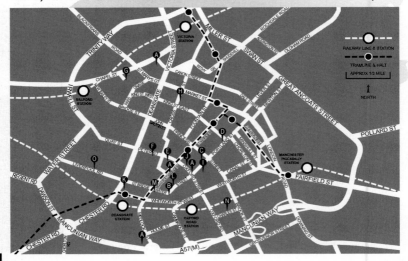

eat!

Crispy duck territory Scoff 'til you drop for a tenner at Buffet City (111 Portland Street) not far from the GMEX Centre. Fresh, tasty and includes crispy duck, which skinflint buffet establishments leave off the menu. *Poppadom paradise* Rusholme's Curry Mile has 70 restaurants covering a stretch of Wilmslow Road, two miles south of the centre. We're fond of Al Bilal at number 87. *Pre-match bite & snacks* An FFG favourite, the Cafe Roma (11 Oxford Street), does a decent all-day breakfast while The Trafford Centre includes 40 restaurants, bars and cafés to choose from. It's near M60 J9&10.

sleep!

The 5-star Forte-owned Lowry (50 Dearmans Place, Chapel Wharf) is apparently among the 32 coolest places to stay in the world (0161 827 4000). Meanwhile... there's a host of budget hotels around Portland St (three Premier Travel Inns within half a mile, and GMEX includes a gym). B&B at Jarvis Piccadilly is about £50 (0161 236 8414) and The Jurys Inn at 56 Great Bridgewater St (0161 953 8888) often runs discount offers. *Staying in Salford Quays* Express by Holiday Inn (0161 868 1000) is a good cheapish option in the lovely setting of Salford Quays, only one mile from Old Trafford. A budget option is the Premier Travel Inn.

enjoy!

Let's rock
Do two things. Check out the Academy at *www.manchesteracademy.net* and The Arena at *www.men-arena.com*. They're both great venues and present the opportunity of turning a weekend into a double-header of football and music.

Head for The Lowry
Fantastic architecture in Salford Quays: the works of LS Lowry alongside contemporary exhibitions and everything from theatre to children's shows. *www.thelowry.com* / 0870 787 5780 Also check out *www.manchestergalleries.org* as plenty of the city's galleries offer free admission.
Museum Of Science & Industry
A brilliant place to spend a few hours – especially if you have children. *www.msim.org.uk* 0161 832 2244

getting around!

Air: From the airport, trains to the centre every 15 mins; average journey time 20 minutes. A taxi costs less than £20.
Train: Most major cities have direct services into Manchester. For information on transport around the city, contact *www.nationalrail.co.uk* / 08457 48 49 50
Metrolink: the light rail system operates a bit like a cleaner version of the London underground system. From outside the conurbation you can buy combined rail/Metrolink tickets. Tickets must be bought before boarding, normally from a machine on a platform.
Free city centre bus: The Metroshuttle service runs three routes connecting main landmarks.

FFG STAR CHOICES

PUB GRUB
The Lass O'Gowrie

BEST BOOZER
The Britons Protection

HEAD REST
Premier Travel Inn

See the sites

Everything you need to make the most of your stay in Manchester
manchester.com

Good tourism website
visitmanchester.com

Info on pubs, nightclubs and bars
manchesterbars.com

London

Introduction

Whichever division your team plays its football in, you'll have the chance to stop off in London – and the country's capital has plenty to offer: landmarks, history, museums, galleries, tourist attractions, theatres, cinemas, clubs, pubs, bars, cafés, restaurants... the list goes on. With so much to see and do you might even decide to stay for longer than the weekend – in the meantime here are a few Football Fans' Guide capital favourites.

drink!

You're spoilt for choice for places to drink in London. From the chain bars and pubs of Leicester Square and Covent Garden to Soho's snazzier drinking dens and the trendy hangouts in Shoreditch and Brick Lane, there's a watering hole for everyone.

The Famous Three Kings on North End Road, Hammersmith is one of the best sports bars around. Or try Sirocco on Shaftesbury Avenue; it has 12 plasma screens and welcomes groups for dining and drinking till late.

The Lamb & Flag in Covent Garden serves a nice pint and decent nosh. Not far away on Maiden Lane, you'll find The Porterhouse, a huge Irish-themed gem of a pub. It offers great Irish stouts and a fine choice of beers from around the world.

One of London's most ancient alehouses, Ye Olde Cheshire Cheese, is a good port of call. This Fleet Street boozer is full of character and you can get a decent steak & kidney pie amongst other things. Another good 'un on Fleet Street is the Old Bell Tavern, serving a range of ales.

At The Bavarian Beerhouse, on City Road (Old Street by tube), you'll find waitresses sporting traditional dress serving steins of Bavarian and German beer. For more refined drinking, try the Match bar on Margaret Street, near Oxford Circus, with its impressive array of cocktails; cuisine is of a high standard too.

Much of the same is on offer at trendy Mahiki, Dover Street, Mayfair. The Green & Red on Bethnal Green Road, Shoreditch attracts a young crowd with its authentic Mexican cuisine and beers, not to mention a popular tequila bar downstairs.

eat!

There's a diverse mix of places to eat in every borough - over six thousand restaurants offering menus from over fifty countries.

Great greasy spoon

Fast food joints are ubiquitous and you're never too far from a café selling cheap eats and lardy breakfasts. For one of the best fry-ups in London try The New Piccadilly Café, on Denman Street, Piccadilly. With no-nonsense breakfasts this Soho caff hasn't changed much since the 1950s but is an institution in these parts.

From the Far East

Wagamama is a good place for cheap Japanese nosh (over 15 branches in London). They serve noodle dishes and rice-based meals. Ping Pong on Great Marlborough Street, Soho, is good if you like dim sum – but if you're keen on Chinese head to Chinatown for a huge choice of authentic food.

Banglatown curries

East London's Brick Lane is the place to head for the best Indian restaurants. Try

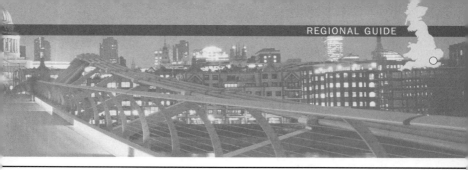

Café Naz (46-48 Brick Lane) for some quality Bangladeshi cuisine. Other recommended places are Shampan, Aladdin and Muhib. If you and your football chums are in a curry mood, you could also check out the Masala Zone on Marshall Street in Soho - you can eat like a king for around a tenner.

Italian style

La Porchetta on Upper Street, Islington, serves wonderful pizzas at incredibe value and welcomes large groups. It's also in Muswell Hill, Finsbury Park and Holborn.

sleep!

Travelodge, Premier Travel Inn are worth considering if you want to keep costs down (if there's a group of you note that Travelodge allows three adults to a room).

If you're visiting north London clubs, the Holiday Inn on Jamestown Road, Camden Lock, is well placed (020 7485 4343). With its market, restaurants and nightlife, Camden is a fine place to stay. A good base for Chelsea and Fulham is Jurys Inn Chelsea Hotel on Imperial Road, near the Kings Road (020 7411 2200).

For something a bit classier, try Hotel La Place (*www.hotellaplace.com*) in the heart of London's West End. This family-run boutique hotel values the personal touch and is value for money. Located at 17 Nottingham Place W1U 5LG, it's just three minutes' walk from Baker Street tube station, 10 minutes' walk to Oxford Street and only 20 minutes to Soho and Piccadilly.

getting around!

Don't bring the car: buy a Travelcard. For about six quid you can use bus, tube and train. If you do drive, then leave the car on the outskirts and tube it. *www.tfl.gov.uk* for information on getting around.

Air: All London's airports have express routes to the heart of the capital. It's under 20 minutes by rail from Heathrow and City; but Stansted (45 mins) and Gatwick (30) take longer.

Train: Frequent services run to all areas of the city and outskirts. For information on tickets and timetables for transport in and around the city, contact National Rail Enquiries. Tel: 08457 48 49 50; web: *www.nationalrail.co.uk*

Tube: The London Underground, which divides the city into six concentric charging zones, is the quickest way of getting around. There are 12 tube lines plus the Docklands Light Railway (DLR) and an connected rail network. The last tube train leaves between 11.30pm and 12.30am.

Bus: Convenient. Timetables, downloadable bus route maps and a good journey planner service are available on the Transport for London website. There is a flat fare throughout the bus network, £1 with pre-pay Oyster Card and £2 if you are paying by cash.

Taxi: Black cabs may be useful at night for short journeys but they're pricey. Minicabs are cheaper but must be hired by phone or from a minicab office. Fix a price before you set off. To book a licensed taxi, call Taxi One: 0871 871 8710.

tip!

Consider investing in an Oyster Card if you're a frequent visitor or staying for a while. It is the

FFG STAR CHOICES

PUB GRUB
Ye Olde Cheshire Cheese

BEST BOOZER
The Porterhouse

HEAD REST
Hotel la Place

cheapest and most efficient way to get around London's public transport network, with substantial cash and queuing time savings, you can use the card on buses, tubes and trams. Buy Oyster Cards at tube stations or online at *www.tfl.gov.uk*.

enjoy!

It's difficult to recommend what to do in London in terms of entertainment: football fans' tastes are diverse and with so much on offer it's difficult to choose. You'll easily find details on all the usual favourites – Madame Tussauds, London Zoo, The Tower Of London – with tourist paraphernalia available at every turn but it's worth checking out the London Eye for some stunning views of the capital including Wembley. The chances are you'll be looking for Friday or Saturday evening entertainment pre- or post-match.

If clubbing's your thing then you'll find plenty on offer in the centre of the city. If you fancy the flicks then head for Leicester Square: you'll find three Odeon cinemas there.

There are plenty of comedy clubs across London but the Comedy Store is the most famous and still the best and attracts some of the biggest names on the stand-up circuit. It's located at 1a Oxendon Street, near Piccadilly Circus tube. Check listings at *www.thecomedystore.co.uk*.

tip!

If you've not got your heart set on one particular show and are happy taking pot luck, then check out the TKTS Booth in Leicester Square for cut-price theatre tickets. There are plenty of other 'official' cut-price outlets, but the one right in the middle of the square is the only genuine official operator.

Brighton

The home of Fatboy Slim is often referred to as London-by-the-Sea due to its cosmopolitan feel. Known for its pebble beach, spectacular Royal Pavilion and trendy nightlife, there's something for everyone. And you can get around easily on foot.

Eat

Gardner St near the station is packed with great eateries including Gourmet Burger Kitchen (23 varieties of burger) and Pokeno Pies for lovely pies and mash. Round the corner in Jubilee St, Carluccio's is an FFG favourite. Preston Street is known as 'Curry Mile' but one of the best Indians, Nooris, is in Ship St.

Drink

There are some brilliant pubs around Brighton station for pints and grub. Walk up Guildford Road for The Battle of Trafalgar and Sussex Yeoman or down to The Basketmakers Arms in Gloucester Road. The Fortunes of War is the FFG's pick of beachfront bars.

Sleep

Cheap Premier Travel Inn is on North St, 10 minutes' walk from the station (0870 9906340). Of many affordable places on the seafront, FFG recommends The Royal Albion (01273

Bristol and Southampton

329202). Other affordables are in Regency Square. Try the Prince Regent (01273 329962) or Adelaide (01273 205286).

Enjoy

Check out the beachfront restaurant/bar scene or have some fun on the Palace Pier. The Aquarium is opposite the pier. Head to The Lanes or North Laine for trendy shops. For late-night laughs look to the Komedia (*www.komedia.co.uk*)

Bristol

Plenty to do in the south west's largest city. Major regeneration has turned the harbourside into a lively centre. The birthplace of trip-hop, which spawned Massive Attack and Roni Size, still produce cutting-edge music.

Eat

Quba Ice on North Street does a hearty full English but FFG recommends York Café in York Place, Clifton, about a mile from the centre, for the ultimate fry-up. Bristol Raj Bari on Hotwell Rd is an award-winning Indian but La Taverna Dell' Artista in King Street an institution. Mazati in Small St offers mouth-watering Middle Eastern and Mediterranean fare.

Drink

Bristol's main nightlife areas are Gloucester Rd, the harbourside, Whiteladies Rd and Park St. Corn St in the old city area is also great for post-match drinking. King St is full of historic pubs and modern bars - try the famous Llandoger Trow. Quayside pubs don't come much finer than The Cottage at Baltic Wharf, while Oceana boasts five bars and two night clubs.

Sleep

Express by Holiday Inn opposite Temple Meads Station is the best city centre location (0870 720 2293). Cheap harbourside accommodation is more attractive. Ibis Bristol is one option (0117 989 7200), Jurys Bristol Hotel another (0117 923 0333).

Enjoy

At-Bristol brings science to life on the harbourside and includes a planetarium. Visit *www.at-bristol.org.uk* or call 0845 345 1235. Nearby Arnolfini is a leading centre for the contemporary arts: fve galleries and it's free. For post-match chuckles, head to Jongleurs on Baldwin Street (0870 0111965).

Southampton

Southampton is a vibrant, cosmopolitan port city with plenty of shopping and a buzzy nightlife. Efficient bus system makes getting around the city a breeze.

Eat

Go to Bargate Shopping Centre for a snack, Oxford Street near the marinas for variety (try Poppadom Express for curries or Olive Tree for Mediterranean) or High Street for a good Chinese called City Beijing.

Drink

The Victory opposite the station is popular, while The Dolphin on Osbourne Rd South next to St Denys Station is an FFG tip for its real ales. Shamrock Quay's bars are also worth sampling.

Sleep

Choices, choices... in the centre you'll find a Premier Travel Inn (0870 238 3308), Holiday Inn (0870 400 9073) and Ibis Hotel (023 8063 4463). But the FFG pick is Southampton Park Hotel on Cumberland Place - perfectly placed for the Bedford Place bar scene (0808 144 9494).

Enjoy

Ocean Village marina is a decent entertainment complex where you can kill a few hours. Alternatively, feast your eyes on funky visual art at The Bargate Monument Gallery on High Street, or catch at gig or some comedy at Southampton Guildhall (023 8063 2601).

A visit to head office

Best in the world

For all their derision about overpriced hamburgers, the media couldn't actually find much wrong with the new £800m Wembley Stadium.

Okay, so the burgers are overpriced, but the owners have to repay the £433m bank loan somehow. The positives outweigh any negatives: ample leg room, brilliant views from every seat, excellent atmosphere, friendly stewards, minimal queuing for the toilets. Perhaps the biggest positive is the time it takes to get away after the match. The £70m spent on upgrading the public transport means you can stay to the end of the game and – service permitting – still be back to any main London station in under an hour.

Negatives, apart from the pricey food? Tickets aren't cheap, but that's football. And driving there remains a nightmare - leave the car at home or head for one of the outlying London Underground stations and take the tube the rest of the way.

GOING TO WEMBERLEY

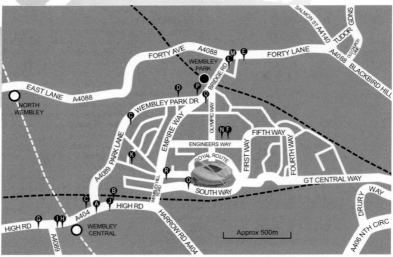

A Burger King B KFC C McDonalds D Wimpy E Asda F Moore Spice G Sanghamam H The Curragh I The New Village Inn J JJ Moons K The Green Man L The Crock of Gold M The Torch N Alisan O The Ibis Hotel P Premier Travel Inn Q The Quality Hotel R The Hilton Wembley Plaza

Facilities

As good as it gets, anywhere. Decent-sized seats with ample leg room; 2,618 toilets, more than any other building in the world, and two giant screens, equivalent in size to 600 domestic TVs. Upper and lower tiers come equipped with bookmakers, sales booths and food and drink bars – at £3.50 a pint the beer's better value than the food.

Food

The food in the tiers is expensive and the biggest blot on Wembley's copy book. The quality isn't bad but the value is. Apparently the pies are handmade, but like everything else they're lumpy in price if not in consistency. Even worse if you're a vegetarian. Last season there was no catering at all for them. No cheese & onion pasties and no chips - they sell these only as part of meal deals - so the only hot-food option was to buy a burger meal, throw away the burger and eat the chips.

Oddly, in a venue promoting sporting excellence, most of the crisps and confectionery also come in super-sized varieties. The best bet is either eat before arriving - there's plenty on offer in walking distance or, if you're heading in via London, check the recommendations in our city guide. Or you might like the more traditional approach and bring your own - but be careful as there have been reports of fans having food and drink confiscated - although the regulations refer only to 'cans, glass vessels, bottles, hampers and cool boxes' being banned.

Outside chance of saving money

There is plenty on offer outside even before Wembley Village opens for business,

but most of it is fast food, Indian or Chinese. All the burgerchains are here. McDonalds' fans will love the walk-thru option which replaces the drive-thru on matchdays and gives very speedy service. Further independent takeaway and restaurant options are available on Wembley Park Drive – including American, British, Chinese, Indian, Italian and more, plus a few sports bars and pubs.

There's an Asda Supermarket on Forty Lane just north of Wembley Park Tube Station. If you fancy a sit-down meal, but nothing on Wembley Park Drive takes your fancy, there's Indian cuisine at Moore Spice (0208 7951966) on Engineers Way in Wembley Retail Park; while Sanghamam (0208 7953555) on Wembley High Road offers authentic Chinese and Indian vegetarian cuisine.

Nearby pubs

There are numerous watering holes within a mile of the stadium, but not too many brilliant ones. But with the area undergoing regeneration over the next five years or so, the standards are likely to go up as hostelries look to capitalise on the increase in visitors to the area. Pubs on the High Road are handy if you're arriving on the tube at Wembley Central. Like most around here on a matchday, places such as The Curragh

---

Pushing the boat out: food prices at Wembley

MEAL DEALS
There are various meal deals for fish, pie, burger, hot dog or pizza, all being served with chips and a drink. The price of these meals is £7–8. You can also buy pies, burgers, hot dogs and pizza for £4–5.

DRINKS
Pint of Carling £3.50
Pint of Tetley £3.50
Bottled beer £3.70
Wine £4
Coca Cola Large £2.90
Coca Cola Small £2.20
Bottled Water £1.80

SNACKS
Chocolate pots £3.80
Walkers Crisps £1.50
Duo chocolate bars 90p

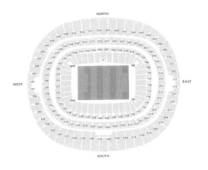

and The New Village Inn get rammed. But they may make a good pitstop on the way to the stadium. JJ Moon's, a Wetherspoons on the High Road, is recommended for its value tucker and cheap beers. One of the best pubs in the area is The Green Man on Dagmar Avenue, just off Empire Way and a stone's throw from the stadium. Up a hill, it overlooks the stadium offering great views of the Venue of Legends. The beer is good, staff friendly and it has a big beer garden. The pub easily accommodates crowds of thirsty pre- and post-match drinkers and also boasts a big car park.

If you're arriving at Wembley Park, check out The Crock of Gold pub or The Torch on Bridge Road. Both do pub grub. En route to the match, you might want to stop off at Alisan at Wembley Retail Park on Engineers Way for a quick jar, if only to enjoy the superb view of Wembley Stadium from the first-floor bar lounge of this Chinese restaurant. Avoid The Greyhound on Harrow Road, near Wembley Stadium station. Staff and doormen aren't the friendliest and you'll pay inflated prices for beers and soft drinks, probably sold in plastic glasses.

Getting there

Wembley has titled itself as a 'public transport destination' with all fans being encouraged to at least use public transport for the final leg of their journey.

Coach and Bus

National Express, as the stadium's Official Transport Provider, has routes to the stadium from 43 towns and cities. Coaches park outside, ideal for immediate access and swift departures. Book at: *www.nationalexpress.com/wembley*. If you are planning to run a private coach, your coach company will need to pre-book a space with CS Parking – a third party company who handle parking. Go to *www.csparking.com/stadium*. There are coach spaces available for all major events, with prices between £30 and £50.

Train and tube

 Wembley Park Underground Station can handle 37,500 passengers in an hour, 70% more than before. It is served by the Metropolitan and Jubilee lines and is less

than 15 minutes' walk from the stadium.

 Wembley Central has Bakerloo line underground services as well as Silverlink overland rail services to Euston and Stanmore, north of Wembley. The walk, via a new covered walkway and White Horse Bridge, is also less than 15 minutes.

 Wembley Stadium Station is on the Chiltern Railways line between London Marylebone and the Midlands via Buckinghamshire and Oxfordshire. It is ten minutes from the stadium via the new White Horse Bridge.

Car

On major event days there is no parking at the stadium and local street parking is restricted so there's a fair chance of getting ticketed and towed. There is limited parking for blue badge holders close to the stadium and they should email *accessforall@wembleystadium.com* to reserve a place. Otherwise, best to park outside town and take public transport.

There are some secure parking spaces at certain Underground car parks within a short ride of Wembley. Better to book in advance *www.ncpwembleyparking.co.uk* than take your chance on the day.

If you are one of the lucky people with a parking space lined up, the most direct route is via the North Circular if you're coming down the M1 or M40/A40 – but this can get severely clogged on matchdays and it's worth having a plan B. If you're coming from the south, use the A4, A40 or even the A316 and then pick up the North Circular as you get closer to Wembley.

Further information

Another feather in Wembley National Stadium Limited's cap is the excellent interactive travel section on the website *wembleystadium.com/gettingtowembley*: click on the area you live in the UK and it will flash up the travel options to getting to the stadium. And for live travel information on event days and in the lead up to events call the Wembley Stadium Travel Information Line on 0845 6000 555.

Accrington Stanley

Accrington Stanley, who are they?

"Enjoy, but wrap up warm and wear a hat." That's the most important advice given by Accies fan Oggy for anyone braving a trip to watch their team play at Fraser Eagle Stadium in the former mill town of Lancashire. "Bring a brolly," says another fan. One of the less desirable aspects of the ground, Oggy says, is the lack of adequate cover from unforgiving weather. He admits that the floodlights aren't great either... so "you might want to bring a torch" too.

Stanley fans are a self-deprecating bunch, and with good reason. They've been on the end of plenty of Accy-bashing down the years, mainly due to the club being namechecked in that advert for milk in the 1980s, featuring two lads with thick Scouse accents. The ad became famous for its phrases: "Accrington Stanley, who are they?" So you may be treated to some tongue-in-cheek chanting from the terraces along the lines of: "Accy Stanley Don't Drink Milk, We Drink Lager!" on your visit.

At the time of the ad, Stanley were a non-league club having resigned from the Football League in 1962 due to financial difficulties. After an absence of 44 years, the club regained league status when they were crowned Nationwide Conference champions in 2006. They won the championship by 11 points. Ironically, the team relegated from League Two was Oxford United, the team chosen to replace Stanley as members of the league in 1962.

The current Accrington Stanley FC was only formed in 1968, although the name dates back much further. The original town team, Accrington FC were amongst the 12 founding members of the Football League in 1888, before quitting the league after just five years. Stanley Villa, based at the Stanley Arms pub, already existed at that time and incorporated the town name to become Accrington Stanley.

Eating out

Lancashire's famous Hollands Pies are served at the stadium, along with the usual burgers 'n' chips. Other than the pubs listed here, you can also eat close to the ground at Tracey's Fish & Chip shop next to the Oaklea pub on Whalley Road. Sahad takeaway on Blackburn Road is "excellent for kebabs and samosas of quality at a more than reasonable price," according to those in the know. For post-match sustenance, try looking further afield, according to one Stanley food-loving devotee. "There aren't that many restaurants in Accy," says Sparkie. "The ones in the surrounding area of Hyndburn are very good." For a Chinese, he recommends Bamboo Garden, 48-50 Union Rd, Accrington, Oswaldtwistle (01254 231459). Some of the best Indian cooking can be found at Mitali Tandoori, 17-19 Warner St, Accrington (01254 381 054). If you like Italian, head for Monte Cristo, 125 Henry Street, Church, Accrington (01254 238400). Or a nice Mongolian at Ger Hana, 411 Blackburn Rd, Accrington, Oswaldtwistle (01254 396777).

Mine's a pint

A few minutes from the ground is the main away fans' pub, The Whitakers Arms. Home-cooked meals and facilities include a pool table, beer garden, darts and Sky.

Club Information Stadium: Fraser Eagle Stadium, Livingstone Rd, Accrington, Lancashire BB5 5BX (Formerly Crown Grnd) Capacity: 5,057 Tel: 01254 356950 Web: www.accrington stanley.co.uk Train: Accrington Colours: Red and white Songs: Although they feature in the title of Waterboys song and have a Beatles tribute act named after them, Accrington Stanley don't

The pub says it can cater for visiting supporters' clubs as it boasts lots of room for coach parties. Book on 01254 392999. About 20 minutes' walk from the ground is The Stanley on Stanley Street. It caters for away fans on match days with 'butties'. The Crown, Whalley Road, is popular with both sets of fans and very near the stadium.

Stopping over in Accrington?

 For an overnight stay in Accrington, try Maple Lodge, 70 Blackburn Road, Clayton-le-Moors, Accrington BB5 5JH. It's AA 4 diamond rated and offers en-suite B&B. Double from £59. Tel: 01254 301284. www.maplelodgehotel.co.uk For a more intimate setting, there's Wendy's Bed and Breakfast, 139 Whalley Rd, Accrington BB5 1BX (01254 871060). Double from £38. Or if you prefer a little more luxury, base yourself at Macdonald Dunkenhalgh Hotel & Spa, a 700-year-old country house set in 17 acres of Lancashire parkland "where you can enjoy excellent food and the sense of well-being conferred by old-fashioned hospitality". It's located on Blackburn Road, Clayton Le Moors, Accrington BB5 5JP. Tel: 01254 398021. Rooms from £80 per night.

If you do one thing in Accy...

You can easily spend time pottering around and enjoying attractions such as Howarth Art Gallery on Manchester Road.

You can follow Accrington's Acorn Trail to discover more about the town's history, visit the oldest market hall in Lancashire and see where the football club was founded. "No trip to Accy would be complete without a stroll up the Coppice," says one local of the area next to the site of the club's original home, Peel Park, which overlooks the town.

Well I never

Jon Anderson, singer with prog-rock band Yes, was born in Accrington. In his younger years, he had wanted to play for the club but reportedly didn't make the grade because of his frail constitution. Author Jeanette Winterson's book Oranges Are Not The Only Fruit is about a lesbian girl who grows up in Accrington.

Don't mention

Milk: in particular that ad in which a young lad memorably claimed that, "Ian Rush says that if I don't drinks lots of milk I'll only be good enough to play for Accrington Stanley."

Do mention

Promotion to the Football League: it completed a remarkable comeback for 'the club that wouldn't die'. Accrington Stanley went out of business in the early 1960s, but reformed and worked their way back up through the non-league scene.

Travel Information

CAR
From the M65: exit at junction 7, following signs for Clitheroe. At the first set of traffic lights turn right onto the A678. Turn right again at the next set of lights, which will take you back over the motorway and towards Accrington on the A680 Whalley Road. Follow this road for less than half a mile, you'll then see Livingstone Road, on the left, which leads to the Crown Ground. From M66: At the end of the M66 follow the A56, then the A680. After negotiating the ring-road through the town centre, you rejoin the A680 Whalley Road. Livingstone Road is approx 400 yards past Accrington Victoria Hospital on the right. Street parking is available, and there is limited free parking at the ground.

TRAIN
The nearest British Rail station is Accrington which is about 20 minutes' walk from the ground. King Street will lead you to Whalley Road, then it's uphill for about a mile until you see Livingstone Road on the right.

have a catalogue of anthems. One of the more popular recent efforts is about a 'cracker' of a goal from Ian Craney at Morecambe Bay. Rivals: Blackburn and Burnley traditionally plus Barrow, Southport and Morecambe.

Arsenal

Gunning for glory

Emirates Stadium opened its doors in July 2006 to great acclaim. The Ashburton Grove venue, constructed in little over three years, is little more than a Tony Adams' punt from Highbury – the Gooners' home since 1913. Arsenal played 2,010 games there; winning 1,196 of those. They scored 4,038 goals and conceded less than one a game.

Highbury is being turned into 700-plus homes, with the Grade II-listed East Stand and West Stand converted into high-spec apartments.

With 60,432 seats, Emirates is the second largest stadium in the Premiership after Old Trafford, a capacity designed to propel the club into the same revenue bracket as the European giants. Emirates expects to average 1,140,000 spectators through its doors every season - Highbury could manage less than 750,000.

Soaring 42m from pitch level to its highest point, the stadium is an impressive beast. Over 60,000 cubic metres of concrete were used in the structure - the equivalent of filling the team bath at Highbury over 7,500 times... apparently.

It's pretty spectacular inside, too. Away fans speak of being struck by its hi-tech facilities. But they agree it'll take time for the arena to forge its own footballing identity beyond flashy architectural motifs.

Gooners' fans have been in good voice to crank up the atmosphere, despite a series of lacklustre displays and a rubbish season by their own high standards. The days when "Boring, boring Arsenal" taunts rang out are long gone.

Away fans are housed in the lower tier of the south east corner. The normal allocation for visitors is 3,000. There's ample leg room in the padded seats and views are generally pretty good, although you can be quite low to the action in that corner. 'Smart' tickets checked via electronic readers allow quick entry.

Eating out

For once in a stadium environment, you can get more than the usual as Arsenal look to cater for their multi-cultural following: authentic imported German smoked Bockwurst sausage, Scottish beef cheeseburgers, freshly battered fish & chips, assorted bagels and even cauliflower bake. Meal deals are available on all snacks, but as you expect at any football stadium it isn't cheap (they've got to pay for the stadium somehow). So you might want to grab a cheaper bite from a burger van. In Islington, the most diverse selection of eating establishments are found in Upper Street. There's everything from cheap cafés to fashionable bistros and tapas bars. Many restaurants cater for a limited budget and offer lunchtime promotions. The White Swan, a Wetherspoons, gets crowded with fans, but it's good for pub grub. Walkabout serves some decent tucker, including bangers & mash and Aussie-inspired stuff such as fillets of crocodile or kangaroo. Upper Street also includes Turkish, Italian, Vietnamese and Cuban eateries (Cuba Libre is a restaurant/bar).

Mine's a pint

By arriving early at the Emirates, fans can take advantage of John Smith's and Fosters promotions running at concourse outlets (£2.50 in 2006/07). Alternatively, soak up

---

Club Information Stadium: Emirates Stadium, Drayton Park, London N5 1BU Capacity: 60,432 (all seated) Tel: 0207 7044000 Web: www.arsenal.com Tube: Arsenal Colours: Red and white. Songs: A favourite from the old days is 'Good Old Arsenal', but you're

the pre-match atmosphere at the Drayton Arms, still the main away pub after the relocation. It's near to Arsenal underground and Drayton Park rail station is just a few minutes away. There's Sky Sports and you can drink outside. The Gunners is one to avoid, for obvious reasons. Chance your pint arm down Upper Street, lined with pubs and bars, but there are few highlights. You'll have a battle to get served in some places, while others like O'Neills and Bierodrome are regularly slated for beers and service. The boozers down Holloway Road are a better bet. Finsbury Park hostelries may be more welcoming and generally less crowded (the tube station is about 10 minutes' walk). Good pubs in Islington are a dying breed, but two worth checking out are The Compton Arms on Compton Avenue and The York on Islington High Street. Both are recommended for their real ales and friendly atmosphere.

Stopping over in Islington?

 Islington is a decent place to stay if you want to venture to London's west end or other central attractions. Kandara Guesthouse on Ockendon Road is a family-run B&B situated in a leafy residential area minutes from the theatres and restaurant district (020 7226 5721). Doubles about £60. Jury's Inn on Pentonville Road offers "superior budget accommodation" (020 7282

5500). It's close to Angel tube and also King's Cross. More expensive rooms are at the Hilton London Islington on Upper Street (020 7354 7700).

If you do one thing in Islington...

Go and see what they've done to Highbury: now a residential development named Highbury Square. It maintains the famous 1930s art deco facades of the old Highbury west and east stands – with new apartments where the North Bank and Clock End once stood. The flats overlook a landscaped garden where Bastin, George, Wright and Henry once bashed in goals a-plenty.

Winning record

Arsenal didn't lose a single Premiership match in 2003/04 - the only time in the modern era a team has remained unbeaten for the duration of a league season.

Don't mention

Bungs: George Graham had to resign as boss due to a row about bungs and ended up being banned from the game.

Do mention

Herbert Chapman: a legendary figure who led the club to their first League championship in the 1930s and oversaw a glorious period in the club's history. Ian Wright: a favourite son of Highbury, and second only to Thierry Henry in the Arsenal goalscoring charts.

Travel Information

CAR
FFG recommends parking at one of the Underground stations (on the Piccadilly Line) on the outskirts and making the final leg of your journey by tube. However, if this isn't possible, then you need to be aware there is very little parking available and you should expect to pay £10 upwards to do so. Leave the M1 at Junction 2 and onto the A1, following the signs for Central London. Stay on the A1 for six miles until you see Holloway Road Tube Station on your right, then take a left at the next set of traffic lights into Hornsey Road and the stadium is a little way down this road. If you're coming from the south or east, you may want to take the M4 or M11 into London and negotiate the North Circular onto the A1.

TRAIN
The nearest tube station is Holloway Road but this is closed on matchdays so go to Arsenal, served by the Piccadilly Line and three minutes' walk from the stadium. You can also opt for Finsbury Park (Piccadilly or Victoria Line and Great Northern Rail) or Highbury & Islington (Victoria or Northern Line and Great Northern Rail) – which are both ten minutes' walk away.

more likely to hear a more modern effort paying homage to one of the current Arsenal stars. Rivals: Without question Spurs, but Arsenal fans also have an extreme dislike for Chelsea.

Aston Villa

Lerner driver

Randy Lerner's arrival spelt the end of Doug Ellis's reign and could signal a resurgence in fortunes. Fans were relieved to see the back of Deadly Doug, chairman from 1968-75 and since 1982. His meddling ways and tempestuous relationship with various managers and supporters seemed only to have a detrimental effect on Villa's progress.

Lerner is ambitious and has pledged to allocate financial resources across multiple fronts, including more transfer funds and upgrades to Villa Park.

The precise nature of his stadium plans aren't yet known. But the billionaire owner of American Football's Cleveland Browns is sure to sink a fair wedge into modernisation.

Rumours of a multi-million pound stadium naming rights deal were played down by the club in late 2006. Lerner is aware of Villa Park's heritage and the likely backlash from fans if he tries to sell the stadium name. Even the stadium label of his NFL team was never auctioned off, which is highly unusual in major league American sports.

Recapturing the glory years for the 1982 European Cup winners may be some time off but improvements are expected soon. Expansion of the North Stand would see the filling-in of the corners, raising capacity to 51,000.

All of which is good news for away supporters who are housed in the lower tier of the North Stand (R block). Visiting fans are also seated in the Doug Ellis Stand (Q Block). The total allocation for the away contingent is around 3,000 tickets. Midlands' rivals will be treated with the utmost disrespect here but travelling fans from anywhere else can look forward to a fine away-day at one of the best 'old' grounds in the Premiership.

Eating out

Food and drink at the club's refreshment bars are of a reasonable standard. Burger trucks line the roads outside Villa Park. On Witton Road you'll find an Indian and chip shop. Star City entertainment complex is five minutes' drive away and convenient for a pre-match meal. Situated just off Junction 6 of the M6, it includes Burger King, La Tasca, Ma Potter's Chargrill, a Mexican, Nandos, Old Orleans and Pizza Hut. The lively Broad Street and Wharfside Street in the city are packed with cafes and restaurants to suit all palates. Canalside eating venues at Brindleyplace offer a more relaxed and sophisticated ambience. Chinatown, by the Hippodrome Theatre, has many excellent restaurants. The Arcadian on Hurst Street has eateries for all tastebuds from modern British cuisine to Mexican, Italian, Chinese and Indian. Birmingham is the 'Capital of the Balti', the spicy dish introduced to the city by its large Kashmiri population in the mid-1970s. Most balti houses are situated in the Sparkbrook, Balsall Heath and Moseley areas of south Birmingham, which form the famous 'Balti Triangle'. Try Ladypool Road in Sparkbrook for a fine choice of Indian food and be aware that many restaurants are unlicensed so you can take in your own booze.

3. ASTON VILLA

Club Information Stadium: Villa Park, Trinity Road, Birmingham B6 6HE Capacity: 42,573 (all seated) Tel: 0871 4238100 Web: www.avfc.com Station: Witton Colours: Claret & Blue Songs: A favourite chant is the (family audience unfriendly) riposte to a Birmingham City song to the tune of 'Roll out the Barrel'. A tune called 'Roll Along Aston

Mine's a pint

Most pubs around Villa Park are best left to home fans. There are quite a number in close proximity to Witton train station, approximately two minutes' walk from the ground. The Cap & Gown on Witton Road is considered to be one of the best away taverns. It's split in two to cater for both sets of fans and there's even a separate entrance for non-Villans. Admission costs a couple of quid. The pub enjoys a friendly reputation and provides a variety of snacks and main courses. The Harriers on Davey Road is another away-friendly haunt. There are several pubs dotted around Aston railway station. Said to be okay for away fans is The Adventurers on Queens Road. The Bartons Arms on High Street, Aston is within walking distance of Villa Park and receives rave reviews. One of the finest examples of Victorian pub architecture anywhere, it's recommended by CAMRA for its selection of ales and imported bottled beers and also noted for its Thai food. It's only a short bus ride from the city centre on the A38. If you only go to one pub, make it this one.

Stopping over in Birmingham?

One attractive option is Campanile Hotel at Aston Locks, Chester Street - a canalside hotel within walking distance of the city centre and easily accessible by motorway (0121 3593 330). There's a Travelodge on Broad Street (0870 191 1564). Or you could bed down at nearby Novotel, which offers rooms for about £60 (0121 643 2000). A cheaper choice is Etap Hotel on Great Colmore Street, with rooms from £35 (0121 622 7575). It's only five minutes from Birmingham New Street train station.

If you do one thing in Birmingham...

There's everything from the National Sea Life Centre to great live music venues, museums and art galleries. See the city guide for more.

Goal record

Aston Villa, one of only seven clubs to have played in every Premiership season, scored the first competitive goal at Arsenal's Emirates Stadium on the first day of the 2006-07 season.

Don't mention

Doug Ellis: the former chairman who was seen by the Villa fans as something of a tightwad and was largely blamed for Villa's recent lack of success on the pitch.

Do mention

1980-82: in 1981 Villa won their first Division One title for 71 years, and followed that up with the European Cup the following season. Paul McGrath: a bit of a legend in these parts.

CAR
Villa Park is only about a mile from Junction 6 of the M6. Whichever way you're coming from exit at this junction onto the A38 Aston Expressway, heading towards Birmingham. After about a mile take the first exit off the Expressway and take the first exit off the roundabout onto Victoria Road; a right at the next roundabout onto Whitton Road leads you straight to Villa Park. There is some street parking available, but with residents' schemes rapidly taking over, it's probably easier and safer to use privately run car parks, such as the one in Aston Hall Road.

TRAIN
Local services are available from Birmingham New Street Station to Witton or Aston. Takes about five minutes to reach Aston station, from where the ground is about a ten-minute walk. Witton is closer (three-minute walk) but it is a further stop down the line and not all trains run to Witton.

Villa' to the tune of 'She'll be Coming Round the Mountain'.
Rivals: Birmingham City. Other Midlands teams are also disliked, such as Coventry, West Brom and Wolves.

Barnet

Characterful

The famous sloping pitch and dated facilities - little has changed at the ground since the mid-1960s - are said to be part of the stadium's charm, and make the Underhill experience different from almost any other ground in the league. Together the club and fans have been actively seeking a site for a new ground for some time – but the local council recently announced they feel that Underhill can be redeveloped.

The club still feel their future lies away from Underhill (possibly at Montrose Park) but nonetheless in the summer of 2007 they lodged a planning application to build new stands behind each goal. That will stave off the looming threat of expulsion from the Football League for failure to meet ground criteria and give the ground a much-needed facelift because in its current state even the staunchest of Barnet followers admit facilities and views are poor, perhaps with the exception of the main stand.

The most vocal Bees fans cheer their team on in the East Terrace opposite the main stand. Visiting supporters will find that the northern section of the stand, allocated for away fans, is one of the best places in the ground to watch matches.

Have a dig at Barnet at your peril. Bees fans are sure to come back with some witty retort. Among the best terrace chants heard by one fan at Underhill was during the foot-and-mouth crisis when Plymouth Argyle were in town. "You're green, you're white, your cows are all alight, Argyle! Argyle!".

Barnet, originally formed in 1888, first gained a foothold in the Football League in the 1990-91 season under chairman Stan Flashman and manager Barry Fry. This was the year the Channel Tunnel was completed, Mikhail Gorbachev was awarded the Nobel Peace prize, Nelson Mandela was freed from prison and Manchester United beat Crystal Palace to win the FA Cup.

Eating out

Snack bars serving matchday staples like burgers and chips are located in a number of places around the ground. Steak & kidney Pukka Pie at £2.20 is a local favourite. But other than the pubs, there are few places to eat close to the ground.

Fast food outlets such as Subway abound on the High Street. And a quick stroll from Underhill, 30 yards south past the Odeon, there's Jose's Cafe which does "good deli food, along with greasy fry-ups and lovely bacon baguettes," according to one local. There's also a Thai restaurant next door and directly opposite is The Fresh Fry which can meet a craving for fish and chips.

More restaurants are just a train ride away in central London.

Mine's a pint

Barnet has lots of good pubs, most of which are located in and around the High Street. Check out The Sebright Arms in Alston Road and The Railway Tavern, near New Barnet station. The Old Red Lion, which virtually overlooks the ground, is known as the 'away pub' and offers "competitively priced beers and good, friendly

---

Club Information Stadium: Underhill Stadium, Barnet Lane, Barnet EN5 2DN Capacity: 5,500
Tel: 0208 4416932 Web: www.barnetfc.com Train: New Barnet Tube: High Barnet Colours:

service".

Other pubs near the ground welcoming away fans are The Weaver on Greenhill Parade, Great North Road - about five minutes' walk from Underhill - and The Queens Arms, next to the Odeon cinema. Described as a friendly, roomy pub with a "lively atmosphere", it serves food till 2pm on matchdays.

Stopping over in Barnet?

 London has the pick of accommodation but if you want to stay in Barnet, The Hadley Hotel, 113 Hadley Road, Barnet is recommended. Tel: 0208 449 0161. It's just a 10-15 minute walk from the ground.

A bit more upmarket is West Lodge Park Hotel in Cockfosters Road, Hadley Wood, Barnet. This four-star country house hotel is set in 35 acres of grounds and is situated a few minutes' drive from the M25 and only 12 miles from the heart of London. Tel: 0208 216 3900.

If you do one thing in Barnet...

Anyone who has been there will vouch for the fact that Barnet is not the most exciting of places.

The Barnet fixture for visitors is the best chance for away fans to stay in London and have it large in the capital for the weekend. Take in some of the capital's attractions such as The London Eye, the Tate Modern and Buckingham Palace. Or just party in the west end.

The ground is 30 minutes from central London by tube or train and an hour by bus.

Watch out, Beadle's about

You might be unlucky enough to bump into TV prankster Jeremy Beadle or ex-Spice Girl Emma Bunton on a trip down Barnet High Street.

Barnet FC's local rivals, Enfield, who now ply their trade in the lower reaches of the non-league pyramid, are dubbed Enfailed by Bees fans.

The late legendary comic Spike Milligan once lived in a spired house close to Hadley Common and regularly frequented the local pubs in Barnet.

Don't mention

The slope on the Underhill pitch: it's a dull topic; and those local politicians who have opposed Barnet's move to a new stadium.

Do mention

The late 1980s and early 1990s: Under the guidance of Barry Fry, the Bees rose to the heights of the third tier of English football.

Travel Information

CAR
From the M25: Exit at junction 23 and follow the A1081/A1000 for about three miles. The ground is at the foot of Barnet Hill near to the junction with Station Road (A110). There is plenty of street parking available, but don't upset roaming clampers. Best car park is at the tube station, which is well signposted from all directions. It costs only a couple of quid and is a short walk from the ground.

TRAIN
New Barnet, about twenty minutes from London Kings Cross. Out of New Barnet station turn right and then left into Station Road. Ten minutes' walking will get you to the traffic lights opposite the Barnet Odeon Cinema. Turn right under the railway. High Barnet Underground Station is five minutes' walk away from Underhill and is the last station on the High Barnet Branch of the Northern Line. London King's Cross also offers a direct connection to this line so you are spoilt for choice really. Turn left out of the station past the car park up the slope and left out onto Barnet Hill (A1000). An alleyway alongside the Old Red Lion pub will take you to the ground.

Amber and black Songs: For some reason 'Twist & Shout' is popular in Barnet. Rivals: Enfield historically, plus Arsenal and Fulham.

Barnsley

Speaking up for Barnsley

Significant redevelopment in the past decade has made 23,000-capacity Oakwell a welcoming arena with good facilities for away fans.

The North Stand housing visiting supporters was built in the summer of 1999 to replace the uncovered seating of the Spion Kop. Visitors are allocated 2,000 seats, although this can be increased to 6,000 for larger away followings.

The Tykes' brief flirtation with the top-flight during the 1997/98 season brought plenty of colour to the Premiership – and just as they did then, Barnsley fans will do their level best to keep the atmosphere bubbling at Oakwell through thick and thin.

Famous fans down the years have championed the cause. Dickie Bird, the eccentric former international cricket umpire, along with Yorkshire cricket legend Darren Gough and TV presenter Michael Parkinson declare allegiance with pride.

But the man who has arguably done most to promote the Tykes is Barnsley FC's poet-in-residence Ian McMillan. Described as "the Shirley Bassey of performance poetry" by the Times Educational Supplement, McMillan became the first poet-in-residence at a British football club in 1997. After the club secured promotion in April of that year, the Yorkshire Post printed a piece headlined 'Barnsley's first Premiership signing'.

McMillan, who has published a book of his football poems, recalls the day of Barnsley's historic scalp in the fifth round of the FA Cup in 1998. "We beat Manchester United 3-2 in an FA Cup game and afterwards a man said to me 'you won't write a poem about this, you'll write a sonnet', which I still regard as one of the best things anyone has ever said about my work."

Eating out

Get your fix of hotdogs, burgers and the like from snack bars located in the North Stand. Or treat yourself to a takeaway of some description from the many cafés and eateries lining Wellington Street in the town centre, a five minute walk from Oakwell. Here you'll find Indians, Italians and Chinese to meet all your dietary desires.

Mortons chippy is one of the finest in Barnsley, while there's another good one on Dodworth Road on the approach to the ground. On Peel Street, China Moon is recommended for its quality Chinese fare, while Franklin's Italian is one of the most popular restaurants of its type in town. Jalsa on Pitt Street offers good Indian cuisine.

However, Barnsley is not known for its restaurant culture, as many who have ventured there will know. One Tykes fan puts it more bluntly: "For anything cultured (like a sit-down meal that doesn't involve gravy) forget it. Go to Doncaster."

Mine's a pint

Away fans can buy alcoholic beverages at the ground. But Metrodome Leisure Centre, a few hundred yards away, is better for pre-match socialising - it has a spacious away-friendly bar and restaurant.

However, The Prince of

Club Information Stadium: Oakwell, Grove Street, Barnsley S71 1ET Capacity: 23,009 (all seated) Tel: 01226 211211 Web: www.barnsleyfc.co.uk Train: Barnsley Colours: Red and white Songs: 'It's Just Like Watching Brazil' was sung with a small sense of irony when Barnsley were in the top flight, in response to fans of other clubs who were of the

Wales on Eldon Street is where most away fans chew the fat over a pint. These are your best options before a match as you may get a hostile reception in town centre hostelries if you openly parade opposition colours. Wellington Street is rammed with pubs and bars and one of the places to head for post-match bevvies.

Barnsley, it has to be said, doesn't exactly stay in at night: it boasts more pubs and bars per square mile than many other towns and cities in the UK.

Peel Street's chain bars cater for the noisy youth of today... probably best avoided if you want a quieter evening session.

But you won't have to look far for friendly locals serving real ales.

Stopping over in Barnsley?

 With Manchester and Leeds within easy driving distance, you may be lured by the city lights.

Nevertheless, there may be a few hardy souls who can't resist some Barnsley hospitality.

The easy solution is the Travelodge on Stairfoot Roundabout, Doncaster Road (0870 191 1621). It's within a mile-and-a-half of the ground. Brooklands Hotel on Barnsley Road, Dodworth, offers four-star B&B treatment at reasonable prices (01226 329100).

If you do one thing in Barnsley...

This large former coal-mining town, located about 15 miles from Sheffield, is surrounded by spectacular countryside dotted with picturesque villages. But the birthplace of straight-talking Mick McCarthy has nothing more than drinking dens and shopping centres to explore. Head to Sheffield and Leeds for weekend sightseeing.

Bald ambition

The late Brian Glover hails from Barnsley and was a professional wrestler before going on to star as the bullying sports teacher Mr Sugden in Ken Loach's film, Kes. Glover accepted many villainous roles and once remarked: "You play to your strengths in this game... and my strength is as a bald-headed, rough-looking Yorkshireman."

Don't mention

The fact that their season in the Premier League was followed by a painful and gradual decline, which eventually ended with the club in administration in 2002.

Do mention

Ronnie Glavin: Scottish midfield maestro of the 80s at Oakwell. Mick McCarthy: an uncompromising defender whilst wearing the red shirt. Clint Marcelle: he scored the goal to get Barnsley into the Premier League élite back in 1997.

Travel Information

CAR
From M1: The club advise you to leave the M1 at Junction 37 onto the A628, which leads right to Oakwell, and then follow signs for visitor's car park. If you're travelling from the south you can also leave the M1 at Junction 36, taking the A61 into Barnsley and pick up the A628 for the stadium. There is also an official club car park located in Pontefract Road, directly in front of the club superstore, but this fills up very quickly on a matchday. Another option is an overflow car park at the end of Queens Road which is well signposted and is a five-minute walk to the away end of the ground.

TRAIN
Barnsley railway station is about a ten-minute walk away. This station is served by trains running between Sheffield and Leeds. From the train station: turn left away from the town centre and head towards the bridge that the dual-carriageway runs over. Go under the bridge and turn left up the slip road and then take the first road on the right and head towards the Metro Dome leisure complex at the top of the hill from where you can see the ground.

opinion that The Tykes were out of their depth. Older fans will remember a version of 'Side by Side' extolling the virtues of Cooper, Currie and Lowndes. Rivals: They detest both Sheffield sides (The Pigs and The Blunts) and Leeds.

Birmingham City

Statement of intent

Blues want to match their aspirations by building a new 55,000-seater stadium on a 50-acre site at Saltley. It forms part of a wider regeneration scheme including a sports village and community facilities.

"It's not just a football stadium plonked in the middle of field," managing director Karren Brady told the Birmingham Mail last March. "The benefits will be felt by many, she said. "It is going to be a community centre, a place where young people can work together, play together, be together." Sweet sentiments indeed.

But it remains doubtful whether the scheme will gain lift-off. There's been much yam-yamming in recent years about this City of Birmingham Stadium as a showpiece multi-purpose venue for the heart of England, but a distinct lack of enthusiasm for it.

Original plans hit the buffers when the city council withdrew support for the proposal that had at one time featured a super-casino. Plenty more hurdles stand in the way. But club officials are back in talks with council chiefs and hope to find investors to fund the project, knowing that if they don't it could be dead in the water.

St Andrews isn't a bad stadium, though it's a little small at around 30,000 seats for a club of Birmingham's stature. The majority of the ground has been redeveloped since the early 1990s, the latest addition being the Railway Stand End completed in 1999.

Away supporters are allocated between 2,500 and 4,500 seats in this stand, depending on demand, and it provides a decent vantage point. The vocal Blues brigade – likely over 25,000 for their Premiership season ahead - keeps the atmosphere highly charged.

Eating out

Chicken balti pies are a big seller at the ground. Burger vans around the venue are numerous. There are two cafés at the retail park opposite the Kop side - found in the 'Big W' store and Morrisons supermarket. A range of fast food outlets and curry houses line the Coventry Road in Small Heath. China Town, a five-minute drive away by the Hippodrome Theatre, has dozens of excellent restaurants. The Arcadian on Hurst Street has eateries to suite all taste buds from modern British cuisine to Mexican, Italian, Chinese and Indian. Birmingham is the 'Capital of the Balti', the spicy dish introduced to the city by its large Kashmiri population in the mid-1970s. Most balti houses are situated in the Sparkbrook, Balsall Heath and Moseley areas of south Birmingham, which forms the famous 'Balti Triangle'. Try Ladypool Road in Sparkbrook for a fine choice of Indian food and be aware that many restaurants are unlicensed so you can take your own booze.

Mine's a pint

 It might be advisable to drink at the ground as pubs for visiting fans nearby are sparse. Most have a 'Blues fans only' policy. The best port of call for the away contingent is The Anchor Inn on Bradford Street in Digbeth, about 15 minutes away but near the city centre:

Club Information Stadium: St Andrews, St Andrews Road, Birmingham B9 4NH Capacity: 30,016 (all seated) Tel: 0871 2261875 Web: www.bcfc.co.uk Train: Bordesley Colours: Blue and white Songs: 'Keep Right on to the End of the Road' is the club's adopted anthem. 'Don't Cry for me Aston Villa' is one of the few printable chants based

constantly changing range of real ales, mostly from small independents. The Wellington, a CAMRA pub on Bennetts Hill in the city centre and five minutes' walk from Snow Hill Station, is another worth checking out. The beers are well kept and selection outstanding. You can bring your own food into the pub.

Just up the road, you'll find The Briar Rose, one of the more refined Wetherspoons pubs, with top ales and friendly bar staff.

Police urge caution - drink in the city centre or on the outskirts and keep colours covered. It takes about 20 minutes to walk to St Andrews from New Street Station. A cab costs little more than a fiver.

Stopping over in Birmingham?

 Birmingham is worth a stop-over, even if it's just to sample the nightlife of Broad Street and the canalside destination of Brindleyplace. There's a Travelodge on Broad Street (0870 191 1564). Or you could bed down at nearby Novotel, which offers rooms for about £60 (0121 643 2000). A cheaper choice is Etap Hotel on Great Colmore Street, with rooms from £35 (0121 622 7575). It's only five minutes from New Street station.

If you do one thing in Birmingham...

There's everything from the National Sea Life Centre to great live music venues, museums and art galleries. Bringing the cultural tone down a bit is Legs 11, a lap-dancing club said to be a favourite haunt of professional footballers. For more info on attractions see page 22 .

Turf trouble

Wembley's spare pitch didn't last long after making the journey from London in January 2007. The £120,000 turf was used to replace the St Andrews pitch. But the club were forced to postpone their game against Leeds because the field, installed in adverse weather, was not fit for play. It was the first time a senior game in English football had been called off due to a newly-laid pitch not being ready.

Don't mention

The fact that City have never won anything of any real significance, a fact that Villa fans are only too keen to remind you of. Penalties: Blues lost their two most vital spot kick contests of recent years, against Watford in a 1999 play off semi-final and against Liverpool in the League Cup Final of 2001.

Do mention

Trevor Francis, who most agree is the most exciting and skilful player ever to have worn a City shirt. Famously became the first million pound player when moving to Forest in 1979. Frank Worthington: the ultimate football showman. Steve Claridge: loveable rogue.

Travel Information

CAR
From M6: exit the M6 at Junction 6 and take the A38(M) (Aston Expressway). Exit at the second exit and at the roundabout head along the Dartmouth Middleway, take the first exit. After about a mile, turn left into St. Andrew's Street.
From M40/M5: Take the M42 northbound. Exit M42 at junction 4 and turn left at the roundabout onto the A34. Continue over four roundabouts, through suburb of Sparkbrook to Camphill Circus roundabout. Take third exit on to A4540 Sandy Lane. At roundabout go straight on to ground. Parking around St Andrews isn't bad for a big city ground: the car park at the ground is for pass-holders only, but there is plenty of street parking around and unofficial car parking facilities for around a fiver.

TRAIN
The nearest station to St Andrews is Bordesley, a ten-minute walk away. You can only get there from Birmingham Snow Hill. If, like most people, you arrive at New Street Station in the city centre, you should take the ten-minute walk to Snow Hill and pick up a connection there, or catch one of the plentiful buses or even walk the twenty minutes or so to the ground.

on rivals Aston Villa; the full words to 'Roll Out the Barrel' being the most obviously unprintable one. Rivals: Aston Villa (The Vile) are the main rivals, but both the Black Country duo of Wolves and West Brom are never popular.

Blackburn Rovers

Bums on seats

Rovers have played at Ewood Park since 1890, making it now the oldest home to a current Premier League club.

Sir Jack Walker's millions transformed the stadium in the 90s when three new stands were built. These were happy days for the Rovers faithful - three years after winning promotion to the top-flight Blackburn were crowned Premiership champions in 1995.

One of the founder members of the Football League, Rovers take great pride in the house that Jack built. It's a compact and homely - but still impressive - venue for both sets of supporters.

Away fans are allocated space in the Darwen End, where up to 4,000 seats are generally available but the entire stand is given over to visitors if the occasion demands it. One gripe heard from visitors is the leg room between the rows of seats.

Average attendances have dipped by several thousand over the past few years - gates were around 21,000 last season. To arrest the decline, the club reduced season ticket prices by more than 25 per cent for the 2007/08 season. The most expensive ticket was cut from £595 to £399 – there's not many charging less now in the Premiership.

If only all club chiefs thought like Blackburn chairman John Williams. "We have recognised the concern of fans who feel that the cost of watching live football has become too expensive," he correctly stated. It's hardly rocket science, the approach, but the hope is Williams is not alone in his actions.

So expect the atmosphere at the 31,367-capacity ground to ratchet up a notch or two this year.

Eating out

Food at Ewood Park is your usual run-of-the-mill tucker, but it does stock the tasty Hollands Pies made locally at Baxenden, says Steve Tinniswood, a sports reporter on the Lancashire Telegraph. McDonald's is opposite the ground, and there are a number of greasy spoons on Bolton Road where Ewood Park is. Best takeaway is a Chinese called The Wok Star: quick, clean and very tasty. Goodfellows (Preston New Road) is the place to go for a pizza. The Akash (Bolton Road, Darwen) is probably the best Indian restaurant in Darwen, about 15 minutes' drive from Ewood Park back past Junction 4 of the M65.

Mine's a pint

Alcohol is available on the stadium concourse. There are two watering holes generally regarded as away pubs. The Fernhurst Hotel directly opposite is very welcoming and, as it's where most travelling fans gather, you can have a good old pre-match sing-song. The venue also has a 70-seat restaurant. The Golden Cup, just off Junction 4 of the M65, tends to be the first port of call for thirsty away fans. Smaller and more intimate, it's 10 minutes' drive from the ground. Blackburn nightlife can be a bit hit and miss, according to Steve Tinniswood. The main pubs centre around North

Club Information Stadium: Ewood Park, Blackburn, Lancashire, BB2 4JF Capacity: 31,367 (all seated) Tel: 08701 113232 Web: www.rovers.co.uk Train: Mill Hill Colours: Blue and white Songs: Rovers fans sing an extravagant version of the famous Irish ditty

Gate. Blakeys is consistently the busiest. Big enough with two bars, a DJ and a dance floor. Opposite is FJ Nicholls which certainly packs in the punters. Loud music, loud clientele - and usually the next port of call for the Blakeys boozers. Around the corner is O'Neills (King William Street), which always has a good atmosphere.

For clubs, try Heaven and Hell (Lord Square), the main club in town blending chart, cheese and techno. Jazzy Kex (Regent Street) is a small dingy place but best for jazz, funk and groove.

Check out its nearby sister pub Barzooka (Victoria Street) - off the beaten track but worth a visit.

Stopping over in Blackburn?

 If you're keen on sampling the local nightlife, Fernhurst Hotel offers reasonably priced rooms (01254 693541). There's also a cheap and cheerful hotel at the motorway services (M65 Junction 4).

Conveniently located in stunning surroundings just four miles from Ewood Park, Whitehall Hotel & Restaurant offers special rates for visitors to Rovers (01254 701595).

If you want to treat yourself, head for the swanky Macdonald Dunkenhalgh on Blackburn Road, Clayton-le-Moors (M65 Junction 7, 15 minutes from the M6). It's a beautifully restored 700-year-old building equipped with every modern comfort and facility – but with prices to match (01254 303407).

If you do one thing in Blackburn...

Go on a tour of Daniel Thwaites Star Brewery, one of the UK's top 10 beer producers, and see how great ale is made.

The brewery is on Penny Street (01254 686868).

Cup feat

The six-times winners of the FA Cup are the only football club to have won the trophy in three consecutive seasons, although it was some time ago (1884-86).

Don't mention

The empty seats: Rovers struggle to sell out all but the biggest games. Kevin Davies: on whom Blackburn once spent a club record £7.25m; he only managed two goals in 29 appearances before a cut-price move back to Southampton, and later a move onto major rivals Bolton.

Do mention

The late nineteenth century: Rovers won the FA Cup five times. The late Jack Walker whose millions saw the glory days return in the mid-nineties. Simon Garner, a proper old-school footballer: he liked a drink and a fag, sometimes at half-time, yet still produced the goods on the pitch and still holds the club goal-scoring record.

Travel Information

CAR
Ewood Park is very clearly signposted from the M65, but nonetheless go prepared to leave at junction 4, join the A666 and head towards Blackburn. Ewood Park is about a mile away on your right. You'll find street parking around the ground is available, and there are also plenty of reasonably cheap car parks on offer.

TRAIN
Blackburn mainline station is about a mile and a half from Ewood Park and at least a twenty minute walk – get a Darwen-bound bus from stand M at the station or opt for a cab. There is also the option of getting a local train to Mill Hill station, but this is still some fifteen minutes' walk away from the ground: turn left onto New Chapel Street, past the shops and left down New Wellington Street and over the canal onto Albion Street. At the end turn left and you'll see Ewood Park.

"The Wild Rover", consisting of several verses, each of which slags off Burnley. The beauty of this tune is that it is easily adaptable depending on who is currently plying their trade at Turf Moor.

Blackpool

Thanks for your hospitality

Bloomfield Road is blooming... slowly. Plans to turn it into a 16,000-all seater are well underway. Phase Two of a project that began in February 2002 is continuing and will eventually see the redevelopment of the south and east stands.

In the meantime, away fans can expect to get battered by seaside gales and that very fine drizzle which soaks you right through. That's because you'll be housed in an uncovered stand.

Club chiefs, in their quaint hospitable northern way, have been kind enough to erect what they call an open temporary 'golf-style' seated stand for away fans on the east side of the ground. In the winter, bring a brolly. The occasional nip of whisky from a hip flask during rain-affected viewing in a cold snap also helps. In the summer, pack your factor 30 sun-block... unless you like the lobster look.

There's space for just over 1,800 travelling supporters, although larger away followings can be accommodated elsewhere.

In June 2006, Latvian businessman Valeri Belokon promised a bright future for the club in the upper echelons of the Football League when he became The Seasiders' new president and director.

He is reported to have sunk £5m into the club and vowed to push stadium redevelopment plans forward and bring better players in to further his ambitions. Belokon also reassured the Blackpool faithful that there were no plans to replace the famous tangerine jerseys with a maroon colour kit, despite a winning sequence of matches played in the strip.

Eating out

Dubbed the "fish & chip capital of England", you won't go hungry up here - the smell of chips fills the salty sea air. At the ground, though, away fans should not get their hopes up. Various concessions kiosks sell tucker like Hollands pies and, erm, you can pay a visit to the famous burger van going by the name of Incredible Edibles. In town, though, you won't struggle. There's a Wetherspoons called The Auctioneer on Lytham Road. "The restaurant in the Big Blue Hotel at the Pleasure Beach is very good as well," says one local. Opposite the ground is a Frankie & Benny's for an Italian meal.

Mine's a pint

Blackpool lays claim to having the highest ratio of drinking establishments per square mile in Britain. Luckily, many of them are conveniently placed near the stadium. Any of the above mentioned pubs are fine. More traditional pubs are better bets for a jar or two. The Old Bridge on Lytham Road falls into this category. It's just round the corner from the ground and, although it'll be wall-to-wall with tangerine shirts, well-behaved away fans are given a cordial welcome. Number One Club on Bloomfield Road has cheap drinks but away fans are not greeted as warmly. A better option is The Bloomfield, a

---

Club Information Stadium: Bloomfield Road, Blackpool FY1 6JJ Capacity: 9,000 Tel: 0870 4431953 Website: www.blackpoolfc.co.uk Train: Blackpool South Colours: Tangerine and white Songs: Mainly based around their hatred of all things PNE and Burnley, Blackpool fans also try

large pub on the same street. The George is not recommended for visiting fans. A good night can be had by sticking to town centre haunts. For dancing and drinking into the wee hours, head for the Sanuk or Syndicate nightclubs.

Stopping over in Blackpool?

There's an abundance of choice. In the non-tourist season, you can just cruise the terraced streets off the Golden Mile, look out for vacancy signs and pick which B&B or hotel takes your fancy. Be advised to book during holidays, as it is unlikely the best stopovers will have rooms. A few options to consider are The Norbreck Castle Hotel, which overlooks the seafront on Queens Promenade. It's a massive hotel and cheap too (rooms from £25) and only a short tram ride away from the centre's many attractions (01253 352341). The Royal Carlton Hotel on South Promenade is also situated on the seafront with the only external scenic elevator in Blackpool. Rooms from £31 (01253 344214). More expensive, but away from the bustle, is the De Vere Herons' Reach on East Park Drive (rooms from £75), including restaurants, bars and a leisure club. There's also a golf centre, with a 12-hole course designed by Peter Alliss. (01253 838866).

If you do one thing in Blackpool...

All the delights of what's billed as "the busiest tourist resort in Europe" await. The club suggests town is "chock-a-block with entertainment and top-drawer shows". And it's not wrong. Blackpool is the perfect destination for a weekend away - climb the Blackpool Tower or scare yourself silly on the Big One at the Pleasure Beach. You could also shed your load of coppers in the Golden Mile of arcades. And there's always the beach.

The old boy done good

After losing out in the FA Cup finals of 1948 and 1951, it was third time lucky for Blackpool in 1953. The Seasiders clinched the cup in a thrilling match against Bolton, dubbed the 'Matthews Final'. Stanley Matthews inspired a comeback from a 3-1 deficit to lead the team to a 4-3 win. He notched 18 goals in 440 appearances for Blackpool before ending his career at Stoke at the age of 50.

Don't mention

Orange or Gold: it's tangerine! Owen Oyston: a mad gamble with the club failed miserably and he was sentenced to six years in prison. He left the club in tatters and facing mounting debts.

Do mention

The glory years of the 1950s: in particular the Matthews FA Cup Final of 1953 which is still considered by many as the best Cup Final ever. Famous ex-players: Stan Mortensen, Stanley Matthews and Jimmy Armfield.

Travel Information

CAR

Leave the M6 at junction 32 for the M55. Continue to the end of the motorway, go straight over the first roundabout into Yeadon Way. Turn right at the second mini-roundabout, and then left at the next mini-roundabout you come to. Turn right at the lights into Waterloo Road and left at the next lights into Central drive. At the next lights turn left into Bloomfield Road for the ground. There is plenty of street parking, plus pay and display car parks all over the place, so take your pick. It's worth checking and comparing prices though, especially during the summer season.

TRAIN

Blackpool South is the nearest station to the ground, and a few minutes' walk away. However it's more likely visiting fans will arrive at Blackpool North, which is a couple of miles from the ground, and worth considering a taxi or bus.

to incorporate the local attractions into their songs. 'You must have come on a donkey' and 'You're only here for the gay bars' two examples. Rivals: Preston and Burnley are the rivals, plus Tranmere.

Bolton Wanderers

Architectural gem?

It's 10 years since the Trotters upped sticks from Burnden Park to move to the magnificent Reebok, kicking off a new era in the Premiership after running away with the Division One title in 1996/97. Club records were smashed in their final campaign at Burnden Park, their home for 102 years, when they netted 100 goals and notched 28 wins. Happy days. Then they were relegated, only regaining a Premiership berth in 2001/02.

Built for about £45 million, the stadium's stunning tubular steel construction cuts an imposing sight on the skyline. The Reebok, incorporating the DeVere Whites Hotel - the UK's first fully integrated hotel facility within a football stadium - established the blueprint for mid-size football stadia in out-of-town locations and many clubs have copied its architectural flourishes.

With the club now well and truly settled in, those traditionalists who yearn for the old style stadium and think the Reebok is nothing more than a functional, soulless arena are very much in the minority.

Whatever your view, when full the Reebok is an awesome arena and there's no doubting the 28,723-seater is a welcoming place for away fans who are normally located in the two-tiered South Stand (3,000-5,000 depending on demand). Seats are fairly narrow but there's enough leg room, and facilities within the stand are of a good standard.

The acoustics are a major plus for a stadium conceived as much more than a football arena. The Reebok has a proud reputation as a multi-sports facility and one of the north-west's leading concert venues. It has held Great Britain rugby league internationals, boxing bouts featuring Bolton's Amir Khan - and even darts!

Eating out

Food and drink at the Reebok is reasonable enough and there's a post office-style queueing system in operation, although sometimes you can expect a lengthy wait unless you get there early doors. Service is efficient when you get to the front, though. The retail park includes a KFC, Burger King, Pizza Hut and a Bolton Wanderers-themed McDonald's. For a sit-down meal, Bolton's increasing restaurant stock in the town centre wins plenty of plaudits.

The Olympus Fish & Chip Restaurant on Great Moor Street and The Royal Balti House in Market Street, Farnworth, were recognised for their high standards at the 2006 Bolton Food and Drink Festival. Frankie & Benny's Italian Restaurant at The Valley, Watersmeeting Road, gets good reviews.

You can buy a pint of Boddington's at La Tasca, the Spanish tapas bar and restaurant, on Bradshawgate, recommended for its tasty menu and quick service.

Mine's a pint

Aside from drinking at the stadium, most of the boozers on the retail park are generally designated for home support. But you can booze merrily at the Middlebrook Tavern on this industrial estate (away supporters are expected to hide colours). Two pubs

---

Club Information Stadium: Reebok Stadium, Burnden Way, Lostock, Bolton BL6 6JW Capacity: 28,723 (all seated) Tel: 01204 673673 Website: www.bwfc.co.uk Train: Horwich Parkway Colours: White and navy Songs: Anti-Man United songs dominate Bolton's repertoire, most of which are unrepeatable. One of the more unusual football

within walking distance of the stadium and probably the most popular for visiting supporters are The Bromilow Arms and The Barnstormers on Lostock Lane, 10 minutes away. The Beehive at the top of the hill on Chorley New Road is OK too. If you don't want the hassle of hunting down grub elsewhere, this place does a two-for-one food deal. It's also a convenient place to park. The Brinsop the other side of the motorway is recommended for its range of ales and bottled beers. Parking is also available. In Bolton town centre next to the station, Sweet Green Tavern is away-friendly. It's 10 minutes on the train to Horwich Parkway station, near to the stadium. For post-match liquid refreshment, Bradshawgate and Churchgate are well populated with pubs and bars.

Stopping over in Bolton?

 If you don't fancy staying in the stadium hotel (check out the club's website) modestly-priced accommodation is available at Holiday Inn on Higher Bridge Street (01204 879988). It's near the station and just over two miles off the M61 Junction 4. Premier Travel Inn is on Chorley New Road. Rooms from £50 per night (08701 977 282). Nestling in a collection of 18th century farmhouses on the edge of open countryside and with fine views of the west Pennine moors, the Last Drop Hotel at Bromley Cross is a more

expensive alternative (01204 591131).

If you do one thing in Bolton...

Have a pint and traditional Lancashire grub in Ye Old Man & Scythe Pub on Churchgate, Bolton's oldest building and pub dating back to the 12th century. Tours are available.

Top of his game

Club legend Nat Lofthouse, the Trotters' record marksman with 285 first-class goals, netted two in the 1958 FA Cup final win over Manchester United. He also scored an incredible 30 goals in 33 England appearances.

Don't mention

That Bolton haven't won a trophy since 1958: they came close in 1995 and 2004 but on both occasions they were runners up in the League Cup.

Do mention

The 1920s: Wanderers won the FA Cup three times. Nat Lofthouse: nicknamed 'The Lion of Vienna' after scoring the winner for England in Austria and getting knocked out cold in the process. A one-club man he played over 500 times for Wanderers and scored the winner in the 1958 FA Cup Final. 'Super' John McGinlay: a more recent Bolton icon who regularly topped the goal scoring charts at Burnden Park and even scored the last goal there before the move to the Reebok.

Travel Information

CAR
Probably the country's easiest stadium to find. Simply leave the M61 at Junction 6. Take the first exit off the roundabout onto the A6027 Mansell Way and at the next roundabout take a left onto Burnden Way for the visitor's car park. There are three official car parks: A is for visiting supporters. Cheaper options are available in some of the nearby industrial units, but there is little or no street parking available.

TRAIN
Travelling by train is even simpler than by car. Horwich Parkway is right next to the stadium and you can get a connection from the mainline station in Bolton.

songs you'll come across is "Look who's Coming up the Hill", which is almost, but not quite, as bizarre as another Wanderers song about chickens, which defies explanation. Rivals: Blackburn are traditional rivals, but Man Utd are hated with a passion too.

Bournemouth

Come on you grockles

The Fitness First Stadium at Dean Court may be a naff moniker for a football club's ground but it's less of the leisure centre its name suggests - more a well-equipped venue for the beautiful game.

It's a massive improvement on Dean Court, the Cherries dilapidated former home which was reduced to rubble to allow for the stadium development on the same site. Opened for the 2001/02 season, the 10,700-capacity ground is in good nick and provides a comfortable experience for visitors.

Having rotated the pitch 90 degrees to cater for the redevelopment, don't be disorientated if this is your first visit in some years. Away fans are now accommodated in the covered, all-seater East Stand, and there are unrestricted views.

Visiting supporters may hear themselves called grockles by Bournemouth types. But it's nothing to get uppity about - the ugly term is simply local slang for tourists.

Far worse would be if you were branded a noggerhead (a blockhead), then you'd have every right to sound off or ballyrag (scold) home fans. If you can weave the word chitterlings (entrails of a pig) into your barbed response, by all means do so.

Funnily enough, the Dorset dialect 'footy' translates as 'insignificant'. Enough said.

Expect some clever one-two's in the home stands. When someone shouts "Up the Cherries", the army of fans replies with the witty riposte "In all Departments". You might also spot a few sad Cherries fans sporting t-shirts bearing the acronym UTCIAD. Amusing only if you are a little drinky (intoxicated).

Eating out

Catering facilities for away fans are located in the East Stand. Lindley Catering complements the usual fare with beef baps, Chinese and Indian options, pizza and soups. Head to Bournemouth town centre, if you're after a sit-down meal. It has over 250 restaurants, bistros, pubs and cafés. There's a Harry Ramsden's along the prom, you can sample fresh seafood on the seafront at Westbeach Restaurant, or wine and dine at Bistro on the Beach while taking in the sea views. It's located in a picture-postcard beach setting on Solent Promenade, just three miles from the town centre. You may also like to get your laughing gear around a Dorset Knob. The local delicacy is a scone-like biscuit, served with sweet or savoury fillings.

Mine's a pint

There's a lively pub and bar scene but one place you won't be welcome is the Cherry Tree, the nearest pub to the ground. However, there are plenty of others. The Queens Park on Holdenhurst Road is close to the stadium and a popular football pub, with away fans welcome. It does food on matchdays, and has Sky TV and a beer garden. The Portman Hotel on Ashley Road is also friendly although the interior is adorned with AFC Bournemouth paraphernalia. There are some tasty ales on tap here. On Boscombe high

Club Information Stadium: Fitness First Stadium, Kings Park, Bournemouth, Dorset BH7 7AF (Formerly Dean Court) Capacity: 10,700 (all seated) Tel: 01202 726300 Website: www.afcb.co.uk Train: Pokesdown Colours: Red and black Songs: Anti-street (Christchurch Road) - a 15 minute walk from the ground - is a Wetherspoons pub, The Sir Percy Florence Shelley. If you want to get served, cover up. For night-time entertainment, popular haunts are Bar Med or Bliss on St. Peter's Road. Old Christchurch Road has many top pubs and bars, including Walkabout, DNA and Label. The Royal Exeter Hotel on Exeter Road has a cool lounge bar called 1812 and serves the best cocktails in town.

Stopping over in Bournemouth?

 This being a busy seaside resort and major conference centre, you'll have no trouble finding hotels or guesthouses. The Best Western Connaught on West Hill Road is a three-star hotel with a restaurant and spa facilities (01202 298020). Rooms are from £40. Quality Hotel Bournemouth is on Gervis Road, East Cliff, and only a short stroll from the golden sandy beaches and town (01202 316316). Rooms are from £24. Boscombe is worth considering. It has plenty of character with its antique and bric-a-brac shops, and it's not far from the stadium. *www.bournemouth. co.uk* is a useful resource for accommodation tips. If you want to splash the cash, why not stay at The Urban Beach, a small boutique hotel close to the beach on Argyll Road (01202 301 509). Rooms are around £115. There's a bistro

lounge and cocktail bar.

If you do one thing in Bournemouth...

Besides Bournemouth's award-winning beaches, there's the winter gardens and pier, oceanariums, surf schools and more. Bournemouth International Centre stages concerts and big shows. If you're driving, the New Forest national park is 15 minutes from the town; in the summer, head for beaches such as Lulworth Cove or Chesil Beach. Great for a family day out is the famous Monkey World, 65 acres of sanctuary for over 150 primates, near Wareham (01929 462537).

Good ole Arry

The Cherries' most successful manager to date is Harry Redknapp. His finest hour came when FA Cup holders Manchester United were knocked out of the cup by Bournemouth in 1984.

Don't mention

The ground: Bournemouth don't own it. They had to sell it to survive, and now rent it back – although with the help of supporters, the club are trying to buy it back.

Do mention

Jermain Defoe: he scored in 11 successive League games for Bournemouth at the start of the 2000/01 season, while on loan from West Ham. Steve Fletcher: a Roger Ramjet look-a-like centre-forward and an absolute hero in these parts.

Travel Information

CAR
Leave the A31 and take the A338 towards Bournemouth. The ground is situated on the left of the A338 on the outskirts of Bournemouth and is well signposted. Exit the A338 onto Little Down Drive and then turn left into Kings Park at the roundabout. There's a large car park at the ground or you can opt for the council-owned one the opposite side of the dual carriageway, which offers a quicker getaway after the game.

TRAIN
The nearest train station is Pokesdown. It's a mile from the ground and at least a fifteen-minute walk. However, most trains arrive at Bournemouth Central, which is a thirty-minute walk. Either try to get a train to Pokesdown, a bus (number 33 to the ground, 34 coming back) or get a cab – which will be about eight quid. If you do get to Pokesdown Station, then exit the station and turn right down the main Christchurch Road. After about 400 metres turn right into Gloucester Road and the stadium is located at the bottom of this road.

Portsmouth, Southampton and Brighton ditties, plus a wide range of traditional terrace anthems, including 'Red Army', 'Keep the red flag flying' and 'We all follow the Bournemouth'.

Bradford City

Modern-day marvel

Intersonic Stadium, formerly the Bradford & Bingley Stadium, is a world away from the ground that people knew before the 1985 Bradford Fire when an inferno destroyed the 77-year-old wooden main stand. Described as the worst fire disaster in the history of British football, the tragedy claimed the lives of 56 fans.

The stadium tragedy on the final day of the Bantams' championship-winning Third Division season - during a match against Lincoln City - led to the launch of new legislation governing safety at football grounds nationwide.

In the wake of the disaster, the Bantams played their home ties at Leeds United, Huddersfield Town and Odsal Stadium, home of rugby league's Bradford Bulls, while the future of Valley Parade was determined.

But a groundswell of support for redevelopment persuaded the local council to provide funding for a £2.6m stadium revamp to allow the Bantams to return to their traditional home.

More significant improvements came in the 1990s under former chairman Geoffrey Richmond who masterminded the conversion of the ground into an all-seater stadium. The Bantams' brief spell in the Premiership led to a second tier being added to the main stand, lifting capacity to 25,000. But by the time it was completed Bradford were facing relegation from the top-flight.

However, the result of Richmond's ambitious endeavour is an impressive stadium. Away supporters are housed in the TL Dallas Stand where there's seating for 1,840. Space for larger away followings is found in the Yorkshire First Stand.

Eating out

The TL Dallas Stand has a catering kiosk selling Shire Pies, Rollover hotdogs and burgers and a range of snacks and drinks. There's not a lot of takeaways nearby, although you'll find a McDonald's not far away in Forster Square Retail Park. Bradford is the unofficial curry capital of Britain - it's said to have more than 200 curry houses. The first opened in the 1950s, at a time when many Asian workers were working in the textile mills. It's inadvisable to choose from any in the immediate vicinity. Best to head into the city. There you'll find some great value curries. Akbar's on Leeds Road promotes itself as "probably one of the best Indian restaurants in the north of England". Restaurants in Centenary Square in the town centre have a growing reputation. Markaz serves a delicious diversity from Indian street foods to Middle Eastern mezze. Or you could try the Cocina Mexican restaurant on Manningham Lane. If money is no object, try the Michelin-starred Box Tree Restaurant in Ilkley - classical French cooking with locally-sourced produce.

Mine's a pint

There's no booze available in the TL Dallas Stand. But if the Yorkshire First Stand is made available - usually for larger followings - then you can make merry with a few pints of Carlsberg or Tetley's. The only

Club Information Stadium: Intersonic Stadium, Valley Parade, Bradford, W Yorkshire BD8 7DY Capacity: 25,136 (all seated) Tel: 0870 8220000 Website: www.bradfordcityfc.co.uk Train: Bradford Forster Square Colours: Claret and Amber Songs: An obscene chant called 'The Bradford Ranger' seems to be popular with the City fans. Other songs seem to be largely divided

11. BRADFORD CITY

pub near the ground is The Bradford Arms on Manningham Lane – although there is a club bar, with a giant screen, located next to the ground. Depending on the visitors, it may admit away fans for a small membership fee.

Probably best to have a few sharpeners in town before a game at various locals or chain pubs like the Wetherspoons' The Sir Titus Salt or the Walkabout on Morley Street.

The Fighting Cock in Preston Street is a proper spit-and-sawdust pub with one of the best selections of real ales in the city and decent food. Another highly recommended is The Love Apple on Great Horton Road. A good option for pre-match or a night out, this café-bar-club serves quality food and drink in a relaxed atmosphere.

Stopping over in Bradford?

 You can gamble on the service and friendliness of cheap B&Bs and guesthouses, or go for reasonably priced hotels. Or stay in the bigger Yorkshire cities. In Bradford, the club recommends the four-star Cedar Court Hotel on Mayo Avenue, off Rooley Lane. It's between Bradford and Leeds at the top of the M606 and just minutes from the M62, M606 and M1 and A1(M) corridor. Rooms around £40. (01274 406606). The Midland Hotel on Forster Square is next to the train station, with rooms from £60. It has a grill restaurant and

three bars (01274 735735). The Hilton Bradford is another option, a few minutes from the station with a restaurant and bar facilities (01274 734734).

If you do one thing in Bradford...

"You'll never be bored in Bradford," trumpets one tourist website.

That's tosh. You'll have more fun in Sheffield or Leeds which offer much more extra-curricular entertainment at the weekend.

However, Bradford does have the National Museum of Photography, Film & Television, home to several galleries, film festivals and the original IMAX.

Snooker loopy

Joe Johnson, the 1986 World Snooker Champion, is a passionate fan of The Bantams. The man who famously beat Steve Davis in that final wore a t-shirt bearing the slogan 'Bradford's Bouncing Back' when he wasn't playing.

Don't mention

The excessive spending under the regime of Geoffrey Richmond: it led to City going into administration and they still haven't recovered

Do mention

Paul Jewell, who guided City into the Premiership in 1999. Stuart McCall: a true club legend who epitomised the spirit required to compete at the top level. Peter Beagrie: fans loved his back flips en route to the Premiership.

Travel Information

CAR
Leave the M62 at J26 for the M606. From here the ground is clearly signposted, but you need to take the A6177 ring road and turn off onto the A650 Manningham Lane. You'll find Valley Parade about 400m on the left as you head south. It's not easy parking at the ground, due to a residents parking scheme. It may be worth considering parking in the town centre and walking to the ground - it's about fifteen minutes' walk – or opt for one of the privately run car parks near the ground.

TRAIN
Aim to get a train to Bradford Forster Square, which is closer to the ground than Bradford Interchange (a half-hour walk or cab ride to the ground). From Forster Square go diagonally across the car park to the main road and turn right into Manor Row then right down Hamm Strasse; and left into Midland Road. You will see the ground to your left.

between hatred for Leeds, for whom they have a special version of 'Marching on Together' and hatred for Huddersfield, who are roundly abused with a large repertoire of songs. Rivals: Bradford fans hate Leeds with a passion. Huddersfield and Burnley are also on their radar.

Brentford

Fancy a beer down the corner shop?

Tune into the buzz at the Bees' nest and you'll hear plenty of chat about the club's plans to move to a new 20,000-seat stadium. Proposals to build a venue at Lionel Road, a triangle of land next to Kew Bridge Railway Station, were first mooted in November 2002 and talks are ongoing with the local council and Strategic Rail Authority.

Bees United, The Brentford Supporters' Trust, acquired 60 per cent of the club on January 20, 2006. It is at the centre of negotiations to acquire land and put a financing package in place to allow construction work to start. The search for investors is underway.

The stadium scheme aims to remedy problems that have beset the club's management for decades - "complex financial arrangements for a new ground, in an area of scarce land availability". Bees United stresses the importance of fundraising initiatives and the club acquiring an alternative stadium "and with it a fresh tranche of revenue streams".

Additional income would come via improved sponsorship deals, better catering facilities, increased attendances and potential ground-sharing with a rugby club.

For the time being, the Bees must content themselves with some short-term improvements to the 12,500-seat Griffin Park, home since 1904.

Away fans will have a better time of it this season. Completion of a new roof covering the Ealing Road terrace will stop visiting fans getting soaked on rainy days.

Of course, there's one massive bonus about Griffin Park for every fan: it's the only ground in British football to have a pub on each corner outside the ground.

Eating out

Curries, pies and chips - along with an assortment of snacks and drinks - are available at catering outlets around the ground. Away fans are also welcome to enjoy the matchday hospitality in The Hive, but you'll pay handsomely for the privilege of a meal deal. If you can't afford this, there are plenty of other choices nearby: Ealing Road has a McDonald's (three minutes' walk from the ground); there are two fish & chip shops in the immediate vicinity; and fast-food outlets line the High Street.

Brentford Tandoori Restaurant is also located on High Street, as is Fatboys Thai, a recommended restaurant for its authentic Thai cuisine. Two of the pubs located at the ground - The New Inn and The Griffin - are known as much for their beers as their pre-match grub.

Mine's a pint

You're never far from a pub at Brentford FC. The New Inn, The Griffin, The Royal Oak and The Princess Royal are conveniently placed at each corner of the ground. All four are away-friendly, so why not complete the Griffin Park pub crawl? Of these, The Princess Royal and The New Inn (fine array of beers, Sky Sports and pool tables) are the favourites among travelling supporters.

After the football, you can

Club Information Stadium: Griffin Park, Braemar Road, Brentford TW8 0NT Capacity: 12,763 Tel: 0845 3456442 Website: www.brentfordfc.co.uk Train: Brentford Tube: South Ealing (Piccadilly Line) Colours: Red, white and black Songs: The usual local rivalry

take your pick from some 70 pubs scattered around Brentford.

The Lord Nelson on Enfield Road, a Victorian pub which has been a centre of its community since 1860, is said to be one of the best around. A range of Fuller's ales are available and it's recommended for its tasty food, which is served in the pub's restaurant area.

Stopping over in Brentford?

 The centre of London is only 12 miles away, so you may prefer to stay there if you're planning to do a spot of sightseeing around these parts.

But if you're determined to make Brentford your base, you could do worse than stopping a night at the Holiday Inn Brentford Lock on High Street, which has moderately priced rooms (020 8232 2000), or Premier Travel Inn on the same road with rooms from £60 per night (0870 990 6304). Travelodge London Kew Bridge Hotel on High Street is another option and offers similar rates (0870 191 1540). It's only half a mile from Griffin Park.

If you do one thing in Brentford...

There's much to do in this borough of London.

There's the Kew Bridge Steam Museum. No doubt there's some very, erm, pretty topiary (hedging clipped in the shape of former chairman Ron Noades, perhaps) on display at Kew Gardens.

And let's not forget The Aquatic Experience at Sion Park, a top family day out where you and the youngsters can see fish, reptiles and amphibians up close (020 8847 4730).

There's also plenty to see in the heart of the capital. For more information, see our city guide.

Pulling the strings

Greg Dyke, the broadcaster credited with introducing the glove puppet Roland Rat to the TV-am breakfast show in the 1980s, was appointed as non-executive chairman of the club following the takeover by the supporters' trust in 2006.

Don't mention

Ron Noades: he acquired the club in 1998, installed himself as manager and chairman and set about running up massive debts.

Noades' ambitious plan to build a stadium near Heathrow never got off the ground, and his suggestion was that the club should relocate to Surrey.

Do mention

Terry Evans: inspirational defender and club captain of the Division Three winning team of 1992, for whom Dean Holdsworth banged in over thirty goals. Terry Hurlock: the term hard-man was invented for him.

Travel Information

CAR
The most direct route is to leave the M4 at junction 2, and follow the A4 until you reach Chiswick roundabout. Take the fifth exit onto the A4 westbound (going back on yourself). Continue for 1 mile, until you reach the traffic lights after GlaxoSmithKline. At these lights turn left into the Ealing Road from where you will see the ground. Fans travelling from the south can also opt for the M3 and head in via the A316, A307, South Circular and A315. You shouldn't have too much trouble finding street parking near the ground – just keep an eye out for residents' parking schemes.

TRAIN
There's the option of train and tube – and both are less than ten minutes' walk from Griffin Park. South Ealing on the Piccadilly Line is the nearest tube station, just head down the Ealing Road for about ten minute. The nearest rail station is Brentford, which is served from Clapham Junction & Waterloo, and only five minutes from the ground. Head up the main road and turn left into Windmill Road then right into Clifden Road. The ground is right in front of you from here.

stuff targeting Fulham, QPR and Chelsea. Also an amusing ditty to the Fred Flintstone theme tune celebrating QPR's FA Cup defeat against Vauxhall Motors. Rivals: QPR, Fulham and Chelsea.

New era for the Albion?

The Albion have been campaigning for a 23,000-seat stadium of their for almost a decade. The club is hoping the government grants permission to build on a site next to the university and the A27 on the outskirts of town.

A decision in Brighton's favour can't come too soon, following the longest-running public inquiry in football history. The then Deputy Prime Minister John Prescott granted permission for the stadium at Falmer in October 2005 but his decision was quashed due to an error in the letter giving permission.

In November 2006, the government asked the various parties to comment on alternative sites, even though the public inquiry had looked at other possibilities and found that none would get planning permission.

The Seagulls have not had a permanent home in Brighton since 1997 when they were forced to leave the Goldstone Ground after it was sold by the previous owners. They spent two seasons ground-sharing at Gillingham's Priestfield Stadium - a 150-mile round trip into Kent for home fans - before the local council granted permission to use Withdean Athletics Stadium.

The running track around the pitch, temporary seating and exposure to the elements makes it one of the most unsuitable grounds in the Football League. Fans are too far removed from the pitch, resulting in a distinct lack of atmosphere.

A limited number of tickets are made available to away fans due to the restricted capacity at Withdean, which holds about 8,800. There's capacity for around 900 visiting supporters in the away end, so make early plans if you want to be among the small army of visitors - but be warned the view isn't great from the away end.

Eating out

Withdean's catering outlets offer hot and greasy grub. The Sportsman pub on one side of the ground does good meals. But there's not much else nearby. You'll have to drive or catch a bus into town. Cheap eats are available on North Street, running down from the Clock Tower. Here you'll find sandwich shops, takeaways, Burger King and Pizza Hut. Preston Street off Western Road is the place for curry houses or a Chinese. China Garden is good value. The Lanes or North Laine area are home to some of the best cafés and eateries. Donatello is an Italian recommended for its good food and quick, no-nonsense service. Family-run Al Duomo next to the Brighton Pavilion makes the best pizza in its wood ovens. Two good fish & chip restaurants for takeaways or sit-down meals are Bardsley's on Baker Street and Bankers on Western Road. If you hanker for tapas, look no further than Pintxo People on Western Road.

Mine's a pint

The Sportsman behind the North Stand is packed on matchdays and has a good atmosphere. En route into town - a 15 minute walk from the ground - is the Preston Brewery Tap and The Crown and Anchor. Both sell Harveys, a popular locally-brewed ale. Within 50 metres of Brighton Station, you'll find some

---

Club Information Stadium: Withdean Stadium, Tongdean Lane, Brighton Capacity: 8,850 (all seated) Telephone: 01273 695400 Website: www.seagulls.co.uk Train: Preston Park Colours: Blue and white Songs: The team run out to the county anthem

fantastic pubs with character and a nice pint to boot. The Lord Nelson Inn on Trafalgar Street is among the finest for its ales and pre-match food. Guildford Road (turn right out of the station) is home to The Battle of Trafalgar and The Sussex Yeoman. Both do excellent food. Nearby is The Evening Star, winner of CAMRA's Regional Pub of the Year 2006, which boasts a large selection of house beers. Brighton has a thriving nightlife. Head down to the beachfront bars for the buzzy atmosphere. Some of the biggest nightclubs are here: including The Beach, The Honeyclub and The Zap. Or for comedy, music and cabaret, visit the Komedia on Gardner Street.

Stopping over in Brighton?

Brighton is packed with hotels and guesthouses. Cheap seafront hotels include The Royal Albion Hotel, directly opposite Brighton's Pier (01273 329202). The Kings Hotel is another option (01273 820854). Quality Hotel on West Street is within easy reach of city centre attractions and nightlife (01273 220033). Boutique hotels with higher room rates offer more character and comfort. Hotel Pelirocco in Regency Square fancies itself as "England's most rock 'n' roll hotel" (01273 327055). More upmarket and extravagant is Hotel du Vin on Ship Street (01273 718588) with its eccentric, gothic revival and mock Tudor buildings.

If you do one thing in Brighton...

There's plenty to keep you occupied. Wander around the town's Lanes and North Laine area, enjoying the café culture and the designer, bric-a-brac and retro clothing emporiums. When the sun's out, there's no better place than the seafront. Brighton Pier holds rides and attractions for all ages. For more info, flick to our regional guide to south coast cities.

Skint by name

Norman Cook, aka DJ Fatboy Slim, owns a minority stake in the Albion. His label Skint Records has been a shirt sponsor since 2000, but he actually supported arch rivals Crystal Palace before he moved to the city.

Don't mention

Bill Archer, Greg Stanley or David Bellotti, responsible for the sale of the Goldstone in the mid-nineties. Front man Bellotti received death threats from irate fans. He was described by a judge as "the most hated man in Sussex".

Do mention

Peter Ward: star of the club's meteoric rise in the late 1970s and darling of the Goldstone faithful. Bobby Zamora: star of back-to-back Championships in 2001 and 2002. Dick Knight: the chairman who took over when the club was bottom of the League in 1997 and saved it from almost certain extinction.

Sussex By The Sea, reworked to a terrace chant 'Good Old Sussex by the Sea'. Rivals: Crystal Palace are their main rivals, although Portsmouth, and Leyton Orient aren't exactly popular visitors.

Bristol City

That's entertainment

Ashton Gate has long been one of the most impressive grounds in the lower tiers of the English leagues, and Championship fans will feel at home in this spacious arena following City's promotion from League One.

Visiting fans will find a pew in the Wedlock Stand at the south-east end of the ground. It was set for a revamp in 2005 but funding problems put paid to the project getting underway.

It can hold up to 5,500 supporters and the low roof ensures good acoustics. Make sure you don't get stuck behind one of the supporting pillars, though.

The stadium has built a reputation as one of the leading sports and leisure venues in the south west of England. Bristol Rugby club have played there on a number of occasions. When the Bristol v Bath clash was held at the ground in 2003, the 20,793 crowd was a record for the Zurich Premiership. Ashton Gate also hosted a World Cup match between the All Blacks and Tonga in 1999.

Boxing remains a popular feature on the stadium's event calendar - the Dolman Exhibition Hall attracts crowds of more than 700 for the 'Bristol Fight Club' shows.

Concerts have also drawn huge crowds. In 1982 the Rolling Stones played in front of 36,000 fans; 18,000 watched Bryan Adams warble away at a stadium gig in 2003. Lucky people! Sir Elton John, Neil Diamond, Rod Stewart, The Who and Ronan Keating have since played the venue.

Eating out

Catering at the ground is fairly standard with all the usual matchday fare such as chicken balti pies. One City fan, however, doesn't see it this way: "The food is bad and exceedingly hot," he warns.

Still, there are choices just down the road which may not take the roof off your palate. North Street, five minutes walk from Ashton Gate, is choc-full of takeaways and cafés, bars and restaurants. Post-match options include Quba Ice, a bar/restaurant recommended for its Afro-Caribbean menu. Traditional jerk chicken or tender goat curry are among customer favourites. It also does a sumptuous Jamaican Platter. British staples are available: full English breakfast and a proper Sunday lunch. Vegetarians are also catered for, and a take away menu is available. Also on North Street is The Lounge, another bar-cum-restaurant that enjoys a good reputation. Ciabattas, steaks and burgers dot the menu and a chalk board features daily specials.

Mine's a pint

Ashton Gate claims to have the biggest bar in the league, but its 1,300 capacity is for home fans only. With no beer available in the away end, you'll have to look elsewhere. The Nova Scotia is a traditional dockside pub popular with home and away fans. It boasts

---

Club Information Stadium: Ashton Gate, Ashton Road, Bristol BS3 2EJ Capacity: 21,479 (all seated) Tel: 0117 9630630 Website: www.bcfc.co.uk Train: Parson Street Colours: Red and white Songs: 'Drink Up Thee Cider' is City's traditional terrace tune, although other clubs have tried to claim it as their own. They also have a couple of tunes

a fine range of real ales. Over the Plimsoll Bridge, you'll find The Pump House. A classy drinking establishment, it's a friendly place with good value drinks and meals. Its beer garden is a great spot for a lunchtime pint on a sunny day.

Another top pub on the quayside is The Cottage (efficient service and a good choice for families). One under-rated venue but a little further away is The Rose of Denmark on Dowry Place. If you're after a quieter pre- or post-match beer, go here. Fans can mix in The Robins but it's mainly for City supporters. Strictly for home fans are The Wedlocks opposite the north end of the ground, The Rising Sun and The Coopers Arms. The waterfront bars are some of the best night-time drinking dens. If you're into clubbing, look up the Syndicate or The Cooler. Jongleurs comedy club on Baldwin Street also stays open into the wee hours.

Stopping over in Bristol?

 There's plenty of reasonably-priced accommodation. The Holiday Inn Bristol Filton (0870 400 9014) on the Avon Ring Road is at the lower end. There's also the Bristol Marriott Royal Hotel on College Green next to the cathedral and waterfront (0117 925 5100). The four-star Jurys Bristol Hotel on Prince Street, along the river quayside, is a more attractive option (0117 923 0333). At the fancy end is the Avon Gorge Hotel, with spectacular views of the Clifton suspension bridge (0117 973 8955).

If you do one thing in Bristol...

'At Bristol', on the harbour side, is an entertainment destination bringing science, nature and art to life. Aimed at families and children, its three attractions include an IMAX theatre, a facility offering over 170 interactive experiences and Wildwalk which provides "a unique journey through the extraordinary variety of life on earth". For further information on sightseeing in the region, see our city guide.

All smiles with the LDV Vans Trophy

2003 was a dramatic season. City scored 106 goals but missed out on automatic promotion and were beaten in the Play-Off semi-finals by local rivals Cardiff City. But they did win the LDV Vans Trophy.

Don't mention

The Wurzels: they did everything possible to reinforce the stereotypes associated with life in this part of the world.

Do mention

Jacki Dziekanowski: Polish superstar - one of the most entertaining players ever seen at Ashton Gate. Gary Johnson: he took the club into the Championship in 2007 after a string of near misses.

Travel Information

CAR
From the M5: Leave at Junction 18, onto the Portway (A4) following signs for the Bristol Airport/Taunton (A38). Go over the swing bridge (Brunel Way), branching left into Winterstoke Road, and you will see the ground on your left.
From the M4: Leave at junction 20 onto the M5. Leave the M5 at junction 19. At the roundabout take the second exit, and follow the A369 towards Bristol.
At the Bower Ashton interchange take the second exit, signposted A3029 Winterstoke Underpass. After 200 yards, bear left into Winterstoke Road. Ashton Road is accessed via Marsh Road. Be warned, parking isn't easy at Ashton Gate; the car park at the ground is for permit holders only and it gets very busy on the streets so you may end up parking some distance from the ground.

TRAIN
Bristol Temple Meads is the mainline station, which is some distance from the ground. Best to get a cab or bus from here as the walk is around 40 minutes. There is the option of a closer train station at Parson Street, a ten-minute walk from the ground, but the rail service is infrequent.

celebrating the 'coincidence' that city rivals Rovers have been struck by arsonists at each of their previous two homes Rivals: Mainly City rivals Rovers (The Gasheads), but Swindon and Cardiff also merit a mention.

Bristol Rovers

Moving on up

Rovers purchased the 12,000-capacity Memorial Stadium from Bristol Rugby Club in 1998, shortly after moving to the venue following 10 years of playing their home matches at Bath City's Twerton Park. Originally built in 1921, Memorial Stadium has been subject to developments over time but is considered archaic by today's stadia standards - there are only about 3,000 seats.

Rovers are pushing ahead with plans for a redeveloped 18,000 all-seater stadium, which they would share with the rugby club. Reservations from locals set the proposals back but now redevelopment could be complete in 2009.

Rugby club officials have talked of moving across town to play at Bristol City's Ashton Gate ground due to their growing popularity - crowds are touching 12,000 for some home fixtures. The Guinness Premiership side requires at least 6,000 seats and a 15,000 licensed capacity to allow it to compete in the top-flight, a minimum standard criterion set for 2010/11. For revenue reasons, Rovers' chiefs are hoping the stadium renovation plans proceed smoothly to ensure their rugby counterparts stay put.

Visiting supporters are housed in the XXXX (The Finest Beer) Stand behind the goal, running along the south side of the stadium, and the Away Terrace, which is situated alongside the Mead Civil Engineering Stand on the east side. For cup and Play-Off matches, away fans are entitled to a greater allocation of overall capacity.

Rovers formed as The Black Arabs in 1883 before changing their name to Eastville Rovers a year later. Thirteen years on, they turned professional and became Bristol Eastville Rovers before gaining their current moniker in 1899. FA Cup quarter-final spots in 1951 and 1958 remain the high points of the Pirates' history.

Eating out

There are food outlets and huts in and around the ground so you can chow down on some proper Cornish pasties and pies. Indian cuisine, Asian foods and continental snacks abound. Fish & chip shops and cafés are within easy reach of the ground.

Recommended eateries include the Bristol Fryer near the Quarington Road junction and the Big Bite Café on Ashley Down Road. For something less lardy, try the freshly-made sandwich and baguette shop opposite the petrol station near the stadium on Gloucester Road.

Meanwhile, bar-cum-restaurant Tinto Lounge on the same street is a stylish and comfortable retreat, boasting an interesting food menu, and you can enjoy traditional Irish hospitality at the Waterfront Pub overlooking the harbour. Nearby Park Street is home to an array of restaurants to suit all tastes and budgets.

Mine's a pint

Gloucester Road is at the heart of studentsville, a two-mile strip running from the stadium to the city centre, and therefore a great place to sink a few jars on matchday. Watering holes in its environs are also billed as "football-friendly zones" on Saturdays and weekday evenings. The Wellington is a popular haunt, while The Anchor and Inn on the Green

Club Information Stadium: The Memorial Stadium, Filton Avenue, Horfield, Bristol BS7 0BF Capacity: 11,916 Tel: 0117 9096648 Website: www.bristolrovers.co.uk Train: Bristol Parkway Colours: Blue and white Songs: Despite having its roots in America's deep south back in the 1800s, Goodnight Irene has somehow been adopted by Rovers' fans as their anthem. Other

serve good ales. Other pubs worth checking out are The Royal George, The John Cabot Inn, The Foresters and The Ashley Arms. You could also venture down to Bristol's quayside pubs for some liquid refreshment.

The Cottage (efficient service and a good choice for families) is a good one. And the waterfront bars are some of the best night-time drinking dens. If you're into the clubbing lifestyle, look up the Syndicate or The Cooler. Jongleurs comedy club on Baldwin Street also stays open into the wee hours.

Stopping over in Bristol?

 When it comes to reasonably-priced accommodation, you're spoilt for choice. The Holiday Inn Bristol Filton (0870 400 9014) on the Avon Ring Road and Forte Crest on Filton Road, Hambrook, are at the lower end. The four-star Jurys Bristol Hotel on Prince Street, along the river quayside, is a more attractive option (0117 923 0333). The city's shops, art galleries, theatres and At-Bristol science museum are just a hop and a skip away.

At the fancy end is the Avon Gorge Hotel, which is two miles from the city centre and has spectacular views of the Clifton suspension bridge (0117 973 8955).

If you do one thing in Bristol...

'At Bristol', located at the city's harbour side, is an entertainment destination bringing science, nature and art to life. Aimed at families and children, its three attractions include an IMAX theatre, a facility offering over 170 interactive experiences and Wildwalk which provides "a unique journey through the extraordinary variety of life on earth".

For further information on sightseeing in the region, see our city guide.

Rod's Rovers refrain

Famous supporters include novelist Jeffrey Archer. The late, great Rod Hull (of Emu fame) released the god-awful single "Singing Bristol Rovers All The Way".

Don't mention

Arson: two of Rovers' recent home grounds have burned down. Weetabix: a terrace craze of chucking the breakfast cereal has led to it being banned at certain away grounds, particularly Shrewsbury.

Do mention

Ian Holloway: A legend at The Memorial Ground following his total commitment as player and manager, where his mad post-match ramblings were first heard. Devon White: particularly his two goals against Bristol City which won the club promotion in 1990. That City's real name is Bristol City 1982, after financial problems forced them to re-form.

Travel Information

CAR
From the M4: Exit at junction 19 for the M32; exit the M32 at junction 2. Head for Horfield and Southmead and follow the signs for the Memorial Stadium onto Muller Road. When you come to a signal-controlled crossroads, Filton Avenue is located almost immediately on the left.
From the M5: Exit at junction 16. At the roundabout head towards Filton and join the A38. After about four-and-a-half miles, just past a set of traffic lights, turn left into Filton Avenue where you'll see the ground is on your right after just a couple of dozen yards. There is ample street parking around the ground. Try Muller Road or Gloucester Road.

TRAIN
Filton Abbey Wood and Bristol Parkway are the nearest stations, but they are still some distance from the ground. Buses 73 and 74 run from Parkway and go past the stadium – or you might be as well to get a cab or bus from Temple Meads Station.

than that most of their songs revolve around the hatred of all things Welsh or from the red half of Bristol. Rivals: Bristol City (The Wurzels). Probably the only thing the City and Rovers fans have in common is a loathing of Cardiff and Swindon.

Burnley

Ageing gracefully

Founder members of the Football League in 1888, Burnley moved to Turf Moor shortly after the club was formed. Only near neighbours Preston North End have been resident at a single ground (Deepdale) for longer.

Turf Moor, one of the few English football stadia with changing facilities behind a goal, is remarkable for having staged football in all four league divisions. However, the Clarets have played outside the top-flight since 1976. The club's most famous fans are legendary weatherman John Kettley and Alastair Campbell, Tony Blair's former spin doctor. And if you've ever seen the Safestyle UK window adverts, the bloke who shouts "Buy one – get one free!" a lot... he's a Claret too!

Since 1994, several developments have sought to bring the ageing Turf Moor into the 21st century, including the creation of two new stands. But it still remains a bit outdated. The next phase of modernisation is to rebuild the David Fishwick Stand (formerly the Cricket Field Stand) to boost the ground's current 22,619 capacity. A suitable site to relocate the adjacent cricket club must first be found thus plans are on hold for the time being.

By the club's own admission, the all-seated David Fishwick Stand, accommodating up to 4,125 away fans, is in need of a makeover. You do at least get a good view from the uncomfortable wooden seats.

Due to the continuing deterioration of the stand, the club says it may need to undertake extensive maintenance to this area during 2007/08 and cannot guarantee it will be available to visiting supporters for the whole of the season. So you might find yourself watching the game from the lower tier of the Jimmy McIlroy Stand.

Eating out

Several snack bars at the ground serve the usual, including Hollands pies, although the concourse gets packed quickly if there's a sizeable visiting crowd.

Yorkshire Street is about one minute from the away turnstiles and has several fast food outlets, chippies and takeaways. The Queen Victoria, a Brewers Fayre used regularly by the away brigade, offers pub grub. It's on Belvedere Road, just past the cricket club. A mix of bakeries, cafés and restaurants are found in the town's main shopping area, St James Street, a 10 minute walk from Turf Moor.

Charter Walk shopping centre also has a few eating places. For an Indian, visit the Shalamar on Church Street. Moon River on Burnham Gate is said to be one of the best Chinese restaurants. Enzo's Pizza Takeaway on Colne Road is a top specialist in its field.

Mine's a pint

The cricket club behind the away end is a popular haunt for visiting fans, with limited parking and food available.

The Queen Victoria, mentioned above, is away-friendly and 10 minutes

Club Information Stadium: Turf Moor, Harry Potts Way, Burnley BB10 4BX Capacity: 22,546 (all seated) Tel: 0870 4431882 Website: www.burnleyfootballclub.com Train: Burnley Central Colours: Claret & blue Songs: Burnley's hatred of Blackburn dominates the terraces, and the

from Turf Moor.

The Sparrow Hawk Hotel on Church Street is a little further away and gets busy with bantering locals and visitors on matchdays. There's a convivial atmosphere and, on the beer front, it's a real treat.

The pub specialises in traditional cask conditioned ales sourced from small breweries all over the UK, Ireland and Belgium.

It also serves some tasty bites, plus cheap pub meals. Another safe haven is The Mercury Tavern on the corner of Todmorden Road.

The local police advise that away supporters avoid the town centre pubs. Certainly, it's best not to wear club strips if you plan on venturing into any.

There are plenty of chain bars and other centrally located hostelries for the nightlife.

Clubs include Lava-Ignite and Fusion, both on Hammerton Street.

Stopping over in Burnley?

The Sparrow Hawk Hotel could make a good pit-stop (01282 421551). It's within easy reach of the ground and town centre amenities. Weekend entertainment includes live acts.

Double rooms are from £53.

If you do one thing in Burnley...

Burnley is a fine Lancashire market town in its own right so you could pick up some bargains at the town's Saturday market.

Bunch of titles

In 1992, the Clarets became only the second team to win all four division titles when they won the fourth division. Wolves were the first. Former Arsenal hitman Ian Wright was one of the biggest signings in the club's history in the 2000/01 season. He scored a handful of goals before hanging up his boots.

Don't mention

Maggie Thatcher, who is generally despised in this part of the world anyway, but even more so by Burnley fans as she supposedly followed the fortunes of Blackburn.

Do mention

Skilful Irishman Jimmy McIlroy: the star of the club's halcyon days of the early 1960s. He is still talked about by those old enough to remember. That Clarets fan John Kettley is your favourite weatherman. One of the funniest own goals of all time: scored by Djimi Traore at Turf Moor, which saw the Clarets knock Liverpool out of the FA Cup of 2004/5.

Travel Information

CAR
From North: Follow the A682 to the town-centre and take the first exit at the roundabout (by the bingo hall) into Yorkshire Street. Continue through traffic lights into Brunshaw Road for the ground.
From East: Take A646 to A671 then along Todmorden Road towards the town-centre. At traffic lights, turn right into Brunshaw Road.
From South/West: Leave M6 at junction 29 for M65. Take the M65 to junction 10 and follow signs for Towneley Hall. The road leads right to the ground. Burnley Cricket Club and the pay & display on Centenary Road are the designated away car parks, but there is also some street parking around.

TRAIN
There are two stations fairly close to the ground, Burnley Central and Burnley Manchester Road (the nearer). From here, exit the station and walk down Centenary Way, from where Turf Moor is clearly visible. From Burnley Central, follow signs for the Town Centre and then head down Church Street and then left into Yorkshire Street.

most popular song is the Turf Moor version of the Wild Rover, which verbally assaults Rovers from all directions. Rivals: Blackburn, although there is also a dislike for Preston and Blackpool.

Bury

Highs & lows & Brucie (not Forsyth)

Two-times FA Cup-winners Bury have played at Gigg Lane for the club's 122-year history. The ground has undergone a major overhaul since 1993, with all four new stands going up and the Cemetery End terracing making way for a 2,500-capacity stand. Visiting fans are housed in this covered east stand offering great views.

FC United (the club formed in the wake of Manchester United's sale to the Glazier family) share Gigg Lane with Bury. While good views of the pitch from all vantage points have allowed the all-seater 11,840-capacity ground to host a variety of other sports down the years - including rugby league, baseball, cricket and, who would've thought it, wrestling and American football.

After winning the FA Cup in 1900 and 1903, the Shakers haven't needed to dust off much silverware since, although winning the Division Two championship in 1997 was a high point.

Sometimes the low points seem more interesting, don't they? The 1980s threw up a few of them. First came the club's biggest ever home defeat when they leaked seven goals without replying in a League Cup match against Nottingham Forest on September 23, 1980. Three years later their record defeat arrived, 10-0 at West Ham United in the Milk Cup.

In 1986, the club recorded its lowest ever crowd for a competitive first team game - the date of February 26 was forever etched in the minds of the 461 poor souls who turned up to watch the Freight Rover Trophy game against Tranmere .

Of course, you can't talk about Gigg Lane without mentioning Bruce Grobbelaar; the eccentric goalkeeping hero of Liverpool's 1984 European Cup final win against AS Roma. He's the oldest player to turn out in a league game at Bury's home, pulling on his gloves for the Shakers at the ripe old age of 40 years and 337 days.

Eating out

The best club grub is the spicy chicken balti pies and hot pasties sold at food kiosks around the ground. There's a bar serving food at Bury Social Club, which opens its doors to visiting fans on matchdays, charging £1 for non-members. It features a large-screen TV and a separate children's area. In addition to the takeaways dotted along the A56 Manchester Road or roads off it, you could try the Jewel In The Crown (Indian, Bolton Street) or Sergio's (Italian, Manchester Old Road). Man Sons Chinese Takeaway on Manchester Old Road is handy for Gigg Lane. A good chippy is The Cornmarket on Haymarket Street. Also recommended is the Trackside Free House on Bolton Street, where you can wash down a meal with a few real ales or bottled beers. Supporters seeking something more upmarket can dine out at EstEstEst Trattoria, the modern Italian restaurant situated on the A56.

Mine's a pint

The Swan & Cemetery on Manchester Road is one of the most friendly for away supporters. Dishing up family meals, the spacious pub offers ample parking and is only 300 yards past Gigg Lane if you're coming from the town centre. Closest to the ground and also said to be very hospitable

---

Club Information Stadium: Gigg Lane, Bury, Lancs BL9 9HR Capacity: 11,669 Tel: 0161 7644881 Web: www.buryfc.co.uk Station: Bury Metrolink Colours: White shirts, blue shorts, white socks Songs: 'You're just a bus-stop in Bury' (to Rochdale) is one of

is The Staff of Life, featuring public and lounge bars. And nearby is The Pack Horse Hotel, a sports-mad family pub housing a big-screen TV, pool table, and a separate room for darts. It's also got a beer garden. The landlord reportedly organises football quizzes and can make you huge home-made butties, if you ask nicely. Elsewhere in town, The Trackside Free House and The Waterloo are favourites for their beer ranges.

Stopping over in Bury?

Hotels are scattered around Bury but you may want to stay in Manchester if you're planning a weekend jaunt up these parts. In Bury, The Rostrevor on the A56 is well-established as a business and tourist hotel (0161 764 3944). Best Western Bolholt Country Park Hotel on Walshaw Road (0161 762 4000) offers rooms from £49 which includes access to its leisure club, while Waterloo Hotel on Manchester Road is another option (0161 764 5864). The Village Hotel at the Waterfold Business Park on Rochdale Road, found off junction 2 of the M66, is the perfect location for a family weekend break, incorporating a footy match and a trip to the Pennines or shopping in Manchester (0161 764 4444).

If you do one thing in Bury...

Locals take great pride in the town's "world-famous" black puddings, so it's worth trying them to find out what all the fuss is about. Basically, the fattier the better. Locals recommend the boiled variety.

Bury Market and East Lancashire Steam Railway make for interesting diversions. Alternatively, after bingeing on those puddings, you could walk off the calories in the nearby Pennines.

If you're staying in Manchester, though, a whistle-stop tour around the city's attractions or a shopping excursion will easily fill a weekend.

No end in sight

Bury's third round FA Cup match against Stoke in 1954/55 lasted a staggering nine hours and 22 minutes. Five replays were needed before Stoke snatched the winning goal in the last minute of extra-time as a sixth game beckoned.

Don't mention

The Cemetery End is aptly named. That winning the FA Cup in 1900 and 1903 really doesn't get you much kudos a century later.

Do mention

You 'own' one of the seats at Gigg Lane, having paid £10 for the right to have your name placed on it during a fund raising event which helped to keep the club alive a few years back. The Neville brothers: who are fans; their parents Neville and Tracy have also worked for the club.

the more original chants, alongside regulars such as the generic 'Hark Now Hear'. Rivals: In Rochdale Bury have a rival who they get to play against.

Travel Information

CAR
From the M60: Exit at junction 17 and take the Whitefield A56 exit at the roundabout. Go straight over the traffic lights, and straight on until you reach the Bulls Head. Here you need to ensure that you are in the right hand lane so you can bear right into Manchester Road. Continue along Manchester Road past the Bluebell, and then follow the directions below.
From the M66. Exit at Junction 3 into Pilsworth Road. Go straight over the next roundabout, past Asda and up the hill and then down to a set of traffic lights. Turn right at the lights into Manchester Road. Go straight through the next set of lights and then over the pedestrian crossing. Gigg Lane is signposted from here, and is a right hand turn. There is plenty of street parking, and a car park at Holy Cross College on Wellington Road.

TRAIN
There are trams from Manchester Victoria and Manchester Piccadilly, but the best bet is to head for Manchester Piccadilly and take the Metrolink to Bury Metrolink Station, which is just under a mile from the ground. Buses 90, 92, 135 and 137 run every ten minutes from down Manchester Road past the end of Gigg Lane.

Cardiff City

Growing the fanbase

The Bluebirds could be stepping out in a plush new 30,000-seat stadium in December 2008 if there are no major glitches in the construction schedule. Work on Cardiff City's new venue on the the site of the nearby Leckwith Athletics Stadium is well underway.

The scheme, comprising a retail park, calls for demolition of the existing athletics facility and a replacement built at a new location before the city's latest sporting palace is erected. The 60-acre development is expected to cost around £100m.

Chairman Peter Ridsdale and rugby union's Cardiff Blues are exploring the potential of a ground-share. Ridsdale is hell-bent on restoring his reputation. It's not easy to forget that he occupied a similar position at Leeds United but fled with the Yorkshire club £103 million in debt. Nailing the business plan for Cardiff is crucial to the club's future economic welfare.

Slapping a naming rights sponsor on the stadium makes perfect financial sense although it may yet be called St David's Stadium.

City reduced season ticket prices at the end of last season as part of efforts to fill the tired-looking Ninian Park, something they couldn't manage during 2006/07 despite a great start to the campaign. Average gates were just over 15,000. So you're likely to encounter bigger crowds and a better atmosphere at the 22,000-seat stadium for this year's campaign - at least until the Bluebirds hit a bad patch.

As the John Smiths Grange End is shared between home and away fans, there'll be plenty of noise generated from under the low roof. The terracing at the back can hold 1,630, while the seating area caters for 545. Best get those vocal chords lubricated.

Eating out

Food at Ninian Park is pretty basic. You're best eating en route to the match. Cowbridge Road East, Canton and Albany Road in Roath are two areas to scout out cafés and takeaways. Happy Gathering is a top Chinese on Cowbridge Road East. Also on this street is La Lupa, a cheap-ish Italian with a mouth-watering and varied menu. Westgate Street is a bit further away but packed with dozens of eateries and again not far from the ground. The Riverside Cantonese restaurant on Tudor Street is recommended for its imaginative menu and quality dishes. If it's chips and greasy food you want, then you'll get it in the city centre's Caroline Street, dubbed 'chip alley'. Dorothy's Fish Bar, one of the oldest chippies in town, provides a nice portion. Cardiff Bay is home to the more upmarket restaurants, if you want a quiet evening out.

Mine's a pint

 Few pubs near Ninian Park actively embrace visiting supporters so stick to the tried and trusted watering holes. Or you might want to cover your colours if you're drinking off the beaten track. The main away pub is The Lansdowne on Lansdowne Road, a spacious establishment and five minutes' walk to the ground. Don't be put off by the City memorabilia in this spacious establishment. Yes,

Club Information Stadium: Ninian Park, Sloper Road, Cardiff CF11 8SX Capacity: 21,432 Tel: 0292 0221001 Website: www.cardiffcityfc.co.uk Train: Ninian Park Colours: Blue Songs: Anything slagging off the English or Swansea is popular, like the chant celebrating how much Cardiff fans prefer using the toilets on the English side of the

you'll see many Bluebirds fans here but it's a welcoming place and trouble-free. Real ales include Cardiff's very own Brains, there's a big screen showing sport on matchdays and it serves hot meals. The Cornwall on Cornwall Street is a lively community pub also frequented by City fans but fine for away support. It has a bright airy bar and comfortable lounge and gets a mention in the CAMRA Good Beer Guide for its ales. There's an extensive menu of light snacks and traditional pub fare. The Cayo Arms on Cathedral Arms is also a welcoming establishment with excellent draught beers, ales and fabulous food at good value prices. The no-colours rule for drinking nearer to the ground is a maxim that must be heeded. Head into the city centre or Cardiff Bay for the nightlife.

Stopping over in Cardiff?

 If you're on a tight budget, Cathedral Road has a fair number of B&Bs and guesthouses. Accommodation options in the city include The Big Sleep Hotel on Bute Terrace (029 2063 6363). A design hotel at affordable prices, it's ideally situated for leisure and pleasure with spectacular views as far as the Severn Bridge. Rooms are from £65. Check into the Travelodge on St Mary Street if you want to be on top of the nightlife (0870 191 1723) - but the area can be noisy at

weekends. Holiday Inn on Castle Street is in a good spot, overlooking Cardiff Castle and the Millennium Stadium (0870 400 8140). On the same street is the more expensive Angel Hotel, which is blessed with plenty of Victorian charm (029 2064 9200).

If you do one thing in Cardiff...

Go on a tour of the Millennium Stadium, a true sporting landmark for Wales, and learn all about the multi-purpose venue's retractable roof, palletised pitch system and how it stages so many different types of events – not to mention a peek inside the changing rooms and a walk up the players' tunnel. Adults: £5.50, children: £3 for a tour.

Cup glory

Cardiff City are the only non-English based club to win the FA Cup. They beat Arsenal 1-0 in 1927 in the first ever final to be broadcast by BBC Radio.

Don't mention

That you don't think Welsh clubs should be allowed to play in the English League. It won't go down well and The Football Fans' Guide enjoys a day out in Wales.

Do mention

That Cardiff remain the only club from outside of England to win the FA Cup, in 1927. Cult hero Robert Earnshaw: a loveable rogue with wonderful talent, who delighted fans with his goalscoring exploits.

Travel Information

CAR
Exit the M4 Motorway at junction 33 and follow signs onto the A4232. Turn off after about six miles onto the B4267 Leckwith Road. Keep following the signs for the city centre and after about half a mile turn right at the traffic lights into Sloper Road. Ninian Park is situated on the left hand side of the road. The main car park is situated in the Athletics Stadium on Leckwith Road, opposite Ninian Park. To enter you need to take a right turn just before Sloper Road. It can take a while to get out afterwards and it's not always the friendliest of places to be hanging around in.

TRAIN
Ninian Park halt is served from Cardiff Central and is right next to the ground. Grangetown station is about fifteen minutes' walk and also served by trains running from Cardiff Central. From here, turn left out of the station, cross the road and head right into Sloper Road for the ground. Another option is to get a taxi from Cardiff Central.

Severn Bridge. Cardiff fans are also known for the bizarre 'Ayatollah' routine which was less of a song and more of a head slapping exercise. Rivals: Swansea (the Jacks). They don't get on with Bristol City – or many clubs from England for that matter.

Carlisle United

Thanks for the memories

Bordering the Lake District, Brunton Park is fairly isolated from the rest of the league's footballing meccas. If you're travelling from way down south, it'll be a long journey to the 16,650 capacity ground - so load up on the snacks.

The Blues are a bit of a yo-yo club, having bounced around the bottom two tiers of the league over the past two decades. They dropped into the Conference in 2004 but returned to the league at the first attempt.

Two appearances at Wembley as runners-up and winners of the Auto Windscreens Shield - in 1995 and 1997 respectively - were brief highlights of Carlisle's rollercoaster ride in the early years of Michael Knighton's strange regime as chairman.

Knighton, it's worth remembering, made a prat of himself in displaying his complete lack of ball skills when attempting keepy-uppies on the Old Trafford pitch back in 1989. The PR stunt was designed to publicise his takeover of the Red Devils, a deal that eventually fell through.

In his time at the club, he even attempted to move Carlisle into the Scottish Football League.

Don't expect any eccentric goings-on at Brunton Park nowadays - he's long since departed and the club is now in better financial shape. Be prepared for a less than lukewarm welcome up here, but you will get a comfortable roost to watch the action unfold. Visitors are usually allocated the North End of the Cumberland Building Society Stand, an all-seated covered section of the stadium.

The uncovered Petteril End terrace can also be opened to accommodate clubs bringing larger followings.

Eating out

The Cumberland Building Society Stand at the ground has a concourse underneath with a shop, bars, a betting shop and food outlets. Burger vans are in the car park. Get your fill here or in town. Warwick Road has a sandwich bar, chippy and the Harbour View Cantonese takeaway. Tebay Services (see page 16) is worth a visit if you're coming by car and fancy a bite immediately prior to or after the match. The home-cooked meals are delicious. You can get some good nosh at a variety of restaurants, including pizza places and a number of Chinese, down London Road at Botchergate. Travelodge on Warwick Road has a Brewsters restaurant and the nearby Toby Carvery has a bar and buffet-style dining. Also there's a Wetherspoons pub, Woodrow Wilson, in Botchergate.

Mine's a pint

The Beehive across the road from the ground welcomes away fans but you're best heading to Carlisle RUFC next to Brunton Park on Warwick Road for pre-match atmosphere. If you're coming by train, The Griffin, with some cheap bevvies, is the first pub you'll come across. Carlisle's 'entertainment strip' is Botchergate with many of the best pubs and bars such as Yates' on Castle Street, Mood (laidback ambience) and The White House (no football

Club Information Stadium: Brunton Park, Warwick Road, Carlisle CA1 1LL Capacity: 16,981 Tel: 01228 526237 Website: www.carlisleunited.co.uk Train: Carlisle Colours: Blue and white Songs: Mostly concentrated on how much they hate Preston, Mackems

jerseys on Saturday evenings). Away fans should avoid Bar Code. Clubbing types can try Terminal One, a bar and nightclub complex on Botchergate. The airport-style venue features two clubs – a New York-inspired disco space: Studio 54 and a dance and R'n'B room: the Helsinki Ice Room. Also there's a Canadian-themed sports bar with pool and snooker and large TV screens, and Paris Rouge - a bar with various cabaret acts.

Stopping over in Carlisle?

A range of B&Bs: the Holiday Inn on Parkhouse Road (0870 400 8166) or Ibis on Botchergate are the pick of the cheap hotel beds (01228 518000). You'll get more for your money at The Lakes Court, a Victorian hotel in the city centre fronting Carlisle's historic Court Square. Adjacent to Carlisle Citadel Railway Station, with the M6 motorway only two miles away and within eight miles of the Scottish border, it's ideal for visiting Carlisle's historic sites and the Lake District (01228 531951).

If you do one thing in Carlisle...

The splendour of the Lake District is right on the town's doorstep. A drive around the spectacular countryside before lunching at a country pub will be time well spent. Carlisle has plenty of shopping and an attractive castle. AMF Bowling, Currock Road is a good family day out.

Aliens in the 'hood?

Liverpool legend Bill Shankly had a spell in management at Carlisle (March 1949 to July 1951). Michael Knighton was publicly humiliated in 1996, following a story headlined 'Knighton: Aliens Spoke To Me' in the local newspaper. Sadly, he didn't carry out his threat to resign, quitting years later.

Don't mention

The aforementioned Michael Knighton: he took over in the summer of 1992, promising to return the club to the upper echelons of English football. Ten years later, after a tireless, well-orchestrated campaign by the club's supporters, he was finally forced to sell up. Carlisle had faced winding up orders, administration, mysterious takeover and consortium rumours, independent 'trusts' uncovered as being Knighton's associates, and 3 consecutive battles against relegation from the football league.

Do mention

The final day of the 1998-99 season: Carlisle needed to beat Plymouth at home or lose the League status they had held for 71 years. Five minutes into stoppage time it was 1-1. United had a corner and on-loan keeper Jimmy Glass ran the length of Brunton Park to score the winner with one second to spare. They were saved and Scarborough were relegated to the Conference. The fact Carlisle are the only league club in Cumbria: they're proud of this.

Travel Information

CAR
It's the same way in and out for everyone... unless you're an exiled fan living in Scotland or even further north. Either way, leave the M6 at junction 43 and take the first exit at the roundabout, signposted for Carlisle city centre. Follow the road through two sets of traffic lights, after going through the second the ground will come into view on the right. The club car park can be found by taking the first right immediately after Brunton Park into Victoria Place and then turn first right onto St Aidans Road. There is also plentiful street parking.

TRAIN
The train is always popular for the trip north to Carlisle. The ground is about a fifteen-minute walk away from the station. Once you arrive at Carlisle station exit north onto Warwick Road – it's immediately opposite the station – and head to the right down Warwick Road. The ground's about a mile down on the left.

and Geordies. Rivals: Starved of local clubs, Carlisle fans have focused on the North Eastern sides for their rivalries, notably Middlesbrough, Newcastle and Sunderland. Plus Preston.

Charlton Athletic

What a crowd puller

After spending seven years in exile, ground-sharing at Selhurst Park and then Upton Park, the Addicks returned to a revamped Valley in 1992. Tiers added to the West and North Stands raised capacity to over 27,000.

Charlton have now embarked on plans to expand The Valley to more than 40,000. The first phase is the addition of another tier on the East Stand, which would be followed by redevelopment of the Jimmy Seed (South) Stand.

Away fans, currently allocated about 3,000 seats in the South Stand, will look forward to experiencing the new-look facilities at this end in the coming years. The stand is long overdue a facelift, although views are fine... that's if you're not stuck behind the only pillar.

Addicks fans are genial and passionate hosts, despite these lean times. The club's underdog tag is fitting but they still enjoy vociferous support, with their fan base extending far outside London and the M25 to the Medway towns of Kent. Two decades ago, gates were as low as 5,000. In 2006/07, Charlton regularly pulled in crowds of 26,000-plus.

And they may well maintain those numbers thanks to an innovative idea from club officials. All those renewing their season ticket early for 2007/08 are due a free Premiership season ticket in 2008/09 should the club bounce back from relegation at the first attempt.

They can also count on the support of a clutch of celebrities, including ITV's Michael Grade and sports presenter Steve Ryder, snooker's Steve Davis and, erm, Karl Howman, decorator Jacko from south London sitcom Brush Strokes.

Eating out

Get a greasy burger or pasty from one of the various outlets. There are separate hot dog stalls. Valley Café is a good eatery by the train station and serves a 'Saturday Special', plus sandwiches. If you turn right out of the station, Golden Fish bar is in the small parade of shops. It offers great sit-down fry-ups and takeaway fare. There's a McDonald's on Bugsby's Way. Kebab Express and Seabay Fish Bar are on Floyd Road. You'll find other takeaways and restaurants on Charlton Church Lane and Woolwich Road. Blackheath and Greenwich are the areas to explore for post-match dining.

Mine's a pint

The Antigallican, a big pub near Charlton station, is the away tavern of choice. It gets very busy and doesn't win plaudits for its looks - but it boasts a proper pre-match atmosphere and serves decent grub. It also offers B&B. The only gripe is that local police insist on fans staying inside the pub. It has two bars, Sky TV and a big screen. The Rose of Denmark on Woolwich Road is another no-frills local for visiting support. Both sets of fans mix in here and its basic selection of beers/lagers is said to be a bit cheaper than The Antigallican. The Charlton Liberal Club, right out of the station and up the hill on the left, also admits away fans for a small payment but you're

Club Information Stadium: The Valley, Floyd Road, Charlton SE7 8BL Capacity: 27,111 (all seated) Tel: 0208 3334000 Website: www.charlton-athletic.co.uk Train: Charlton Tube: North Greenwich Colours: Red and white Songs: The most renowned song, celebrating the Floyd Road Stand, came to the fore during their exile from The Valley. To the tune of 'Mull of Kintyre' they

expected to hide colours. It's quieter, more family-friendly and only a short walk to the ground. The Royal Oak on Charlton Lane is always a convivial place and serves a good meal. The Bugle Horn in Charlton Village is another good pub. If you want to sup in London, *www.addickted.net* has a useful pub guide. Near King's Cross/St Pancras/Euston stations is The Flying Scotsman on Caledonian Road - large and popular with an assortment of fans. The Duke of York on Platform 8 at King's Cross is very convenient and rather pricey. O'Neills on Euston Road is cheaper.

Stopping over in the Charlton area?

 Budget beds can be hard to find in central London. Pickwick B&B on Woolwich Road is near the ground and recommended by *www.addickted.net*. For a bit more money try Express By Holiday Inn on Bugsby Way, Greenwich (020 8269 5000) or Novotel on Greenwich High Road (020 8312 6800). Novotel is next to the station and 12 minutes from Canary Wharf. Custom House Hotel on Victoria Dock Road is good value at about £50 (020 7474 0011). In Docklands, it's 25 mins from J30 of the M25.

If you do one thing in the Charlton area...

Visit the impressive O2 Arena in Greenwich. The first music venue in London since The Royal Albert Hall in 1871 also contains a 2,000 capacity live music club, 11-screen cinema, as well as bars and restaurants.

Stupid plonker

In 'Only Fools and Horses', Plonker Rodney's middle name was Charlton because his mum was apparently a Charlton fan.

However, the sitcom's series' creator, Balham-born John Sullivan, is a Fulham supporter.

Don't mention

The 1980's: Charlton were homeless after a rescue package saving the club did not include ownership of the freehold to The Valley. The club were forced to ground-share at Selhurst Park and Upton Park for seven years. They returned home largely thanks to the efforts of the fans who formed The Valley Party, which won over 10% of votes in a local election. Carl Leaburn: largely remembered for famously hitting the post against Spurs from two yards out, which spawned sales of 'I Saw Leaburn Score' t-shirts.

Do mention

Jimmy Seed: Athletic's most successful manager who turned Charlton from a Third Divison (South) side to FA Cup winners (1947) pushing for the league title. Derek Hales: classic centre-forward and Valley icon of the '70s. Clive Mendonca: his 28 goals in season 1997-98 was the major factor in Charlton returning to the top flight.

Travel Information

CAR
From M25: Exit at J2 and follow the A2 until it becomes the A102(M). Continue until you turn right onto the A206 Woolwich Road: the ground is on the right. From the A205 S Circular: Head to Woolwich and turn left into Woolwich Road at the roundabout for the free ferry. From central London: South through Blackwall Tunnel, come off at second junction and take first exit at the roundabout for the Woolwich Road. Street parking restrictions are vigorously enforced.

TRAIN
Train services to Charlton run from central London and north Kent. The station is very near to the ground; just follow the crowd down Floyd Road. Frequent services from Charing Cross, Waterloo East and London Bridge, with limited departures from Victoria and Cannon Street. Some services come through Dartford and continue to Charlton, while connections for others can be made at Blackheath, Lewisham and London Bridge. The DLR from east London connects with rail services from Greenwich and Lewisham to Charlton, while the underground station at North Greenwich is a short bus ride from The Valley.

lament the sadly missed stand. Most others revolve around their dislike of Millwall and Crystal Palace. Rivals: Millwall, Palace and West Ham.

Chelsea

Growing out of the Bridge

Chelsea are seeking to expand the 42,449 capacity of Stamford Bridge to 55,000 in a bid to capitalise on their recent success and growing fan base. Club chiefs had reportedly been assessing new stadium sites in Earls Court and White City due to the constraints on extending their current pad in the built-up area of west London. But these plans were abandoned in 2006 when Chelsea announced their intentions to stay put.

It's not that the Blues need the financial muscle to compete with Arsenal, Manchester United and a host of European high-flyers - billionaire backer Roman Abramovich isn't counting the pennies after all. It's a matter of pride. When Emirates Stadium opened in 2006, The Bridge became the seventh largest ground in the Premier League.

Vacating the stadium in the London borough of Hammersmith and Fulham would have meant leaving behind a venue with a vast footballing heritage. The club have played here since their inception in 1905. Stamford Bridge was in existence before that: the stadium was offered to Fulham, but after they declined, preferring to stay at Craven Cottage, Chelsea Football Club was formed to make use of the stadium.

Former chairman Ken Bates oversaw a massive revamp of the club's home, started in 1994 and completed in summer 2001. It transformed a dilapidated and crumbling ground with poor sightlines into one of the most impressive arenas in English football.

A remnant of the past is the back wall of the famous Shed terrace – now outside of the new-look stadium. A huge sprawling mecca for their most vociferous supporters, it was demolished in 1994 and replaced with the all-seated Shed End stand in 1997. Away fans are housed in the south east corner of this two-tiered stand, with the normal allocation pegged at 3,000 tickets.

Eating out

Catering at the ground is expansive but also expensive – so a better option is to take advantage of what's on offer along the Fulham Road. There is the usual array of fast food joints you would expect – but there are also some hidden gems. You'll come across any number of delicatessens and trendy restaurants. There's a decent Italian called Barbarella. The Butchers Hook nearby is a gastropub offering good value British cooking. Kishmish (formerly Blue Spice) is a fancy Indian right next door to the ground. Blue Elephant is a fantastic Thai restaurant on Fulham Broadway with a fine reputation – and you'll also find a whole range of chain restaurants at the redeveloped Fulham Broadway Station (it's a shopping mall, with the first floor devoted to food). Kings Road also has an abundance of eateries. La Rueda is a lively Spanish restaurant with a huge tapas menu. For gourmet Indian head to Chutney Mary. The Big Easy is an American crab shack and barbeque. If you're feeling flush book a table at Gordon Ramsay's restaurant – on Royal Hospital Road – but be warned you need to book well in advance and they won't let you in wearing jeans or football shirts!

Mine's a pint

Alcohol is available at Stamford Bridge. There are a few dozen pubs and bars within

Club Information Stadium: Stamford Bridge, Fulham Road, London SW6 1HS Capacity: 42,449 (all seated) Tel: 0870 300 1212 Website: www.chelseafc.com Tube: Fulham Broadway Colours: Blue and white Songs: Chelsea fans have been keeping the 'Blue Flag Flying High' for many years. Another song Chelsea fans claim as their own is the 'One

21. CHELSEA

10 minutes' walk of the ground, but those nearest are packed with the blue army. The Slug and Lettuce next to Fulham Broadway station - the nearest tube stop to the ground on the District Line - is a firm favourite among away fans. The Goat in Boots on Fulham Road and the White Horse near Parsons Green tube are also good drinking spots. The Earls Court Tavern, Earls Court, provides a warm welcome. As an area, Earls Court - a couple of stops away from Stamford Bridge on the tube - is fairly neutral and therefore one of the better areas in which to sup before a game. You get a good crowd of mixed fans, keen for a chinwag about football. The Blackbird is the kind of drinking den where you can chew the cud with Chelsea supporters without any grief. It sells Fullers beers and tasty pub grub in a friendly environment. Away from the hustle and bustle of Earls Court Road is The Kings Head, on Hogarth Place, a good pub with a relaxed vibe.

Stopping over in the Chelsea area?

 Chelsea Lodge is a budget hotel on Fulham Road, within easy reach of London's major attractions (020 7823 3494). Comfort Inn on Penywern Road, Earl's Court, is another bargain for this trendy area and a great sightseeing base (020 7373 6514). It's just a stone's throw away from Earls Court tube station. Slightly more

expensive is Jury's Inn near the fashionable Kings Road. This three-star hotel is on Imperial Road, Imperial Wharf (020 7411 2200).

If you do one thing in the borough...

Visit Riverside Studios on the banks of the Thames in Hammersmith - west London's leading centre for contemporary and international performance, film, exhibitions and tv production. It presents a diverse programme of events, including cutting-edge theatre and comedy.

Giving some stick

In 2002, three Chelsea fans were charged with "throwing celery without lawful authority" after being caught hurling the vegetable during the club's FA Cup semi-final against Fulham at Villa Park.

Don't mention

That you can remember when Chelsea used to have cars parked around the edge of the pitch and crowds of 15,000.

Do mention

Gianfranco Zola: he is adored to this day at the Bridge for his talent and general all round good-blokishness. Ron 'Chopper' Harris: the archetypal 'hard man' of football. Peter Osgood: he typified the Kings Road image of the club in the 70s and led the team to FA Cup glory over 'dirty' Leeds in the FA Cup final of 1970.

Man Went To Mow' classic. 'Carefree' we are the famous CFC, to the Lord of the Dance tune is also popular. Rivals: Arsenal and Spurs; also Leicester for some reason, and recently Manchester United have become just as unpopular.

Travel Information

CAR
Probably best to aim for the outskirts of London and use the tube – but if you want to take your chances exit the M25 to junction 15. Follow the M4 which becomes the A4 up to Hammersmith. Stay on it over the Hammersmith flyover before turning off for Earls Court. Go past Earls Court station and down the one way system until you hit Fulham Road. Take a right at the traffic lights and straight on for 600 yards – the ground is on your right. If you're coming from the south, and not using the M25 cross the Thames via Wandsworth bridge and head straight up Wandsworth Bridge Road. At the junction with New Kings Road turn right and then immediately left This will take you up to Fulham Broadway. Turn right onto Fulham Road.

TUBE
Fulham Broadway is on the District Line – you'll probably need to change at Earls Court and pick up a Wimbledon-bound train. Fulham Broadway is one of the best (if not the best) Underground Stations in London when it comes to accommodating football fans. The massive platform and steps mean a rapid exit straight out onto Fulham Road – it also makes for a swift exit for everyone after the match. Just follow the crowds a few hundred yards left to Stamford Bridge. West Brompton (also on the District Line) is within walking distance too.

Cheltenham Town

Up and at 'em

The Robins have come a long way since the late 1990s, with modernisation of Whaddon Road keeping pace with their on-field success.

All of their football was played outside the Football League until the club gained promotion from non-league's top-flight in the 1998/99 season. Cheltenham secured the Conference championship with a goal scored in the seventh minute of injury time against Yeovil Town.

Redevelopment of the Whaddon Road End - providing a 990-seat stand for away supporters - was completed in December 2005. Known as the Carlsberg Stand, it offers unrestricted views for visiting fans. Construction of the stand was the culmination of seven years of extensive ground improvements.

Whaddon Road remains an intimate stadium. But when the sections of terracing are rammed with noisy diehard Robins fans and the ground is full to its 7,066 capacity you get a cracking atmosphere.

The In2Print Stand adjoining the Carlsberg Stand also accommodates away fans for teams bringing a larger travelling support.

The Robins beat Grimsby Town in the League Two play-off final to clinch promotion to League One for 2006/07, playing in front of 29,196 fans at Cardiff's Millennium Stadium - the biggest crowd ever to watch Cheltenham.

Eating out

At the ground, there are plenty of snack bars and the Sports Bar at Whaddon Road also welcomes away fans on matchdays. A widescreen TV shows live sport and you can buy hot food between midday and 2.45pm. There's a chippy and Chinese takeaway close to the ground. You'll find more eating options in the town centre, only 10 minutes away. The Moon Under Water, a Wetherspoons on Bath Road, has cheap meals.

For the more discerning palate, head for The Hewlett Arms on Harp Hill, a wine bar/restaurant. Oriental bar and restaurant Jim Thompson's on Clarence Street offers pan-Asian cuisine. If you're driving, you might want to consider the Golden Heart Inn, about five miles outside the town in Nettleton Bottom, Birdlip, on the A417. In addition to its real ales, ciders and range of wines, this traditional country inn has a wide and varied menu, with fish, vegetarian, and award-winning meats sourced locally.

Mine's a pint

Pubs are at the centre of friendly Cheltenham so you can't go far wrong if you're looking for a place before the game. Whaddon Road's Sports Bar is a friendly place. In the town centre, Regent Street has a number of pubs including a Slug & Lettuce, while on Clarence Street you'll get a tasty Belgian brew at the

Club Information Stadium: Whaddon Road, Cheltenham GL52 5NA Tel: 01242 573558 Website: www.ctfc.com Capacity: 7,066 Train: Cheltenham Spa Colours: Red and white Songs: The Town fans are quite self deprecating, as illustrated by the 'We Can

Belgian Monk. The Kemble Brewery Inn on Fairview Street is tricky to find but worth the effort. Formerly a Victorian butcher's shop, it serves a great selection of cask ales and home-cooked food. After the football, you could head to places like It's A Scream, a large pub in town which gets busy with revellers. There are five or six nightclubs in town to choose from, with 21 Club on Regent Street a popular choice.

Stopping over in Cheltenham?

 Options include the Thistle Hotel on Gloucester Road, located on the outskirts (0870 333 9131). It has a restaurant, lounge, bar and health and leisure club. Also good value is the Travelodge on the A40, just one mile south of Cheltenham (0870 191 1701). Exit junction 11 of M5 and follow signs for Cheltenham. The hotel is situated at the first roundabout. If you're after something a little trendier, why not stay at The Big Sleep Hotel, a "designer budget hotel" on Wellington Street. It's simple yet stylish, with bedrooms from £70 (01242 696999). Elsewhere, Macdonald Queen's Hotel on The Promenade might be a little more expensive but it's one of the nicest Regency hotels around (0870 400 8107).

If you do one thing in Cheltenham...

One of Britain's finest spa towns, Cheltenham is located in the picturesque Cotswold Hills. It's best known as the home of National Hunt racing, the highlight of which is the Cheltenham Gold Cup in March. It's very good for cultural festivals - there's one for jazz, folk, science and literature. And one for cheese. That's if you count the legendary Cooper's Hill Cheese Rolling and Wake where a bunch of nutters hurl themselves down a very steep hill in pursuit of a 7-8lb double gloucester cheese. It has to be seen to be believed.

In Blind Faith

Sky Sports pundit Andy Gray is a former Robins player. Steve Winwood, a former member of Blind Faith and Traffic, is a Robins fan.

Don't mention

That Cheltenham, in a sporting sense, is probably known primarily as a horse racing venue. That Cheltenham is in Gloucestershire: Town fans steadfastly refuse to accept its existence, and are often heard referring to their home county as Cheltenhamshire.

Do mention

Dave Lewis, prolific striker of the 1970s who once scored 53 goals in a single season. Steve Cotterill: he made his name as a manager at Whaddon Road before moving on to bigger things. Steve Book: fancied himself as a bit of a latter day Bruce Grobbelaar and could often be found deep in 'conversation' with the crowd.

Travel Information

CAR
From The North: Leave M5 at junction 10 and take the A4019. After about four miles turn left onto the A435 (Portland Street) and then second right onto Wellington Road – then right onto Prestbury Road and left into Whaddon Road.
From The South: Leave the M5 at Junction 11 and and follow A40 and A4015. Then pick up the A46, which leads onto the A435 Portland Street. Take the second right onto Wellington Road – then right onto Prestbury Road and left into Whaddon Road There is no car parking on offer at the ground, and some street parking near the ground is restricted. There is a park and ride facility from the racecourse, which takes ten minutes and may be worth a punt.

TRAIN
Cheltenham Station is around two miles from the ground. If you fancy walking, you can head along Gloucester Road. A right turn on to St Georges Road will lead you onto Clarence Parade which becomes Royal Well Road, Clarence Street and then North Street. Hang a left down Albion Street and immediate left onto Portland Street. After 400 metres turn right into Clarence Road, which forks left into Prestbury Road. Whaddon Road is about 600 metres on the right. Best bet is a bus.

Drive A Tractor' song, which is likely to be heard on most matchdays coming from both home and visiting fans alike. Rivals: Gloucester City, Kidderminster and Rushden (The Annies).

Chester City

The Deva's in the detail

Deva Stadium - Deva is Roman for Chester - is said to be the first ground built to meet all the specifications required by the Taylor Report, the study into the 1989 Hillsborough Stadium disaster which recommended that all major football clubs should convert to all-seater stadia.

Opened in 1992, the 6,000-seat venue boasted disabled spaces on both sides of the ground, automatic turnstiles and exits among other safety features. The move was a huge relief for fans who had been forced to watch City play their home games at Macclesfield's Moss Rose under a two-year ground-share scheme following the sale of Sealand Road in 1990.

Strange-but-true stats on Deva Stadium include the use of 171 doors, 48,000 bricks and 4.5 tons of nails and screws in its construction.

Ground improvements are continuing, with plans mooted for new executive boxes in the west and east stands and expansion of, or a new, supporters' club.

Formed in 1885, Chester turned professional 17 years later and were renamed Chester City in 1983. Most of their time has been spent playing in the lower divisions. After going into administration in the late 1990s, the club had a four-year spell in the Conference before regaining their berth in the Football League in 2004.

If you're a fan of arch-rivals Wrexham, don't expect any red-carpet treatment. Chester wags will bid you the warmest of welcomes with a few choice chants. Be prepared for some verbal jousting.

Eating out

Mobile catering vans on Bumpers Lane offer such delicacies as chicken balti pies. At the ground, the stadium catering is okay but a little pricey. You'll find a great chippy, in Sealand Fish & Chips on Sealand Road, which is popular with home fans. There's a burger bar at the top of Northgate Street while bar food at the Mill Hotel on Milton Street is recommended by others. For a sit-down meal, most of the decent restaurants are along Grosvenor Street and Pepper Street including: Pasterazzi, Ego and Piccolino. Closest to the ground is Frankie & Benny's on the Greyhound Retail Park. Locals also highlight the buzzy Chez Jules on Northgate Street for some contemporary French cuisine with value-for-money pricing. And The Chester Tandoori on Brook Street serves up a good Indian.

Mine's a pint

The Eight Rights on Cousens Way with good beer and bar food, along with The Watergate Inn, Watergate Street, a friendly pub near the racecourse, and The Dublin Packet in the city centre once owned by Everton great Dixie Dean, are tips for matchday guzzling. And the gents from Chester's WC Brewery have designed a pub crawl, "for visiting football fans who'd like to down quantities of real ale ready to numb the pain of a

---

Club Information Stadium: Deva Stadium, Bumpers Lane, Sealand Industrial Estate, Chester CH1 4LT Capacity: 6,012 Tel: 01244 371376 Website: www.chestercityfc.net Train: Chester Colours: Blue and white Songs: Most are aimed towards their hatred of

certain away defeat". See *http://wc brewery. com/ footballcrawl.html*.

Stopping over in Chester?

 The Holiday Inn on Wrexham Road close to the racecourse is only 10 minutes by car from the stadium (0870 400 9019). Also handy is The Stafford Hotel on City Road, near the railway station (01244 326052).

For something a little classier, The Queen Hotel on the same street, built in the 19th century, offers quality at a higher price (01244 305000).

The Mill Hotel on Milton Street (01244 350035) is close to the canal, offering diners the chance to eat aboard a canal barge. City fans frequent the main bar.

If you do one thing in Chester...

Visit Chester Zoo, one of Cheshire's most popular visitor attractions. It includes the Fun Ark adventure play area as well as a wide range of shops and cafés.

Or immerse yourself in Roman history by visiting The Deva Experience, off Bridge Street. You could have a flutter on the gee-gees at one of the race meetings held at Chester racecourse.

Alternatively, a pleasant stroll around Grosvenor Park and a ride on a steam train on the miniature railway might fill a few hours.

Famous son

Sealand Road was the old stamping ground of the mighty Ian Rush in the late 1970s, who later signed for Liverpool in a club record £300,000 transfer deal. He played 34 league games, scoring 14 goals, before he was snapped up by Reds manager Bob Paisley. Rush returned to manage City for a short stint in 2004/05.

Don't mention

Terry Smith: who purchased the club in 1999 and promptly installed himself as manager, rapidly becoming the most hated man in the city. Fans boycotted the stadium and Smith's failure to finance ground safety led to games being cancelled. Even his choice of club strip was roundly despised. Although his controversial reign ended in 2003 he persisted with a claim for £300,000, which came close to winding the club up. It took them a long while to recover.

Do mention

Season 2003/04, when the 49 goal partnership of Daryl Clare and Darryn Stamp helped City win promotion back to the Football League. Gary Bennett: Like Rush, another prolific goal scorer, he notched 63 times in three spells at the club. Grenville Millington: he came out of retirement at the end of the 1982/83 season to keep goal in Chester's last game before they were reformed as Chester City. He also caused a game to be abandoned in 1981 after colliding with a post!

Travel Information

CAR
From the town centre follow the Queensferry signs into Sealand Road (A548) and after a little over a half a mile turn left at the traffic lights into Bumpers Lane where you'll find the ground in the heart of an industrial estate. There is plenty of parking available at the ground – but it can take a while to get out afterwards. There are also other options in the surrounding industrial estate.

TRAIN
The station is a good two miles from the ground, so it's best to get a cab or bus. The railway is on the opposite side of the city to the ground. If you do choose to walk from the station, head straight up City Road to the end and turn right down Foregate Street, which becomes Watergate Street at the Cross. Carry on down Watergate Street past the Racecourse (on the left) and this becomes Sealand Road. Turn left at set of lights into Bumpers Lane and the ground is on your right.

the Welsh – and of Wrexham in particular. All the usual unrepeatable songs make an appearance. Rivals: Wrexham and Chester really don't get on. Shrewsbury aren't popular either.

Chesterfield

Planning a bright future

The Spireites hope to be playing in a new stadium within the next few years. Plans to build a 10,600 all-seater with a price tag of £10m are well advanced. It will be located on a 25-acre site on the old A61 at Whittington Moor. The North Stand of Chesterfield's new home is earmarked for away fans.

The plans gained momentum following a meeting of the Chesterfield Football Supporters' Society (CFSS) earlier this year. CFSS became the majority shareholder six years ago when it saved the team from expulsion from the Football League and bankruptcy. When Chesterfield emerged from the dark days of administration, CFSS handed over the day-to-day running of the Spireites to the club's board.

In January 2007, the organisation rubber-stamped a plan that allowed the board to take full control, allowing it to seek funding for the stadium scheme from bodies such as the Football Foundation.

The board also wants to raise around £3.5m from an issue of preference shares, a move club chiefs say "will continue the theme of the club being owned by the supporters".

Some say the 8,500-capacity Recreation Ground, Saltergate, is a stadium with 'character'. Others put it a little more bluntly, describing it as a knackered facility way past its prime. Either way, it seems few tears will be shed over its redundancy.

Away fans will welcome news of the Spireites' relocation. Notwithstanding the improved loos, the current facilities are drab and you can get drenched very quickly on the Cross Street open terrace, which has a 1,600 capacity. Visitors can also sit in the more comfortable confines of the covered Cross Street Far Wing stand.

Eating out

The Recreation Ground wasn't built with hospitality facilities in mind but there is a food hut for visiting supporters which sells typical matchday fare. As the ground is only five minutes from the town centre, it's best to eat there. Burger King, Pizza Hut and various other cafés and takeaways are dotted around. There's a KFC, chippy and Indian on Chatsworth Road at the B&Q roundabout. Linda's on St. Margaret's Drive is a very good sandwich shop and popular among football fans. It does hot and cold food, and breakfasts. Chinese restaurants, including Simply Chinese, are easy to spot in the town centre. There's a Thai on Saltergate and the Thai Pavilion Restaurant on Glumangate. For a cheap meal, visit one of the two Wetherspoons pubs.

Mine's a pint

Chesterfield's proud boast is that the town has more pubs in a quarter of a square mile than anywhere else in the country. 100 yards from the away end are The Chesterfield Arms and The Industry pubs, which are the recommended venues for travelling support.

If you're not parading your team's colours, you could try The Barking Badger (near the train station) and Slug & Fiddle. Real ale drinkers should head to The Market Tavern.

Club Information Stadium: The Recreation Ground, Saltergate, Chesterfield S40 4SX Capacity: 8,504 Tel: 01246 209765 Website: www.chesterfield-fc.co.uk Train: Chesterfield Colours: Blue Songs: Odes to David Elleray and bitterness towards Mansfield-

Pubs to avoid (they are for home supporters only) are mainly found on Saltergate and include Local Heroes, The Gardeners Arms and The Barley Mow.

If you want to boogie the night away, try one of three nightclubs in town: Livingstone's, Holywell Street; Lava & Ignite, Knifesmith Gate; Escapade on Cavendish Street.

Stopping over in Chesterfield?

 Hotel Ibis Sheffield South on Chesterfield Road, Barlborough is the cheapest (0870 752 2235). Slightly more expensive is The Chesterfield Hotel on Malkin Street, opposite the town's railway station and within easy reach of the motorway network. It includes a restaurant, bar and leisure club (0870 832 9907).

Ringwood Hall Hotel, set in a Georgian Grade II listed manor house at Brimington, is a little more extravagant and minutes from the M1 (01246 280077).

If you do one thing in Chesterfield...

Gape in awe at the town's 14th century 'Crooked Spire' Church - the largest church in Derbyshire. The spire was twisted when unseasoned wood was used during its construction. The 32 tons of lead tiles were placed on top and as the timber dried out the weight of the lead twisted the spire. Then head for the Peak District. Sheffield,

Nottingham and Derby have more to see and do (see our more detailed guides).

Keeping up appearances

The team are nicknamed the Spireites after the famous crooked spire. The club has produced two outstanding goalkeepers in Gordon Banks and Steve 'Oggy' Ogrizovic.

Don't mention

Darren Brown: as owner of Chesterfield in 2000, he bankrolled the assembly of a promising squad by manager Nicky Law. Unfortunately for them, the Football League discovered a series of financial irregularities and deducted them nine points along with a hefty fine, thus ruling them out of any chance of winning a tight championship race. David Elleray: his refusal to award a goal in the FA Cup semi final of 1997 against Middlesbrough when the ball had clearly crossed the line denied The Spireites an historic FA Cup Final appearance.

Do mention

Despite the loss of the FA Cup semi final it was the proudest day in the club's history. Jamie Hewitt's sensational last minute header earned the club a replay and another big pay-day. Ernie Moss: an honest and dedicated striker who was top scorer in three different spells with the club spanning three decades and helped the club to the Fourth Division title in 1970.

Travel Information

CAR
Leave the M1 at Junction 29 and take the A617 towards Chesterfield. On reaching the edge of the town centre go straight across the first roundabout and then the next, passing the crooked spire of Chesterfield Church to yourleft. As the road divides, keep to your left, going around an open car park. This road leads into Saltergate, where you will pass the Barley Mow pub on your left and the Town Hall car park, before reaching the ground on your right. There are plenty of car parks in the town centre to choose from, one at the town hall and one next to Manor College. There is a pay and display in Ashgate Road as well, but you should easily be able to find space on the surrounding streets, especially if you are there relatively early.

TRAIN
Chesterfield Station is less than a mile from the ground. Go straight out of the station and turn left into Corporation Street, going straight across the crossroads. The Chesterfield Hotel will be on your right hand side. Go over the footbridge, and cross over Tapton Lane and head up Saltergate. The ground is on the right hand side.

based miners aside, not a lot to report. Rivals: Chesterfield's rivalry with Mansfield (The Scabs) has its roots in the Miner's Strike. Nor do they particularly like either of the Sheffield sides.

Colchester United

Scaling new heights

Colchester's dream of a new 10,000-capacity all-seater community stadium at Cuckoo Farm could become reality by the start of the 2008/09 season. The local council agreed to the stadium's business plan and funding of the £14.2 million project at a meeting on November 13, 2006. About 250 members of the public attended the full council meeting that evening – with another 200 awaiting the verdict outside the town hall. More good news came in January when the borough council granted permission for the stadium to be built ahead of the new A12 junction. Talk of relocation to a new stadium has been an ongoing saga for more than 30 years. Numerous expansion plans and stadium proposals dating back to 1970 all failed.

The Cuckoo Farm site first emerged as the most viable site in 1998 since when the club has fine-tuned the plans to address local concerns. The new stadium is set to be a regional landmark venue for the provision of community, sporting and social activities for residents of Colchester and forms part of the wider regeneration of north Colchester.

The U's Layer Road has been home turf since the club's formation. The 6,180-capacity ground has two terraces for away fans (standing for 909) and just over 400 seats.

Colchester have experienced an upturn in fortunes of late. In 2007, they enjoyed their highest ever league finish, following promotion from League One the previous season and after many years playing in the lower divisions.

The U's might have one of the lowest average gates in the Championship, but their enhanced footballing credentials are finding new fans to bolster the loyal fanbase. The old adage "If we build it, they will come" is likely to ring true when the new stadium is constructed.

Eating out

If you don't fancy making use of Layer Road's basic catering facilities, Colchester town centre is 10 minutes' walk from the ground and has a plentiful supply of eateries. McDonald's, Burger King, KFC, bakeries and chippies are easily found on the main streets. Pizza Hut has outlets on High Street and at Turner Rise Retail Park a bit further out. Sloppy Joe's, a family American-style bar and diner on High Street, is recommended not just for the generous portions. It has special offers and meal deals throughout the week.

China Chef on Crouch Street is not cheap but you're paying for quality nosh here. Jade Palace is fairly near the ground on Barrack Street and worth a visit for its all-you-can-eat buffet. Zizzi's - on Headgate - has received plaudits for its fine Italian cuisine.

Mine's a pint

The Maypole is the main away fans' hostelry. Located on a street off Layer Road called Berechurch Hall Road, it's a friendly place to neck a few jars and tuck into some fine pub grub before a game. Sky Sports will keep you in touch with the latest footballing stories.

Nearest the ground is The Drury Arms, a no-nonsense local where you'll find home and away fans chewing the fat

Club Information Stadium: Layer Road, Colchester CO2 7JJ Capacity: 6,375 Tel: 0871 2262161 Website: www.cu-fc.com Train: Colchester Town Colours: Blue and white Songs: Plenty of songs having a bash at erstwhile Ipswich manager George Burley are still doing the rounds. The club song is a traditional number called 'Up the U's' which is

over pints and hot snacks.

The Dragoon on Butt Road is another pre-match haunt. The landlord and staff will go out of their way to make you welcome here. Pub meals are available on matchdays and it has pool, darts and a beer garden. Adnams beers and guest ales are on tap.

Evening drinking choices range from Yates's and Edwards and Hub on Head Street (the latter being the pick of these for its music policy) to Odd One Out on Mersea Road near St Botolph roundabout. This is touted by some as Colchester's best pub due to its terrific choice of ales and relaxed ambience. You might have to ask for directions as it's tricky to find.

Stopping over in Colchester?

 Stay at The Red Lion Hotel on High Street and you'll be right on top of the action (01206 577986). The three-star hotel offers B&B from £37 per person per night.

There's a Holiday Inn three miles from town on Abbotts Lane, located just off the A12 (0870 400 9020). Bedding down in London is also an option, if you want to make a weekend of your trip to Essex. It's about a 45-minute train ride away.

If you do one thing in Colchester?

Colchester Zoo on Maldon Road, Stanway, is considered to be one of the finest zoos in Europe with over 200 species living in 60 acres of beautiful parkland. You should be made aware that the new enclosure for orang-utans is expected to open in late 2007. By splashing out £110 to adopt an animal, you can help fund the £16,000 a day running costs of the zoo.

So go on, p-p-p-pick up a penguin.

DJ backing

DJ and journalist Steve Lamacq, a massive Colchester United fan, became sports editor of The Harlow Gazette at the age of 21. Lamacq is as enthusiastic about The U's as he is about discovering new bands. "I've seen it all before, I've been to Wembley with Colchester United, but every season there's something different and it's still as exciting," he told BBC Online.

Don't mention

The away toilets: Just about every single away fan who visits Layer Road bangs on about how terrible they are.

Do mention

If you want to blend in refer to Colchester as Col U. That you are looking forward to the club moving to Cuckoo Farm: it's the site of the club's proposed new all-seater home. The famous 3-2 FA Cup fifth round win over Don Revie's Leeds United in 1971. Lomano LuaLua: he was only at the club a year, but left a lasting impression with his silky skills and unpredictable finishing.

Travel Information

CAR
Leave the A12 at Stanway (signposted the A1124), and turn right at the next roundabout. Take the exit into London Road (signposted Mersea/Stanway). Go over the mini-roundabout and travel one mile to a set of traffic lights. Turn right into Straight Road and go right to the end. At roundabout, turn left and then take a sharp right into the right into Gosbecks Road. Go straight over the first roundabout and at the second roundabout turn left (Kent Blaxill factory on the left) for Layer Road. The ground is on the left. There is a little bit of street parking around the ground. If you drive a bit further away parking restrictions are more relaxed. There is also the park and ride which runs from Sobraon Barracks - well signposted as you head towards the ground.

TRAIN
Colchester's main station is a good 45 minute walk, so best to catch a cab or bus from there. Better still get a connection to Colchester Town station which is within walking distance. It's also close to a bus stop which will get you to the ground. For the bus turn right outside the station and cross the road at the pedestrian crossing. Match day buses stop outside the bingo hall in Osborne St.

obviously quite old as it uses phrases such as "what a game we'll see" and "we're as strong as the old oak tree". Rivals: Ipswich and Southend are the local opposition, but there is a longstanding rivalry with Wycombe, dating back to their Conference battles.

Coventry City

Bring back the glory days

The 32,000-seat Ricoh Arena is a fine football mecca for the Sky Blues. The move from Highfield Road in 2005 appears to have rejuvenated the club. Gates have increased by an estimated 20 per cent since relocation.

Some think the glory days may be just around the corner. But Sky Blues fans aren't getting their hopes up. After all, it's been 20 years since the club's finest hour. Memories of tricky wing play from Mickey Gynn and Keith Houchen's diving header in the pulsating 3-2 FA Cup final victory over Spurs in 1987 have long since faded.

Like any new stadium, the Ricoh Arena is labelled 'state-of-the-art'. The £113 million multi-purpose complex is considered a benchmark for its conference, banqueting, exhibition and various sports facilities – not to mention a 71-bed hotel.

The Ricoh has become a popular concert venue, too. Canadian soft rocker Bryan Adams performed the first ever gig there before an 8,000 audience in the Jaguar Exhibition Halls.

It's easily accessible - within two hours' drive of almost 75 per cent of the population in England. And it's less than 30 minutes away from two major railway stations and international airports.

Away fans are located in the Jewson South Stand, which accommodates 3,000. The precise allocation varies on a game-to-game basis. Views and acoustics are okay but you're a fair distance from the pitch and leg space is just adequate.

'Gary Mabbutt's Knee' is a brilliantly named Coventry City fanzine, which also has a web presence. It refers to the Sky Blues' winning goal in the FA Cup final against Spurs at Wembley Stadium, when the barrel-chested defender deflected a cross into his own net.

Eating out

The stadium bowl is served by 19 bar and food outlets, offering things like steak & kidney pies. You can get a pie & pint deal. There are no cafés or takeaways near the ground due to its edge-of-city location. About 400 yards away is a retail park housing a Tesco.

Simply Scrumptious, a three-minute drive from the Ricoh along the A444, is no ordinary sandwich shop. It does a fantastic selection of succulent fillings for sarnies or baguettes such as minted lamb and beef & chilli. Coventry boasts some very good restaurants of all descriptions. Recommended dining establishments near the city centre include Ristorante Da Vinci on Earlsdon Street, a traditional Italian with an upmarket flavour. Earlsdon Cottage Restaurant on Warwick Street has built a good reputation for fine dining with a varied menu. It incorporates a pub with guest ales on tap, and a wine bar.

Mine's a pint

 Get to the Ricoh early and you could shift a few pints of Carling or John Smith's. It might be the best decision you make all day, as there are few pubs within walking distance and the city is a few miles away. Go ahead and check out the pubs along Longford Road but most tend to be bustling with Sky Blues fans. The main away fans

Club Information Stadium: Ricoh Arena, Phoenix Way, Foleshill, Coventry CV6 6GE Capacity: 32,000 (all seated) Tel: 0870 4211987 Website: www.ccfc.co.uk Train: Coventry Colours: Sky blue Songs: 'Let's all sing together' is the fans' anthem. 'In Our Coventry Homes' an ode to the fact that the city has two cathedrals (one in ruins in case

pub is The Black Horse at the top of this road. It features a large outdoor area with seating and tables, shows Sky Sports, has a pool table and serves food. From here go across the roundabout on to Bedworth Road where you'll find The Longford Engine. It's mainly for home fans but does admit away supporters and family groups. A mix of food is offered, while a pool table and cash machine are available.

It's a 15-minute walk to the Ricoh. The Old Windmill on Spon Street in the city gets good reviews - it's in the CAMRA Good Beer Guide 2007. Locals say the venue is snug and full of character with a great range of tasty ales. For post-match drinking activities, hit High Street, Whitefriars Street or Gosford Street.

Stopping over in Coventry?

The stadium hotel "heralds a new and exciting concept in overnight accommodation for the city of Coventry" (0870 8116 500). Hmmm, not sure about that, even if the boutique-style hotel does offer 46 pitch-view double rooms. You could stay here, but it's not so handy for city centre shopping or entertainment.

If you're on a budget, there are numerous guesthouses close to Coventry railway station.

Novotel on Wilsons Lane offers reasonably priced rooms and is walkable from Ricoh, just off junction 3 of the M6

(0870 811 6397). Also recommended is four-star Ramada Hotel in the city. Located on The Butts, it's a high quality alternative with prices to match (0870 890 3722).

If you do one thing in Coventry...

Visit Coventry Transport Museum, located at Millennium Place on Hales Street, and see displays of the world's largest collection of British road transport, including 240 cars, commercial vehicles and buses, 100 motorcycles and over 200 bicycles. Admission is free.

That's a Jimmy Hill isn't it?

It was Jimmy Hill's idea to change the club's nickname from the Bantams to the Sky Blues. He later became Coventry's chairman.

Don't mention

Terry Butcher: as popular as he is with many of the nation's football fans for his blood-stained heroics for England, he had a disastrous spell at Coventry City. Villa Park: Coventry have only ever won one League match there and that win in 1999 came after more than a hundred years of trying.

Do mention

The 1987 FA Cup Final: City famously beat Spurs 3-2 after extra time in one of the all-time great cup finals. Keith Houchen: he scored a superb diving header in the 1987 final.

Travel Information

CAR
From the M6, leave at J3 and take the A444 towards the city centre. After a mile you'll see the stadium on your left. If you're coming from the south on the M40, exit at J15 and take the A46 towards Coventry. Stay on the A46 and head for the M6 to reach the stadium – it's longer, but quicker as you avoid the built-up area. Parking at the stadium is for permit holders only and nearby residential areas have parking restrictions but there are schools and businesses which offer matchday parking for about a fiver. The club has a Park & Ride scheme: £7 per car (incl. bus travel for occupants). At the Jaguar Research & Development in Whitley Coventry, it is primarily for supporters coming up from the south and going to the stadium via the M1, J17 and then the A45 to Coventry. Continue on the A45 towards Coventry and pick up signs for the 'Jaguar/ Racquet Centre' to take you to the park & ride. Pre-book your space on 0247 6236986.

TRAIN
Coventry station is about five miles away from the ground. Best to catch a bus, first to the Pool Meadow Bus Station – most buses from the station go there. From Pool Meadow get one to the stadium: every ten mins matchdays. A £3 matchday ticket gives you unlimited bus travel around Coventry. Buses depart after the match from outside the North Stand.

you're interested) is another local favourite. Rivals: Just about every club in the West Midlands: Aston Villa, Birmingham City, Leicester City, Walsall, West Bromwich Albion, Wolverhampton Wanderers.

Crewe Alexandra

Charm offensive

For the Railwaymen, Alexandra Stadium will always be plain Gresty Road. The same cannot be said of the stands whose sponsors have created some daft tongue-twisters thanks to their bold commercial statements.

Ten years ago, Crewe fans could surely never have imagined they'd be having conversations about the merits or otherwise of the Air Products Stand, the Charles Audi Stand or, ahem, the Advance Personnel Stand.

The away end is not exempt from this sponsorship trend. Crewe may have been slow to replace boss Dario Gradi - his stewardship began in June 1983 - but they had no qualms about calling the visitors' section the Blue Bell BMW Stand.

Still, the Alexandra Stadium remains one of the most popular grounds in the country. It made the shortlist of three stadiums in the 2007 Football League Best Away Ground.

That it's a favourite venue is down to a slew of upgrades over the past decade. The £6 million redevelopment of what is now the Air Products Stand was the final piece in the makeover and helped deliver a well-equipped 10,153-capacity venue.

The Blue Bell BMW Stand is quite spacious, holding around 1,600 visiting fans and providing close-up views along the side of the pitch.

Stoke City are fierce local rivals and, naturally, much sneered at by The Alex when they visit for derby games. Crewe fans are quick to rip the mickey out of the Clayheads. Take the following gag as a particularly, erm, fine example of the Crewe (t)wit: A Clayhead walks into a bar with a toad on his head. "What the hell's that?!" asks the barman. "I don't know," said the toad. "It started as a wart and just kept growing!"

Eating out

There's a tea and snack bar for away fans, with pies, hotdogs and chips on sale. Or you can grab some tucker and mix with home fans in the Alexandra Suite. Top-notch fishy fare and fries are available from the chip shop opposite the ground. Nantwich Road has a wide selection of cafés and takeaways, including a sandwich shop, bakery, burger bar and a Chinese. The Golden Palace, a Chinese off Nantwich Road, is popular on Saturday nights so booking is advisable.

Giovanni's Italian restaurant, along with the Persian Kebab House and a Greek diner, are also on this road. Cheshire Cheese, a bar-cum-restaurant on Crewe Road, has a varied menu and is recommended for a slap-up meal. Passage to India is a curry house near The Barrel pub. Family pubs serving fine grub include The Brocklebank on Weston Road (A5020) and The Rookery Wood (Tom Cobleigh), which is further down Weston Lane by the roundabout.

Mine's a pint

There are no pubs which are said to be out of bounds if you're togged up in away colours. People don't tend to venture into the town centre, though, settling instead for the refreshments on offer in the Nantwich Road taverns. Why not make up your own

Club Information Stadium: Alexandra Stadium, Gresty Road, Crewe CW2 6EB Capacity: 10,153 (all seated) Tel: 01270 213014 Web: www.crewealex.net Train: Crewe Colours: Red and white Songs: An old Elvis number gets the treatment: 'Wise men sing only fools go to

pub crawl? Duck into The Royal for a snifter and put a few down the hatch in The Brunswick (large, friendly boozer and popular for away fans), The Barrel and The Bank and your mission will be complete. Don't forget the family hostelries mentioned above, if you want to avoid crowded pubs on matchdays. Or The Borough Arms, one of the best real ale pubs in Cheshire. For some bar tipples and a lively atmosphere in the evenings, you could try Square One on Mill Street or Tonic on Nantwich Road.

Stopping over in Crewe?

Manchester and Liverpool are popular places to stay for away fans as both are less than one hour away on the train. One of the most popular hotels for those away fans who do want to stay in Crewe is The Royal Hotel. It's good value accommodation and handily placed opposite the train station (01270 257398). Travelodge is handy for the motorway - just off junction 16 off the M6 and A500 between Nantwich and Stoke-on-Trent (0870 191 1571). Sleepers Hotel on The Wharf, Thomas Street, is another option (01270 585555). The Malbank Hotel in Nantwich is said to be a good stopover for a midweek match, with cheap pints and cheap rooms (01270 626011).

If you want to blow some cash on a more upmarket hotel with marble fireplaces

and stained glass features, Crewe Hall on Weston Road could be just what you're looking for (01270 253333).

If you do one thing in Crewe...

Crewe is great for a few drinks before and after a game, but there isn't a huge amount on offer – unless of course you're a railway enthusiast. Nearby Alton Towers is a fun day out.

Otherwise you could make a beeline for the cultural attractions in Liverpool or Manchester if you're looking to make a weekend of things.

What's in a name?

Crewe Alexandra is often the subject of pub quizzes. It's one of only two Football League clubs with an 'x' in their name. The others? Wrexham.

And Alexandra – like Forest, Villa, Academicals, Argyle, Hotspur and Wednesday - is a unique name for a British professional football club.

Don't mention

That Crewe lost their first FA Cup match 10-0; nobody will remember - it was against Queens Park of Glasgow in 1884.

Do mention

Dean Ashton, David Platt, Robbie Savage: all kicked off their careers at Gresty Road and are still held in high regard by the fans. Dario Gradi: Super Dario managed the club for 24 years before moving upstairs.

Travel Information

CAR
Exit the M6 at Junction 16 and take the A500 and then A5020 (Old Park Road and Weston Road) into Crewe. Then as you come towards Crewe Station turn left at the roundabout, onto the A534 Nantwich Road. Gresty Road is just past the Railway Station on the left. There is street parking available around the ground, as well as some limited parking at the stadium. Also as you come into Crewe on Weston Road you'll see a sign for away fans' street parking. This directs you to an industrial estate about fifteen minutes' walk to and from the ground.

TRAIN
Crewe aren't nicknamed the Railwaymen for nothing: the town once housed a bustling railway works and today remains a major rail junction and is a thoroughfare for a number of train services. With that it mind, it should come as no surprise that it's easy getting there by train. It's also only a short walk to the ground. Exit left out of the station and along Nantwich Road; then turn left into Gresty Road and you'll find the stadium is a short way down on the left.

Stoke... but I can't help falling in love with Crewe.' Other efforts pay homage to Dario. Rivals: Stoke and Port Vale at a push... but these two are too consumed with one another to strike up a major rivalry.

Crystal Palace

Genial hosts

Palace are looking at the possibility of relocating from Selhurst Park to the site of the National Sports Centre. Flamboyant Eagles chairman Simon Jordan made enquiries about relocating the club to the site of their original home two years ago but the London Development Agency put the mockers on plans due to "logistical issues". Proposals for a 25,000-seater would raise objections from local residents near Crystal Palace Park while poor transport links are a major drawback.

The perma-tanned chairman bought Selhurst from the club's previous owner Ron Noades in November 2006 and has made no secret of his intentions to relocate. But a lack of alternative sites in the area means that Palace are likely to stay put for a while yet.

Fans either love or loathe Jordan who can come over as an arrogant egomaniac at times. Still, he produces some choice soundbites, such as "I'd rather support Millwall than sell Andy Johnson".

Selhurst Park is unique in English football for ground-sharing with two professional football clubs at different times. Charlton Athletic were temporary tenants for five years before Wimbledon left Plough Lane and replaced them at Selhurst in 1991. This arrangement lasted over a decade. In 2003, Wimbledon controversially departed to Milton Keynes 60 miles away.

The Eagles' 26,309 all-seater ground is also one of very few football stadia still to have an original wooden construction from when it was first built. Away fans are located in one corner of the Arthur Waite stand, near to the Holmesdale Road End, seating just over 2,000. The worst seats in the house are at the rear of the stand, where you'll struggle to get a good view. Aim to sit in the first 15 rows from the front or you'll get a pillar-box view of the game.

Eating out

The usual football-style refreshments are available in the Arthur Waite Stand but it's pricey and not particularly good. The catering bar gets busy and you could find yourself queuing. In short, best not to bother. Sainsbury's next to the stadium is good for parking on matchdays and grabbing a bite to eat. Lap Hings outside the ground on Whitehorse Lane is a big hit for takeaway fried food. A bit further down nearer Thornton Heath is Doneagles for fish & chips, served at tables if you prefer. Thornton Heath is probably the best area for the away posse - it's also the site of a Wetherspoons pub serving cheap food and drink and only 10-15 minutes' walk to the ground. Crystal Palace is the best location for evening eating and pubs. All tastes are catered for in this area. Westow Hill is loaded with eateries. Among the favourites is Joanna's, which offers breakfast, brunch and à la carte food - a mix of British favourites and international flavours.

Mine's a pint

The Wetherspoons seems to be the pub of choice for visiting fans. Other pubs around Thornton Heath may prove welcoming but you might come up against some strict bouncers here and there. Real ale houses abound in the Selhurst Park area and you shouldn't experience any

Club Information Stadium: Selhurst Park, London SE25 6PU Capacity: 26,309 (all seated) Tel: 0208 7686000 Web: www.cpfc.co.uk Train: Selhurst/Thornton Heath Colours: Red & Blue Songs: 'Glad All Over' is the Palace anthem: the team

trouble getting into them. Beer from two main independent brewers, Young's and Fuller's, is not hard to find. The Railway Telegraph on Brigstock Road is a large Young's pub and popular with away fans. Likewise the Clifton Arms on Clifton Road, the closest hostelry to the ground. William Stanley on South Norwood High Street is another Wetherspoons. It's yards away from The Alliance, which is smaller but has a much better ambience and range of ales.

Croydon is a drab part of London but has plenty of drinking dens perfect for a session before or after a match. Get off the train at East Croydon and do some exploring. The Dog and Bull on Surrey Street is tipped as one of the finest ale houses with quality Young's Special and Ordinary among the beers on tap. The Saturday market is close by. It has a big beer garden at the rear and the food is reasonably priced.

Stopping over in Croydon?

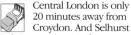

Central London is only 20 minutes away from Croydon. And Selhurst Park is easy to get to from London Victoria train station, so you're best staying up in town where you'll be spoilt for choice for accommodation. If you've set your heart on Croydon, though, there's the no-frills Express by Holiday Inn at Priddy's Yard (020 8253 1200) and a Jury's Inn on Wellesley Road, a five-minute walk from East Croydon train

station (020 8448 6000). But if you're planning on sightseeing or going on the razz in London, a better idea is to stay at Express By Holiday Inn on Belgrave Road, near London Victoria (020 7630 8888) or Thistle Westminster, on Buckingham Palace Road (0870 414 1516).

If you do one thing in Croydon...

There's not a huge amount on offer in Croydon – football and athletics are the main attractions. So head into the City of London where you're bound to find plenty to do. Check out the city guide for more information on the capital's top sights.

Anthem from a Spurs fan

Palace have The Dave Clark Five's 1964 hit 'Glad All Over' as their anthem. The band apparently formed in north London to raise funds for Dave Clark's football team, Tottenham Hotspur.

Don't mention

Ron Noades: former chairman who sold the club, but kept the freehold for Selhurst Park causing major financial problems.

Do mention

Ian Wright: plucked from obscurity he went on to score more than one hundred goals for Palace. Steve Coppell: he had four successful spells in the Palace hotseat and led the club to third in the top flight and an FA Cup Final.

Travel Information

CAR
Leave the M25 at Junction 7 for the A23 to Croydon. After the roundabout junction with the A236, this becomes Thornton Road. As you come towards Thornton Heath take the fourth exit at the roundabout onto the A235 and an immediate left onto the B266 (Brigstock Road). Then bear right on to the High Street. At the next roundabout go left into Whitehorse Lane, the ground is on the right. An alternative route is to exit the M25 at Junction 10 and follow the A3 towards London. After about ten miles take the A240 towards Epsom; then the A232 towards Sutton and then pick up signs for the A23. You should be able to find street parking close to Selhurst Park.

TRAIN
Three stations: Selhurst, Thornton Heath and Norwood Junction. Selhurst and Thornton Heath are both served by trains from Victoria, Clapham Junction and East Croydon. It's a short walk from Selhurst Station to the ground. Thornton Heath is about a ten-minute walk: turn left out of the station and walk down the High Street. Norwood Junction is served by trains from London Bridge, Charing Cross and East Croydon.

run out to it. 'Eagles, Eagles' and anything defamatory about Brighton, Millwall and Charlton. Rivals: Millwall and Charlton for geographical reasons and Brighton (dating from the 70s).

It's party time

Nationwide Conference champions Dagenham & Redbridge secured promotion to League Two for the first time in April 2007. It was the fulfilment of a dream for Dave Andrews, club chairman for 35 years, who estimates the 1996/97 FA Trophy finalists will make £400,000 "by going up".

Naturally, Daggers fans are in good cheer ahead of their League Two adventure. "It's a great thing for the town. We'll be playing West Ham in the league in a couple of years!" quipped one chirpy supporter to the local paper.

Clearly, that's wishful thinking, but there's certain to be a party atmosphere at the Victoria Road ground with the league newcomers entertaining a host of better-known clubs.

Dagenham & Redbridge have only been in existence since 1992, although their origins date back to four amateur clubs from east London and Essex - Ilford, Leytonstone, Walthamstow Avenue and Dagenham FC. Redbridge Forest won promotion to the Conference in 1991 before the merger into today's club.

For the 2007/08 season, two sections of the 6,078-capacity ground are designated for away fans – 240 seats and a 1,200-capacity terrace.

Victoria Road has existed as a football ground since 1917. Substantial work at the stadium has brought it up to a good standard. The club has two years to install another 1,000 seats to comply with league rules for a 2,000 seating capacity; these are expected to be built on the Pondfield Road End.

The Daggers fan base is fairly diverse due to the club's mixed heritage, but the passionate followers are a friendly shower.

Eating out

One snack bar at the away end will cater for most needs. If you crave chips, burgers or just a cuppa, you'll find prices cheaper than most other clubs.

For larger away followings, a mobile catering van is brought in to dispense matchday fare. An assortment of fast food outlets are scattered around the ground, including two chippies in the area opposite Dagenham East Station and on Rainham Road between the station and Victoria Road.

For some traditional 'East End' tucker, there's a pie & mash eaterie just beyond The Eastbrook pub in Dagenham Road. If you're driving, you could stop off at the McDonald's on the A1306. Oxlow Lane is a few minutes' walk from the ground and has a pizza parlour, Indian and Mr Wong's Chinese restaurant. Romford, three miles away, is the best place to go for a sit-down meal after the match. Faraglioni is a recommended Italian on Rush Green Road and Asia Spice does a good Indian.

Mine's a pint

Beer is not sold at Victoria Road. In previous seasons, away fans were

Club Information Stadium: Glyn Hopkin Stadium, Victoria Road, Dagenham, Essex RM10 7XL (Better known as Victoria Road) Capacity: 6,078 Tel: 0208 5921549 Web: www.daggers.co.uk Tube: Dagenham East Colours: Red and white Songs: A rousing rendition of 'Digger Dagger' goes something like: "Digger dagger, digger dagger, Oi, Oi, Oi".

allowed to drink in the Dagenham & Redbridge FC clubhouse at the ground for a small admission charge. The venue holds about 800.

There are other good watering holes nearby for a pre-match pint. The Railway, a large pub with a big screen TV, is popular among away fans due to its close proximity to the tube stop and ground (five minutes away). There's a good chippy opposite.

Another place catering for large numbers of travelling supporters is The Eastbrook. This is a family pub with a beer garden. The Bull is further down the Rainham Road on the roundabout at the top of Ballards Road (from Dagenham East tube station turn right, away from the ground). It serves pub grub on matchdays and includes a garden and seating at the back.

The advice from locals is to avoid The Beacon in Oxlow Lane - it's not a welcoming pub for visitors. If you want to paint Romford red on a night out, start your pub crawl in South Street's bars.

Stopping over in Romford?

 Some might say it's not an attractive proposition, but, if you've

trekked from afar, a gallon of Old Speckled Hen down town and a few hours' kip in a local hotel may not be such a bad idea. Premier Travel Inn on Mercury Gardens is reasonably priced (08701 977 220). Or you could rest up in Travelodge on St Edwards Way, Market Place, for a similar cost (0870 191 1756).

If you do one thing in Romford...

Hmmm. Have a flutter on the dogs at the Coral Romford Greyhound Stadium, or head for the bright lights of London to the west, easily accessible by tube.

Coffin up for the club

The club is the only league team to be sponsored by an undertakers (shirt sponsors are local funeral directors West & Coe).

Don't mention

East London: the club's postcode is Essex, the local radio station is BBC Essex but despite this they are referred to in some media circles as East Londoners.

Do mention

& Redbridge: they're proud of their full name and like to distinguish themselves from the forerunners Dagenham FC.

CAR
Leave the M25 at Junction 27 and take the M11 towards London. At the end of the M11 take the A406 towards Docklands, and then the A13 towards Dagenham. Exit the A13 onto the A1306. At the third set of traffic lights turn left into Ballards Road. At the large roundabout turn left into Rainham Road. After about half a mile turn left into Victoria Road. There is street parking around and a fair sized car park at the ground which is free, but be warned it can fill up 45 minutes ahead of kick off.

TUBE
Take the District Line to Dagenham East. The tube journey is about 40 minutes from London, another option is to get a train from Fenchurch Street to Barking Station and then a tube to Dagenham from there. Exit left out of the station and the ground is clearly signposted. It's about a five minute walk up Rainham Road; Victoria Road is on the left.

It can be heard at most home matches. Rivals: These have been any of the non-league sides in the Essex area who've come into money. Notably Grays Athletic, Hornchurch and Canvey Island in recent years. Things may change with Football League status.

Darlington

Naming and shaming

In the summer of 2003, Darlington bade farewell to its home at Feethams and moved into an ambitiously large 25,000-seat stadium on Neasham Road. It was the brainchild of flamboyant local entrepreneur George Reynolds, the man who rescued the club from financial ruin in 1997.

The controversial chairman behind the construction of the stadium badged it the Reynolds Arena. Reynolds wanted to bring Premiership action to the arena, but he didn't invest in quality players and his dream quickly died. The club couldn't sustain the 11,000-plus attendances seen during the stadium's honeymoon period and - just four months later - it again fell into financial trouble, sinking into administration in December the same year with the ground still not completely finished.

Darlington's main creditors launched a takeover of the club, eventually removing Reynolds, the Good Samaritan-turned-villain of the stadium project. The ground was soon rebranded the Williamson Motors Stadium. For the 2005/06 season, it acquired an even less attractive moniker and one which doesn't exactly trip off the tongue if you're a footy commentator - still the 96.6 TFM Darlington Arena, named after the town's radio station, is at least finally finished.

Dominating the skyline as you drive down the bypass to the A1, the roof of the venue's stands is free of supporting pillars ensuring an unobstructed view for all visitors. The stadium sits 1.9km from the town's train station (25 minute walk) and away fans can purchase tickets at turnstiles 36-43 in the East Stand.

If the stadium looks half-empty on the telly, that's because it usually is. But Quakers fans claim the atmosphere will defy your expectations as the roof helps to keep the noise in.

Eating out

Concourse food kiosks offer sausage rolls and Taylor's pies and pasties, supplied by the renowned Darlington butcher - apparently you can actually see some proper meat and they don't fall apart. Places to eat nearby are few and far between. Try the chippy on Neasham Road or the East End fish bar close to the Yarm Road junction. There's a good sandwich bar on Yarm Road opposite The Albion pub. It serves all-day breakfasts in a bap. Near the station are some takeaways and cafés in Victoria Road, including Scotties Fish Bar and Rocky's. Coronation Hotel, a B&B option, on the corner also has a café where you can grab breakfast and a cuppa. In town, the fast-food chains are easily located. Good curry houses are Spice Garden and Radhuni on Parkgate, while you can also find Phutawan Thai Restaurant there. For modern Indian food, go to Reema on Coniscliffe Road or The Garden of India on Bondgate. An excellent Chinese buffet is offered at Central Park in Northgate. For an Italian, La Sorrentina on Parkgate is recommended.

Mine's a pint

 Many pubs are fan-friendly. At the stadium, The Tinshed and The Corner bars welcome away fans and concourse bars for away supporters are also housed in the South Stand. Good pubs

---

Club Information Stadium: 96.6 TFM Darlington Arena, Neasham Road, Darlington DL2 1DL Capacity: 25,000 (all seated) Tel: 01325 387000 Web: www.darlington-fc.net Colours: Black & White Train: Darlington Songs: Most popular nearby are The Copper Beech and The Tawny Owl on Neasham Road. Town centre pubs - about 30 minutes' walk from the ground - are some of the best. Look for the market square's clock to get your bearings. Family pub The Pennyweight serves good ales and lunches. At The Hole in the Wall get Magnet or Greene King IPA and eat a Thai dish while watching Sky Sports. On Skinnergate, there's a Yates's and Wetherspoons, The Tanners Hall, and Bar Risa. The Railway Tavern, High Northgate is a rockers' pub Friday nights and hosts live music. Number 22 on Coniscliffe Road offers bottled British and continental beers. Another friendly CAMRA pub is The Quaker Café, Mechanics Yard, off High Row.

Stopping over in Darlington?

 At the budget end, try Arcadia Guest House, or The Dalesman B&Bs near the station on Victoria Road. Also, the Grange Guest House on Grange Road and The Argyll on Corporation Road. On the other side of town is the Greenbank Hotel on Greenbank Road (01325 462624). Darlington Arts Centre on Vane Terrace offers basic rooms and good canteen breakfasts. For a little more money, go for The Coachman Hotel on Victoria Road (01325 286116) or The Cricketers on Parkgate (01325 384444). A bit more expensive is Blackwell Grange, Grange Road, 20 mins'

walk from the stadium (0870 609 6121). A comfy alternative is Hotel Bannatyne, Southend Avenue (01325 365858).

If you do one thing in Darlington...

Check out the Darlington Railway Museum, attend a concert at Darlington Arts Centre or visit an exhibition at the Civic Theatre. If you have the time, the North Yorkshire Moors or the Yorkshire Dales are worth exploring.

Lucky losers

Darlington became the first modern day team to lose in the FA Cup and still qualify for the next round in 1999/2000. Manchester Utd didn't enter due to their participation in the FIFA Club World Championship and the Quakers were picked out in a lucky losers' draw from the 20 teams eliminated in round two.

Don't Mention

The aforementioned George Reynolds: former chairman who built the club's stadium, was reported to have invested £27m in the club and once tried to sign Faustino Asprilla. However, in January 2004 the club went into administration and Reynolds quit. Two years later he was jailed for three years for tax evasion.

Do Mention

Marco Gabbiadini: voted the club's all-time greatest player. Fred Barber and David Speedie: two famous faces from the early 1980s.

---

seem to be anti-Hartlepool songs, with many of the classics reworked to belittle the Poolies. Rivals: Hartlepool United (Poolies) are the main rivals.

Travel Information

CAR
From the south: Exit the A1(M) at Junction 57 and take the A66 towards Darlington. Continue on this road and you will eventually see the ground ahead of you. When you do, turn left at the roundabout into Neasham Road for the stadium. From The North: Leave the A1(M) at Junction 59 and take the A167 towards Darlington, then the A1150 towards Teeside, and finally the A66 towards Darlington. You will see the stadium on your right. There's a fair sized car park at the stadium which costs £5 per car – but it can take a while to clear. Some street parking to be found towards the city centre, but this can be quite a walk.

TRAIN
Darlington train station is around one and a half miles away from the stadium. Cross the covered footbridge back over the railway into Albert Road and take a right into Neasham Road. The stadium is about a mile further on down this road on your left. It should take about 25 minutes to walk it or you can get a bus to and from the ground for just £1 from Tubwell Row in the city centre – which is a short walk from the station.

Derby County

Feel the noize

The Rams were racking up gates of 25,000-plus at the back end of last season as Billy Davies' high-flying team strung together a dazzling run of performances.

Such strong and passionate local support makes any visit to Pride Park a real occasion. The hordes of hollering Rams followers, together with the away contingent, can produce a big noise in this totally enclosed stadium.

With two sets of two identical stands, the 33,597-seat venue is built in the mould of many grounds erected in the past 15 years. But a decade after opening on the outskirts of the city, the stadium is still held in high regard by many visitors and stadium anoraks for its top-notch fan amenities, including good concourse facilities with TV screens.

Derby's old Baseball Ground is a distant memory but will always be remembered fondly as the setting for the club's glory years under Brian Clough's regime from 1967-73. During his successful tenure, they won the league title in 1972 and made the European Cup semi-final a year later.

Away supporters are seated in the Cawarden South Stand behind one of the goals, which can accommodate up to 4,800.

According to some, parking at Pride Park is a bit of an issue as the roads in and out of the business park in which it is situated often get jammed up on matchdays. Be prepared for a wait or go elsewhere. You could park near the railway station in a public car park and walk to the ground (15 minutes) or get the shuttle bus from the city centre. The club advises away fans to park at Catalyst, which is on London Road (A6) opposite The Navigation pub.

Eating out

Fast food and drinks are sold from concourse outlets at Pride Park, where you can watch the pre-match build-up on plasma screen TV. American-style fare is available at Old Orleans on the stadium site. There's also a Harvester restaurant-bar conveniently placed here, which is perfect for a pre-match feed – however, cover your colours up to be sure of getting in.

With over 350 restaurants and eating establishments to choose from in Derby, you'll have no trouble finding what you want. Near the train station on Midland Road is a café called Sara's Snax and also an Italian restaurant, Antibos.

The Shalimar is a recommended Indian on this road. For good value Chinese cuisine, head to Shing-Do on Wardwick opposite the library. Cornmarket has several restaurants including a Deep Pan Pizza. If you're coming from the north, you could pop into the Meteor Centre complex on the A61 for a quick bite.

The Foresters Leisure Park, south west of the city centre on the A5111 ring road, has a KFC and other places to eat.

Mine's a pint

The Crown and Cushion on Midland Road is just up from the train station and recommended as an away-friendly pub. It serves a nice pint and decent food. There are other pubs you could try on Midland Road/Railway Terrace. One in particular - The Brunswick - curries favour among many visiting fans and gets crowded on matchdays. You can sup on an excellent choice of ales and guest brews and there's a friendly atmosphere at this pub on Railway Terrace. The Waterfall and The Alexandra Hotel are friendly joints nearby, both offering tasty beers on tap. Some of these places serve food but not always on Saturdays.

Market Place and Irongate are two good areas to head for a pub crawl after the match. For somewhere with character, go to The Dolphin on Queen Street - it's Derby's oldest pub, dating back to 1530. An old coaching inn, it is thought to have been a stopping-off point for highwaymen and is reputed to be haunted.

Stopping over in Derby?

 On Wheelwright Way at Pride Park there's Express By Holiday Inn (01332 388000). It's good for a stop-over in the week if nothing else. Located on Prospect Place off Derwent Parade, Sleep Inn is another option near the stadium and within easy reach of the A52 and M1. Rooms are priced from about £50 (01332 611 980).

If you want to spend a night in the city centre, your best bet is to book a cheap

room (from £30) at Legacy Aston Court Hotel on Midland Road (0870 832 9941). It's just a minute from the train station.

If you do one thing in Derby...

Derby has a rich industrial and cultural heritage but there's nothing much to recommend on the attractions front. However, it's a great base for exploring the Peak District.

In spring 2008, QUAD will open on Corporation Street, a welcome attraction to Derby, which should make an interesting destination if you're a film buff or fancy gawping at some contemporary visual art. It will contain two cinema screens and a couple of gallery spaces.

Pitch perfect

One stadium anorak has calculated that mowing the Pride Park pitch one way is a seven-and-a-half mile route.

Don't mention

A 5-1 defeat at Real Madrid in 1975: even worse when you consider Derby were 4-1 up from the first leg of this European Cup tie.

Do Mention

Dave Mackay: inspirational left-half who not only played for the club, but was manager too – leading the Rams to the 1974/75 League Championship. Steve Bloomer: legendary centre-forward from the early 20th century.

Travel Information

CAR
Leave the M1 at Junction 25 for the A52 towards Derby, the ground is about seven miles away and well signposted. There is not a great deal of parking available around the stadium so try the cattle market car park for about two quid. Go past the normal turning for the stadium and to the Pentagon Roundabout. Take the first turning off there and then turn next left and drive about 300 yards back on yourself for the car park. It's about a five-minute walk back to the stadium.

TRAIN
It is a short walk from Derby Station to the stadium; simply cross over the pedestrian bridge into Pride Park and follow the crowd.

classic seventies number: "Derby, County, Derby, County". Also popular is 'We Are Derby, Super Derby' and any anti-Forest chants. Rivals: Forest. Leicester aren't popular either.

Doctcaster Rovers

Community spirit

With the opening of Doncaster's £32million Keepmoat Stadium in December 2006, Rovers are the envy of other clubs around the league seeking to get community stadium projects off the ground.

Named for Keepmoat plc, the UK's leading regeneration and social housing specialist, the eye-catching venue forms part of the town's Lakeside Sports Complex. This includes a running track with a 500-seater stand, an outdoor amphitheatre for concerts, a 350-seat restaurant, a health & fitness club and a number of floodlit football pitches.

The move from the rundown Belle Vue marks a massive turnaround in fortunes for a club which faced the prospect of being wound after dropping out of the league in the late 90s.

"Our new ground is another world compared to Belle Vue," says a Rovers fan, "the setting, adjacent to a lake, is fabulous."

Completed on schedule and on budget, the 15,300-capacity stadium is situated close to junction 3 of the M18 (follow stadium signs) less than a mile from the club's former home at Belle Vue. It's also home to Doncaster Rovers Belles, rugby league side Doncaster Lakers and Doncaster Athletic Club.

Visiting supporters are housed behind the goal in the North Stand. One big plus point is the spacing between rows of seats, giving ample leg room for every fan. If you're driving here, it'll cost you about £5 to park at the stadium.

Eating out

Food stands around the concourses serve the usual football fare. Some say it's pricey but service is generally quick and efficient. There are mixed reports about the chicken balti pies. "The Rollover hotdogs are the best grub in the ground," one fan says, "and are the best value too." You'll find plenty of burger vans nearby, while the Lakeside Village shopping centre has a McDonald's, KFC, Pizza Hut and various cafés. For a good sit-down meal, head into town. There's the China Palace Cantonese Restaurant on Silver Street and a host of others to choose from. The Lakeside and The Cheswold pubs on the retail and commercial parks close to the ground do food and are fine for families.

Mine's a pint

Beer is sold on the concourses beneath the stands at the stadium. The pubs mentioned above get packed so best to get there early. You can get liquid refreshment at The Salutation, an away-friendly pub on South Parade, near the Odeon. It also runs a free bus to the ground. The Park Hotel on Carr House Road is also said to be welcoming on matchdays. After the match and into the night, make a beeline for Priory Walk in the town centre - it's littered with cracking pubs and bars. According to a

Club Information Stadium: Keepmoat Stadium, Stadium Way, Lakeside, Doncaster DN4 5JW Capacity: 15,231 (all seated) Tel: 01302 764 664 Web: www.doncasterroversfc.co.uk Train: Doncaster Colours: Red and white Songs: 'In Dublin's fine city' has been reworked to

102

club source, Doncaster's nightlife is "rated". "There's been documentaries about it." Make of that what you will but there's probably something for everyone.

Stopping over in Doncaster?

 If you want to sample the nightlife, stay local. Sheffield is 20 miles down the road, but you can go there next time. Cheap hotels include the Travel Lodge on Great North Road (0870 191 1631), Premier Travel Inn on Wilmington Drive (0870 197 7074) and the Holiday Inn on High Road, Warmsworth (A1(M), junction 36). Like the others this hotel is within easy reach of the stadium (0870 442 8761). If you stop at the reasonably-priced Danum Hotel, an impressive Edwardian building at the top end of High Street, you'll be right on top of the nightlife (01302 342261). Dominating an attractive square of 18th century architecture on the edge of town, The Regent Hotel provides a more luxurious stay (01302 364180). Rooms are priced from £65.

If you do one thing in Doncaster...

Conisbrough Castle dates back to the 12th century and boasts "the finest circular Norman keep tower in the UK". Whether you gamble or not, you'll always have a good day out at Doncaster races. For some family fun, head to The Dome, a sports and entertainment complex, including a climbing wall and ice rinks. It has an aquatic experience comprising seven inter-linked pools, geysers, water cannons, whirlpool spas and giant flume rides.

Donny Dog in distress

Rovers' mascot 'Donny Dog' (alias Andy Liney) was bizarrely barred by police from entering The Galpharm Stadium for a match against Huddersfield Town in 2006. The decision was based on unspecified "police intelligence". Despite receiving written permission sanctioning an appearance at the ground just days earlier, Donny Dog was down on his luck. Liney's offer to remove his mascot head and sit in the away end was also declined. As he had no other clobber to change into, he went back to the supporters' coach with his tail between his legs and missed the match.

Don't mention

Ken Richardson: former owner of the club, who paid an arsonist to burn down the main stand at the old ground Belle Vue (for which he served time), took the club into the Conference and very nearly out of business.

Do mention

John Ryan: Richardson's replacement; a local businessman and Rovers fan who has taken the club from the Conference to League One and into a stunning new stadium.

Travel Information

CAR
From either the A1(M) or M1 pick up the M18 towards Doncaster. Exit at Junction 3 and take the A6182 towards Doncaster. The stadium is well signposted from Junction 3. Stay on the A6182, turning left at the second roundabout and then right onto the industrial estate at the next. And past the Tesco distribution centre, turn right at the bottom of the road and the stadium is further down on your left. There are just 1000 parking spaces at the stadium; 60 spaces are reserved for disabled fans, but these must be booked in advance. The cost of parking at the stadium is £5. A number of businesses on the nearby business park offer matchday parking a little more cheaply and there is limited street parking to be had in this area.

TRAIN
Doncaster Station is about twenty-five minutes' walk to and from the stadium – so you may want to opt for a taxi. If you're walking: head out of the station and turn right and follow the dual carriageway until you reach the turning for Middle Bank on the right.

pay homage to the girls of Donny and the town's football team. Rivals: Half of Yorkshire: Barnsley, Hull, Rotherham, Scunthorpe. The other half won't be on the Christmas card list either.

Everton

Visiting the grand old lady

Fans breathed a sigh of relief when the ground-sharing plan with Liverpool was killed off in April 2007. But they're a tad bitter, the Reds having got the go-ahead to build a new stadium in Stanley Park when Everton - Liverpool's first pro club - might have to move out of town. Club chiefs are currently exploring new stadium ideas, with a Kirkby site in neighbouring Knowsley now under scrutiny for possible relocation.

But Blues fan group Keep Everton in Our City is fighting to keep the club's stadium in Liverpool, claiming that relocation outside the city boundary would be a huge mistake.

Chairman Bill Kenwright says he doesn't want to move Everton away from Goodison Park, but the city council have confirmed it would be impossible to expand the ground, known affectionately as 'The Grand Old Lady'.

Kenwright insists it is no longer financially viable to remain at the 40,569-seat Goodison Park - the first purpose-built football stadium in England and the first with a four-sided stadium with two-tier stands.

Everton's last plan to move to a 55,000-seater waterfront stadium at King's Dock was abandoned in 2003, after the club failed to raise their funding contribution towards the multi-purpose arena project.

The Bullens Road Stand can house up to 3,000 away supporters. Like the rest of the ground, it has a certain ramshackle charm, but is in dire need of an update. Some of the vantage points from the lower tier are far from fantastic due to several supporting pillars restricting sightlines. In fact, putting the romance of the place aside, the fact is Goodison Park offers a below-par view for visiting fans.

Eating out

There's a decent variety of matchday staples sold at the ground. Goodison Supper Bar next door cooks up traditional fish & chips, while County Road nearby offers a selection of fast food outlets and cafés. In the city, St John's is Liverpool's largest shopping centre with a McDonald's, Subway and KFC. For the more discerning palate, there's an abundance of choice in a city with a thriving restaurant and café-bar scene. Chinatown (around Berry Street) is one option for eating out. 60 Hope Street, four times Best Merseyside Restaurant of the Year, is a recommended haven for European cuisine at very reasonable prices... best to book early though. Another top tip is just down the road; The London Carriage Works, Merseyside's Restaurant of the Year 2006. It includes a relaxed brasserie area and dishes up classic meals with a modern twist. If you want top-notch Japanese food, try Sapporo Teppanyaki Restaurant Sushi & Noodle Bar on Duke Street, East Village: light meals and snacks served at lunchtimes.

Mine's a pint

Down a few Changs at the ground or fill up elsewhere. Anfield Hotel on Walton Road is a popular venue for pre-match drinking. Good range of beers and outside seating. The Winslow, outside Goodison, offers a warm welcome and

Club Information Stadium: Goodison Park, Goodison Road, Liverpool L4 4EL
Capacity: 40,569 (all seated) Tel: 0870 4421878 Web: www.evertonfc.com Train:
Kirkdale Colours: Blue and white Songs: The wonderful 'It's A Grand Old Team To

has a buzzing atmosphere on game days. Sink a few pints and scoff some food while watching sport on one of the many televisions. The Arkles on Anfield Road is another favourite for away fans due to its host of amenities - two big screens and some nice ales. Avoid The Stanley Park, known as 'The Blue House', wall-to-wall with bluenoses. Check out County Road's hostelries, many of which will be full of Toffeemen but are generally away-friendly. You'll be fine at any of the pubs near Lime Street station (two miles from Goodison) as long as you cover colours and don't get too lippy. Of these, The Crown gets good reviews for its cheap food and beers - including Cains bitter - and friendly service. Also worth a visit is The Vines, better known as 'The Big House', one of a number of grand Victorian boozers in the centre.

Stopping over in Liverpool?

There's a wide range of accommodation. Carey's is a small B&B on Walton Breck Road close to Goodison and extends a warm welcome to visitors (0151 286 7965). Another is Litherland Park B&B, four-diamond rated accommodation which is excellent value and is only 15 minutes by car from the city centre (0151 928 1085). Budget hotels in the heart of Liverpool include Hotel Ibis at Wapping (0151 706 9800) and Premier Travel Inn on Vernon Street, off Dale Street (0870 238 3323). The extravagant choice with tariffs to match is Malmaison Hotel situated at Princes Dock (0151 229 5000).

If you only do one thing in Liverpool...

Liverpool was not crowned the European Capital of Culture 2008 for nothing. You're spoilt for choice. Obviously, the Beatles are a huge part of the city's heritage. But don't forget about innovators like OMD, Echo and the Bunnymen and, erm, Atomic Kitten. The Beatles Story visitor attraction within Liverpool's Albert Dock is one of the top sights.

World Cup first

Goodison Park was the scene of the first goal scored in the 1966 World Cup and no other stadium witnessed more goals throughout the finals.

Don't mention

That famous Bill Shankly quote: the ex-Liverpool boss once said he'd pull his curtains if Everton were playing in his garden. Another of his remarks was: "There are only two teams on Merseyside: Liverpool and Liverpool reserves."

Do mention

The mid 1980s: a fantastic time for Everton which saw the Toffeemen vying for the major domestic honour with their red city rivals: the Blues' haul included the FA Cup in 1984 and League title in 1985 and 1987.

CAR
Follow the M62 until you reach the end of the motorway. Then take the A5058 towards Liverpool. After three miles turn left at the traffic lights into Utting Avenue and after a mile turn right at the corner of Stanley Park into Priory Road and you'll find the ground at the end of this road. Early birds may find street parking. Otherwise you may find it over towards Anfield or there's a car park in Stanley Park; it costs just over a fiver and the entrance is in Priory Road. You can also park at the Warton Sports Centre for £3. It's just off the A580 (a right-turn off the A5058, just before you reach Utting Avenue) a 15min walk.

TRAIN
Kirkdale Station (served by trains from Liverpool Central) is about fifteen minutes' walk. Turn right out of the station and cross the railway bridge and go up Westminster Road. Turn left into Goodall Street and into Harlech Street. Cross over the County Road at the traffic lights and go down Andrew Street and into Goodison Road. Another option is Sandhills Station (also served by Liverpool Central) which has a Soccerbus to the ground. It runs for a couple of hours before games and about an hour afterwards. Buy a return train ticket to Goodison Park – it's £1 extra, but covers your bus travel and is cheaper than paying separately.

Play For'. An anti-Liverpool effort talks about throwing Liverpool and Rangers fans in the Mersey. Rivals: Liverpool (and Rangers, because of their historical association with the Reds).

Fulham

Down by the riverside

On the banks of the Thames, Craven Cottage is one of the most idyllic settings in English football. Founded in 1879, Fulham are the oldest professional football club in London and have plied their trade at the stadium since 1896.

The Whites are famous for their bond with Craven Cottage, a quaint badge for a club with fine traditions but few honours. Their rapid ascent to the Premiership, bankrolled by Mohamed Al Fayed, meant the stadium did not comply with the Taylor Report's all-seater requirements - it had terracing as recently as 2002.

Fulham were forced to relocate to Loftus Road under the expectation that they would return to a brand new pad. But plans to build a lavish 30,000-seat replacement never came to fruition. Major refurbishment of the outdated Cottage eventually took place and Its capacity has since been increased to 24,600 - still one of the smallest in the top tier.

The Cottage retains a distinct charm, though. The Johnny Haynes Stand built in 1905 is a Grade II listed building protected by English Heritage.

Visiting supporters are housed to one side of the Putney End Stand, previously terracing open to the elements. Away fans are allocated about 3,000 seats. Several supporting pillars may obstruct your view, so prepare to seat-hop for the best view. Oddly, there's space in this stand designated for so-called neutral supporters, which the club says is suited to fans with no affiliation or "for home and away supporters happy to sit together". How sweet.

Half a dozen rows of seats are uncovered, then rows are labelled from 'A' up to the back 'UU' and offer covered seating.

Eating out

All stands in the stadium sell food and drink; with pies, burgers, pasties and similar available here and also at the burger stands around the ground. Situated at the Bishops Park end of the Johnny Haynes Stand is the Café at the Cottage, a great place to get fresh breakfast pastries, Belgian buns, char-grilled wraps, baguettes, bagels and even fish pie - basically, posher nosh delivered from Al Fayed's Harrods but at value prices. Rolls and filling wraps are from £2.50. For a brilliant all-English breakfast, The River Café outside Putney Bridge tube station (15 mins' walk to the ground) is a must. Tasty's is a recommended takeaway on Fulham High Street. Three restaurants on Upper Richmond Road might take your fancy if you're hungry for something different. Bayee House restaurant is a popular Chinese with excellent food and service. The cheerily-attired Chakalaka specializes in all South African cuisine. The Hare & Tortoise is an open-kitchen Oriental noodle bar where you can enjoy inexpensive Japanese cuisine in a laid-back atmosphere.

Mine's a pint

Eight Bells on Fulham High Street at Putney Bridge is the usual stop for away fans - decent beers and friendly staff. You could also try The

---

Club Information Stadium: Craven Cottage, Stevenage Road, London SW6 6HH Capacity: 24,600 (all seated) Telephone: 0870 4421222 Website: www.fulhamfc.com Tube: Putney Bridge Colours: Black and white Songs: A nice ode to Mohammed Al Fayed which cleverly rhymes 'He want's to be a Brit' with what

Temperance on the same road, a good choice for its range of beers. Swerve The Golden Lion... it's gone downhill, say some locals. Also steer clear of The Cottage, a Whites fans' pub on Colehill Lane. Most of the other taverns on this south side of the river are fine for pre-match drinks, although it's a bit of a mixed bag. The Crabtree on Rainville Road, Hammersmith, is one of the picks. This Thameside pub offers good pub grub and has a huge beer garden. If you keep your colours covered, The Boathouse on Brewhouse Street on the Putney side should be fine. Spread over three floors, it's become a firm favourite locally for its unfussy, friendly feel and quality drinks. And the beauty of many of these options is that you get a chance to walk off any excess with a stroll to the away end entrances.

Stopping over in Fulham?

Putney Bridge's Premier Travel Inn is conveniently located if you're staying in this area, although not cheap from £77 per room (0870 238 3302) it is convenient for London's west end, Earls Court and Olympia Exhibition Centre.

There are a couple of Express by Holiday Inn hotels in the surrounding area - one on King Street, Hammersmith, and another on North End Road, Earls Court (0800 556 5565).

If you do one thing in Fulham...

Visit Riverside Studios on the banks of the Thames in Hammersmith. It's west London's leading centre for contemporary and international performance, film, exhibitions and television production. It presents a diverse programme of events, including cutting-edge theatre and comedy.

Rock bottom

Fulham dropped into the football basement in 1994 and two years later were staring non-League football in the face. Home gates averaged just 4,000, but Micky Adams steered them out of danger then got them promoted the following year.

Don't mention

That you think Chelsea are the premier team in Fulham: yes Stamford Bridge is actually in Fulham, and the ground was originally offered to the Cottagers. They turned it down and the owners formed Chelsea FC (for obvious reasons they couldn't opt for Fulham).

Do mention

Micky Adams: legendary boss who cut his managerial teeth at the Cottage started the upward rise from the lower reaches of the Football League's basement to the Premiership. He led Fulham to their first promotion in 15 years in 1997.

CAR
From the M1: Leave the M1 and take the North Circular towards Harrow for about four miles. Then take the A40 into London and head west on the A402 for a few hundred yards before heading south on the A219. This takes you into Hammersmith, turn right onto the A315 and almost immediately turn back onto the A219 heading south. After about a mile turn right into Harbord Street, which leads into Stevenage Road. From the M4: This becomes the A4. After around two miles branch left into Hammersmith Broadway. Take ring road around Hammersmith and take the A219 Fulham Palace Road and look out for Harbord Street. From the south: Exit M25 at Junction 10 and take the A3. After eight miles take the A219 towards Putney. As you go over Putney Bridge you'll see the ground to your left on the Thames. Street parking around the ground is pay and display. It's about a fiver for three hours – although parking is free in the evenings and on Sundays.

TUBE
Putney Bridge on the District Line is nearest. The ground is about a fifteen minute walk. Come out of the station and take Station Approach and cross over Putney Bridge Approach into Bishop's Park and walk along the riverbank to the ground. The park is closed after evening games.

they think of QPR. They also reworked 'Keep The Blue Flag Flying' to tell Chelsea fans precisely what they should do with it. Rivals: Chelsea, QPR (with whom they ground-shared while the Cottage was redeveloped) and to an extent Brentford.

Gillingham

Heading for the Medway

A new stadium is in the pipeline for the Gills, who look set to up sticks from Priestfield Stadium within the next few years. Potential sites to build a palatial pad within and around Medway are being examined. Complete with conferencing and banqueting facilities, and possibly with a hotel on site, it would house between 16,000 and 26,000 fans.

Big ideas, then, for a club whose average attendance in 2006/07 was just 6,300. But club officials and local council chiefs firmly believe they could put a larger stadium to good use with a wide range of sporting events and concerts.

Kent's only league ground has benefited from significant investment in the past decade or so, with three new stands going up since 1995. Before that the venue had seen little redevelopment since the 1920s.

Away fans are allocated the Brian Moore Stand, named after the late former Gillingham director and legendary ITV football commentator. This stand was a replacement for the Town End terrace demolished during the 2003/04 close season. It may be all-seater but it's also open to the elements, so come prepared for bad weather or hire a waterproof from a steward. Yes, these kind people apparently offer them.

The away turnstiles are at the top of Priestfield Road and, if you're on foot, the walk from the station is no more than 10 minutes.

The Gills haven't had many honours to shout about in recent times, although the FA Cup run to the quarter-finals in 1999-2000 sticks in the memory. As does the 5-0 drubbing they received at the hands of Chelsea which ended their cup campaign.

Eating out

Visiting supporters' food and drink facilities inside Priestfield amount to concourse outlets in the Brian Moore Stand and a burger van. The stadium food is average at best say Priestfield regulars. Best to avoid the Blues Rock Café next to the stadium as it will be chocca with home fans. There are local chippies. Sandhu's Takeaway in Franklin Road does fish & chips, burgers and kebabs and is not far from the station. Step off the train and you'll be facing Gillingham's high street, which is lined with takeaways, pizza palaces, the odd bakery and a noodle bar. You could dive into the Co-op on Gillingham Road for pre-packed snacks or duck into the Livingstone Arms pub - it welcomes both sets of fans and is well-known for its complimentary pre-match bar food: hot roast potatoes, sausages and onion rings. Post-match, head into the town centre for Indian restaurants among others.

Mine's a pint

You can buy beer at the ground but you'll probably want to make merry in warmer, more comfortable surroundings. The Livingstone Arms is the away supporters' pub just 100 yards from the ground. It's lively on matchdays and has a good selection of beers. If

Club Information Stadium: Priestfield Stadium, Redfern Avenue, Gillingham ME7 4DD Capacity: 11,582 (all seated) Tel: 01634 300000 Web: www.gillinghamfootballclub.com Train: Gillingham Colours: Blue Songs: There's a bit of a Chelsea influence with popular anthems being the 'Over Land And Sea' song

you're arriving by train, it would be rude not to pop into The Southern Belle opposite the station exit. Another option for a pre-match appetiser is The Star on Watling Street. There's a decent food menu and wide range of drinks, plus a beer garden with a kids' play area. The Roseneath in Arden Street has a beer garden and serves guest cask ales. Don't bother with The Cricketers on Sturdee Avenue, it'll be packed to the Gills. The Jubilee in Darnley Road, Rochester, has an intimate atmosphere and welcomes families. For a lively evening out, try the Medway Queen in Chatham. The suburb of Rochester is packed with pubs and bars for late-night boozing. Recommended are The Crown, The Queen Charlotte and The George Vaults, the latter runs three bars and spins cutting-edge house music at the weekends.

Stopping over in Gillingham?

 Gillingham isn't too far from picturesque Canterbury, or London for that matter, but if you do want to make the Medway town your base for the weekend check in at the Premier Travel Inn en route to the stadium (0870 197 7105). Rooms are from £55. The Honourable Pilot Brewers Fayre pub is next door for food and beers. Another low-budget option is

The King Charles Hotel on Brompton Road (01634 830303). Four-starred Bridgewood Manor at Walderslade Woods, Chatham, comes with terrace bar and bistro, a swanky restaurant and a spa and leisure club (01634 201333).

If you do one thing in Gillingham...

Try knocking down ten pins at Chatham Bowling Alley. If you like castles, Rochester has some nice turrets but the better one is Leeds Castle in Maidstone. Canterbury has plenty of historic sights.

All right at the back

Steve Bruce, touted as the best centre-back of the 1980s and 90s never to play for England - began his footballing career with the Gills, joining the club straight from school in 1977. Bruce was a first-team regular for six years before moving to Norwich and later starred for Manchester United.

Don't mention

The 1999 play-off final: 2-0 up with less than two minutes left to play, Manchester City fought back to equalise and then win 3-1 on penalties.

Do mention

The 2000 play-off final: twelve months later the Gills were back at Wembley to banish the memories of 1999. They beat Wigan 1-0 to secure promotion under the guidance of Peter Taylor.

Travel Information

CAR
Leave the M2 at Junction 4 and take the A278 towards Gillingham. Turn left at the third roundabout onto the A2 towards Gillingham town centre. At the traffic light junction with the A231, turn right into Nelson Road and then right into Gillingham Road. You should be able to find ample street parking to the south east of the ground around Toronto Road and Sturdee Avenue. There is also a cheap pay and display car park on Railway Street near Gillingham station where you can park for a couple of quid.

TRAIN
The ground is about ten minutes' walk from Gillingham Station – which is well served by London Victoria and Charing Cross. Turn left out of the station and follow Balmoral Road which leads into Priestfield Road at the cross roads and right to the visitors' end of the stadium. To get to the Gordon Road Stand, turn right at the crossroads and then first left into Gordon Road. For the Medway Stand turn left at the crossroads and then first right. Both routes will also lead to the Rainham End.

and the Stamford Bridge favourite 'Celery'. Rivals: They don't like Millwall, but the Lions are more consumed with Chelsea and West Ham. There's also a rivalry with Brighton dating back to the time the Seagulls were tenants at the Priestfield.

Grimsby Town

A big catch at Great Coates

The Mariners are seeking a move away from the outdated Blundell Park in Cleethorpes which they have called home since 1899. "Like a Victorian cottage Blundell Park has period features," jokes our Grimsby correspondent.

Relocating to a 21,100-seater venue at Great Coates, called 'Conoco Stadium', is the preferred option and the latest plans were submitted to the local council last season (2006/07).

Residents near the site of the proposed stadium - just three miles from Blundell Park - had raised objections to a previous planning application in January 2006. North-East Lincolnshire Council had backed a similar scheme tabled in 2001.

This time club chiefs are confident the stadium scheme, which includes commercial and leisure facilities, will win approval from all parties.

Club chairman John Fenty called for a "champion in the political arena" to push the project through. Local MP Shona McIsaac is backing the initiative and believes there is plenty of support from the Grimsby public. "The vast majority of people who have been in touch with me are supportive of the plans for the new stadium and retail development," she said, adding: "Apart from one Scunthorpe fan who thought the best place for the Mariners to relocate to was one mile east of Blundell Park!"

Grimsby hope to move in 2009 but, for the time being, there's space for 2,200 away fans in the Osmond Stand, at one end of Blundell Park. Expect a noisy home crowd ("We piss on your fish, yes we do, yes we do" may well be heard). A word of warning: you'll have to brace yourself against the icy winds coming off the North Sea, so scarves, hats and gloves are key.

Eating out

A major fishing port for centuries, you must try Grimsby's famous haddock & chips. A couple of chippies are sited between the away fans' pub called The Leaking Boot and Blundell Park, one by the name of Hobsons. There's also a MacDonald's on this stretch of road. On Cleethorpes seafront outside the bus station is another recommended chippy - at Seaway you get a massive chip butty for around 75p. Cold and hungry at Blundell Park? Pie and peas is a favourite. Pop into Scotties Bar in the Osmond Stand for a good feed. Catering especially for visiting fans, it's open from 1.30pm on a Saturday.

Mine's a pint

Don't expect an over-friendly reception at some of the town's pubs, advises one fan of the Mariners. Your best bet for a slice of Cleethorpes hospitality is to go to the away-friendly Leaking Boot pub five minutes' walk from the stadium. Other nearby pubs are to be found along Grimsby Road and up Isaac's Hill. One pub not to step into if you're not a Mariner is The Imperial outside the ground on Grimsby Road, though you're not likely to miss the prominent 'Home supporters only' sign on the gate. The Rutland Arms next

Club Information Stadium: Blundell Park, Cleethorpes DN35 7PY Capacity: 9,546 (all seated) Tel: 01472 605050 Website: www.gtfc.com Train: Cleethorpes Colours: Black and white Songs: 'I'd rather be a Cod Head than a...' and other defamatory songs about

door to Ramsdens on the same street is a mere 10 minutes' walk from the stadium and serves very quaffable beverages supplied by the Old Mill brewery. Decent alehouses in the town centre deserving your drink money include Swigs on Osborne Street and The Tap & Spile, found behind Freshney Place car park. The Tap is comfy and affordable and sometimes plays host to live bands. Despite the name, Willy's Wine Bar on Cleethorpes seafront is a distinguished hangout, known for its beers including the black and white porter Mariners Gold.

Stopping over in Grimsby?

 There are plenty of cheap B&Bs and guesthouses and moderately priced hotels when you head towards Cleethorpes, along Isaac's Hill past the roundabout. You'll find others if you continue up past Alexandra Road, along High Cliff Road and down Kingsway where you'll find The Kingsway Hotel (0845 126 0580), and Kings Royal Hotel (book online). Other tips in Cleethorpes are The Brentwood on Princes Road (01472 693982), Holmhirst Safari Hotel on Alexandra Road (01472 692656), Tudor Terrace Guest House on Bradford Avenue (01472 600800) and Comat Hotel on Yarra Road (01472 694791).

If you do one thing in Grimsby...

Head to the National Fishing Heritage Centre at Alexandra Dock to learn about the fascinating history of the town's fishing industry. If that's not your thing, you can while away the hours on Cleethorpes seafront, picking your way through a bag of fish & chips (curry sauce or gravy optional).

Frankly, it would be rude not to.

Famous exes

Famous ex-managers include Bill Shankly and Lawrie McMenemy. Former England boss Graham Taylor played 189 games for Grimsby (1962-68).

Don't mention

That Grimsby fans only sing when they're fishing: they don't. In fact those that do fish, probably don't actually sing while they're doing it – they're much more likely to sing at football. Brian Laws: wasn't a success as a manager and even broke star striker Ivan Bonetti's cheekbone in a dressing room row. To make matters worse Laws went on to huge success at rivals Scunthorpe.

Do mention

Alan Buckley: despite the likes of Bill Shankly and Lawrie McMenemy managing the club he ranks above Shanks as most fans' choice as top boss of all-time.

Travel Information

CAR
The stadium isn't actually in Grimsby, it's in Cleethorpes. It's well signposted and you'll find it on the A180 which runs between Grimsby & Cleethorpes. If you're coming from the M1 take the M18 onto the M180, which becomes the A180 and the ground's on the left. If you're coming from the south on the A1, go via Lincoln on the A46. As you come into Cleethorpes, pick up the A180 towards Grimsby and the ground is on the right. There are plenty of sidestreets in which you'll find ample parking.

TRAIN
It is about a fifteen-minute walk to the ground from Cleethorpes Station. Exit the station and turn right; then turn left onto Station Road and into College Street. At the end of the road turn right onto Isaac's Hill and into Grimsby Road. After less than half a mile and you will see the floodlights of the ground on your right. The main entrance is just off the main road, but you'll need to turn right into Neville Street and then left onto Harrington Street for the away end.

the team from the north side of the Humber Bridge. The reworked Annie's Song also is popular... and includes the lyric 'a night out in Nunsthorpe'. Rivals: Lincoln, Hull and Scunthorpe.

Hartlepool United

Monkeying around and Meat Loaf

Away fans will be greeted warmly at the 7,629-capacity Victoria Park. Some ear defenders might come in handy, though, as the passionate home supporters have been voted among the noisiest in the league.

It could be worse though - chubby rock warbler Meat Loaf is a fan and once threatened to lend his vocal support to the team on a regular basis when he considered moving to the area. Sky Sports' Jeff Stelling is another famous Pools fan – as his antics on his Soccer Saturday show always prove.

Visiting fans are housed in The Rink End at the north end of the ground (961 seats). The ground is within walking distance of the town centre and there's plenty of parking available at Jackson's Landing shopping centre and other retail parks.

Watch out for the entertaining antics of the club's mascot H'Angus the Monkey, who's become something of a legendary figure.

The most famous person to pull on the H'Angus the Monkey suit was Stuart Drummond who brought the mascot to life in 1999. In 2001, he caused controversy at one match by playing with an inflatable doll and, in a separate incident, was booted out at Scunthorpe for simulating sex on a female steward.

Posing as the mascot, Drummond stood for election as mayor of Hartlepool in 2002. He won with a 52% share of the vote and was re-elected to the post in 2005 with an increased majority.

Formed as a professional club in 1908, the Pools joined the league in 1921. During the First World War, the ground's main stand was destroyed by a German Zeppelin. The temporary stand built was only replaced by the Millhouse Stand in the 1980s. Further ground improvements took place in 1996.

Eating out

Opposition fans have sung the praises of Victoria Park's meat pies. For a good value sandwich, nip into Hungry Jack's at the marina. There are two McDonald's in town, one on the way to the ground, the other in the main shopping centre. There's also a Burger King close to the stadium, next to Asda on the retail park. Chip shops and pizza parlours are never far away. For more sophisticated palates, a variety of restaurants - from Chinese to Mexican - are found in the centre of Hartlepool. Al-Syros on Upper Church Street offers Mediterranean fare. A plethora of Indian dishes will tickle your taste buds at Café India on Whitby Street. Joe Rigatonis on Church Street delivers exceptional Italian and continental cuisine at great prices.

Mine's a pint

The most popular haunt for visiting fans is The Corner Flag at the ground, which is located between the Cameron's Brewery Stand and the Rink End. Open 1pm-11pm, it enjoys a fine reputation among both home and away fans. There's a cover charge on the door for visiting supporters, who can gain access to a good selection of beers and lagers, plus soft

Club Information Stadium: Victoria Park, Clarence Road, Hartlepool TS24 8BZ Capacity: 7629Tel: 01429 272584 Web: www.hartlepoolunited.co.uk Train: Hartlepool Colours:

drinks and hot beverages Children are also made to feel welcome. Nearest the ground is The Millhouse, though this is generally frequented by home fans. It's only a short walk to the town centre pubs. Yates's on Victoria Road is perfect for a quick tipple and a bite to eat. Over the road, you'll get cheap drinks and food at the Wetherspoons pub, King John's Tavern. Jackson's Wharf at the marina is another recommendation.

Stopping over in Hartlepool?

Cosy B&Bs and family-run hotels abound. Another cheap choice is the Premier Travel Inn on Maritime Avenue at the marina, which is linked to a Brewers Fayre restaurant and play zone (08701 977127). You'll pay a little more at The Staincliffe Hotel, a picturesque pre-Victorian hotel situated on Seaton Carew road with sea views (01429 264301). Its elegant, affordable themed rooms are complemented by the award-winning seafood on offer.

The Grand Hotel, built in the style of a French Chateau, is another destination for those looking for something a bit special (01429 266345). Located on Swainson Street, it's conveniently placed in the town centre for visits to the marina, maritime attractions and shopping facilities.

If you do one thing in Hartlepool...

It's well worth a walk around the Historic Quay. Guided tours of HMS Trincomalee, the second oldest British warship afloat are available. There's also an award-winning museum at the marina, featuring a children's maritime adventure centre, as well as plenty of places to shop and a cinema. The Camerons Brewery is another of the town's top attractions.

Cloughie's first team

Hartlepools United was the first team managed by the late great Brian Clough. He took the helm in 1965 and was in charge for less than two seasons before joining Derby as manager. Pools finished 18th in Division Four in his first season and eighth the following year.

Don't Mention

Monkeys: during the Napoleonic Wars the fishermen of Hartlepool hanged a monkey washed up on the coast from the wreckage of a ship, because they believed it was a French spy and feared an invasion. (Hence the mascot being a monkey called H'Angus.)

Do Mention

Cloughie: Poolies are proud of the fact he cut his managerial teeth at Victoria Park. Cyril Knowles: led the club to promotion in 1989, but sadly died soon after.

Travel Information

CAR
Exit the A1(M) at junction 60 onto the A19 and then pick up the A689 to Hartlepool going straight on at two roundabouts and two sets of traffic lights. The left turn into Clarence Road takes you to the stadium. There is a fair sized car park at the ground or ample street parking past the stadium and off Clarence Road.

TRAIN
Hartlepool railway station (served by routes from Newcastle and Darlington) is a short walk to and from the ground. Leave the station and walk down Station Approach and right onto Church Street, over the junction with the A689, and into Clarence Road – the ground's on the left.

Blue and white Songs: Anything with a distinctly anti-Darlington flavour goes down well in these parts. Rivals: Darlington.

Hereford United

No Bull

Edgar Street has played host to the Bulls since their inception in 1924. United reportedly paid the Hereford Athletic Ground Co. just £82 and two shillings to rent the ground in their first season.

The 1971/72 season is one of the biggest talking points in the club's history. United, at that time playing non-league football, took Newcastle United back to Edgar Street after drawing 2-2 in the FA Cup Third Round at St James's Park. Ricky George's extra-time winner gave the Bulls a famous 2-1 win in what is regarded as one of the competition's greatest ever giant-killing acts.

The Meadow End of the ground, described by home fans as "the life and soul of Hereford football", witnessed jubilant scenes when their cup hero smashed home the last-gasp goal and prompted a pitch invasion.

Away supporters are accommodated in the two-tier Len Weston Stand of the 8,843-capacity ground, which combines terracing and seating. Half the stand is reserved for visitors. You'll get a good atmosphere on the terraces but the seats offer the best views. Blackfriars Street stand is all terracing and also split in half, with an overspill section for travelling fans.

Some form of redevelopment is expected soon. Edgar Street is in dire need of a makeover, according to many of the United faithful. One says: "I love the Street. I love its uniqueness and I love it that other people call it a cow shed. But we know something needs to be done for the best interests of the club".

Eating out

Catering at the ground is not rated too highly but the balti pies sold here are a very popular choice. The usual fast-food outlets, including KFC, Domino's Pizza and McDonald's, are located in the town centre. A good chippy is found next to the Oxford Arms on Widemarsh Street. For a more nourishing meal, locals recommend The Palace (Chinese on Commercial Road, near the train station) and, strangely, Rockfield Road DIY stores - upstairs you can apparently feast on cheap and good quality food.

Mine's a pint

Enjoy a pre-match pint in the ground's bar, Legends, which has a friendly atmosphere and offers views across the ground. Edgar Street's city centre location makes all the local hostelries accessible on matchdays. If you're driving, dump the car and seek out some liquid refreshment at places like The Barrells, a fine pub on St Owen Street with real ales brewed in Hereford. The Victory on the same street is another sound choice for the away brigade and real ale lovers. The Oxford Arms and the Exchange are nearest the

Club Information Stadium: Edgar Street, Hereford HR4 9JU Capacity: 8,843
Tel: 01432 276666 Web: www.herefordunited.co.uk Train: Hereford Colours:
White and black Songs: 'Hereford United We All Love You' is popular and anything

ground and come
recommended for pre- and
post-match drinking. Karos,
a sports bar with pool
tables and large screen, is
also nearby. However,
visiting fans should avoid
the Newmarket Tavern on
Newmarket Street, and
JD's.

Stopping over in Hereford?

 For a budget
overnight stop, try
anywhere down
White Cross Road for
B&Bs. The Cedar Guest
House (01432 267235) and
Rowan Tree Guest House
(01432 274132) are among
the alternatives. And
they're handy for the
stadium, just 10 minutes'
walk away.

Family-run Charades
Guest House on South
Bank Road (01432 269444)
is reasonably priced and
close to the station.

The city has an
abundance of cheap hotels.
Decent options include the
Three Counties Hotel on
Belmont Road, a modern
purpose-built hotel with 60
en-suite bedrooms set in
over three acres of
landscaped gardens (01432
299955).

If you do one thing in Hereford...

The Bulmer's cider factory,
the world's largest cider-
producing plant, is one of
the highlights of this rural
county.

There are also
numerous small producers
of cider and perry in
Herefordshire, producing
traditional unfiltered
beverages from local apples
and pears. To explore the
history of cider-making and
sample some ciders, apple
brandies and apple
liqueurs, pop along to the
Hereford Cider Museum,
located at the King Offa
Distillery on Ryelands
Street. Go easy on the
scrumpy!

Radford's belter

Ronnie Radford's 30-yard
screamer in that FA Cup
match against Newcastle
United is one of the most
talked about and televised
goals in the competition's
history. The goal levelled
the match after Malcolm
Macdonald had put the
Magpies ahead. Supersub
Ricky George did the rest.

Don't mention

The final day of the
1996/97 season: Hereford's
failure to beat Brighton
meant they were relegated
out of the Football League.

Do mention

Promotion back to the
Football League: the Bulls
bounced back, winning
promotion via the
Conference play-offs in
2006. John Charles: the
Gentle Giant was
player/manager when the
club were elected to the
Football League in 1971.

Travel Information

CAR
From the north: Keep
on the A438 into
Hereford and stay on
the inner ring road
through the town centre
and take the A49 Edgar
Street.
From the M4: Exit at
junction 15 and take
the A417 to Gloucester.
Then follow the A40 to
Ross-on-Wye and then
the A49 to Hereford. As
you enter the town
centre simply continue
on the A49 into Edgar
Street.
From the South West:
come over the New
Severn Bridge on the
M4. Exit at junction 24
taking the A449 / A40 /
A4137 route before
joining the A49 which
eventually leads to
Edgar Street. Exit Edgar
Street into Blackfriars
Street, just before the
ground as you head
north, where you'll find
a large pay and display
car park. It's less than
a quid to park for four
hours.

TRAIN
Hereford Station is
served by trains from
London Paddington,
Birmingham and Crewe
– and it is a short walk
to and from the ground.
Walk out of Station
Approach onto
Commercial Road. At
the traffic lights, go
right into Blueschool
Street, and immediately
right into Widemarsh
Street, then it's left
into Blackfriars Street.

anti-Shrewsbury also goes down well at Edgar Street. Rivals:
Shrewsbury and Kidderminster; Cheltenham and Cardiff aren't
too popular either.

Huddersfield Town

Down at the Pharm

The white arches of The Galpharm Stadium, formerly the McAlpine, are an arresting sight on the approach to the venue. Rebadged in 2004 when Pharmaceutical company Galpharm struck a 10-year stadium naming rights deal, the multi-use venue is home to both the Terriers and rugby league outfit Huddersfield Giants.

Its high-spec facilities make the 24,500 capacity ground one of the best equipped in the lower tiers of the league. All vantage points, including the Pink Link Stand housing away fans, offer top-notch views of the pitch.

The Terriers moved here from Leeds Road in 1994. A year later the ground played host to the American rock band R.E.M, who attracted around 70,000 people to their two concerts. Other acts to have graced this west Yorkshire stage include Sir Elton John, Bon Jovi and the Beautiful South.

In the last decade, the £40 million stadium complex has become an important regional, national and international sporting venue, holding major rugby union and rugby league games. If you get bored with the football, or simply want to spend the morning of the match doing something constructive, there's plenty on offer at this sports and entertainment destination, particularly if you're bringing the kids. Go for a dip in the swimming pool or see a film at the 10-screen multiplex cinema next to the stadium. Golf enthusiasts can test their skills at Stadium Golf, voted as one of Britain's top 10 golf driving ranges by Today's Golfer publication.

The facilities include a 30-bay driving range, two teaching studios operated by five PGA professionals and an all-weather putting green. You can also hire all the golf gear here.

Eating out

The pies sold at the ground are decent, but the Rollover Hot Dogs don't always resemble the pictures. Eateries at the stadium complex include a Pizza Hut, while The Rope Walk pub next door also serves food. Burger vans, chippies and cafés line the Leeds Road near the venue. Huddersfield town centre is about 20 minutes' walk away and it's here you'll come across the best restaurants. John William Street caters for an assortment of tastes with Thai, Italian and Chinese among them.

Mine's a pint

There's a bar at the back of the Pink Link Stand but beer at the stadium is pricey and not especially good, some say. The Rope Walk is modern and away-friendly but you'll need to get there early.

A word of warning: door staff have been known to take objection to certain team colours, so you might want to cover up. In town, there are two Wetherspoons: Lloyds on Kings Street and the Cherry Tree, John Williams Street. Kings Street has many other pubs and bars.

The wonderfully-named Slubbers Arms on Halifax Old Road is a gem of a pub for real ale fans and gets busy on matchdays. It's cosy alright but worth squeezing in for the quality beers such as Timothy

---

Club Information Stadium: Galpharm Stadium, Huddersfield HD1 6PX (Formerly the McAlpine Stadium) Capacity: 24,500 (all seated) Tel: 0870 4444677 Web: www.htafc.com Train: Huddersfield Colours: Blue and white Songs: 'Those Were The Days My Friend' draws on the fact Huddersfield won the championship three

116

Taylor's Landlord and various other guest ales. Seek it out and you won't be disappointed. Recommended nightclubs are Tokyo's in the town centre and Visage in the Folly Hall Mills area. Nearby Leeds has a greater variety of night-time taverns and clubs to meet all demands.

Stopping over in Huddersfield?

 Turn up unannounced and you could easily find a B&B or guesthouse. Reasonably priced beds are available at the Travelodge on the A62 Leeds Road (0870 191 1646) and Holiday Inn in Brighouse towards Leeds (0870 400 9013). Cheapish rooms with more character are offered at The George Hotel opposite the railway station on the main square in Huddersfield (01484 607788). This hotel is an elegant Grade II listed building, which is famous as the birthplace of rugby league - the meeting that founded it was held at the hotel in 1895.

Prices for B&B per night at The Old Golf House Hotel on New Hey Road, Outlane, start from £35 (0870 609 6128). The M62 runs directly behind it. Hotel facilities include a restaurant, lounge bar and 5-hole pitch and putt.

Also recommended is the more expensive Waterfront Lodge on Huddersfield Road, Brighouse, which offers designer accommodation on the banks of the Calder & Hebble canal (01484 715566).

If you do one thing in Huddersfield...

Fancy dropping into the Titanic Spa for a facial or, erm, tranquillity scalp treatment. No, thought not. Still, the UK's first eco-spa situated in a traditional textile mill on the edge of the Pennines does promise "exceptional results-driven spa treatments".

If the sound of that makes you want to run for the Yorkshire Dales, then there should be no stopping you.

It's either the Dales or the attractions of Leeds, then.

Chapman's success

Town entertain Arsenal in summer 2008 as part of their centenary celebrations. The connection is Herbert Chapman who managed the Terriers during one of their most successful periods before moving to London in 1925. He then guided the Gunners to their first ever trophy in 1930 - an FA Cup at the expense of... Huddersfield.

Don't mention

Phil Parkinson: after accepting the post of manager in 2007, he changed his mind and called the club an hour before he was due to be unveiled to the fans and media.

Do mention

The late Harold Wilson: the former PM was a fan of the club. The fact Huddersfield won three League Championships in a row and the FA Cup in the 1920s.

Travel Information

CAR
From the M62: Exit at junction 25 and take the A62 to Huddersfield which will lead you to the stadium on your left by turning into Gasworks Street and then Stadium Way. From the M1: leave at Junction 38 and take the A637 and then A642 into Huddersfield. Stay in the right hand lane as you start to negotiate the ring-road around the town as you will need to turn right onto the A62 Leeds Road. The stadium is on the right. There is a car park at the ground where you can park for a fiver and a number of unofficial car parks nearby which are a little cheaper.

TRAIN
The ground is about fifteen minutes' walk from Huddersfield train station – which is well served by trains from Manchester, Leeds and Sheffield. To get to the ground exit the station and walk down Northumberland Street and on into Leeds Road. Turn right down Gasworks Street and straight on into Stadium Way.

times in a row and the FA Cup. Other popular songs are 'Smile A While' and an old favourite which begins 'There is a team that's dear to its followers'. Rivals: Bradford City and Leeds United.

Hull City

Roaring, roaring Tigers

By any standards, Hull City's Kingston Communications Stadium is a magnificent venue. Opened in 2002 with 25,400 seats, the £44m arena is located in a scenic parkland setting and has become an architectural icon in this part of east Yorkshire. It hosts the football and rugby league's Hull FC as well as a plethora of other sports and entertainment. Future expansion of the East Stand could lift capacity to 30,000.

Most away fans have a good experience at the Premiership-standard KC Stadium due to its modern facilities. Don't let the sometimes intimidating police presence spoil your day - on the whole, Tigers fans have a good reputation as friendly folk.

The North Stand holds up to 4,000 away supporters. You're guaranteed a comfortable 90 minutes here with no annoying pillars to ruin your view. It's a far cry from visiting fans' experiences of the decrepit Boothferry Park, the club's home for over 50 years. In its later years, when club finances were tight, the stadium was affectionately dubbed "Fer Ark" as lack of scoreboard maintenance meant they were the only letters of Boothferry Park signage to be illuminated.

Happier days characterised the early years of City's residency at KC Stadium. Attendances around the 20,000 mark were some of the best in the division and the first two seasons after the move saw Hull complete back-to-back promotions into the Championship. Yet it's the largest city in Europe never to have fielded a football team in the top division of its national league.

Hull City also gets a mention at pub quizzes across the land for the question "What is the only football club in the country spelled entirely of letters you can not colour in?".

Eating out

Concourse catering facilities are more than adequate. Take your pick from the takeaways outside the ground. The city centre is only 15 minutes' walk from KC Stadium. Hull has a huge selection of eating venues as befits a large city. The Boars Nest is an established English restaurant on Princes Avenue. If you can stomach the fact that Mr Chu's at St Andrew's Quay is John Prescott's Chinese of choice, then give it a whirl. You could enjoy contemporary à la carte dining in Two Rivers Restaurant at Hull's award-winning aquarium The Deep. Old Custom House, meanwhile, is a family-run restaurant on Market Place specialising in seafood. Scarlett Café Bar on Princes Dock Street is also highly rated for its fish dishes. Venn on Scale Lane offers an eclectic brasserie menu on the ground floor, while upstairs you can sample modern British cooking.

Mine's a pint

Alcohol is on sale at KC Stadium for most matches. Do not go seeking out pubs near the ground, otherwise you'll be asking for trouble - the majority are strictly for Tigers fans only. Avoid any of the locals around Boothferry Park where some City fans congregate - The Silver Cod on Anlaby Road for instance. City centre pubs will extend a friendly welcome. For a taste of

Club Information Stadium: Kingston Communications Stadium, The Circle, Walton St, Hull HU3 6HU Capacity: 25,504 (all seated) Tel: 0870 8370003 Web: www.hullcityafc.net Train: Hull Paragon Colours: Amber and black Songs: 'We All

history with your pint, nip into Ye Olde White Harte on Silver Street - one of the best ale houses in Hull - and Ye Olde Black Boy on High Street, or enjoy the views of the Humber Estuary from The Minerva on Nelson Street. There's a high concentration of pubs and bars on Spring Bank - the Polar Bear for atmosphere and the Tap & Spile for real ale. Hull is not short of trendy bars either. Worth mentioning are Jaz Café Bar on Lowgate, which transforms into a thriving music bar with live bands and cocktails in the evening, and Lattitude - a chilled-out bar-bistro on Newland Avenue.

Stopping over in Hull?

 If you're coming from afar, Hull is well worth a weekend stay for the city's attractions and nightlife. The Portland Hotel is within walking distance of the stadium, marina, shopping and the station (01482 326462). Rooms from £58. Holiday Inn at the marina on Castle Street has accommodation at similar rates and also makes an ideal base for Hull sightseeing and night-time excursions (0870 400 9043). Kingston Theatre Hotel is a small friendly hotel set in the Georgian splendour of Kingston Square (01482 225828). Doubles cost around £55. If you don't mind staying on the outskirts of Hull, go for Hotel Elizabeth in North Ferriby, a hotel with affordable rooms and stunning views of the Humber Bridge (01482 645212).

If you do one thing in Hull...

Rapidly-evolving Hull has much to offer visitors, from the waterfront - a stunning focal point and location of festivals and events - to a burgeoning arts and culture scene. For something unique, make for The Deep, "the world's only submarium". It contains a stunning collection of sharks and other exotic species and the deepest viewing tunnel in the world. And don't forget to go and gawp at the feat of civil engineering - the Humber Bridge - one of the longest single span suspension bridges in the world.

Second Choice Steve

England boss Steve McClaren joined Hull City as an apprentice and spent the best part of his playing career at Boothferry Park, chalking up 178 appearances from 1979-85.

Don't mention

David Lloyd (of tennis and health club fame): took over as chairman in 1998. His tenure saw the club on the verge of bankruptcy and relegation out of the Football League.

Do mention

Warren Joyce: former player, who in a stint as player-boss masterminded the Great Escape of 1998/99 and kept the club out of the Conference. Adam Pearson and Peter Taylor: the chairman-manager combo who guided Hull to back-to-back promotions and into the Championship.

Travel Information

CAR
If you used to approach the old ground down Anlaby Road, pass the ground on your right, go under the railway bridge, and at the second set of traffic lights, turn left into Walton Street and you're there.
From the M62: Exit at Junction 38 and take the A63 to Hull. Exit the A63 onto the A15 which becomes the A1105 at the big roundabout. Stay on the A1105 which becomes Anlaby Road. Walton Street is about half a mile further on from the third roundabout on the left.
From The North: Exit the A164 just before the Humber Bridge onto the A1105 and into Boothferry Road. Walton Street is about three miles down the A1105 on the left.
There is ample parking at the stadium for around £3 – but it takes a while to get away. Hull Royal Infirmary has parking for around £2; it's ten mins' walk but you won't have a long wait at the end. There is some street parking to the north of the stadium.

TRAIN
The Stadium is about fifteen mins' walk from Hull Paragon Station. Exit the station on the south side and turn right along Anlaby Road, eventually you'll reach the turning for Walton Street on the right.

Follow The Black And Amber Team' to the tune of Yellow Submarine. 'The Tigers' and 'Only Fools Rush In' are also popular at the KC Stadium. Rivals: Bradford, Grimsby, Leeds and Scunthorpe.

Ipswich Town

Who are you calling Tractor Boys?

Don't get Town fans started on their 'Tractor Boys' tag. There are mixed feelings around these 'ere parts 'bout the nickname coined to mock Ipswich's agricultural roots.

The label became common currency during the club's 2000/01 season in the Premiership. Self-deprecating Town fans responded to taunts from opposition supporters with ironic jeers of "One nil to the Tractor Boys".

They may hail from a small backwater in rural East Anglia - a meeting with rivals Norwich City is dubbed the 'Old Farm Derby' - but some sensitive Suffolk types think the name derogatory and slightly embarrassing.

Jim Magilton is one of these. The former Northern Ireland international said it drove him mad. He clearly failed to understand the irony in the chanting, telling a national newspaper in 2000 that it conjured up images of "carrot-crunching yokels coming out of the tunnel with straw stuck between their teeth".

Most local fans see it for what it is - a bit of harmless fun. After all, the other option of The Blues is hardly unique. Tractor Boys fans' chanting and dressing up as farmers provides an injection of humour and colour on a footballing occasion at Portman Road.

Portman Road's capacity is up to 30,300 - with an allocation of 3,000 seats for away fans at the south end of the Cobbold Stand. It's comfy enough but the ageing stand, built in the 1970s, could do with a refurb. Check out the statues of legendary managers Sir Alf Ramsey and Sir Bobby Robson when you're here.

Eating out

Depending on the number of visiting fans, there's at least one catering bar in the ground serving alcoholic drinks, pies, burgers, etc. There are several fast food stands along Portman Road on matchdays but the offerings pale in comparison to the stuff sold from mobile burger bars at the NW corner of the ground on Sir Alf Ramsay Way behind the Cobbold Stand. Get your egg & bacon butties at Jenny's burger bar. Cardinals Park, 10 minutes' walk away, has a McDonald's and KFC. The ground is a short walk from town. Another option is to eat a basic and cheap meal in Buttermarket Shopping Centre food hall beforehand. On St Stephens Lane, it includes Potato Bakehouse for traditional filled spuds, and Fresh and Coffee Express for sandwiches and savouries. Café Giardino offers freshly prepared hot or cold meals and snacks, including its signature gourmet beef sandwich. Post-match appetites can be satisfied at an Italian called Artista on Northgate. For those rushing to the game, it offers a 'fast lunch'. The Chinese on Majors Corner, opposite the Odeon cinema, is recommended.

Mine's a pint

Away fans gather at The Drum & Monkey on Princes Street or the Station Hotel, ideal for those arriving by train.

Club Information Stadium: Portman Road, Ipswich IP1 2DA Capacity: 30,300 (all seated) Tel: 01473 400500 Web: www.itfc.co.uk Train: Ipswich Colours: Blue & white Songs: 'Ooh Aah We're The Tractor Boys' has obvious local connections,

Basic as they are, this is where the banter takes place and both are close to the ground. Avoid the Curve bar on Princes Street - it's home fans' turf. The Black Horse Inn on Black Horse Lane is another recommended pre-match drinking venue. Take your pick from town centre pubs but you might not endear yourself to locals if you go around flaunting your away strip. With its mix of bars and clubs, Cardinals Park is a popular place to spend a night out. The Fat Cat on Spring Road, about 15 minutes' walk from the town centre, is well worth seeking out if you're a connoisseur of real ales. Expect to see around 20 beers on draught at this award-winning ale house. The Dove - on St Helen's Street and nearer to the centre of Ipswich - was CAMRA's Suffolk Pub of the Year and East Anglian Pub of the Year 2006. It also sells around 20 different whiskies.

Stopping over in Ipswich?

 The Lattice Lodge on Woodbridge Road on the eastern side of Ipswich is said to be a great B&B. Located in a large Edwardian property 15 minutes from town, it offers a homely atmosphere, friendly service and wireless broadband (01473 712474). Novotel is conveniently placed for the football and town centre. It's on Grey Friars Road, less than 1km from the ground (01473 232400). The Salthouse Harbour hotel at Neptune Quay is expensive with rooms from £100 but a very attractive alternative to the budget accommodation (01473 226789).

If you do one thing in Ipswich...

Fancy a bit of outdoor off-road rallying? Make a pit-stop at Beacon Rally Karts for a few hours and open up the throttle on one of their mean machines around a variety of race tracks. There's something for all ages and families are welcome. Situated in a six-acre site on the edge of Ipswich, the centre is at Beacon Hill Farm, Martlesham, near Woodbridge (0845 644 1592).

Dutch courage

Ipswich are said to be the first English club to bring Dutch flair to their team, with the addition of Arnold Muhren and Frans Thijssen, the former joining the club in 1978.

Don't mention

The play-offs: Town may have won promotion to the Premiership via the end-of-season lottery, but that was at the fourth attempt. Since relegation, they've lost a further two play-off semi-finals – both to West Ham.

Do mention

Former England managers Sir Alf Ramsey and Sir Bobby Robson: both managed Ipswich and Sir Alf led them to the League Championship, while Sir Bob won the FA Cup and UEFA Cup.

CAR

Take the A14 and then A1107 into Ipswich – after you come over the river turn right into W End Road and then left into Portman Walk, which leads into Sir Alf Ramsey Way and to the ground. Parking is difficult, but there are three pay and display parks in Portman Road but with limited spaces. An early arrival is recommended to ensure a space close to the ground. There are several town centre car parks which are about ten minutes' walk and a multi- storey car park located next to the railway station. Wherever you park you should be able to do it for under a fiver.

TRAIN

The ground is about ten minutes' walk from the station. Simply exit the station and walk straight on down Princess Street – over the river and two roads – and left into Portman Road. Ipswich Station is served by trains from London Liverpool Street and Peterborough.

while Ipswich fans also like 'Singing The Blues' when Ipswich win and Norwich lose. Rivals: Norwich City and Colchester United.

Leeds United

Fierce rivalries

Elland Road has played host to some memorable domestic and European encounters through the years. But the Whites' recent slump in fortunes has led to dwindling attendances and the club rarely fills the 40,200 capacity nowadays.

Ambitious plans to relocate under former chairman Peter Ridsdale's troubled stewardship of the club have long since been forgotten. That was 2001. That was before Leeds borrowed £60m against future gate receipts in attempts to turn the club into a European powerhouse. Everyone knows what happened next.

Debt-ridden Leeds are not planning to move or expand the ground any time soon, although the stadium could do with a revamp to bring facilities up to today's standards. But that doesn't bother the players or United faithful who love the atmosphere here.

It's still ranked the 10th largest stadium in English football. Manchester United boss Sir Alex Ferguson thinks it's right up there for home advantage. He once branded Elland Road "the most intimidating venue in Europe".

Elland Road is not the hostile ground it used to be. But fans of the Whites' many rivals - any of the Premiership giants and several Yorkshire clubs - can still expect some barracking from home fans.

If you are sporting the colours of the Red Devils, Bradford or another fierce rival, it's advisable to keep a low profile around the stadium - and in the city centre on matchdays.

For derby day or a cup clash, one big bonus is the sizeable allocation of seats for visiting supporters. Normally, the south-east corner of the South Stand accommodates 1,700 but this rises to 4,800 for larger away followings.

Eating out

The food's not bad at Elland Road. Chicken & chips and other greasy fare is available. Behind the away end is United Fisheries, a popular chippy on matchdays so prepare to queue. The Cracked Egg Café next door also does a lively trade; serving tasty fry-ups, breakfast baps and hot rolls. McDonald's and Subway are nearby. TGI Friday's in City Gate offers "fresh food and generous portions". Dino's, a family-owned Italian on the train station's doorstep, is very welcoming and serves a great lunch and evening menu - everything from sandwiches, seafood, and meat and vegetable pastas, to grilled fish and rotisserie chicken.

For more classic Italian dishes, try Bibis Criterion off Sovereign Street. Maxi's high-class Chinese restaurant on Bingley Street is perfect for a relaxed post-match dinner. Curry lovers could head to Akbar's balti restaurants in either Eastgate or Greek Street.

Mine's a pint

 The majority of pubs around Elland Road are designated for home support. Nearest for visitors is the Old Peacock behind the South Stand. Visiting supporters are admitted but you might get some serious stick from the assembled Leeds posse.

Leeds is the kind of place

Club Information Stadium: Elland Road, Leeds LS11 0ES Capacity: 40,204 (all seated) Tel: 0113 367 6000 Web: www.lufc.com Colours: White Songs: 'Leeds, Leeds, Leeds' and 'Marching On Together' are widely recognised as top of the charts at Elland Road.

where covering your away colours can make all the difference for pre-match drinking.

The Britannia on Top Moor Side, a few minutes' walk from the ground, is said to welcome visitors. So too does The Bulls Head on St Matthews Street, another Yorkshire local in the very finest tradition.

Not a football pub but worth a visit during the evening, The Duck and Drake on Kirkgate is an unpretentious, no-frills ale house. Its range of beers and excellent food marks it out as something special amongst the hordes of trendier pubs and bars in the city centre. Another great pub for real ales is Whitelocks on Turks Head Yard. It's hidden down an alley so ask for it by name.

Stopping over in Leeds?

 Bewleys Hotel on City Walk, Sweet Street, is recommended by the football club for all away fans. It's 10 minutes from the ground. The hotel's website says it offers "the epitome of affordable chic in this cosmopolitan and vibrant young city". But don't let the marketing blah put you off. It's reasonably priced - rooms are from about £70 - bang in the city centre and not far from the M1/M62/Leeds junction (0113 234 2340). Travelodge on Blayds Yard, off Swinegate, provides a cheap bed and is a quick stroll to the train station (0870 191 1655).

If you do one thing in Leeds...

Not keen on city life? Do you not fancy visiting Leeds City Art Gallery and one of the best collections of 20th century British art outside London? Then go and explore the Yorkshire Dales. If you're on a weekend trip, return from an invigorating hike in the hills and hit the town. You should always make time to sample the nightlife.

Silver where?

Leeds United have been overshadowed in recent years by the success of rugby league's Leeds Rhinos. The team were crowned Super League champions in 2004 and came runners-up in the finals of both the Challenge Cup and Super League the following season. The football club's last major trophy was the 1992 league title.

Don't mention

Peter Ridsdale: his bad financial management is seen as the root of Leeds' horrendous slide through the leagues. Brian Clough: lasted only 44 days at Leeds after arriving from Brighton in the 1970s, shortly before taking the Nottingham Forest job.

Do mention

Don Revie: his team were feared across the land when they won the League title in 1975. Howard Wilkinson: he repeated the feat with Leeds in 1992.

Travel Information

CAR
Relatively easy to find, once you work your way onto the M621. Exit at junction 2 and simply head south on the A643, which is Elland Road and leads straight to the ground. There is a large car park right next to the ground and you can park there for three pounds – and it's a fairly quick exit at the end.

TRAIN
Leeds train station is around a 35 minute walk from the stadium – but there are shuttle buses from just outside the station to the ground. The buses drop off and pick up at the corner of the North and East stands. Leave the station from the rear exit, and get onto Whitehall Road. After going under the railway bridge fork left down Springwell Street, then turn left at the roundabout onto the A58 Domestic Road, which runs into Domestic Street. Turn right down Willoughby Terrace, then at the end of the road, right into Shafton Lane, then turn left onto Ingram Road, which forks left into Tilbury Road. Cross the M621 via the footbridge onto Elland Road.

Rivals: Bradford, Huddersfield and both Sheffield clubs; Cardiff aren't popular either... and from happy days in the top flight contempt was reserved for Manchester United and Chelsea.

Leicester City

Mind your step at the Foxes' Den

"From a barren desolate piece of waste ground has risen a stunning futuristic collaboration of steel and glass that dominates the skyline of Leicester." So says the Foxes' official website. But away fans might beg to differ.

The £37m Walkers Stadium, Leicester City's 32,500-seat home since 2002, is what the Americans might call a 'cookie-cutter' stadium - one based on a functional blueprint lacking any defining features.

Up to 3,000 visiting supporters can be accommodated in the north-east corner of Walkers Stadium. Away fans do commend the enclosed design for wrapping in the noise, allowing boisterous fans to generate an electric atmosphere. And the high and low level seating around the stadium bowl offers good views.

But mind your verbals and gesticulations during the game. Heavy-handed stewarding with fans being ejected for nothing more than vociferous chanting has angered some visitors. The treatment of fans by local police outside the ground has also come in for criticism.

There is plenty of parking around Walkers Stadium, but you could face problems if rugby union's Leicester Tigers are at home.

Gary Lineker, a former Leicester hero and face of Walkers Crisps, opened the stadium, which replaced the decaying facilities at Filbert Street, a few hundred yards away, in 2003.

Lineker played for the Foxes from 1978-1985 and has fronted numerous ad campaigns for the crisps maker.

Eating out

Concourse facilities are very good at Walkers Stadium with the usual refreshments available. Freemans Common is four minutes away and features various eateries including a Nando's Chicken restaurant. Narborough Road has numerous cafés and takeaways. The Shark is a nearby chippy on Walnut Street. And there's Wing Way, a Chinese takeaway on Grasmere Street. There's also a decent chip shop on Aylestone Road. The Quay on Western Boulevard shows sport on TVs and dishes up some fine pub grub. For an evening meal, make for Granby Street in the city centre. It's packed with a plethora of restaurants. San Carlo is a top Italian with an extensive menu. It produces the freshest pizzas for miles from its wood burning oven. The Case restaurant on Hotel Street is recommended for "modern European cuisine with an English accent". And of course, Leicester is also renowned as a place for good Indian food.

Mine's a pint

No alcohol is served in away supporters' areas at the venue and most pubs nearby are for Foxes fans only. The Victory on Aylestone Road is one to avoid. The stadium is just 15 minutes from the city centre.

Club Information Stadium: Walkers Stadium, Filbert Way, Leicester LE2 7FL
Capacity: 32,500 (all seated) Tel: 0870 0406000 Web: www.lcfc.co.uk Colours: Blue
Train: Leicester Songs: 'When You're Smiling' is the main fans' song and often sung

Many away fans congregate at pubs near the train station on London Road such as The Hind. This spacious old-fashioned real-ale boozer has a trouble-free atmosphere, serves a fairly cheap pint and includes a big screen and pool table. You could also try The Wyvern on Granby Street or The Barley Mow, a down-to-earth, comfortable place with a range of well-kept real ales. Supporters from both sides mix well in The Counting House on Almond Street, Freemans Park. The Gateway on Gateway Street is only five minutes from the ground, very away-friendly and touted as one of the best for its Batemans ale and other brews.

Stopping over in Leicester?

 If you can bear to stay close to opposition territory, Express by Holiday Inn adjacent to Walkers Stadium might work for you (0116 249 4590). Spindle Lodge is a family-run hotel handily placed for the station, stadium and city centre with rooms around £50. Great service and food is offered by the friendly owners (0116 233 8801). Best Western Belmont House Hotel on De Montfort Street offers the facilities expected of the hotel brand (0116 254 4773). It's a short walk from the centre and includes a restaurant. It's a bit pricier, although lower rates are available at weekends.

If you do one thing in Leicester...

Book your seat on Human Spaceflight: Lunar Base 2025, an interactive astronaut experience at The National Space Centre.

The UK's largest attraction dedicated to space is brilliant fun for all ages. It's signposted off the A6, two miles north of the city centre, midway between Leicester's inner and outer ring roads.

Join the club

Leicester City have lost a record four FA Cup finals but they are one of only 10 teams never to play outside the top two tiers of English football.

Don't Mention

Former managers Mark McGhee and Peter Taylor: McGhee jumped ship for Wolves, when there was little between the two clubs; while Taylor is blamed for starting the decline early in the new millennium which ended in relegation and administration.

Do Mention

Martin O'Neill: the former Foxes boss took Leicester into the Premiership, won the League Cup and led them into Europe. Gary Lineker: a proper son of Leicester, he began his career with the club and after hanging up his boots – despite his many media commitments – still gets involved with the club.

Travel Information

CAR
Exit the M1 at junction 21 or follow the M69 which meets the M1 at that junction. Follow the A5460 towards the city centre. After about three miles, turn left at the traffic lights into Upperton Road, cross the river and then a left turn into Eastern Boulevard will lead you to the ground. There's plenty of street parking around the Upperton Road area, or you can use one of the many unofficial car parks around, such as the one at Leicester Rugby Club – which is ten minutes' walk from the stadium.

TRAIN
It's about twenty-five minutes' walk from the station to the ground. Come out of Station Street and go left down Waterloo Way, with the road on your left. The pathway deviates away from the main road, but does rejoin the main road as pavement again. Turn right into Lancaster Road, cross the park, then cross the main road and head left down Ayestone Road. Take a right into Walnut Street, left into Burnmoor Street and you can see the stadium.

with passion by the Leicester faithful. Rivals: Derby County, Nottingham Forest, Coventry City.

Leyton Orient

Olympic ambitions

Brisbane Road, the O's home for 70 years, is set to have a shiny North Stand for the start of the 2007/08 season, turning the Matchroom Stadium into a four-sided venue once again.

More interesting is the tantalising prospect of seeing your team take on Leyton Orient at the plush Olympic Stadium after the 2012 Games has come and gone. The showpiece venue will convert from 80,000 seats to 25,000 and have an athletics legacy once the sporting extravaganza has left town.

West Ham wanted to take over the Stratford facility but the club's desire for a 40,000-seater proved unworkable and time was against them too. Enter the O's. The club's negotiations with Games planners, spearheaded by chairman Barry Hearn, could pay dividends - although the O's priorities remain consolidating their League One status and completing the revamp of Brisbane Road.

Hearn reckons a move to the Olympic Stadium could rejuvenate Orient and turn them into a major club. He says: "There is a long way to go before 2012, but our involvement with the community would put us in prime position for us to be involved as part of the Olympic legacy." For now it's just a dream and, like all dreams, it could easily be shattered. Talks between the club and Olympic organisers are still at early stages and could lead nowhere.

Fear not, though, Matchroom Stadium is really not as bad as its name suggests. That's if you're an O's fan. They benefit from well-equipped facilities on matchdays, while visiting supporters are housed in the oldest part of the ground. The views aren't all that great and tickets are pricey for this level of football. You'll be sat in East Stand South, which has space for 1,450 fans.

Eating out

Normal football fare is available in the East Stand South. Leyton High Road has a number of cafés and takeaways. Check out the greasy spoon called Royal Café, 50 yards from the stadium, or Orient Kebab House further up the road. Chicken lovers will appreciate the presence of a KFC. But there's not much else in the immediate vicinity of Brisbane Road. Restaurants in Leyton are a mixed bag but there's big variety, including Thai and West Indian eateries. Chingford is always good for a sit-down meal. The pick of the crop are La Trevi Restaurant, a fantastic Italian on Larkshall Road, Highams Park, and the Indian called Star of India in Leytonstone.

Mine's a pint

The away fans' favourite is Coach and Horses on the High Road. Looking rough on the outside, this traditional boozer is friendly on the inside and within stumbling distance of Matchroom Stadium. London Pride and Adnam's are on tap and well priced. But there's little in the way of food, save for a few ham & cheese rolls. Home fans make a beeline for Birkbeck Tavern on Langthorne Road. But away fans should receive a warm welcome. It can get a bit crowded before and after

Club Information Stadium: Matchroom Stadium, Brisbane Road, Leyton, London E10 5NF Capacity: 9271 (all seated) Tel: 0870 3101881 Web: www.leytonorient.com Colours: Red, white and black Tube: Leyton Songs: 'Orient Til I Die' gets a regular airing, as do a few anti West Ham songs – including a

Orient play, so get there early if you want a pew and not a queue. Guest real ales nestle up against the lagers on the drinks menu and there's a big outdoor area for summer supping. Don't ask for food as there's not much on offer here.

One of the most highly rated pubs in the area is The William IV and Sweet William Micro Brewery. The cluttered, cosy interior lends some character, while the ales are consistently well kept. Fullers ESB, London Pride and Discovery are usually available.

Other pubs on High Road to pay a visit include The Lion and Key and The Three Blackbirds.

Stopping over in Leyton?

 Twenty minutes on the Tube and you're in the heart of London where the accommodation options are endless.

If you do want to stay close to Leyton, there's a Travelodge on Clements Road in Ilford (0870 191 1693) and Holiday Inn Express in Buckhurst Hill (020 8504 4450). Situated almost 11 miles from central London (or 35 minutes by Tube), the Inn is close to the North Circular Road (A406) which gives access to the M11 motorway.

If you do one thing in Leyton...

Watch the football, have a few pints and make haste for London's myriad attractions and nightlife.

If you're with the family, you could take a ball, Frisbee and picnic to nearby Epping Forest and have a very good time indeed. As the largest public open space in London, it's a nice place to while away a few hours.

For more information on London's sights, see the city guide.

Pot the reds then screw back

Barry Hearn rescued the club from going out of business in 1995 when it was put up for sale for just £5 by the then chairman Tony Wood.

Hearn had a brief cameo in Chas & Dave's cockney send-up about snooker called 'Snooker Loopy', a comic song name-checking the star talents in his dominant Matchroom stable of the 1980s.

Don't mention

That you'd rather go to Upton Park if you lived in East London: West Ham are Orient's main rivals.

Do Mention

Mr Hearn: although not met with 100% approval rate, the way in which he's transformed Orient has to be applauded. Martin Ling: finally led them out of the basement doldrums after two near misses under Tommy Taylor.

Travel Information

CAR
Exit the M11 onto the A406 North Circular heading south towards the A12. If you're coming from the south east, exit the M25 at junction 29 for the A12. Take the A12 into the city and exit onto the A106 into Leyton and then take the fourth right onto the A112 Leyton High Road, heading north. After a few hundred metres you will see a right turn into Buckingham Road.

TRAIN
Leyton is on the Central Line and a short walk along Leyton High Road. Turn right out of the station until you reach Buckingham Road on your left. Turn down here for the ground.

reworking of the Mary Poppins classic 'Chim Chimney, Chim Chimney, Chim Chim Cheree' – which of course rhymes with claret and blue. Rivals: West Ham, Brighton and Southend.

Lincoln City

The Queen, the Imps... and some sheep

Renovations to Sincil Bank Stadium have been staggered over many years, resulting in an all-seater venue at the start of the 1999/2000 season. But they're not finished yet. Under the 'Goal 2010' campaign, the club is equipping itself to play in the Championship, with improvements to training facilities, bars and catering among the plans. Whether the perennial Play-Off losers make it out of League Two to fulfil these ambitions is another matter.

Imps' fans are hopeful of a replacement for the main stand, but nothing is yet planned. Such development might help attract new events to the 10,130-capacity ground, which already boasts an illustrious history as a venue for non-sports activities.

Queen Elizabeth II once flashed her trademark robotic wave to adoring crowds on a visit in 1958, while legendary bands such as The Who, The Kinks and The Small Faces rocked the rafters in a concert eight years later. Less illustrious, however, were the sheep dog trials held in the summer of 1943. Not a sight you'd see nowadays, of course. Still, locals seem thrilled enough watching a few lost souls chasing each other aimlessly around a patch of grass on a Saturday afternoon.

The Stacey West Stand gets its name from the two Lincoln City victims of the 1985 fire at Bradford City FC's ground - a tragedy which claimed 56 lives.

In 1987, the Imps suffered an ignominious exit from the Football League, becoming the first team to be automatically relegated. But they bounced back at the first attempt.

Away supporters share the Lincolnshire Co-operative Stand with Imps' fans. There's space for 1,600 visitors in blocks 1 and 2.

Eating out

Join the ranks of home fans for a bite and some banter in The Centre Spot social club at the south end of the ground. Visiting supporters are made very welcome. Wash down one of the legendary Lincoln City hot pork rolls with a few pints and you'll be match-fit. Sky Sports and Imps TV will keep you in touch with the day's big footballing stories. Local catering firm Double M sells hotdogs, burgers and similar fare at kiosks around the ground. It's only a 15-minute walk into town for the best fast-food emporiums and takeaways. Sit down with a pie in Lincoln's famous Browns Pie Shop at the top of Steep Hill in the Cathedral Quarter. Or grab some pub grub for between £5 and £10 at The Nosey Parker on Crusader Road (the steaks are said to be good). For a slab of pizza, head for Zizzi's in the centre. Big Wok on Beaumont Fee offers a standard Chinese buffet for about £4.99. One place for lovers of spicy chicken dishes is Nando's on Brayford Wharf North.

Mine's a pint

Sincil Bank's Centre Spot bar will see you right for a pre-match tipple. The club also recommends The Millers Arms, an away-friendly pub on High Street and only five

Club Information Stadium: Sincil Bank Stadium, Lincoln LN5 8LD Capacity: 10,130 (all seated) Tel: 0870 8992005 Web: www.redimps.com Train: Lincoln Central Colours: Red and white Songs: 'We Are The Imps' to the tune of the Quadrophenia classic 'We Are The

minutes from the stadium. High Street is home to many other pubs. There's also a good selection at Brayford Wharf North, including Quayside, The Royal William IV and The Square Sail. And don't forget The Nosey Parker (see above).

Stopping over in Lincoln?

 Lincoln has enough going on to make it worth staying a night. You'll find plenty of B&Bs scattered around. The Lincoln Hotel opposite the cathedral on Eastgate in the city centre is recommended (01522 520348). It's not the cheapest but has the prime location for sightseeing, and a restaurant and bar to boot. Another option is Courtyard by Marriott Lincoln located at Brayford Wharf North (01522 544244). Easily accessible from all major routes to the city, it includes a brasserie and café-bar and is perfectly placed for shopping, entertainment and local attractions.

If you do one thing in Lincoln...

Whether you'll want to discover the city's Roman, Norman, Medieval, Tudor and Georgian heritage is up to you. Nevertheless the cathedral and castle at the heart of historic Lincoln are pretty stunning and worth a peek - in between pubs perhaps. In fact, you could easily spend a few hours walking around the cobbled streets, checking out the antique shops and getting a feel for the city's rich heritage.

Or settle into an eaterie or drinking parlour at Brayford Waterfront, kick back and enjoy the views.

Graham Taylor's debut

Former England boss Graham Taylor started out as a manager at Lincoln City in 1971 at the tender age of 28.

He guided the team to the Division Four championship in 1975/6, one of the most successful campaigns in the club's history in which the Imps netted 32 wins and lost only four games. A year later, Taylor sought a new challenge at Watford. In 1996, more than 10,000 turned out to watch Newcastle United's £15million hitman Alan Shearer make his debut in a pre-season friendly at Sincil Bank.

Don't mention

1987: a bad year for the Imps, they were relegated from the Football League into the Conference – but did bounce back 12 months later.

Do mention

Andy Graver, Grant Brown, Mick Harford, Gareth Ainsworth: all members of the Lincoln City League Legends.

Travel Information

CAR
Take the A46 towards Lincoln and branch off onto the A1434 Newark Road towards the city and then pick up the A15 South Avenue. After about 400m turn left into Sincil Bank for the ground. There is plenty of street parking, an official car park behind the west stand for around a fiver, or try South Common at the beginning of South Park Avenue.

TRAIN
Turn right out of the station and take the bridge over the railway. Go over the bridge and follow the road (Sincil Bank) straight to the ground.

Mods' is popular at Sincil Bank. As is 'Give Us A C' with the final line "put 'em together and what have you got". Rivals: Anyone from: Scunthorpe United, Mansfield Town, Hull City, Grimsby Town, Peterborough or Boston.

Liverpool

A new red heaven

Liverpool FC have embarked on the development of their new 60,000-seater in Stanley Park, with construction due to be completed by 2010. The project is part of the comprehensive regeneration of the Anfield area and the transformation of the park itself.

New owners George Gillett and Tom Hicks, along with chief executive Rick Parry, are driving the scheme forward. Hemmed in by residential properties, there was never any hope of expanding Anfield, Liverpool's home since 1892.

Like Goodison Park across the field, Anfield has aged gracefully. And it's got plenty of northern soul - it may only squeeze in 45,362 but the ground erupts like no other when the Reds score.

You're reminded of the club's two most successful managers when you walk through the Paisley Gates or the Shankly Gates, where 'You'll Never Walk Alone' is writ large in wrought iron.

Liverpool commandeered the Gerry & the Pacemakers classic as their own in the 1960s. Belted out from under The Kop roof, it creates a deafening wall of sound unmatched in English football.

In the wake of Hillsborough, The Kop became something of a shrine to the 96 victims of the 1989 stadium tragedy. It was later demolished and replaced with an all-seater stand. You can also pay tribute to those who died at the Hillsborough Memorial on Anfield Road.

Away fans are located in the lower tier of the Anfield Road Stand, with almost 2,000 seats for visiting fans in a stand shared with home supporters. Make sure you don't end up with a restricted view ticket, it could well put a downer on what should be a terrific matchday experience.

Eating out

Refreshment kiosks sell the usual, including a 'Scouse Pie'. Burger vans and nearby chippies cater for most appetites. In the city, St John's is Liverpool's largest shopping centre and has a large food court featuring McDonald's, Subway and KFC. There's an abundance of choice in a city with a thriving restaurant and café-bar scene. Chinatown (around Berry Street) is one option for eating out. 60 Hope Street, four times Best Merseyside Restaurant of the Year, is recommended for cuisine at very reasonable prices... best to book early though. Another top tip is just down the road; The London Carriage Works, Merseyside's Restaurant of the Year 2006. It includes a relaxed brasserie area and dishes up classic meals with a modern twist. If you want to see creative flair in the preparation of top-notch Japanese food, try Sapporo Teppanyaki Restaurant Sushi & Noodle Bar on Duke Street, East Village. Light meals and snacks served at lunchtimes.

Mine's a pint

Alcohol is not always available on the concourses, so neck a few pre-match jars en route. The Albert and The Park are both no-go zones. The Arkles on Anfield Road is your best bet for a cool fizzy beverage, the main away pub because of its proximity to the visitors' end. Otherwise, trek

Club Information Stadium: Anfield, Anfield Road, Liverpool L4 0TH Capacity: 45,362 (all seated) Tel: 0151 263 2361 Web: www.liverpoolfc.tv Train: Kirkdale Colours: Red Songs: 'You'll Never Walk Alone' with Liverpool scarf held aloft is a

across Stanley Park to the cluster of pubs near Goodison Park. Anfield Hotel on Walton Road is a popular venue with a good range of beers. The Winslow, outside Goodison, offers a warm welcome. The Stanley Park, known as 'The Blue House', is a haven for bluenoses but okay for non-Reds. You should get no hassle in County Road's hostelries, many of which support the blue half of Liverpool. And you'll be fine at most pubs near Lime Street station as long as you cover colours and don't get too lippy. Of these, The Crown garners good reviews for its cheap food and beers, including Cains bitter, and friendly service. Also worth a visit is The Vines, one of a number of grand Victorian boozers in the centre. Red and White Kop offers an informative guide to Liverpool *www.redandwhitekop.com*.

Stopping over in Liverpool?

 Carey's is a small B&B on Walton Breck Road close to Anfield and extends a warm welcome to visitors (0151 286 7965). Another recommended is Litherland Park B&B, four-diamond rated, which gives excellent value for money and is only 15 minutes by car from the city centre (0151 928 1085). Budget hotels in the heart of Liverpool include Hotel Ibis at Wapping (0151 706 9800) and Premier Travel Inn on Vernon Street, off Dale Street (0870 238 3323). The

extravagant choice with tariffs to match is Malmaison Hotel situated at Princes Dock (0151 229 5000).

If you only do one thing in Liverpool...

Liverpool was not crowned the European Capital of Culture 2008 for nothing. You're spoilt for choice. Obviously, the Beatles are a huge part of the city's heritage. But don't forget about innovators like OMD, Echo and the Bunnymen and, erm, Atomic Kitten. The Beatles Story visitor attraction within Liverpool's Albert Dock is one of the top sights.

Quote, unquote

Bill Shankly on the Blues: "If Everton were playing at the bottom of the garden, I'd pull the curtains." And a pearler from Gerard Houllier: "Our job is to make the fans happy. When we win, 45,000 people go home happy. When we lose, it not only affects them, it affects their cats."

Don't mention

The European Cup Final v AC Milan 2007: Liverpool lost 2-1, when really they should have had enough about them to have beaten their opponents.

Do mention

The European Cup Final v AC Milan 2005: in one of the best (if not the best) finals of all time, Liverpool came back from the dead to beat their Italian opponents. Trailing 3-0 at the break, they drew level and then won on penalties.

Travel Information

CAR
Follow the M62 until you reach the end of the motorway. Then take the A5058. After three miles turn left at the traffic lights into Utting Avenue and after a mile or so, just past Stanley Park, turn right into Anfield Road for You may find street parking. Otherwise there's a car park in Stanley Park and also one at Goodison Park – home of Everton – turn right into Priory Rd just before Stanley Park.

TRAIN
Kirkdale Station (served by trains from Liverpool Central) is the closest; about twenty minutes' walk. Turn right out the station and cross the railway bridge and follow the Westminster Road. Turn left into Bradwell Street and cross the A59 and turn right a few hundred yards down to Luton Grove, which leads into Florence Street. You'll come out on Walton Lane; turn right and then left for Anfield Road. Another option is Sandhills Station (also served by Liverpool Central), which has a Soccerbus to the ground. It runs for a couple of hours before games and about an hour afterwards. Buy a return train ticket to Anfield – it's a pound extra, but covers your bus travel and is cheaper than paying separately.

fantastic audio-visual experience for any football fan. 'Poor Scouser Tommy' and 'Fields Of Anfield Road' are other Liverpool originals. Rivals: Everton and Manchester United.

Luton Town

Falling apart

Kenilworth Road is falling apart and Luton Town chiefs have made little attempt to spruce it up in recent years. Redevelopment is out of the question because the stadium is hemmed in on three sides by terraced housing. Fresh plans to move to a new stadium always seem to be in their infancy and the omens are not looking good for the preferred site.

The club wants to built a 22,000-seater on a parcel of greenbelt land off Junction 12 of the M1, so that they can "pursue our ambitions of pushing towards a place in the Premiership". Officials bemoan the fact that years of uncertainty over a new venue have seen similar-sized clubs such as Reading and Bolton leap-frog them and go on to reap the financial rewards of top-flight football. Sadly, South Bedfordshire District Council don't share the vision. Not yet, anyhow. Councillors insist the scheme doesn't fit in well with the existing and current local plan and considers the best site to be at Junction 11a.

The Hatters have been here before. A previous stadium scheme spearheaded by former chairman David Kohler proposed a development on a site off Junction 10 of the M1 - but was fiercely seen off by councillors and residents.

For now the saga shows no signs of an ending, happy or otherwise, so for the immediate future Luton away means a trip to Kenilworth Road - once voted the worst ground by the Observer.

To access the covered and all-seater Oak Road Stand you even have to go down a narrow alleyway. There's space for 2,000 fans in the stand – just. Leg room is non-existent and facilities pitiful – but the one positive is that visiting fans can get a good atmosphere going inside the cramped away end.

Eating out

Two catering bars for away fans with pies, burgers and the like. There's a fish & chip shop around the corner from the ground, which does a roaring trade with football crowds. Sainsbury's is just down the road for all your food needs. Nearby Dunstable Road is crammed with options such as takeaways and Alankar Indian Restaurant. The Bluebird One takeaway on the corner of Clifton Road and Wimborne Road is highly rated. The ground is only about half a mile west of the town centre. Luton's Arndale Centre houses plenty of coffee shops, bakeries and fast food places. Aroma Restaurant in The Galaxy Centre is renowned for its value-for-money Oriental buffets. Diners can choose from as many as 30 lunchtime or 60 dinner dishes offering culinary delights from the Far East.

Mine's a pint

No alcohol is served at the ground and there are few pubs in the immediate vicinity. But you'll find a number within easy walking distance. The Bedfordshire Yeoman on Dallow Lane is a spacious establishment popular with away support on matchdays. It has pool, darts and TV. Nelson's Flagship is around the corner from the ground on Dunstable Road. Check out the West Indian cuisine on the menu. The Whitehouse is packed

Club Information Stadium: Kenilworth Road, Luton LU4 8AW Capacity: 10,300 (all seated) Telephone: 01582 411622 Website: www.lutontown.co.uk Train: Luton Colours: Black and white Songs: Mostly anti-Watford songs: 'He's Only A Poor Little

with home fans on matchdays, so don't go snooping. The English Rose on Old Bedford Road keeps its real ales in tip-top condition and is well-loved by CAMRA types, as is The Bricklayers Arms on High Town Road, a friendly local selling guest beers from small breweries. Also does a nice sandwich. The Galaxy Centre, "the area's premier leisure venue" in town, is choc-full of chain bars and pubs, if that's what you're looking for. One stylish club worth mentioning is Charlie Brown's on Midland Road. At the weekends, DJs spin old-school soul tunes downstairs and house and club classics on the upper level.

Stopping over in Luton?

 Stockwood Hotel on Stockwood Crescent is central and cheap: rooms from £35 (01582 721000). This non-smoking hotel is easily accessible from the town's railway station and M1 motorway. The Royal Hotel on Mill Street is right in the centre and handy for shops, pubs and restaurants (01582 400909). Doubles from £59. Hotel St Lawrence, Guildford Street is a small independent family-run hotel that "fizzes with style, informality and warmth" (01582 482119). You're promised brasserie-style cooking and there's also a lobby bar. Rooms are priced about £60.

If you do one thing in Luton...
Visit Whipsnade Wild Animal Park in Dunstable, a short drive away but well worth it. It's home to more than 2,500 animals, including many rare and endangered species, and holds daily demonstrations. It's open every day of the year except Christmas Day. Active sorts might fancy the Xscape sports and entertainment complex up the road in Milton Keynes. It offers a combination of extreme sports and leisure activities for all ages, with an indoor snow slope, indoor skydiving and a climbing experience.

Morecambe & Luton
Eric Morecambe was a Hatters fan and a former club director of Luton, one of a small group of teams to have played in all four divisions of the Football League.

Don't mention
That the only reason Luton did so well during the 1980s was because they had a plastic pitch – and nobody else (apart from Oldham, Preston and QPR) were used to playing on them. Former chairman Bill Tomlins: he has been tied up in a payments-to-agents scandal which hasn't done him or the club any good.

Do mention
The 1980s: a great time to be a Hatter as the club spent most of it in the old First Division and shocked the nation by beating Arsenal in the 1987 League Cup Final. David Pleat: the architect of promotion to the top flight.

Travel Information

CAR
Leave the M1 at Junction 11 and take the A505 Dunstable Road towards Luton which will lead you right to the ground – Kenilworth Road is about a mile and a half in on the right. There is a residents' parking scheme in operation near to the ground and street parking is difficult but not impossible. You can find paid-for parking at the nearby Sainsburys supermarket and there are other unofficial operators – all for under a fiver.

TRAIN
Luton Station (don't go to Luton Parkway – as this serves the airport) is around fifteen minutes' walk from the ground. Exit the station, turning left along the railway bridge. Then turn right into Bute Street and through the Arndale Shopping Centre coming out onto the Dunstable Road turn right and Kenilworth Road is on the left.

Hornet' is a very popular and much heard Luton original. 'Come On You Hatters' can also be heard ringing round Kenilworth Road on matchdays. Rivals: Watford.

Small crowds for a club with a big heart

Average attendances at Macclesfield Town's Moss Rose stadium are among the lowest in the league, perhaps because they've spent so long as a non-league side. Ex-Manchester United star Sammy McIlroy turned the Silkmen into Conference champions in 1995 but they were denied a league place as their ground failed to meet league requirements. Ground improvements were duly made and the Silkmen eventually sealed promotion two years later.

These days, the intimate 6,335-capacity stadium is in decent shape but offers a somewhat low-key atmosphere due to gates hovering around the 2,500 mark. Still, you'll get a good view of the action. The £1.3 million Alfred McAlpine Stand that replaced the old 'tented village' and major renovation to the concourse behind the away end now makes for a better day out for visiting fans.

The stand can accommodate 403 away fans, and there's space for 1,530 standing uncovered in the Silkmen End. In a bid to swell numbers, there's free entry for all Under-12s.

Construction of the Alfred McAlpine Stand was not without controversy - the latest in a series of financial crises through the decades to threaten the club's survival. Club chiefs were ordered to pay a substantial fine to the Football Foundation for breaching FA rules relating to funding of the development. A 'Save Our Silkmen' fundraising appeal rescued the club from going under.

Macclesfield's fiercest rivals are Altrincham. They met each other regularly in the Conference and lower leagues but the clubs have not played in the same division since 1996.

Eating out

At the stadium, you can pick up some tasty snacks such as burgers and hotdogs but be prepared to splash the cash. "The balti pies are great if you can stomach paying twice the going rate," says one local. Before the match, get to the Railway View on Byrons Lane earlyish for some good pub grub. The Society Rooms on Park Green is a Wetherspoons pub, so there's plenty of dirt-cheap food here. You could even treat yourself and book in for pre-match hospitality in the McIlroy Suite - always excellent food and away fans very welcome. After the match, why not try the Balti Kitchen on Park Green (not far from the railway station). It's touted as one of the best Indians in the area.

Mine's a pint

On the one-mile trek from the railway station to Moss Rose, you'll pass The Albion - a good place to catch your breath and quench your thirst. The Railway View, mentioned above, has a great atmosphere and a fine selection of real ales. The Golden Lion on Moss Lane is the nearest pub to the ground - about 10 minutes' walk away. Home and away fans mingle well and it's child-friendly. Other recommended pubs include

---

Club Information Ground Name: Moss Rose, London Road, Macclesfield SK11 7SP Capacity: 6,335 Tel: 01625 264686 Web: www.mtfc.co.uk Train: Macclesfield Colours: Blue & white Songs: 'Maccy Maccy Maccy Maccy Macclesfield' and 'You

the Boarhound on Brook Street and the Jar Bar on Park Green. For some post-match merriment or a big night on the tiles, a pub crawl finishing with a curry will do the job nicely.

One fan suggests starting at Chester Road Tavern, before heading to The Barnfield on Catherine Street and The Castle on Church Street. Neck a pint in Waters Green Tavern followed by a jar in the Nags Head - both on Waters Green - and end your jaunt in the Society Rooms. You'll be famished by then but the Balti Kitchen will attend to your needs.

Stopping over in Macclesfield?

 There's a mix of accommodation in the town but nearby Liverpool and Manchester might be more up your street, if you're intending to spend the weekend in this area. At the budget end, Premier Lodge on Congleton Road (0870 700 1466), The Travellers Rest on Cross Street (01625 422822) and 60-room Best Western Hollin Hall on Jackson Lane, Bollington (01625 573246), are possibles. More upscale is the four-star De Vere Mottram Hall Hotel on Wilmslow Road, Mottram St Andrew, which is described as "one of Cheshire's most exclusive leisure, gold and business hotels" (01625 828135).

If you do one thing in Macclesfield...

Go hiking in Macclesfield Forest or tour around the beautiful countryside of the Peak District. The Jodrell Bank Science Centre and Arboretum, offering interactive activities for youngsters, is a good family day out. If that proves too taxing, there's an abundance of attractions and shopping facilities in Manchester and Liverpool. Both cities are only a short drive or train ride away. For further information, check out our regional guides.

Cup joy

The Silkmen have enjoyed Wembley success twice, picking up the FA Trophy in 1970, the non-league's cup competition inaugural year, and again in 1996.

Don't mention

The new club crest: supposed to be launched at the start of the 2007/08 season, supporters weren't happy with the modern design so the plans were scrapped and the club reverted to the old crest.

Do mention

Sammy McIlroy: not only did he take the club out of the Conference and into the Football League in only his second season in charge; he then won promotion again to lift the Silkmen into the same division as nearby Manchester City.

Travel Information

CAR
After leaving the M6 you need to pick up the A54 to Macclesfield (exit at Junction 17 if you're coming from the south and take the A534 towards Congleton; exit at 18 from the north and you'll find yourself on the A54). Follow the signs for Buxton and then turn off onto the A523 to Macclesfield, which leads to the ground as you come towards the town centre. There is plenty of street parking around the ground.

TRAIN
Macclesfield Station is on the Manchester-Stafford branch line of the West Coast Main Line. It's about twenty minutes' walk from the ground. Exit the station and turn left into Sunderland Street. Turn left onto Mill Lane at the traffic lights and follow this road into London Road and to the ground. Buses also run this route every half hour or so – catch a number 9 or 14.

Are My Silkmen' are regularly heard ringing around Moss Rose when things are going well. Rivals: Altrincham from non-league days, but more recently Stockport County.

Manchester City

Growing up fast

Built for the 2002 Commonwealth Games at a cost of £110 million, the spectacular City of Manchester Stadium has been home to the Sky Blues since 2003, when they moved out of Maine Road.

Alterations to the stadium after the sporting extravaganza added 10,000 seats to bring capacity up the present-day 48,000. Oasis attracted 60,000 for a 2005 concert - the highest non-football attendance to date.

Also known as Eastlands, the venue's bowl has two tiers all the way round the ground and third tiers along the two side stands. Every vantage point affords excellent views - even if you are seated way up in the South Stand housing away fans.

Around 3,000 visitors can be seated in one side of this stand, 4,500 if demand requires. You might find yourself perched fairly close to the Blue brigade, so be prepared for some barracking and banter.

Smart card technology is in operation at the ground. Away supporters are issued with a paper version, which can be swiped at card readers to gain quick access through the appropriate entrance.

Eastlands is the site of the tallest sculpture in the UK, 'B of the Bang', which was built to commemorate the success of the 2002 Commonwealth Games. The 1969 FA Cup winners' home also houses the widest pitch in English football.

Staging of the 2008 UEFA Cup final at Eastlands will cement the venue's reputation as a footballing mecca. The City of Manchester Stadium is expected to have its own Metrolink station sometime between 2008 and 2010.

Eating out

Spacious concourses complete with TVs showing the game can make any visit to the concessions bars a less rushed affair. Burger stalls around the ground cater for most needs. City Social café at the ground is a family-orientated sports bar which runs a breakfast menu daily from 9.30-11am. Other pre-match main meals and snacks are available. There's an Asda and a McDonald's, both on Ashton New Road, for a cheap feed. Yasmin Garden and British Raj Balti House are Indian restaurants along here. The wonderfully-named Glamorous Chinese Restaurant on Cassidy Close is near the stadium and comes recommended. For anything else, you're best eating in the city. Eastlands is easily reached by rail and bus and is about 25 minutes' walk from Manchester Piccadilly Station. Here there are any number of fast food outlets and takeaways. The Trafford Centre is a good place to head for: it has about 40 restaurants. Manchester's cultural diversity means there's a great range of places to eat after a match. From Chinatown to Rusholme's Curry Mile, satisfaction is guaranteed. Check out the city guide for more info.

Mine's a pint
Booze is available at the stadium but don't go hunting pubs

Club Information Stadium: City Of Manchester Stadium, Rowsley Street, Manchester M11 3FF Capacity: 48,000 (all seated) Tel: 0870 621894 Web: www.mcfc.co.uk Colours: Sky blue and white Train: Ashburys Songs: 'Blue Moon' is

around it as most are designated for City supporters. The Grove is most popular among visiting fans. It's about 10 minutes' walk from the away end along Ashton New Road past Asda, and does excellent Holts Bitter. A similar distance from the ground on Bradford Road is the Bradford Inn, which also gets jammed with travelling fans. Mary D'bemish Bar on Grey Mare Lane, not far from the South Stand, is also a decent pub. Three Arrows Inn on Middleton Road, just off the M60 and behind Heaton Park, is a top recommendation for its cask ales, fantastic food at cheap prices and relaxed ambience. City centre pubs and bars are plentiful. If you're coming by train, Deansgate is littered with taverns and chain bars. Hop off the train and go past the CIS building, up Miller Street and left onto Rochdale Road to find The Marble Arch, a traditional boozer renowned for its range of ales and chatty atmosphere. For brilliant tips on Manchester drinking visit *www.manchesterbars.com*.

Stopping over in Manchester...

 Manchester offers all styles of accommodation. Some of the cheapest for fans: Express by Holiday Inn on Hyde Road, two miles from the stadium - there's another at Salford Quays (0800 556 5565). Jarvis Piccadilly hotel is on Portland Street in the city centre, ideal for the local sights (0161 236 8414). B&B is from £52 a night. Thistle Hotel on Portland Street offers rooms from about £70 (0161 228 3400). For three-star accommodation in Piccadilly, you could try Gardens Hotel, which has reasonably-priced rooms (0161 236 5155).

If you do one thing in Manchester...

There are lots of things to do in Manchester – and much of it is free of charge, such as the Museum of Science & Industry. Check out our city guide for more information.

Power players

The stadium will soon become the first in the world to be powered by its own wind turbine. The 85m turbine, also built to generate power for nearby homes, is provided by power company Ecotricity and will produce about two megawatts of electricity.

Don't mention

Manchester City's relegation to the third tier of English football: their local derby game for the 1998/99 season was against Macclesfield.

Do mention

That City relegated their rivals Manchester United on the final day of the 1973/74 season – and that it was United legend Denis Law, then a City player, who scored the goal in the 1-0 win.

Travel Information

CAR
Leave the M60 at Junction 23 for the A635 towards Manchester. Exit onto the A662 towards Droylsden/Manchester and after around three miles you'll see the Stadium on your right. Alternatively you can leave the M60 at Junction 24 and take the A57 (Hyde Road) towards Manchester. Turn right onto the A6010 Pottery Lane which will lead you to the stadium and you'll also find a few unofficial car parks charging around a fiver. There is also an official car park at the ground for a similar price.

TRAIN
The closest train station is Ashburys which is on a local line from Manchester Piccadilly Station. The stadium is easy to find and about ten minutes' walk. Turn left out of the station and the stadium is up the road on the left.

the City fans' anthem, City-supporting Oasis have had a few of their songs reworked by the faithful, and other well-aired tunes are anti-Manchester United songs. Rivals: Need you ask?

Manchester United

Giants by name...

Old Trafford is one of the world's finest stadiums. With a 76,100 capacity, it towers above its Premiership counterparts, with recent developments having seen the north-west and north-east corners filled in.

In the future, further rebuilding and corner-filling could boost capacity to a staggering 96,000. However, this expansion is hampered by a railway line and residential area.

The Theatre of Dreams has witnessed the highest average attendances in English football for over 30 years (with the exception of the late 1990s when it was under redevelopment).

Unfortunately, getting to and from the ground can be a complete nightmare. Be prepared for long delays if you're coming by car/coach.

Some fans have experienced trouble-free getaways by parking their cars in Old Trafford cricket ground. United advises drivers to use official, secure car parks identified by brown signs. Coming by public transport? The nearest Metrolink stations (for Manchester's trams) are Old Trafford and Trafford Bar.

Squeezing onto the trams after a match can be an unsettling experience - you may want to wait a while, especially if you're with youngsters. A train service runs from Piccadilly/Oxford Road stations to the ground. Buses go from Manchester Chorlton Street Station.

Away fans are located in one corner of the ground (sections of the south and east stands), where the normal allocation is 3,000 seats. Views are excellent from these areas. The atmosphere varies depending on United's opponents. It can be a wee bit quiet. Listen out for the rowdy rabble in the Stretford End/West Stand - United fans that wouldn't touch a prawn sarnie with a bargepole.

Eating out

Old Trafford catering bars sell the usual matchday delights. Burger vans and fast food stalls line the roads around the ground and there's a fish & chip shop on the corner of Sir Matt Busby Way. If you get off the Metrolink one stop early at Trafford Bar you'll discover the Tollgate Inn (Seymore Grove), which serves hot food. Other places to eat can be found in nearby Salford Quays. A Wetherspoons pub, The Bishops Blaize, on Chester Road, is a decent pit stop. For anything else, you're best eating in the city. You can fuel up at any number of fast food outlets and takeaways near Manchester Piccadilly station. The Trafford Centre is good for a pre-match bite; it has about 40 restaurants. There's a great range of places to eat after a match, from Chinatown to Rusholme's Curry Mile in Wilmslow Road. Check out the city guide for more info.

Mine's a pint

Pubs near the ground and in the canalside area of Salford Quays are generally restricted to the Red Devils clan. Chester Road has a good supply of pubs, but it's wise to hide colours down this stretch. The Bishops Blaize and The Gorse Hill are fine for pre-match drinking. The Trafford is likely to be full of the beer-swilling United faithful, so give it a miss. To get away from the

---

Club Information Stadium: Old Trafford, Sir Matt Busby Way, Manchester M16 0RA Capacity: 76,100 (all seated) Tel: 0870 4421994 Web: www.manutd.com Colours: Red, white and black Train: Old Trafford Metro: Old Trafford Songs: Contrary to rumour there's a vast array. The pick of the bunch: 'The Manchester Calypso', 'Take

crowds, try The Quadrant on Great Stone Road, (about 10 minutes to Old Trafford). It sells pretty cheap bevvies and there's a chippy next door. The Bridge Inn on Dane Road, Sale (two stops from Old Trafford on the Metro), is away-friendly and you can sup outside next to the canal in warm weather. Otherwise, the best place for a good pint is in the city. Pubs around St Peters Square are perfect for the tram on matchdays. Deansgate is littered with taverns and chain bars all within reach of Victoria Station. The Moon Under Water is okay if you're after a cheap meal and pint. Hop off the train and go past the CIS building, up Miller Street and left onto Rochdale Road to find The Marble Arch, a traditional boozer renowned for its ales and chatty atmosphere.

For more top tips try *www.manchesterbars.com*

Stopping over in Manchester...

The Old Trafford Lodge at Lancashire's Test cricket ground is excellent value with rooms for around £50 per night (0161 874 3333). It's adjacent to the Old Trafford Metrolink tram station. Salford Quays is a picturesque location to stay. There are plenty of hotels here, with Express by Holiday Inn among the more modestly priced (0161 868 1000). Copthorne Hotel is more stylish and the Metrolink tram stops directly opposite. B&B is from £79 (0161 873 7321).

In town, the Jarvis Piccadilly on Portland Street is the ideal base to explore sights (0161 236 8414) - B&B about £52 a night. Thistle Hotel on the same street provides rooms from £70 (0161 228 3400). And there's always the Gardens Hotel in Piccadilly (0161 2365155).

If you do one thing in Manchester...

The Lowry is a real jewel in the crown. In Salford Quays, this landmark brings together a wide variety of performing and visual arts under one roof. Take in a show, catch the latest exhibition, have a great family day (*www.thelowry.com*). Check our city guide for information.

Keeping up appearances

Ryan Giggs could make history this season by surpassing Sir Bobby Charlton's record of 759 appearances for the club.

Don't mention

That most Manchester United fans don't come from Manchester: the club has worldwide support, but equally they have a huge following in the city and surrounding areas of Greater Manchester.

Do mention

Sir Alex Ferguson and Sir Matt Busby: two of the greatest managers in English football. Best, Law and Cantona: not just legends at Old Trafford, but football legends full stop.

Travel Information

CAR
From the south: Exit M6 at J19; take the A556 towards Altrincham then the A56 towards Manchester. After six miles Sir Matt Busby Way is on your left - take it if you can but it may be closed to traffic. From the north: Exit M6 at J30 onto M61 'Bolton' which becomes M60. At J9 take A5081 to Manchester, Sir Matt Busby Way is about two miles along on right. From the west: Take the M56 then the M60 (west and north). Exit at J7 onto the A56 towards Stretford; Sir Matt Busby Way is on the left after 2 miles. There's parking at Old Trafford for £8, but it has to be pre-booked: call 0870 442 1994. There are small private car parks nearby or street parking. Old Trafford Cricket Ground has parking for around a fiver, but the later you arrive, the longer it takes to get out. An excellent place for a quick exit is just off the A56 as you're heading north. You'll see signs for the car park just before you reach Sir Matt Busby Way. It's about a fiver.

TRAIN
Old Trafford Station is directly behind the South Stand; on matchdays you can catch a train there from main city centre stations. Or get the Metrolink from Manchester Piccadilly to Old Trafford.

Me Home, United Road' and the yuletide special 'Twelve Days Of Christmas'. It's devoted to Cantona and ends "...three Cantonas, two Cantonas and an Eric Cantona'. Rivals: Manchester City, Liverpool and Leeds United.

Mansfield Town

Stags lock horns with rivals

Any survey canvassing the views of Mansfield Town fans on the things they care most passionately about will reveal the same finding: they love to hate Chesterfield - both the place and the football team. For the rivalry between the teams is among the fiercest in the lower realms of the Football League.

Stags' fans will take any opportunity to have a pop at Chesterfield, but they also have a healthy disrespect for the former mining town in which they live. Football isn't so much the talk of the town among local supporters. Instead, there's rising crime and whether or not Mansfield is above or below Chesterfield as one of the worst places to live in the UK. Their self-deprecation knows no ends. Top tips for a visit to Mansfield? "Innoculations, as many as your doctor can give you," says one local. "Watch Deliverance - this is regarded as a documentary on Mansfield."

Not that any of this nonsense and east midlands bickering should deter you from visiting Mansfield: they're nice people really and it can be a welcoming town and football club – just not to folk from Chesterfield!

Field Mill, where football has been played since 1861, holds about 9,500 seated spectators. Plans to build a new stadium in the mid-90s were scrapped in favour of a redevelopment. Three new stands resulted, but it's still not the prettiest of venues. Visiting fans can watch games from the North Stand, which is accessible from the Portland Industrial park and small alleyway to the rear of the ground.

Eating out

A small food kiosk, selling a mixture of hot and cold snacks and drinks, serves the North Stand and matchday hospitality packages are offered. But for cheap nosh, you're best popping into Burger King at the retail park close to Field Mill. In fact, within walking distance of the ground there's a fair number of choices. McDonalds and KFC are just a few hundred yards away. You can find a fish & chip shop and a Chinese takeaway on Nottingham Road. For a quick sandwich or meal, nip into the Safeways supermarket and café or dive into one of the local pubs (see below). If you're after a hearty bit of post-match food, Mansfield caters for all tastes. Among them are: Chand Indian Cuisine on Toothill Road, a two-floor restaurant which can accommodate large groups; The Cheeky Monkey in the Handley Arcade offers a great range of tapas; Kularb Dang Thai Restaurant in the arcade is the town's only Thai; and Chicago Rock Café on Clumber Street has an extensive menu, plus hot and cold buffets.

Mine's a pint

Away fans aren't greeted warmly everywhere, so be careful where you choose to quench your thirst. For instance, avoid the

---

Club Information Stadium: Field Mill, Quarry Lane, Mansfield NG18 5DA Capacity: 10,000 (all seated) Tel: 0870 7563160 Web: www.mansfieldtown.net Colours: Yellow and blue Train: Mansfield Songs: 'Oh When I Die' is a weird song about being buried with

Old Victoria, which is only for Stags' fans. The Market Tavern in the town centre is also for the home brigade. It's best to stick to the recommended watering holes. The Early Doors pub across the road from Field Mill is away-friendly, welcomes families and serves a decent range of food. It positively encourages friendly interaction between home and away fans. The Famous Talbot, also on Nottingham Road, is a popular place for post-match pints and reflection on the goals scored or the missed chances. It serves good quality food in a friendly, family atmosphere. The Lord Byron at the top of Quarry Lane welcomes all supporters and is a brisk stroll to the ground. Red On The Square downtown welcomes well-behaved and responsible fans. DJs crank up the music on weekends, making for a lively night out. Most bars and clubs will not admit fans wearing football strips and trainers in the evening.

Stopping over in Mansfield?

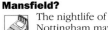 The nightlife of Nottingham may beckon, but if you fancy a quiet night then there are plenty of guesthouses offering cheap rooms if you do want to stay here. The Clifton Hotel on Terrace Road is one of the best choices. Located just five minutes away from the city centre, it promises a friendly welcome and has rooms from only £35 (01623 623876). There's also a Premier Travel Inn in South Normanton, Alfreton: rooms around £50 (08701 977 180).

If you do one thing in Mansfield

Not a huge amount on offer in Mansfield (described by D H Lawrence as that once romantic now utterly disheartening colliery town) - but the Palace Theatre might have something on worth a look. If not, check out our city guide for nearby Nottingham.

When the trophy cabinet was full...

Does anyone remember the Freight Rover Trophy? Well, the Stags certainly do. They won it in 1987 after beating Bristol City in a penalty shootout. It's the only time they have appeared at Wembley Stadium to date.

Don't mention

Carlton Palmer: the former England midfielder was manager at Field Mill but wasn't a popular appointment from day one.

Do mention

Ray Clarke: legendary striker from the 1970s, who was reluctantly sold to Sparta Rotterdam for a club record £90,000. He later played for Ajax.

Travel Information

CAR
From the north: Leave the M1 at Junction 29 onto the A617 to Mansfield. After about six miles, turn right into Rosemary Street and after a further mile turn right into Quarry Lane. From the south: Exit the M1 at Junction 28 onto the A38 to Mansfield. Stay on this road for around six miles and then turn right at the crossroads into Belvedere Street and right again into Quarry Lane. There is ample parking at the ground for about two quid, otherwise street parking can also be found fairly easily.

TRAIN
Mansfield Station is served by trains on a local line from Nottingham. Getting to Field Mill is easy: you can see the ground from the station. It's about ten minutes to walk it: turn left along the dual carriageway and then turn right at the second set of traffic lights into Quarry Lane.

alcohol – but it's a favourite at Field Mill – as are any anti-Chesterfield songs. Rivals: Mainly Chesterfield, but Nottingham Forest, Notts County and Lincoln City aren't exactly popular either.

Middlesbrough

The only way was up

Knocked up in 32 weeks, the Riverside Stadium is the pride of Teesside. When it opened its doors for the 1995/96 season, it was the biggest new football stadium to be built since the war.

Another 5,000 seats were added in 1998 with the £5m corner extensions to the West Stand, lifting capacity to a respectable 35,100.

Boro fans prefer not to dwell on the dark days at Ayresome Park, the club's home for 92 years. And there were quite a few - 1986 was a real annus horribilis. Boro were relegated to Division Three and the club went into liquidation, suffering from massive debts.

A consortium rescued the club and Boro bounced back with successive promotions in the following years. Current chairman and lifelong fan Steve Gibson has been instrumental in not only saving the club but investing huge sums towards its further progression.

February 2004 signalled the completion of Boro's turnaround in fortunes when they won their first piece of major silverware - the Carling Cup - in the club's 128-year history. And there's been a UEFA Cup final since just to frank the progress.

"Sometimes we don't appreciate how far we've come. This is our 10th consecutive season in the Premiership," says Steve Goldby, editor of ComeOnBoro.com, the best Middlesbrough fan site. (For 'Connoisseurs of Middlesbrough Football Club', the website boasts contributors including ex-referee and Boro fan Jeff Winter.)

Nicknamed the Breezeblock Stadium by the north-east rivals, at least the Riverside provides decent views. Up to 4,000 away supporters can be accommodated in the South Stand, and the wide concourses mean there's little congestion during the rush for refreshments at half-time.

Eating out

Cheeseburgers and pizza slices are among the staples sold at the Riverside. More than a dozen burger bars on Dockside Road do a brisk trade - the one nearest the railway level crossing does a fantastic steak burger for £2, according to regulars.

If you walk towards the town centre and go through the underpass, you'll find a shopping complex with McDonald's, Pizza Hut and Burger King. Go through the complex and opposite Doctor Browns pub is an Indian and The Purple Onion Restaurant, which is highly recommended for its matchday menu - everything from pasta meals to sausage & mash, curries and fish & chips. Marton Road has other eateries and there's a Nando's chicken restaurant nearby. Barnacles is an excellent chippy on Linthorpe Road, the main shopping street in the town centre with an array of restaurants dishing up all manner of gastronomic delights. The Masala on Borough Road is "the best Indian in town", says ComeOnBoro.com's Goldby. Best to book if you want to eat on a Saturday night.

Mine's a pint

Alcohol is available at the Riverside. If you want to avoid

Club Information Stadium: Riverside Stadium, Middlesbrough, Cleveland TS3 6RS Capacity: 35,100 (all seated) Tel: 0844 4996789 Web: www.mfc.com Train: Middlesbrough Colours: Red Songs: 'Who's That Team They Call The Boro' and

the more boisterous teenage drinkers on a Saturday night the advice is to steer clear of those next to the train station. "It's a really friendly town and away fans will experience no problems or animosity," says Goldby. Unless, that is, they show their faces in The Navigation. This is the nearest pub to the ground and as such the most partisan. Avoid.

Doctor Browns on Corporation Road is the usual port of call for away fans. It's perfectly located for pre-match ale but expect to find it heaving an hour or more before kick-off. Home and away fans mix well here, and it shows sport on large and small screen TVs. Mohans on Bedford Street, 10 minutes' walk from the station, is recommended as one of the best pubs in town.

If you want to avoid the young local riff-raff on a Saturday night, head for Southfield Road, just off the centre - it contains the more refined drinking establishments and trendy night spots.

Stopping over in Middlesbrough?

 Longlands Hotel on Marton Road is a recommended mid-market choice (01642 244900). It's situated about 10 minutes' walk from central Middlesbrough and has en-suite rooms from

£30. Further up the road is the Baltimore Hotel, offering basic but comfortable accommodation (01642 224111). It's about £60 for the cheapest room.

There's an Express by Holiday Inn also on Marton Way (01642 814444).

If you do one thing in Middlesborough...

If you've got a motor, drive over the famous Transporter Bridge spanning the River Tees... then make haste for Newcastle and its wealth of attractions.

What a shocker

Ayresome Park, chosen ahead of St James' Park to host three group games at the 1966 World Cup, was the scene of the tournament's biggest upset when North Korea beat Italy.

Don't mention

The year 1986: the club was forced to reform after financial difficulties (a far cry from today) and the players and staff even found themselves locked out of Ayresome Park.

Do mention

Juninho: the Brazilian international had three separate spells on Teesside – in his first he helped them to two Wembley finals – and he is still adored by the Boro faithful.

Travel Information

CAR
Take the A66 through the centre of Middlesbrough and you will pick up signs for the Riverside Stadium. There is no parking at the stadium, but you'll find a number of independent car parks nearby for under a fiver.

TRAIN
It's likely you will have to change at Darlington for Middlesbrough Station, although there are some direct services. Once you get there it's a short walk to the stadium from the station. Exit out of the front of the station left onto Zetland Road, then turn left again into Albert Road. Then take a right into Bridge Street East and right again into Wynward Way. The stadium is down this road.

many other traditional generic efforts in homage to their favourites or derision of their rivals. Rivals: Sunderland and Newcastle United.

Millwall

Hear the Lions roar

The New Den – now just back to being called The Den - has been home to the Lions since they departed their old ground a few yards down the road in 1993. It was the first new football stadium built for a league team in London since 1937. And it's a vast improvement on the old stadium.

While the ground hardly ever reaches its 20,146 capacity, you'll always get a vociferous local crowd as Lions fans roar their support. There's no denying that Millwall followers are among the most passionate and boisterous in the league. Former manager George Graham once remarked that Lions fans reminded him of his days in Glasgow: "The people up there are really fanatical about their football, they eat it and sleep it - and the Millwall fans were exactly the same."

"No one likes us, we don't care," is the common refrain reverberating around The Den, a song of defiance which has its roots in Millwall's dark history of hooliganism. Their troubles over the years, due in large part to the notoriety of their 'firm', have been well-documented but greatly exaggerated for easy headlines.

Millwall fans' tough-nut image dates back to the start of the 20th century when they changed their nickname from The Dockers after being referred to as 'Lions' for their giant-killing antics in their FA Cup journey in 1900. They later adopted a lion emblem, bearing the slogan We Fear No Foe.

The New Den - the sixth ground Millwall have occupied since they formed in 1885 - is a comfortable place to watch football, although known as an intimidating place for visiting teams. The North Stand holds 2,300 away fans with the lower tier a further 1,500 if called for.

Eating out

Refreshment bars on the concourse serve football grub such as chicken & chips and Pukka pies. There are burger vans dotted around the ground and The Millwall Café opposite the club shop offers fish & chips and other cheap fills. You won't go hungry in this area of London. By South Bermondsey Railway Station, only a few minutes' walk from the ground, you'll find a Greggs bakers and café as well as an Indian and Chinese.

Elephant & Castle shopping centre has plenty of cafés, takeaways and restaurants and is just a short bus ride away. Meanwhile, both Greenwich and Blackheath have a mixture of tapas bars, noodle joints, Mexican restaurants and Italians. It's also the location of the best local pubs, many of which do food. Windies Cove, billed as south east London's finest Caribbean restaurant, offers a delicious menu. It's located on Trafalgar Road in Greenwich.

Mine's a pint

Most home fans drink at the ground, creating a buzzy atmosphere on matchdays. Bars at the back of the away stand offer a selection of lagers and real ales. The best matchday pubs are found in the New Cross area and include the

---

Club Information Stadium: The Den, Zampa Road, London SE16 3LN Capacity: 20,146 (all seated) Tel: 0207 232 1222 Web: www.millwallfc.co.uk Train: South Bermondsey Colours: Blue and white Songs: 'No One Likes Us, We Don't Care' has been synonymous

New Cross Inn, Walpole Arms, The Paradise Bar (a gastro pub), The Hobgoblin (with beer garden) and Goldsmiths Tavern. Marquess of Granby on Lewisham Way is also recommended. For a top evening out in this part of town, Greenwich's Up the Creek cabaret comedy club on Creek Road gets a big thumbs up. It has a bar and Thai restaurant upstairs.

Stopping over in the Millwall area?

 There are no hotels near the ground. But you'll find a Novotel on Greenwich High Road with rooms at reasonable rates (020 8312 6800) and an Ibis on Stockwell Street, Greenwich (020 8305 1177).

It's an ideal base to do a spot of sightseeing in the Big Smoke. The Clarendon in Blackheath is in a picturesque setting 10 minutes from Greenwich Park. Doubles are from £90 but it's perfectly placed for a weekend stay.

If you do one thing in the Millwall area...

Stay in Greenwich or Blackheath and there's an abundance of London's most famous attractions right on your doorstep.

Take your pick from the Maritime Museum, The Royal Observatory and Greenwich Market. In addition, Buckingham Palace, The Tower of London, St. Paul's Cathedral and the West End's theatreland are only 20 minutes' away.

For more information, consult our city guide to London.

Short stay for the journeyman

Former Millwall star Steve Claridge - legendary journeyman of English football with over 15 league clubs to his name - became player/manager in June 2005. But club chairman Jeff Burnige quit two months into his job and changes in the boardroom led to Claridge being unceremoniously sacked after just 36 days and without a competitive match in charge.

Don't mention

Sergei Yuran: the Russian international joined in January 1996 as the club looked to push for promotion to the Premiership. Instead they were relegated and Yuran's colossal wages contributed to financial problems which left the club in administration.

Do mention

Harry Cripps: inspirational player from the 1970s who still has legendary status with the Millwall faithful. George Graham: led the club into the Second Division, before being snapped up by Arsenal.

Travel Information

CAR
The park-and-train approach is worth considering for Millwall as parking isn't easy around the ground. If you are driving the whole journey, depending on where you're coming from, there are a number of ways to get to Millwall. If you're coming from outside the M25 it's probably best to head in on the A2 from Junction 2 of the M25 (although those coming up from the south may prefer to head in via the A23 or A3 and then into Bermondsey via Peckham). Follow the A2 to the City/ Westminster and this takes you straight to the ground. You need to exit the A2 a mile or so after New Cross Gate tube station (you'll see this on your right). Street parking can be found around the ground, but there isn't much in the way of parking – official or otherwise.

TRAIN
If you're coming by rail aim for South Bermondsey Railway Station, you can change at London Bridge. Away fans have a special walkway to the ground. The nearest tube stops are Surrey Quays and New Cross Gate – but it's best to get the 'rattler' as it's known in these parts.

with Lions fans for years, as has the 'Millwall' roar which can be quite intimidating for visiting fans. Rivals: West Ham United, Crystal Palace, Chelsea and Charlton Athletic.

MK Dons

Who is that mad music bloke?

The Dons kick off the season in their new Denbigh North stadium situated next to the A421 spur junction with the A5. Bletchley railway station is nearby.

The £44 million stadium with an initial capacity of 22,000 (only the lower tier) will eventually rise to 32,000 within a couple of years under the club's proposals. It will be one of just five stadia in English football to meet UEFA's four-star requirement. Designed by Emirates Stadium architects HOK Sport, the development will eventually house an indoor concert venue, hotel and basketball arena for the MK Lions.

It is the brainchild of Pete Winkelman, Dons' chairman, former record-label executive and self-styled evangelist for Milton Keynes. He heads the InterMK consortium which controversially relocated Wimbledon to the city in 2003.

Since then the Dons have had to make do at the National Hockey Stadium. The 8,800-seat hockey venue has never amounted to much as a football ground - visiting fans were seated in the uncovered North Stand, making it a miserable day out when the heavens opened.

The new Denbigh stadium, just a couple of miles away, is far from basic. It features some of the latest innovations in football stadia, including open concourses overlooking the pitch, meaning fans won't miss any of the action on a trip to the burger bar. The venue also contains a synthetic-enhanced natural grass pitch and the most comfortable seats in English football.

Average gates are not even expected to reach 12,000 but Winkelman reckons the stadium will grow with the club and be one that will stand the test of time: "In 50 years hopefully they will still be using the stadium built by that mad music bloke."

Eating out

Catering kiosks and burger vans will do a roaring trade in and around the stadium until other cafés and restaurants are erected. For a Scotch egg or pre-packed sarnie go to the nearby Asda or Tesco. Central Bletchley's bars and restaurants are about one mile from the ground. Saap Thai on Chandos Place is described as a bit of a gem. Modestly priced eat-in and takeaway food includes a range of curries, spicy salads and noodle dishes. Jeff & Chele's Pie, Mash and Liquor shop on Oliver Road is a big hit for its authentic Cockney fare. On Midsummer Boulevard in Milton Keynes there's a good Mexican restaurant called Chiquito and the Royal Lido, a Chinese restaurant serving the best steak dish in the city. Jaipur on Grafton Gate East, the fringe of the city's business district, serves a good Indian in a fine dining environment. For more eating establishments, head to the theatre district. The Spice Lounge is an Indian restaurant noted for its quality and wide range of dishes.

Mine's a pint

 Away fans previously frequented pubs close to the city's main train station including

---

Club Information Stadium: Stadium MK, Denbigh, Milton Keynes MK1 1SA Capacity: 22,000 (all seated) Tel: 01908 607090 Web: www.mkdons.co.uk Train: to be inserted

the Wetherspoons called Secklow Hundred on Midsummer Boulevard. But their allegiances are sure to switch to pubs and bars in the Bletchley area near the stadium. The Old Swan on Shenley Road is tipped as one of the best for cheap food and ale, while The Enigma Tavern on Princes Way has a friendly atmosphere and a decent pint. There are a few drinking dens on Buckingham Road. Near the Fenny Stratford train station, The Bull and Butcher garners good reviews for its range of beers. Re-hydrate after a match in the lively theatre district of Milton Keynes, which includes Hogshead, Lloyds, the Rat & Parrot and Yates's. The Fountain Harvester on London Road is good for families, offers an extensive food menu and has a large beer garden.

Stopping over in Milton Keynes?

 Not much reason to stay here unless you don't fancy a long return trip somewhere. The Holiday Inn on Saxon Gate West is one idea for a cheap-ish bed (0870 400 9057). It's just a few minutes' walk from the Centre MK shopping precinct - one of the largest covered shopping areas in Europe. Jurys Inn is close to Milton Keynes train

station and the city's retail district (01908 843700). Rooms are from about £50.

If you do one thing in Milton Keynes...

Xscape offers extreme sports and leisure activities for all ages.

It contains the country's biggest indoor snow slopes, Europe's first purpose-built body flying tunnel, rock climbing walls, bowling and a multiplex cinema (*www.xscape.co.uk*).

Franchising - the end

Ahead of the 2005/06 season, the Football League introduced six new rules on club relocation, effectively preventing franchising from ever taking place again.

Don't mention

That MK Dons is franchise football and not what English football is about: even if you think it, it won't go down well with the locals. It's not their fault, and why shouldn't they embrace the move now it's happened.

Do mention

What you think of the new stadium: locals are proud of the new MK Stadium. However it came about, there is no doubt that it is one of the best arenas in the land. Pete Winkelman: he's as popular in MK as he was unpopular with Wimbledon supporters.

here Colours: White Songs: 'MK Army' appears to have taken off since the move up the M1 to Milton Keynes. Rivals: Luton Town.

Travel Information

CAR
Exit M1 at J14 following signs for Central Milton Keynes. At the first roundabout take the third exit (H6 Portway) go straight over the next nine (yes, nine) roundabouts. At the tenth roundabout take the first left onto the A5, and at the next get in the right hand lane and take the fourth turning (V6 Grafton Street) for the stadium. From the north exit the M1 at junction 15 and take the A508 for 14 miles. At the roundabout junction with the A5 turn left and at the third roundabout get in the right hand lane and take the fourth turning for V6 Grafton Street. There is limited street parking near the stadium; paid-for parking available at the stadium on a first-come first-served basis: it is recommended to pre-book by calling the club. Or park in town and catch a bus.

TRAIN
Bletchley is two miles away so best to opt for a taxi or bus: the bus station in the town centre or alight at Milton Keynes Central: opposite a bus station. The half-hour walk: exit left out of the station and walk down to the main road, turn left and at the roundabout bear left along Saxon Street; head over roundabout and a double-mini roundabout. As you reach the large roundabout on the A5, you will see the stadium to your left.

Morecambe

Seaside welcome

Morecambe clinched promotion to the Football League for the first time in their 87-year history with a 2-1 Conference Play-Off victory over Exeter City. Danny Carlton became a folk hero with his 20-yard piledriver late on to secure victory and propel the Shrimps into the big time.

Club officials spent the summer sprucing up Christie Park, the Shrimps' 6,400-capacity home. Nestled on the outskirts of this Lancashire seaside town, it's a tidy ground that won't be out of place in the fourth tier of English football. Gradual improvements over the past 10 years have given it a modern sheen but it still oozes character.

There's seating for 1,200 in the Main Stand and the only part of the ground which isn't covered is the magnificently-named Car Wash Terrace, which takes its name from the car wash behind it. The turnstiles at the side of the Umbro Stand are intended for away supporters. For those who don't fancy standing in this covered terrace, you're best buying a ticket for one of the 200 seats allocated to visitors in the Main Stand.

Plans are afoot to redevelop the Car Wash Terrace to increase seating capacity at the ground. To comply with league requirements, the club is also introducing a CCTV system around the ground, computerised turnstiles and extra toilet facilities.

Average attendances for 2006/07 were about 1,700 but club chiefs believe promotion will swell gates to 2,300 this season. The novelty factor of a trip to Morecambe should be enough to lift crowds at Christie Park. And there are some tasty derbies in store. Accrington Stanley, just 35 miles away, are sure to bring an army of boisterous fans - while Bury, Rochdale, Stockport County and Macclesfield Town will doubtless make their presence felt.

Eating out

A few years back Christie Park's pies were voted the best in English football by a footy mag - and they're still winning plaudits. The range of pies are inexpensive and available from the burger bar open to away fans at the Umbro Stand end. The pie, peas & gravy combo was selling for £1.50 in the ground last season, although this may not be available to travelling fans from the burger stall. Atkinsons Fish & Chip shop is behind the away end and there are a couple of other chippies nearby. The town is a 15 minute walk from the ground and there's a wide selection of cafés, sandwich shops and chippies scattered along the promenade. Crescent Coffee Lounge on Marine Road is a good place for a variety of foods. You'll find a number of restaurants down this stretch of sea-front road. Honey Tree Chinese Restaurant is recommended for its quality fare. It offers a range of cuisine styles including Cantonese, Pekingese and Szechuan. Pebbles Restaurant, located at the Crown Hotel on the prom, is recognised as one of the best places to eat. It serves quality classic à la carte and traditional meals with a modern twist. Pedder Street in the town centre contains quite a few eateries. If you're a pie-eater, there's only one place to head: Pott's Pies. Alfredo's in Skipton Street does a good steak.

Club Information Stadium: Christie Park, Lancaster Rd, Morecambe LA4 5TJ Capacity: 6,400 Tel: 01524 411797 Web: www.morecambefc.com Train: Morecambe Colours: Red and white Songs: Not a huge repertoire, with mostly

Mine's a pint

Previous years saw away fans mix with the Shrimps faithful in the stadium's JB's Bar when there was no crowd segregation. But it may not be accessible to visitors this season with rival supporters likely to be kept apart. In the Conference, home and away fans mingled happily in the welcoming York Hotel on Lancaster Road, less than 10 minutes' walk to the ground. The pub has Sky TV and serves food on matchday. If the York Hotel is out of bounds, your best option may be to head down Pedder Street or Queen Street, although there's nothing fancy down here. The Eric Bartholomew, a Wetherspoons pub on Euston Road named after the legendary local funnyman's real name - is good for cheap food and beer if nothing else.

Stopping over in Morecambe?

Due to its far-flung location and close proximity to the Lake District and Yorkshire Dales, it's worth considering a weekend stay. Broadway Hotel on the East Promenade does a decent B&B deal (01524 410777). Lothersdale Hotel on the Central Promenade, also gets the thumbs up from locals for its service and comfort. Rooms are from about £50 (01524 416404). All local attractions are within easy reach and by taxi it's only two minutes from the station. York Hotel on Lancaster Road also offers £35 B&B "for weary away travellers" (01524 425353). The Crown Hotel on Marine Road Central is another good value alternative (01524 831841). The hotel is directly in front of the Eric Morecambe statue.

If you do one thing in Morecambe...

Wander down the prom - enjoy the fantastic views across Morecambe Bay to the Lake District and get your picture taken with the statue of the town's most famous son, Eric Morecambe. If you're driving and have time, go and explore the Lakes just 25 miles away.

Shrimps net honours

The 1960s and early 70s were Morecambe's golden era. This period saw the club win a hatful of non-league trophies, appear in the FA Cup third round and revel in an FA Trophy success at Wembley in 1974.

Don't mention

Ipswich Town: twice they have faced Morecambe in the FA Cup in recent years, and twice have ended glorious cup runs.

Do mention

Winning the FA Trophy at Wembley in 1974: a great day in the club's history. Promotion from the Conference: after finishing as runners-up in 2003 (in the days of one up, one down), Morecambe finally clinched their place in the Football League via the play-offs in 2007.

Travel Information

CAR
Exit the M6 at junction 34 onto the A683 towards Lancaster, then take the A589 to Morecambe. At the third roundabout take the second exit into Lancaster Road. The main car park is for pass holders only, but the small car park behind the Umbro Stand is free. Otherwise you should easily find street parking.

TRAIN
Morecambe Station is a ten-minute walk to and from the ground. Come out of the station and turn right down Central Drive and then bear right into Euston Road, which leads straight into Lancaster Road. Morecambe is on a branch line and served by trains from Lancaster.

generic favourites being reworked to pay tribute to the Morecambe – and Lancashire, they're proud to come from the county. Rivals: Lancaster and Southport.

Newcastle United

Room at the top

The Magpies are pushing ahead with a ground expansion under a £300 million three-phase development of St James' Park. The plans, which will take capacity from 52,387 to 60,000, include creation of a major conference centre, hotels and luxury apartments.

Dubbed the Number 1 St James' Park project, it will be funded completely independently of the football club's revenues. Phase One is the development of a 140-bedroom hotel complex on the site of the old Magpie Supporters' Club. Another hotel with so-called "superior apartments" is planned for the rear of the Leazes End.

If the plans gain approval, capacity will be increased at the Gallowgate End as Newcastle bid to remain one of the largest grounds in the UK. Club chiefs insist a 60,000-seater is the minimum target for a club backed by "the most loyal and passionate supporters in the game".

As it stands, the Toon's current stadium ain't half bad. Rebuilt with improved facilities over the past decade, it makes an impressive architectural statement on the Newcastle skyline.

Away fans are allocated 3,000 seats in the north-west top tier of the Sir John Hall Stand, the one responsible for the cacophony of noise at the ground. It's a fair old trudge to the top - 14 flights of stairs - and the views aren't great. It's a long way from the pitch. Not for those who have a fear of heights, then. Bring your high-powered binoculars if you want some close-ups of the action.

The atmosphere in Level 7, the height at which away fans sit, can't be faulted. When this stand fills up, there's nothing like the deafening roar of the Toon Army to enhance a matchday experience. Naturally, local derbies get a bit tasty but, for other supporters, a bit of sarky Geordie banter is the order of the day.

Eating out

Concourse catering offers the usual matchday food, including some tasty pies, and queues are kept to a minimum. Not far from St James' Park you'll find the Stowell Street area, better known as Chinatown. Charlies on Gallowgate gets top marks for its buffet food, all-you-can-eat for about £6. Wok This Way is another top tip. In the city centre, numerous pavement café bars, fast food joints and pie shops are within easy reach of the stadium. Recommended is Munchies takeaway chain. Newcastle's own shopping mall in Eldon Square and the Metro Centre shopping precinct across the Tyne in Gateshead are good places to find cheap snacks and cafés. Fish & chip afficionados in the north-east say Seashells at Monkseaton, Whitley Bay, is one of the best. You won't find better haddock at Kristians chippy, North Shields Quay, according to locals - good for an eat-in meal. Rupali in Bigg Market is one of the best Indians.

Mine's a pint

Refreshment areas at St James' Park serve alcohol in branded plastic glasses. Around the ground and in the city, away fans should hide their colours.

Between St James' Park and the station (about half a mile walk away), you'll find the Bigg market area, which is full

Club Information Stadium: St. James' Park, Newcastle-upon-Tyne NE1 4ST Capacity: 52,387 (all seated) Tel: 0191 2018400 Web: www.nufc.co.uk Train: Newcastle Colours: Black and white Songs: Famed for their 'Blaydon Races' chant

of pubs. For more refined drinking dens visit the more traditional Haymarket area or Quayside part of town, to the south of the market.

Hostelries near the station on Neville Street are most popular for visiting fans. Look out for The Lounge and O'Neills. But there are better options elsewhere. The traditional Adelphi, Shakespeare Street, is great for a pre-match beer.

As for real ale pubs, The Crown Posada on The Side is a must-visit on the way to the Quayside from the station or Wetherspoons. This traditional Victorian pub has an abundance of character and fantastic range of ales, some from local micros. The Newcastle Arms on St Andrews Street is said to be one of the friendliest pubs and provides an excellent choice of real ales. One option is the roomy Bridge Hotel on Castle Square, which has a beer garden.

Topless bars such as Idols and Vaults on the Bigg market attract rowdy pre-match crowds and offer cheap pints.

Stopping over in Newcastle?

 The Jesmond Hotel on Osborne Road, one of the best areas to drink and eat on Saturday nights, is the perfect spot to stop over. The hotel is at the quieter end of the road (0191 281 5377). St. James' Park is a 20-minute walk from here and B&B starts at £42.50. Osborne Road is home to plenty more hotels, although some are a bit pricey.

Travelodge at Gateshead is decent, cheap and only a few minutes in a taxi to everything you need (0870 1911783).

If you do one thing in Newcastle...

The top tourist attractions in this vibrant city are in Gateshead. Go to a concert at the architectural wonder that is The Sage Gateshead or explore the Baltic Centre for Contemporary Art, with a dynamic, diverse and international programme of art. Don't forget the Angel of the North; it's worth a look and doesn't take long. For more information turn to the city guide.

Scoring sensation

Alan Shearer scored 131 of his 206 total tally for Newcastle at St James' Park - 65 at the Leazes End, 66 in front of the Gallowgate.

Don't mention

Alex Ferguson: as Sir Alex vied with Kevin Keegan's Entertainers for the Premiership title in 1995/96 the Toon Army weren't impressed by his mind games with their beloved King Kev. It was match-point Fergie, after an explosive rant from the former England captain on live TV after a 1-0 win over Leeds.

Do mention

Alan Shearer, Jackie Milburn, Hughie Gallacher: the Toon Army loves (if not needs) a goalscorer and you don't get much better than these three.

Travel Information

CAR
At the end of the A1(M) continue on the A1 and take the A184 and A189 to Newcastle. Take the Redheugh Bridge over the River Tyne and straight up the dual carriageway to the ground. St James' Park is located right in the middle of the city; hence you'll find a number of pay and display car parks in walking distance from the stadium.

TRAIN
Newcastle Central Railway Station is about ten minutes' walk through the city centre. Come out of the station and head right onto Grainger Street and turn left onto Newgate Street which will lead you to the Gallowgate roundabout.

and the 'Toon, Toon, Black And White Army' cry. Rivals: Sunderland and to a lesser extent Middlesbrough.

Northampton Town

What a load of Cobblers

Northampton ply their trade at Sixfields Stadium - a 7,653 capacity ground that sits adjacent to a community athletics facility. Proposals to redevelop the site have gone before the local borough council but political wrangles and red tape have held up progress. The club wants to increase capacity to around 15,000 and add executive boxes and conference facilities.

The Cobblers shared the County Ground with Northamptonshire County Cricket Club for 97 years before moving to Sixfields in 1994. Designed as a multi-purpose stadium, the venue has since hosted American football games and rugby league matches among other events.

Car boot sales, for instance, are a regular feature on the calendar at Sixfields. Some wags have said they're a cheaper and more entertaining way to pass 90 minutes than watching the football, although the derbies against Peterborough United are definitely worth the ticket price. Check out the club's websites for future car-booters. You might go home with a bargain. Or you might go home with a load of old tat.

Like any out-of-town stadium-leisure development Sixfields is a nice enough place to come for visiting supporters. The South Stand can hold up to 900 away supporters, with an additional 300 seats available in the Alwyn Hargrave Stand if required.

A large hill overlooks the ground, offering oblique views of the action. Some enterprising fellows watch the game for nothing from this vantage point but they aren't able to see the entire pitch. Nice for a picnic, mind – or if you're short of a few quid.

Eating out

Snack at the ground on pies or pasties or grab a cheap bite from the burger van at the main entrance to the stadium. Alternatively, fill your face at the fast food joints in and around the leisure complex housing the stadium. These include McDonald's and Burger King, TGI Friday's, Old Orleans and Bella Italia.

There's also a Frankie & Benny's, the 1950s-style New York Italian diner, and Buddies USA. You can get breakfast, lunch and evening meals at Buddies, a place where they encourage you to "order in diner speak, watch the large-scale train set trundle around, listen to great music and eat great food".

If this puts you off, and well it might, try the other healthy eating outlets and restaurants on site. En route to the ground is an Oliver Adams bakery and also Rainbow Fish & Chips. Also on Weedon Road is the Indian Brasserie, a perfect pit stop for a pre- or post-match curry.

Mine's a pint

The away supporters pub is the Sixfields Tavern next to the ground, although you might have to cover up your jerseys. Old Orleans sells a decent selection of ales and is family-friendly but staff may cold shoulder visiting supporters if you're not on your best behaviour. The Megabowl, the white building

Club Information Stadium: Sixfields Stadium, Northampton NN5 5QA Capacity: 7,653 (all seated) Tel: 0870 8221997 Web: www.ntfc.co.uk Train: Northampton Colours: Claret and white Songs: 'The Fields Are Green' (aka 'The Nene Boat Song'), which starts: "The

at the top of Sixfields, is good for families and has bowling and pool tables. TGI Friday's opposite the main stand serves what's expected from the chain pub/restaurant and has become a favourite haunt for away fans.

Avoid Chevys Music Bar at the Sixfields complex - for home supporters only. A couple of good locals near Northampton Saints rugby ground are The Rover and The Foundry. Thomas A Beckett is a good Irish boozer on St James Road. King Billy on Commercial Street is a bit of a biker's pub but it has a friendly atmosphere, hosts live music and serves a decent range of drinks. For late-night partying, Fever nightclub on Horseshoe Street is the place to be and be seen.

Stopping over in Northampton?

 An unlikely overnight destination due to its central location, but if you reconsider there are conveniently-placed hotels for a quick getaway. Express by Holiday Inn is located on Cheaney Drive, off Junction 15 of the M1 (01604 432800). Park Inn is situated in the heart of the town centre on Silver Street (01604 739988). Travelodge is just off Weedon Road on Upton Way (0870 085 0950).You'll get cheap room rates at all three.

If you do one thing in Northampton...

Apart from the football and rugby in Northampton, there's precious little else for footy fans to feast their eyes on. Unless, that is, you want to be touched by the award-winning exhibition, Diana: A Celebration at nearby Althorp, the country estate where the Princess of Wales is buried.

Santa Pod, the home of drag racing, at Podington, Wellingborough, may be more your scene. A major venue for high speed cars and bikes, it holds over 50 events during the race season Jan-Nov, ranging from the European Drag Racing Championships to 'bring your own' public race days. *www.santapod.co.uk*

Growing out of Northampton

Radio 1 DJ Jo Whiley and writer and broadcaster Andrew Collins were both born in Northampton.

Collins charted his formative years in the town in his memoir 'Where Did It All Go Right?'. He even has a website dedicated to the themes of the book - *www.wherediditallgoright.com*

Don't mention

Terry Fenwick: lasted just seven weeks in the Cobblers' managerial hot-seat, before being sacked in February 2003.

Do mention

Walter Tull: he was one of the first black players to appear for an English team. He joined the club in 1910 and one of the roads near the stadium is named in his honour.

Travel Information

CAR
If you're coming from the south exit the M1 at Junction 15A and take the A43 towards Northampton and you will come to the ground on your right. And coming from the north is just as easy. Leave the M1 at junction 16 onto the A45 to Northampton and the ground will appear on your right. You can park at the ground for around two pounds. There is also a council-owned car park behind the away stand which costs around three quid. Be careful if you're tempted to park in one of the restaurant or leisure complex car parks as parking restrictions may result in your car being clamped.

TRAIN
Northampton is well connected, but it's a lengthy stroll of over two miles to the ground, so consider a taxi or number 1, 1A or 40 bus from the stop at the south end of the station, which won't take you right to the stadium, but within five minutes' walk. If you fancy the walk: turn right from the station and follow the main road, you'll eventually see the stadium appear on the horizon.

fields are green the skies are blue, the river Nene goes winding through". Rivals: Peterborough United, Rushden & Diamonds and MK Dons are slowly working their way on to the radar.

Norwich City

Let's be 'aving you

Upgrades to Carrow Road in the noughties have turned it into one of the finest mid-size stadia around. The venue's facelift was complete following the building of the £8 million Jarrold Stand.

The club's £15m securitisation deal re-financed the existing debt and provided funding for the 8,182-seat Jarrold Stand. It was the first ever such deal to be agreed with an English football club outside the Premiership.

The refinancing package partly helped the club to buy three strikers in December 2003, assisting their assault on the then First Division title. The Canaries won eight of their last nine games to seal a return to the Premiership after a nine-year absence. But they were relegated the following season.

Delia Smith, the elegantly-bouffanted club director and best-selling cookery author, displayed her feisty side in a legendary on-field outburst over the PA in 2005. Her drunken half-time rant in a Premiership game against Manchester City came after the Canaries had thrown away a two-goal cushion. TV cameras caught her bawling: "We need a 12th man here. Where are you? Where are you? Let's be 'avin you. C'mon!" The You Tube clip is priceless.

In January 2007, majority shareholders Delia Smith and her husband Michael Wynn-Jones announced that they were open to selling their shares. But they say any prospective buyer would have to invest heavily in the squad.

With its modern fan amenities, Carrow Road is an enjoyable day out. Visitors are allocated about 3,000 seats in the Jarrold Stand. Another seating tier on the City Stand could raise the 26,034 capacity to around 30,000 in future. But this will happen only if the Canaries secure a Premiership berth and go on to consolidate their position in the top flight.

Eating out

Delia Smith has overhauled the catering since her arrival at the club. At the food kiosks, slices of pizza, pasties and pies with various fillings are available, among other matchday staples – and they are tasty. You can pick up some cheap kebabs, chips and Domino's pizza near the railway station. Or there's a Morrisons across the road from the stadium. Walk through the Riverside shopping complex, five minutes from the ground, and you'll find a number of cafés, American-style tucker at Frankie & Benny's, Nando's Chicken Restaurant, Old Orleans and Pizza Hut. The city centre is probably the best place to head for finer dining.

Mine's a pint

The Compleat Angler right in front of the railway station is the away fans' choice. It's plenty big enough, there's a tasty selection of real ales and food. Outside seating by the river provides a pleasant spot for warm weather drinking. KFC is a few yards down the road if you're after a quick bite on the way to the match. Most pubs between here and Carrow Road are away-friendly. In the Riverside centre, both Lloyds No1 Bar, a Wetherspoons outlet, and

Club Information Stadium: Carrow Rd, Norwich NR1 1JE Cap: 26,034 Tel: 01603 760760 Web: www.canaries.co.uk Train: Norwich Colours: Yellow & green Songs: 'On The Ball City' is believed to be the oldest football chant in the world. It goes: *"Kick it off, throw it*

Squares next door are popular with both groups of fans. Squares shows Sky Sports on large and small screens and sells a nice pint of ale - but you might have a wait to be served. Old Orleans is less crowded, with a better food menu and best for families.

Stay away from these chain bars at night unless you want to socialise with youngsters getting off their rockers. Instead, head for city centre pubs and bars for the craic. The Trafford Arms on Grove Road is recommended. Located on the edge of town, it has 10 hand-pumps for cask beers and good value food. The Rose on Queens Road is football-friendly with top ales and an eclectic evening food menu.

Stopping over in Norwich?

 Opened in spring 2007, the Holiday Inn at Carrow Road is a good base for the footy and town centre attractions (0870 890 1000).

Travelodge on Queens Road is basic and cheap, though you'll have to use the adjacent St Stephens NCP car park (0870 191 1797).

For more luxurious accommodation at higher rates, try Marriott Sprowston Manor Hotel (with golf course) on Wroxham Road (01603 410871).

If you do one thing in Norwich...

Good for cheap knick-knacks is Norwich's open-air market which is apparently the biggest in Europe.

The city's medieval past is evident in its ancient buildings but Norwich is also a major hub of arts and culture excellence.

The Sainsbury Centre, designed by Norman Foster, features a gallery and museum exhibiting international artists. It also hosts national shows.

European glory

Norwich followed up their third place in 1992/93, the inaugural season of the English Premier League, with a famous victory over Bayern Munich in the UEFA Cup the year after. That Jeremy Goss volley sealed a shock 2-1 victory.

Don't mention

Robert Chase: very unpopular former chairman, whose 'sell, sell, sell' policy was seen by fans as the reason Norwich went from being a top three team to a second tier team in the 1990s.

Do mention

Mike Walker: silver-haired manager who guided the Canaries to third in the Premier League and into the UEFA Cup, where they were unlucky to be knocked out by Inter Milan.

Travel Information

CAR
The likelihood is you'll be heading in on either the A11, A47 or possibly the A140. Whichever route you take, pick up the A47 (southern bypass) heading east and then the A146 into the city centre. At the first set of traffic lights turn right and then take a left at the roundabout and right at the next lights into King Street. Bear right and once you cross the river you'll see the ground is on your right. There is limited street parking, but a good place to park is Norfolk County Hall, which is well signposted on the left of the A146. It costs around three quid and can hold up to two thousand cars – although it can take a while to exit if you're late arriving.

TRAIN
It's a short walk to the ground from Norwich train station. Turn left and head for the retail park and you will see the ground behind that.

in, have a little scrimmage; Keep it low, splendid rush, bravo, win or die; On the ball, City, never mind the danger; Steady on, now's your chance; Hurrah! we've scored a goal." Rivals: Ipswich Town.

Nottingham Forest

Football in the clouds anyone?

Forest have experienced many ups and downs at the City Ground over the years. Most of the highs were under the stewardship of the mighty Brian Clough (1975-1993), the man who once said: "I wouldn't say I was the best manager in the business, but I was in the top one."

Since Ole Big Ead's reign, the number of managers who have taken the helm at Forest has run into double figures, a sign of the club's miserable fortunes in recent years.

These days the European Cups of 1979 and 1980 are but a distant memory as the club battles to regain its former glories. Forest have the ignominious honour of being the only team to have won the European Cup and then be relegated to the third tier of domestic football.

With a 30,602 capacity, Forest's stadium - their home since 1898 - is one of the largest outside of the Premiership.

The lower tier of the Bridgford Stand can accommodate around 4,750 away supporters. Access to the visitors' turnstiles is through The Brian Clough Stand car park via Scarrington Road off Lady Bay Bridge.

Things have changed dramatically at Forest – but there are still bold reminders of Forest's glorious past. Fans still yearn for a return of the days of that Clough brand of attractive passing football. He memorably poured scorn on purveyors of the long ball game: "If God had intended for us to play football in the clouds he wouldn't have put grass on the ground".

Eating out

There are concourse snack and beer bars underneath the Bridgford Stand and burger vans outside the ground. A parade of shops on Radcliffe Road next to the ground includes McDonald's, Domino's pizza, a chippy and kebab outlet – and there are the locally-renowned roast pork cobs to be found too. Pappas, a Greek takeaway is also on this stretch of road. You can get decent food at The Larwood & Voce, the 'unofficial' pub for away fans a few hundred yards from the Bridgford Stand and adjoining Trent Bridge cricket ground.

The Trent Bridge Inn does not let away supporters in. Take a 10-minute walk to West Bridgford and you'll find a Pizza Express, along with various Chinese and Indian restaurants. The legendary Hooters is 400 metres from the train station (15-minute walk to the ground) and is incredibly popular with away fans. They don't care that the food and drink is a wee bit expensive when they're being served by semi-naked women.

Mine's a pint

Check out the Larwood & Voce Tavern on Fox Road for the atmosphere on matchdays. The South Bank Bar is a stone's throw from the City Ground and another popular choice. It sells a wide range of beers and lagers and also does some food. Best to

Club Information Stadium: City Ground, Nottingham NG2 5FJ Capacity: 30,602 (all seated) Tel: 0115 9824444 Web: www.nottinghamforest.co.uk Train: Nottingham Colours: Red & White Songs: 'You've Lost That Lovin' Feelin' sung by

avoid The Lady Bay Inn on Trent Boulevard as it's a haven for Forest fans. The Stratford Haven on Stratford Road, West Bridgford, is said to be one of the best pubs in the area, known for its great range of real ales. Casa bar has a riverside location on Arkwright Street. It welcomes families, features Sky Sports and has seating outside. The Pitcher and Piano, housed in a deconsecrated church at High Pavement, does good food and is a lively party place in the evenings. For late-night, value-for-money cocktail action, try Cucumara, found at Hurts Yard off Market Square.

Stopping over in Nottingham?

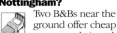 Two B&Bs near the ground offer cheap accommodation: the Riverside Guest House, 42 Holme Road, West Bridgford (0115 982 0915); and Castle Hotel, 82 Radcliffe Road, West Bridgford (0115 945 5784). Stay in the centre if you plan to explore the city's sights or nightlife. If you want something reasonably cheap, how about The Premier Travel Inn on London Road near the BBC studio and train station (0870 990 6574). The 166-room Britannia Nottingham Hotel on St. James Street is an inexpensive alternative - with Nottingham Castle, Trent Bridge Cricket Ground and the Victoria Shopping Centre right on your doorstep (0115 988 4000). The design-led, four-star deluxe Park Plaza

Nottingham on Maid Marian Way is a bit special and more expensive (0115 947 7200).

If you do one thing in Nottingham...

There's plenty to do, including City of Caves, Green's Windmill & Science Centre, Nottingham Castle and the Tales of Robin Hood museum. The city is also flanked by Sherwood Forest and the Peak District. For more info, turn to our Nottingham city guide.

Too close for comfort

The City Ground is only a few hundred yards from Notts County's, making the grounds the closest in English football. Little-known Brian Clough trivia: Ole Big Ead was a prolific marksman before his playing career was cut short by a knee injury. He scored 251 goals in 274 league games for his home town club Middlesbrough and Sunderland.

Don't mention

David Platt: a disastrous spell in charge led to financial strife. Gary Megson: was in charge of Forest as they were relegated from the Championship in 2004 and never really looked like turning things around in League One.

Do mention

Brian Clough: he led the club to the Championship and two European Cup successes in 1979 and 1980 – and also fathered Nigel, one of the club's finest players.

Travel Information

CAR

From the north: Exit the M1 at junction 26 and take the A610 towards Nottingham. Negotiate your way through the town centre and eventually pick up the A60. Just after crossing over the River Trent you will see the ground on your left.

From the south: Exit the M1 at junction 24 and take the A453 towards Nottingham. Then take the A52 East towards Grantham and then onto the A6011 into Nottingham and you will see the ground on your left. There is parking available at the ground, otherwise it is a choice between street parking and the council car park, which charges around three quid, on the Victoria Embankment on the ground side of the river.

TRAIN

Nottingham Station is about a twenty-minute walk. Turn left out of the station's main entrance and then left again. Once you reach the dual carriageway (London Road) turn right towards the ground – it's just over Trent Bridge.

Tom Cruise in the film Top Gun is popular with Forest followers as are any anti-Derby or pro-Forest songs. Rivals: Derby County and Leicester City.

Notts County

The oldest club in the world

Yes, that's Notts County's proud boast. Formed in 1862, the club also takes great pride in its fan amenities at Meadow Lane. The ground received a major overhaul in the 1990s, offering benefits for all who visit the 20,300-capacity, all-seater venue. It's one of the better stadia in the lower divisions and the stands are right on top of the action, allowing great vantage points for all away fans who are housed in the massive Kop End behind one of the goals.

This section of the ground is split into two tiers and holds 5,475 supporters. Views from the back of the stand are among the best in the ground, though the upper tier is only open to clubs who bring a fairly large following.

Feel yourself unlucky if the wind carries the immortal words of the Magpies' legendary chant to your lugholes. Called the 'The Wheelbarrow Song', it's beauty lies in its sheer simplicity. 'I had a wheelbarrow, the wheel fell off', repeated ad nauseum, will lighten the mood if your team is having a shocker. Possibly.

It originated at an away match against Shrewsbury Town in 1990 when disenchanted Notts County fans decided to take the mickey out of the local fans' accents, twisting the Shrews ditty to come up with their surreal response. The chant took off and became a lucky omen as the Magpies made it to Wembley and went on to win the Division Three Play-Off final that year.

Another favourite chant is 'Always shit on the red side of the Trent', to the tune of Monty Python's 'Always look on the bright side of life'.

Eating out

The Kop Stand provides two catering bars for away supporters and you'll also get beer here. But if there are many visiting fans, serving times can be slower than elsewhere in the stadium. Or venture to the comfy Meadow Club, located at the rear of the Family Stand, where bar snacks, hot food and beer are on the menu. Open to home and away fans, it also has a big screen and a number of televisions showing Sky Sports. The Jimmy Sirrel Stand has two tea-bars, with pre-match alcohol served at one of them. In addition, there are eight catering outlets around the ground vending a variety of snacks and refreshments. Away fans with a few quid to blow can shell out for a VIP package, including parking space, a pre-match three-course carvery meal, programme and padded seating. The only drawback is that you'll be away from the rest of the travelling fans. Hooters on London Road - just two minutes' walk from the away end - serves up a decent dish. Food's not bad either!

Mine's a pint

At the ground, alcoholic beverages are on sale in a number of areas but they must be consumed in the concourse/snack bar areas. Nottingham is littered with fabulous drinking dens - you can't go far wrong in this

Club Information Stadium: Meadow Lane, Nottingham NG2 3HJ Capacity: 20,300 (all seated) Tel: 0115 9529000 Train: Nottingham Colours: Black and white Songs: The 'Wheel Barrow' song goes: "I had a wheelbarrow, the wheel fell off", while County fans will also sing "It's just like watching Juve" in reference to the fact that the Italian

hospitable city. Hooters is a popular choice with away fans, while The Globe on London Road is also football-friendly. South Bank Bar on Bridgford Road is one of the city's premier sports bars, and close to the ground. As is Casa, which has a riverside location on Arkwright Street. It welcomes families, features Sky Sports and has seating outside. The Pitcher & Piano, housed in a deconsecrated church at High Pavement, does good food and is a lively party place in the evenings. For some late-night, value-for-money cocktail action, try Cucumara, found at Hurts Yard off Market Square.

Stopping over in Nottingham?

Stay in the centre if you plan to explore the city's sights or nightlife. If you want something reasonably cheap, how about The Premier Travel Inn on London Road near the BBC studio and train station (0870 990 6574) or The Best Western Westminster Hotel on Mansfield Road (0115 955 5000). The 166-room Britannia Nottingham Hotel on St. James Street is an inexpensive alternative - with Nottingham Castle, Trent Bridge Cricket Ground and the Victoria Shopping Centre right on your doorstep (0115 988 4000). Another is the Strathdon Hotel on Derby Road (0115 941 8501), which is close to the Rock City nightclub and bus station.

If you do one thing in Nottingham...

There's plenty to keep you entertained. Highlights include City of Caves, Green's Windmill & Science Centre, Nottingham Castle and the Tales of Robin Hood museum. The city is also flanked by Sherwood Forest and the Peak District. For more information, see our Nottingham city guide.

Strange moniker

Notts County sealed a sponsorship deal with Aaron Scargill Estate Agents in 2002, which led to the stadium getting the rather clumsy tag The Aaron Scargill Stadium. Luckily, the local company went bust before the season started and the ground reverted to its original name.

Don't mention

Colin Murphy: most fans blame him for the club's relegation to the bottom division in 1996/97. That the City Ground and Meadow Lane are the two closest grounds in England: people will think you're an anorak!

Do mention

Neil Warnock: led the club into the top division, against all the odds, in 1991. They beat Brighton 3-1 in the play-off final and also enjoyed an FA Cup quarter-final against Spurs that season. Sam Allardyce: dragged the club out of the doldrums in 1997/98 as Division Three Champions, before Bolton spotted he was a very talented boss.

Travel Information

CAR
From the north: Exit the M1 at junction 26 and take the A610 towards Nottingham. Negotiate your way through the town centre and eventually pick up the A60. Just before the River Trent you will see Meadow Lane on your left.
From the south: Exit the M1 at junction 24 and take the A453 towards Nottingham. Then take the A52 East towards Grantham and then onto the A6011 into Nottingham; as you cross Trent Bridge turn left into Meadow Lane for the ground.
There is plenty of street parking as well as a club-run car park and an independent option at the cattle market next to the away end – both are under three pounds.

TRAIN
Nottingham Station is about a twenty-minute walk. Turn left out of the station's main entrance and then left again. Once you reach the dual carriageway (London Road) turn right. Meadow Lane is just before Trent Bridge.

giants' first kit was given to them by Notts County; hence the same strip. Rivals: Forest, but they're nice folk in Nottingham and it's more of a brotherly rivalry, particularly from the Forest end. Mansfield, Chesterfield and Derby are also unpopular.

Oldham Athletic

Hoot, hoot hooray!

Work on a multi-million pound revamp of Boundary Park was due to get underway this summer to provide the Latics with a 16,000-seat stadium. The ambitious scheme to rebuild three of the stands, incorporating office space and conferencing facilities, hinged on provision of a residential development to fund the project. A three-star 80-room hotel is also proposed.

But the Rochdale Road End for away fans will remain intact. The all-seater covered stand is a comfortable spot to watch your side do battle against the Lancashire club. Bring your woollies in the winter months as the 13,624-capacity Boundary Park is known as the coldest league ground in the country. It's also the second highest behind the Hawthorns. With the surrounding area being quite open, be prepared to get battered by the wind.

Oldham enjoys many rivalries in the Greater Manchester area - derbies against Manchester City, Bolton Wanderers, Blackburn Rovers, Rochdale or Bury are special affairs.

At any game, watch out for club mascot Chaddy the Owl making a fool of himself pitchside. A fixture at Boundary Park since the early 1990s, Chaddy is famous for his 100-yard run-ups to fluff penalties during the pre-match entertainment.

In the mascot world, Chaddy was once among the fittest around, notable for his lightning turn of pace. Portrayed by someone going by the name of Kevin from 1999 to 2004, Chaddy scooped the Mascot Grand National in 2002 and 2003. Allegedly sabotaged in the following year's race, he missed out on the hat-trick. These days someone slower, by the name of Wayne inhabits the mascot costume. However, you might get a good imitation of a Tawny Owl's plaintive hooting... if you ask nicely.

Eating out

Burgers and hotdogs are some of the football staples sold at the ground along with a variety of snacks and drinks. Boundary Park is tucked away in a residential area so you don't have to go far to get some tucker. The retail park off the A627 has a Pizza Hut, McDonald's, Burger King and KFC.

Two minutes from the stadium on Rochdale Road you'll find the Chinese Chippy, while there's a couple of sandwich bars in close proximity. Tesco - on Featherstall Road - is the nearest local supermarket, a good snack stop if you're driving. The town centre is about two miles away and the biggest concentration of takeaways and restaurants for pre- or post-match appetites is on Oldham Road and Yorkshire Street. Some of the pubs mentioned below dish up good food.

Mine's a pint

Slake your thirst with a beverage from the licensed bar in the Rochdale Road End. Due to the stadium's location, there's not much choice of boozers around Boundary Park. The Blue Bell Inn on Broadway is within walking distance and has a wide-ranging food menu and spacious beer garden for summer drinking. The Old Grey Mare on Oldham Road is a haven for

Club Information Stadium: Boundary Park, Sheepfoot Lane, Oldham OL1 2PA
Capacity: 13,624 (all seated) Tel: 0871 226 2235 Web: www.oldhamathletic.co.uk
Train: Oldham Werneth Colours: Blue Songs: Two Chelsea originals are popular:

Latics' fans but away fans are welcome. It also serves food. As does The White Hart just down the road. Alternatively, wash down a plate of decent pub grub with a pint at The Clayton Green Brewer's Fayre, situated next to the Premier Travel Inn at Westwood Retail Park, Chadderton Way.

For the post-match analysis into the night, conduct a pub crawl along Yorkshire Street. Baileys hosts a DJ at weekends and is open into the small hours. The Last Orders boasts cheap drinks and friendly bar staff. The Walkabout is described as a bit rough and The Litten Tree characterless and overpriced. Number Fifteen has a lot more charm.

Give The Queens Arms a wide berth. You'll get nothing but grief from home fans, if you're allowed in at all.

Stopping over in Oldham?

 With Manchester seven miles away there's no particular reason to stay in Oldham, unless you plan on exploring the local nightlife.

The Premier Travel Inn on Chadderton Way offers rooms from £48 at weekends (08701 977203). Menzies Avant, a couple of miles from the ground, is the luxury option. The four-star hotel east of Manchester includes a gym, brasserie and cocktail bar.

If you do one thing in Oldham...

Seek out a bargain at the town's Tommyfield Market before enjoying a bite and a beer prior to kick-off. If you like the great outdoors, explore the Saddleworth landscape. For more information on Manchester's many attractions, see the city guide.

Plastic disaster

Oldham installed an artificial pitch in the 1980s but, like the plastic surfaces at QPR, Luton Town and Preston, it gained a bad reputation and was eventually replaced with natural turf. Players hated the synthetic pitch because the ball bounced all over the place and it made them look rubbish. They also got carpet burns and sand in their pants. Still, it stopped them diving.

Don't mention

Chris Moore: chairman of the club between 2001 and 2003, he promised lots and delivered little, eventually leaving the club in a financial mess.

Do mention

Joe Royle: legendary manager of the club, who took them to the top flight and kept there by masterminding one of the greatest escapes of all times in 1992/93 with three victories in their last three matches. Paul Scholes: the former England midfielder is a mad-keen Oldham fan.

Travel Information

CAR
Take the M62 onto the A627(M) towards Oldham, exiting towards Royton on the A663. Take an immediate right into Hilbre Avenue which leads to the massive car park, behind the ground, where you can park for a couple of quid.

TRAIN
Oldham Mumps and Mill Hills are both long walks, so get a train from Manchester Victoria to Oldham Werneth. If you arrive at Manchester Piccadilly you can catch the Metrolink to Victoria station (included in your fare if you have a ticket to Oldham). Oldham Werneth Station is about fifteen minutes' walk to the ground. Exit right out of the station along Featherstall Road South and over the mini-roundabout. At the large roundabout you need to turn left onto Chadderton Way, but use the underpass to get onto the right side of the road as you will need to turn right into Boundary Park Road. Then turn right up Sheepfoot Lane for the ground.

'Keep The Blue Flag Flying' and 'Zigga Zagga'. Rivals: Stockport County, Bolton Wanderers, Huddersfield Town, Leeds United and both Manchester clubs.

Peterborough United

Who are you calling Posh?

Peterborough United's London Road stadium is conveniently located in the city centre but Posh fans are relishing a move to more modern facilities.

Posh chairman Darragh MacAnthony is pressing ahead with proposals to build a new ground away from London Road within five years. The multi-millionaire Irishman dreams of seeing his team playing in the Premiership at a swanky new out-of-town replacement for the current 15,314-capacity venue.

For the time being, London Road provides a decent roost for travelling fans - there's plenty of parking and a huge away end. The away supporters' allocation is 850 seats in 'A' block of the Main Stand and 3,475 in the Moyes End Terrace – from where a terrific noise can be generated if enough like-minded folk have made the journey to the Fens with you.

The stadium, where football has been played for over a century, is only about three-quarters of mile from the train station - a 10-minute walk.

The ground is rarely bursting at the seams though - in fact it's often only one-third full - so it can be lacking in atmosphere. Remedy the situation by throwing in a few Northampton Town gags (Posh's arch rivals) and you'll liven up proceedings!

When the club, formed in 1934, gained admittance to the Football League in 1960, attendances were regularly over the 20,000 mark. To date, the record attendance is 30,096 for the team's FA Cup fifth round encounter with Swansea City in 1965.

Eating out

At the ground, the mobile burger stall on the corner of the car park sells food before and after the game. London Road has some fast-food shops, with Papa Luigi Dial a Pizza a popular choice. Grab a pizza slice and fries for around £2.50 on matchdays. Take away pizzas are half price. KFC and Turkish Delight are on the same street. There's a nice chippy near The Office on Oundle Road. The Posh Independent Supporters' Association, based at Ebeneezer's on Grove Street, does a mean beef roll and selection of fresh sandwiches. Away supporters are greeted with open arms. With a large screen for live games, it's very close to London Road. The Drapers Arms, a Wetherspoons pub on Cowgate near the bus station, is OK for food and close to the stadium. Recommended for a sit-down Thai meal is real ale pub The Brewery Tap on Westgate. Charter's Bar & Restaurant, a tastefully converted Dutch barge on the river at Town Bridge includes a 100-seater oriental restaurant called 'East' on the upper deck. Gladstone Street's Marisquiera does tasty Portuguese food and drink.

Mine's a pint

Posh Venue Pub at the ground is open to all, selling food along with hot and cold drinks. It also shows football on big screens. Nearby pubs - many of

---

Club Information Stadium: London Road, Peterborough PE2 8AL Capacity: 15,314 Tel: 01733 563947 Web: www.theposh.com Train: Peterborough Colours: Blue and white Songs: 'It's Posh We Are' is the favourite of the fans; anti-

which rely heavily on matchday custom - aren't looking forward to the club moving away from London Road. They have everything you want from a football pub. The Office at Woodston is a friendly venue and welcomes families. Good for some post-match analysis, it has two TVs showing sport. Away supporters can also mix easily in The Cherry Tree just down the road. Hot meals are available here. There's also The Peacock on London Road opposite the ground. Packed out on matchdays, this is a family pub with a lounge and public bar, pool tables and a TV. Meanwhile, Ebeneezer's is air-conditioned and offers some of the cheapest beers in town, plus guest ales on tap. For a cracking selection of real ales, drop into Charter's Bar & Restaurant. Located on the river at Town Bridge, it's also close to the popular Metropolis Lounge nightclub.

Stopping over in Peterborough?

 If you are planning to stay in town, your options are fairly limited. The Travelodge in the city centre, on Chapel Street, is a good call. It's behind the market and just 20 minutes' walk from the stadium (0870 191 1803). An alternative is The Best Western Orton Hall Hotel, dating from the 17th century, at Orton Longueville (01733 391111). Pricier but offering a bit more charm is the Bull Hotel at Westgate, a quarter of a mile from the train station

(01733 561364).

If you do one thing in Peterborough...

The city is not over-blessed with attractions but the Nene Valley Railway is a good family day out. Take a trip from Wansford Station, Stibbington, which is less than 10 minutes from the ground.

Alternatively, you could drive out to the Fens or spend a few hours in Stamford, a lovely stone town 14 miles down the A1.

Up the Posh

The team's Posh nickname is said to have its origins in the 1920s when the player-manager of Fletton United - an early incarnation of United - was heard to say he was seeking 'Posh players for a Posh team' to play in what was once the Northamptonshire League. 'Up the Posh' had moved into the lexicon of home fans by the 1930s.

Don't mention

Big Ron Manager: they say that there's no such thing as bad publicity, but the Sky TV football reality programme didn't show the club in a terribly brilliant light.

Do mention

The 1992 play-off final: Barry Fry led the Posh into the post-Premiership new-look First Division. The fact that Peterborough managed a record 134 goals in 1960/61, their first season in the Football League.

Travel Information

CAR
Located on the outskirts of the town centre London Road is the A15. The ground is fairly well signposted around the town centre. From the North/West: Drive into the centre of Peterborough on the A605 or A47 and follow signs to pick up the A15 on the south side of the town centre. Heading south on the A15 London Road you will eventually see the ground on your left. From the South: Best to exit the A1 onto the A15 towards Peterborough and after a few miles you will see the ground on your right.
There is a car park at the ground and a council pay & display car park between the ground and the town centre, just off London Road. You can park in either for under a fiver.

TRAIN
Peterborough station is around a mile away from the ground. Turn right out of the station and follow the main road, passing an Asda store on your right. At the traffic lights near to Woolworths, turn right. Go over the bridge and you can see the floodlights of London Road, over on your left. It takes about 20 minutes to walk from the station to the ground. Thanks to Andrew Dodd for providing the directions.

Cambridge and Northampton ditties are also well aired at London Road. Rivals: Cambridge United, Northampton Town, Rushden & Diamonds.

Plymouth Argyle

Pilgrims seek home comforts

Protracted plans to finish rebuilding Home Park appear to be back on track. Argyle are working with the city council to conclude redevelopment of the ground, which first started in 2001.

Phase one saw the completion of three sides of the ground, leaving only the main grandstand to be replaced. But little work has been carried out since 2002.

Various obstacles delayed phase two, including the Pilgrims spending £2.7m on buying the Home Park freehold from the council.

In March, the club announced that they hope to submit a planning application for the £27 million scheme later this year. This would include work on the new stand, along with development of commercial and leisure facilities on site.

Home Park is mostly seated with a 20,922 capacity. The Mayflower Enclosure of the main grandstand, along one length of the pitch, is still terracing but this will be converted to seating under the next stage of the revamp.

Argyle are the most southern and western league club, meaning that the nearest away game during 2006/07 was Cardiff (approx 153 miles) and the furthest Sunderland (just over 400 miles). But distance is no object for the enthusiastic Green Army who always boast an impressive presence up and down the country, thanks in part to hordes of exiled fans.

Away fans are accommodated in the five-year-old Barn Park End, where the allocation is up to 2,000 seats. Views and refreshment facilities are good. Due to the intimate nature of the ground and the raucous local support, you normally get a cracking atmosphere at Home Park. Don't be put off by the sometimes heavy police presence around the ground.

Eating out

Hot and cold food in many different guises is available in the ground, including local favourite Ginster pasties. The ground's out-of-town location means there aren't many cafés and takeaways nearby. Stop off at Stoke Village shopping precinct (10 minutes' walk from the ground) or Mutley Plain's shops (15 minutes') for a quick feed before the game. Any visitor to the West Country should try a traditional pasty. In both areas you'll find bakeries, fish & chip shops, cafés, pubs and restaurants. The historic Barbican area surrounding Plymouth's ancient harbour has all manner of eateries for post-match dining, from the pizza and pasta bars to the more upmarket restaurants, but if you get the chance (and are hungry enough) you should try a Cap'n Jasper's quarter-pounder or half-yard hotdog – you'll find it at the Barbican on Whitehouse Pier. The China House, a pub-cum-restaurant, is recommended for its beer and food. For a little sophistication, fine food and fine wine, head to Tanners Restaurant on Finewell Street.

Mine's a pint

Alcohol is served at the ground but you'll get a better pint at a local. The Britannia Inn, a Wetherspoons across the road from the ground, welcomes away fans and has cheap drinks and meals, but gets

Club Information Stadium: Home Park, Plymouth PL2 3DQ Capacity: 20,922 Tel: 01752 562561 Web: www.pafc.co.uk Train: Plymouth Colours: Green and white Songs:

packed. There are few others close to Home Park.

The Pennycomequick between the railway station and the stadium is another worth ducking into. If you want some great old-fashioned boozers, stroll down to the Barbican. Sink a few at The Dolphin - "basic and unpretentious but a really great pub" is the local view. The Bass from the cask is quite something. Why not make a pub crawl along the waterfront, stopping off at the Navy Inn? This area is full of quality pubs and champagne/wine bars. As it's not walkable to the ground, you're best hailing a taxi to Home Park at least an hour before kick-off. The centre of Plymouth's nightlife is Union Street, full of chain bars and clubs attracting boisterous revellers. It's the place to go for a wild night out. But the Barbican area of old Plymouth is unbeatable for its diverse mix of drinking dens.

Stopping over in Plymouth?

You'll never be lost for something to do in Plymouth. For that reason and the fact Plymouth is an epic round-trip, it's well worth staying there. It's easy to get a B&B or hotel of a good standard and with some character at Plymouth Hoe, adjacent to the seafront and 25 minutes' walk to Home Park. Out-of-season rates are cheap and there are always rooms to fill. The town's Travelodge and

Holiday Inn hotels are centrally placed but, like all chain hotels, lack the charm and friendly service of independently-run guesthouses.

If you do one thing in Plymouth...

Plymouth has a rich history as a seafaring port - Drake and Raleigh once weighed anchor here. You can stand where the Pilgrim Fathers stood before they embarked on the Mayflower and find out plenty more about the ship's historic voyage down at the Barbican, home to Britain's maritime heritage. The quayside's restaurants, bars and speciality shops provide a relaxing environment for a day out.

Funny name

Plymouth Argyle's name was taken from the Argyll and Sutherland Highlanders football team of the late 19th century. Argyll comes from the Gaelic word meaning "the boundary of the Gaels".

Don't mention

Peter Shilton: the legendary England keeper couldn't save Argyle from relegation in 1992 and again in 1995 as they sunk down two divisions.

Do mention

Paul Sturrock: after saving the club from relegation out of the Football League in 2000/01 he led the club to promotion in his first full season and laid the foundations for promotion to the Championship in 2003/04.

Travel Information

CAR
Very easy to find. Take the M5 to the south west and at the end of the motorway onto the A38. Exit onto the A386 towards Plymouth and after about a mile you will see the ground on your left. There is a huge car park at the ground, which is free – and the earlier you arrive the quicker you'll get away at the end – although it only takes about twenty minutes for the car park to empty. There is limited street parking to the north of the ground.

TRAIN
It's about a twenty-minute walk from Plymouth Station to the ground. Turn right out of the station and under the railway bridge and keep walking along Alma Road until you see the ground on your right.

'Green Army' and various generic odes to Plymouth, including the Molly Malone song. Rivals: Exeter, Torquay and Bristol City.

Portsmouth

It's a cover-up

Pompey have unveiled plans for a new £600million waterfront football stadium and residential development on reclaimed land in the city's dockyard and at Fratton Park. The 36,000-seat stadium is being designed by Herzog and De Meuron, the Swiss architects behind Beijing's National Stadium.

Pompey and Sellar Property Group will build the stadium, along with waterfront apartments and a large new public space, together with a mixture of leisure facilities, restaurants and cafés. In spring 2007, the club and property company also announced proposals for the redevelopment - including about 750 homes - of Fratton Park, the club's home since 1899.

Planning applications for the ambitious projects are due to be submitted in autumn 2007. If everything goes according to plan, construction of the new stadium could begin in 2009 and be ready for the start of the 2011 season.

In the meantime, Pompey fans and long-suffering visitors to Fratton Park can look forward to some improvements. Fans in the uncovered Inter-cash Milton End - the only roofless stand in the Premier League - have often been drenched by a downpour or blown senseless by sea breezes.

In April, the club submitted a planning application for a roof over the Milton End, bowing to pressure from the footballing authorities to upgrade the stand for fans. It was scheduled to be erected by the start of the season.

This comes as some relief to away fans who've wearily tripped to the south coast club in the knowledge that the Milton End is the worst stand – and that's being generous - in the top-flight. There's normally an allocation of about 2,000 seats for visitors.

Despite its ageing facilities, the 20,288-capacity stadium is never found wanting in atmosphere.

Eating out

Food at the ground is nothing special and runs out quickly, according to some fans. Bring snacks, use the burger vans or head across the road to the Pompey Centre for fast food needs (McDonald's and KFC). Gunwharf Quays at Portsmouth Harbour has a fine range of cafés, delis and restaurants for pre- and post-match dining. Here you'll find a Burger King, Nando's, Subway and Café Rouge. The Carvery in Central Square is great for a quick and filling bite Ha! Ha! Bar & Canteen, La Tasca, the Spanish tapas bar and restaurant, and Italian eateries Zizzi and Frankie & Benny's are good places for a sit-down meal. Southsea has its own identity which extends to a variety of individual and stylish restaurants. The Bangkok on Albert Road is a decent place to grab a Thai curry, and there are other eating options on this street. For some great French food that doesn't break the bank, try a place called 8 Kings Road.

Mine's a pint

The Good Companion on Eastern Road, a large pub with a beer garden, is one popular haunt for both sets of supporters. Beer and food is okay, it has Sky Sports and is only five minutes' walk from the ground. Do not set foot in any pubs up close to the stadium. Places to avoid like the plague include The

Club Information Stadium: Fratton Park, Frogmore Road, Portsmouth PO4 8RA
Capacity: 20,288 (all seated) Tel: 02392-731204 Web: www.pompeyfc.co.uk Train: Fratton Colours: Blue, white and red Songs: The famous Pompey Chimes ring out for the

Shepherds Crook, Milton Arms and Mr Pickwick. The Brewers Arms on Milton Road is recommended, an away-friendly Gales house where the ales are kept in fine nick. Fratton Station is only 10 minutes' walk from the venue, but watering holes nearby are generally for Pompey. One of the safe havens near this station is The Connaught Arms at the junction of Penhale Road and Guildford Road. It is described as "a lovely, friendly, backstreet pub". Dubbed "The Pastie Pub of Portsmouth", it offers home-made pasties and a strong range of real ales on tap. Matchdays see a number of Pompey fans, but visitors are very welcome. Fratton Park is a 20-minute stroll from the city centre pubs. Post-match, sup at the pubs/bars on Portsmouth's Guildhall Walk, Southsea seafront or Gunwharf Quays.

Stopping over in Portsmouth?

 Gunwharf Quays is home to the Express by Holiday Inn, a good location for an overnight stop for harbour attractions and nightlife (0870 400 9093). There are myriad cheaper accommodation options in Southsea. Waverley Road has a plentiful supply of them. Family-run Arden Guest House on Herbert Road, near Southsea seafront, is recommended. Doubles are from £40. (023 9282 6409). Victoria Court Hotel on Victoria Road North is centrally located and the station is within easy walking distance. Doubles are priced approx £50 (023 9282 0305). Queens Hotel on Clarence Parade offers high standards of comfort and style with beds from £60 (023 9282 2466).

If you do one thing in Portsmouth...

Experience the views from the "elegant, sculptural and awe-inspiring" Spinnaker Tower, soaring 170m into the sky above the historic harbour of Portsmouth. Glide to the top in the panoramic glass lift and step out at three different viewing platforms, where you can watch the history of this navy port unfold through unique Time Telescopes.

All-time low

The lowest gate for a first-team match involving Pompey is 502, at the Anglo-Italian group match at Ascoli in Dec 1992.

Don't mention

Terry Venables: not the most successful chairman. He had a penchant for signing average Australians; he was national coach of Australia at the same time as owning Pompey.

Do mention

Harry Redknapp: legendary manager who lead Pompey into the Premiership in his first spell as boss. A stint as Southampton boss saw his popularity wane only temporarily, particularly as he returned to Fratton Park after taking Saints out of the Premiership.

Travel Information

CAR
If you're heading west go along the M27 (ignore the M275 turn off) and continue on to the A27. Once on the A27, or if you are coming west along this road: exit onto the A2030 and head towards Southsea and Fratton. Eventually you will see the ground to your left. There is little on offer in terms of official or unofficial car parks, so it's a case of finding street parking.

TRAIN
The nearest local train station is Fratton, which is a ten minute walk away. Take a left along the footbridge on which you leave the platform and exit the bridge left in Goldsmith Avenue. Frogmore Road is half a mile down the road on the left.

duration of every Pompey match and to accompany them the favoured song is 'Play Up Pompey'. Rivals: Southampton (Scummers), and to a lesser extent Brighton and Bournemouth.

Port Vale

Let them entertain you

Vale Park in the town of Burslem, one of six making up the city of Stoke-on-Trent, has been home to the Valiants since 1950 after the club moved from the Old Recreation Ground in Hanley.

Some bright sparks cooked up plans to build a 70,000-capacity stadium. It was dubbed 'The Wembley of the North' but the project never got off the ground due to financial problems and the club settled for something considerably smaller.

The Valiants have had a taste for the 'Wembley of the South' three times. They even picked up silverware on one occasion, although you'd be hard-pressed to find anyone outside Stoke who doesn't use the words 'mickey' and 'mouse' when the Autoglass Trophy of 1993 is mentioned. Port Vale chiefs often have to tell their fans to "Quit your mithering" because for years they've complained about away fans having the best seats in the 23,000-capacity house. Enjoy the comfort of the Hamil End, housing around 4,500 visiting supporters, in the knowledge that Vale fans are whingeing in the cheap seats.

Stoke folk refer to everyone else as 'duck' and have some strange local dialect. 'Dunner werrit', for instance, which apparently means stop moaning in normal persons' English.

In 2006, Robbie Williams - the cocky cabaret entertainer - became a shareholder at the club he's supported all his life. The former member of Take That, reportedly worth a cool £100 million, dug deep into his meagre resources and splashed out £240,000 in the cash-strapped club. The LA-based singer is lucky enough to have a confident and cocky tribute act supporting Vale on his behalf. He operates under the rather splendid moniker of Dodgie Williams.

Eating out

Oatcakes and Wrights pies are the local specialities in the Potteries. You'll get the meat pies at the ground, along with a range of other snacks and drinks, at the refreshment kiosks in the Hamil End.

Not far from the away end you'll discover the fabulous Strawberry Café, which serves huge baguettes loaded with a cooked breakfast - and all for about £2.30. Vale players tucking into fry-ups are frequently spotted there during the week. It also serves Caribbean-style food. Also nearby is Vale Café where you can spend a few quid on a different version of the egg-and-bacon staple, and much more besides.

In the summer, the park opposite the ground is a good place to picnic. Burslem is only 10 minutes' walk from Vale Park and has a number of decent places to eat.

If you're after some classy British cuisine, head for Denrys, a restaurant over two levels in an old Victorian building on St. Johns Square. The food is reasonably cheap and staff are friendly and efficient.

The neighbouring town of Hanley offers plenty in the way of Chinese, Indian and Italian restaurants as well as the best nightlife around. Roberto's on Pall Mall is an Italian restaurant which has a good reputation.

Club Information Stadium: Vale Park, Hamil Rd, Burslem, Stoke On Trent ST6 1AW   Capacity: 23,000 (all seated) Tel: 01782 655800 Web: www.port-vale.co.uk Train: Longport Colours: White and Black Songs: Elvis seems to feature

Mine's a pint

The Vine is the away pub located a stone's throw from the ground. It's small but has a good atmosphere and serves a few real ales but is not renowned for its food, The Bull's Head, is also recommended for visitors, particularly for its range of ales. The lounge has a roaring fire for the cold winter months and an outdoor bar for the summer.

Locals view The Red Lion on Moorland Road as one of the finest for food and its selection of ales. The Leopard on Market Place is worth a visit too. Tommy Cheadle's is strictly for Valiants fans. Hanley and Newcastle-under-Lyme are further afield and have an assortment of pubs and bars. If you're planning on a big night out, make tracks for Hanley.

Stopping over in Stoke?

The Swallow George Hotel on Swan Square, Burslem, is 15 minutes' walk from the ground and offers reasonably priced accommodation (01782 577544). The four-star Best Western Stoke-on-Trent Moat House on Festival Way, Stoke, is a short drive from either junctions 15 or 16 of the M6 (01782 609988). Also recommended is Manor House Hotel, a converted farmhouse in Alsager on the Cheshire and Staffordshire border (01270 884000). It's eight miles from Stoke-on-Trent but a pleasant place to stay. Rooms from £50.

If you do one thing in Stoke...

Alton Towers is a short drive from Stoke city centre and well signposted off the M6. The waterpark is splashing fun and the theme park features the Dung Heap adventure playground. If that's not enough you could always spend a few hours at Jodrell Bank Observatory towards Macclesfield. The centre is home to the Lovell Radio Telescope and has interactive exhibitions devoted to the thrill of space and space travel.

Who are you?

Port Vale is one of a handful of teams not to be named after a geographical location. It's just a made-up place in the Potteries, right? The precise origins of the name are a mystery but it is believed that the club took its name from a canal wharf near Burslem.

Don't mention

Administration: Vale legend Brian Horton returned to the club as manager in 1998, but his spell in charge was hampered by constant financial problems off the pitch.

Do mention

Robbie Williams: the pop singer is a massive fan of Vale and even has a major shareholding in the club.

Travel Information

CAR
Firstly there is no such town as Port Vale: the ground is in Burslem. Exit the M6 at junction 15 or 16 – depending on which direction you're heading - and take the A500 towards Stoke on Trent, then the A527 towards Burslem. Follow the signs for Burslem town centre, turning right after a few hundred metres. Continue into the town centre and on over the traffic lights at the cross roads and turn left into Hamil Road. There is a large car park next to the ground, where you can park for under a fiver, otherwise street parking.

TRAIN
Longport Station is the closest to the ground, but it is not well served, and it's still at least a thirty-minute walk away. It's better to head to Stoke-on-Trent Station. It's some four miles to the ground, so walking isn't really an option for most fans, but for under two quid you can get a return bus ticket to Burslem town centre. As you come out of the entrance to Stoke station the bus stop is on the left. Catch the 29 to Bradeley, (coming back from Burslem, you'll need the 29 to Keele).

almost as much as anti-Stoke feelings in the Vale song repertoire: 'Can't Help Falling In Love' and 'The Wonder Of You' have both been given the Vale treatment. Rivals: Stoke.

Preston North End

What a pitch

Deepdale has a rich history dating back to 1875 when the Lilywhites first moved to the ground. Thirteen years later North End became a founder member of the league. The stadium is the oldest continuously-used league venue.

Modernisation of the ground over the past decade has elevated Deepdale's reputation among football fans. The 22,225-capacity stadium is three-quarters done. The ageing Pavilion Stand is set for a facelift to increase capacity to 30,000.

Construction of the Bill Shankly Kop, named after the former PNE defender and opened in 1998, was the second phase of the redevelopment. Away fans share the stand with PNE fans. Usually there's space for 3,000 visitors, but for large away followings this can be increased to 6,000.

Remember 1986? This was the year Preston successfully applied for re-election to the league after finishing 91st, and when some bright spark thought it would be a good idea to put down a plastic pitch at Deepdale. The hard, bouncy pitch was rubbish and the team performed shabbily on it. Apart from clinching the Division Four runners-up spot the following season, the club had no honours to speak of until after the miserable artificial surface was ripped up in 1994.

The National Football Museum is based inside two stands: the Sir Tom Finney Stand and the Bill Shankly Kop. Check out the skidding statue of Finney outside the ground, arguably the best ever football work of art. The orthodox winger dazzled in 433 league appearances for Preston over 14 years, scoring 187 goals.

Shankly once said of Finney: "He would have been great in any team, in any match and in any age - even if he had been wearing an overcoat."

Eating out

Concourse refreshments include a decent range of hot and cold food. On the menu are hot dogs served in baguettes and three types of pie: meat and potato, steak, and butter. If you're coming by train, there are plenty of takeaways and cafés on Fishergate, which you'll pass on the 25-minute walk to the ground. Eateries are a bit thin on the ground around Deepdale, says Steve Tinniswood, a sports reporter on the Lancashire Telegraph. Preston town centre is the best place for some cheap pre-match nosh. Buffet at Preston (Friargate) is a Chinese restaurant with a difference. Charges vary depending on what time you get there. But once you're in, pay your money, grab a plate and eat as much as you like. The Chop House (Winkley Square) is the place to go if you want to treat yourself. A bit pricey but very trendy it uses the best local produce to cook up some classic British dishes. Below the Chop House is the Olive Press, an upmarket pizzeria.

Mine's a pint

The best bet for a good pint and lively atmosphere is The Sumners, just up the Tom Finney Way from the ground. Home and away supporters mingle freely, decent pub grub is available, it's child-friendly and also has a large beer garden. Across the

Club Information Stadium: Deepdale, Sir Tom Finney Way, Preston PR1 6RU
Capacity: 22,225 (all seated) Tel: 0870 4421964 Web: www.pnefc.net Train:
Preston Colours: White and navy Songs: Anti-Blackpool, Burnley and Blackburn

road is The Garrison, a traditional boozer also popular on matchdays. If you're driving to the ground from the M6, you'll pass the Hesketh Arms, which is welcoming enough. Arriving from Junction 32 of the A6, you'll find The Withy Trees, excellent for beer and food. Preston is roughly split in two when it comes to a night out - the student quarter and the towny quarter. Friargate has student drinking dens and is fine for those wanting to relive their grant-stretching days. The Adelphi (Fylde Road) at the bottom end of Friargate is the main student pub. Roper Hall is a lively and loud pub-cum-club, while O'Neills is more than welcoming. Heading in to the town centre, he recommends The Black Horse, Preston's oldest pub, where you'll find Robinsons Bitter on tap. The Exchange (Fox Street) is the towny equivalent of the Adelphi and, if you head up to Fishergate, there are some trendy bars hidden down the side streets. Squires is Preston's premier club but Fives (Guild Hall Street) and The Loft (Glovers Court) are pretty good, too. The Warehouse (St John's Place) is an indie end-of-night joint, the best place for a Smiths-singing hoedown.

Stopping over in Preston?

 A few sherbets and friendly chat in the locals can sometimes put the brakes on heading elsewhere. The Holiday Inn is

right in the middle of town (0870 400 9066). For a more upmarket option try the Marriot Hotel (Garstang Road) at the other end of town (01772 864087). A bit off the beaten track for Preston's nightlife but if you can afford to stay here, you can afford a taxi into town.

If you do one thing in Preston...

Visit the National Football Museum at Deepdale, packed with fascinating hands-on interactives.

It includes the finest single collection of FIFA and English FA football memorabilia in the world.

Back of the net

When David Nugent hit the net in the Euro 2008 qualifier against Andorra in March 2007, he became the first North End player to score for England in 49 years. Finney was the last, scoring against Northern Ireland in 1958.

Don't mention

Craig Brown: after a few years of good progress, North End stood still during the former Scotland boss's tenure at Deepdale.

Do mention

The fact that Preston North End were the first team to do the double: in 1888/89, during the League's first season, but they're proud of this - who are also the Invincibles - the only team not to lose a league or cup game in one season.

Travel Information

CAR
Exit the M6 at junction 31; when you reach the roundabout on the A5085 (the first normal roundabout) turn right into Blackpool Road. Just before the fourth set of traffic lights turn left down Parkside and you will see the ground to your left. Parking is mainly in the streets, but there is a pay and display opposite the ground on Deepdale Road, and for three pounds you can park at Moorfields School. Use the directions as above, but at the last set of traffic lights continue straight on for about 200 yards and the school is on the left.

TRAIN
It is about twenty minutes' walk from Preston Station to Deepdale. Turn right out of the station approach road into the High Street. After a mile or so you reach the ring road, you head straight over the large traffic lights, heading towards a pub called the County Arms opposite the prison. Turn left along the road here passing the County Arms (which is not recommended for away supporters) and continue along Deepdale road. The ground is now another half mile in a straight line along this road. Thanks to Kevin Wrenn for supplying the directions and general information.

songs are very popular, with 'Chim Chimney' reserved for Burnley and a special 'Who's That Jumping Off The Pier' for Blackpool. Rivals: Blackpool, Burnley and Blackburn Rovers.

Queens Park Rangers

Turning it round

Loftus Road looks a bit shabby these days but it's still great for watching football as fans are so close to the pitch.

QPR would renovate the 19,100-capacity ground if they weren't up to their eyes in debt. Club chairman Gianni Paladini admits it must be paid off before any investment is made in upgrades to Loftus Road. Meantime, investigations into building a 30,000-seat stadium are ongoing. But exploratory discussions will remain just that until the club sorts out its finances.

The Italian tycoon and former football agent took control of the club following a bitter power struggle in 2005, knowing he had a job on his hands to lift QPR out of the doldrums.

There's been plenty of hostile criticism from some R's diehards opposed to his regime. Paladini was even threatened with violence - he was allegedly held hostage at gunpoint during a match against Sheffield United at Loftus Road.

Paladini labelled the naysayers the "enemy within" and has spent a good chunk of the last two seasons trying to patch up his rocky relationship with Super Hoops fans. The end of turbulent times is not nigh.

Away fans are situated in the two-tiered School End, which has space for 3,400 supporters. Normally only the upper tier is open unless extra demand requires use of the lower tier. In the upper tier, try to avoid the 115 restricted view seats and 65 severely restricted places. The best seats are in the first five rows and you feel right on top of the action. It's worth turning up at the ground earlier than normal as slow turnstiles at the School End can lead to lengthy delays.

Eating out

Catering kiosk offerings at Loftus Road do not garner good reviews. Aside from the balti pies, some fans say burgers and the like are completely tasteless, the chips are undercooked and drinks overpriced. Head down Uxbridge Road for cafés, fried food outlets and traditional chippies. There are Indian, Chinese, Thai and Lebanese restaurants to fulfil all your needs prior to the match. Goldhawk Road has many others, while The Central Bar (Wetherspoons) and Walkabout at Shepherds Bush Green are top tips for cheap pub meals. The centre of London isn't far away for swankier post-match drinking and dining venues.

Mine's a pint

 The Springbok on South Africa Road is closest to the ground and admits home and away fans. You'll always get a lively atmosphere in the Wetherspoons and Walkabout. There are mixed reports on The Green found on Uxbridge Road - still, it makes a good stop for a real ale. As does The Defector's Weld across the road, which comes recommended for its platters of food and speedy service. The White Horse not far away will appeal to

Club Information Stadium: Loftus Road Stadium, South Africa Road, London W12 7PA Capacity: 19,100 (all seated) Tel: 020 87430262 Web: www.qpr.co.uk Tube: Shepherd's Bush Central Colours: Blue and white Songs: 'Come On You Rs' and

those who like to drink in proper little boozers with character. It also has TV screens, pool, jukebox and beer garden. There's an O'Neills nearby, if you fancy a pint of the black stuff. Goldhawk Road's drinking establishments are hit and miss. The Bush Bar and Grill is fine, more upmarket and stylish than most bars in this area - but with prices to match. Head for the city in the evening. The Argyll Arms on Argyll Street, Soho, is one of the best examples of late Victorian pub design in the West End, and the drinks and service are highly rated. Afterwards, newly-refurbished Club 49 on Greek Street is a classy little venue.

Stopping over in Hammersmith and Fulham?

 The London borough may not be the first on your hit list for accommodation when the city is a train ride away. But you could do worse than staying at the Premier Travel Inn on King Street near Ravenscourt Park tube with rooms from £77 (0870 850 6310). Express By Holiday Inn is down the road (020 8746 5100). Brook Green Hotel on Shepherds Bush Road is another option (020 7603 2516). Doubles are from £60.

It's a five-minute walk from Hammersmith tube and bus station.

If you do one thing in the borough...

Loftus Road is only a 20-minute tube ride – on the Central Line - from central London, and west end attractions are much closer. This is theatre land. But if you don't want to see a former soap star warble their way through a below-par musical or some luvvies hamming it up in a much-hyped production, dive into Soho's weird and wonderful drinking dens for a serious session on the pop.

Butch at the Loft

Raymond 'Butch' Wilkins is the oldest player to turn out for QPR. He had two spells at the club, playing his last games for Rangers a few days shy of 40. Wilkins then went on to play for four other clubs before retiring.

Don't Mention

Chris Wright: the former chairman isn't popular after proposing a merger with Wimbledon and leaving the club with millions of pounds of debt.

Do Mention

Dave Sexton: legendary manager during the 1970s, who led Rangers to runners-up spot in the First Division. Stan Bowles and Rodney Marsh: Rangers playing legends from the past.

Travel Information

CAR
From M25/M40: Follow the M40 and then A40 towards Central London until you reach the right turn for the A219 Wood Lane, and right again into South Africa Road for the stadium. Other routes: From the south, you may use the A23, A3 or A4 to head into the centre of London. Follow signs for Central London and then for Hammersmith/ Shepherd's Bush (use the A306 if you're coming on the A3; and exit the A23 onto the A214 and A217). Eventually you will find yourself on the A219 Shepherd's Bush Road. When you come to the Shepherd's Bush Common, exit left onto the Uxbridge Road and Loftus Road is the fourth turning past the Underground Station. No parking at ground; metered street parking is available or park in the industrial estate at the BBC TV Centre in Wood Lane for around seven quid.

TUBE
There are two Shepherd's Bush tube stations - Shepherd's Bush (Central) Station is nearer to the ground, about five minutes' walk along Uxbridge Road. If you end up at the other station, cross the common and head down Uxbridge Road. White City (Central Line) is also very close to the ground.

'Rangers' are popular rallying cries for the team. The Loftus Road faithful also like to tell Chelsea fans what they can do with the blue flag. Rivals: Brentford, Fulham and Chelsea.

Reading

Bring on the crowds

Virtually every game in 2006/07 was a sell-out at the 24,200-seat Madejski Stadium, testament to the club's success in its first Premiership season - the zenith of the club's 135-year history.

August 2008 marks the 10th anniversary of their new ground, built on the site of a household waste dump at a cost of more than £50m. The stadium complex, which incorporates a 150-room four-star hotel, has won plenty of praise.

Ambitious chairman John Madejski has rejuvenated the club since his arrival in 1990, a period when the Royals were toiling in Division Two at Elm Park, Reading's home for 102 years.

Madejski, who earned his fortune from Auto Trader magazine, is spearheading efforts to expand the stadium. An additional 6,000 seats in the East Stand should be ready for the start of 2008/09. Work on the South and North Stands is proposed to raise capacity to about 38,000.

Reading boss Steve Coppell agreed a new two-year contract extension in March 2007, saying: "With the stadium expansion we'll get bigger crowds, bigger income and therefore better players. That's the only way to compete."

The normal allocation for away fans is 2,327 seats in the South Stand, where you're treated to excellent views of the pitch.

One of the downsides of the Madejski is its location. Handy for those driving off the M4 - although parking is extremely limited close to the ground (use the speedway track car park next door) - but a pain to reach if you're coming by train. Reading Central railway station is three miles away. Shuttle bus services are provided between the station and the stadium.

Eating out

As there are few places to buy food and drink around the ground, you're better off grabbing a bite in the South Stand or from burger vans in the immediate vicinity. Pizza Hut, KFC and McDonald's are in the nearby retail park.

If you're feeling peckish on the drive to the stadium, pop into The World Turned Upside Down Harvester on Basingstoke Road (the old A33) and chow down on a flame-grilled meat dish. For something more exotic, try Eastern Pearl on the same road. This large restaurant serves a good choice of Southeast Asian dishes. Shinfield Road in Shinfield, just off the M4, has a host of other eateries, such as Honeymoon Chinese Restaurant, providing good traditional Chinese food. Also on this road is The Black Boy Inn, a family-friendly pub offering a wide selection of pub grub. It has a large outdoor seating area for summer drinking and dining.

In Reading town centre, Art of Siam and Topo Gigio, a Thai and Italian respectively on Kings Walk, are recommended. One of the Reading area's premier gastro pubs is The George and Dragon, dating back to the 16th century. It's a traditional and relaxing pub with open fires and exposed beams, serving exceptional food. It's situated in the village of

Club Information Stadium: Madejski Stadium, Bennett Road, Reading RG2 0FL Capacity: 24,200 (all seated) Tel: 0118 9681100 Web: www.readingfc.co.uk Train: Reading Colours: Blue and white Songs: Not a huge history of songs – most of them are the generic ones. Until recently Reading fans were always regarded as

Swallowfield, four miles south of Reading and close to the M4 (Junction 11). A useful online resource for Reading eateries: *www.readingrestaurants.com*

Mine's a pint

Apart from the alcohol available inside the ground, you'll struggle to get a good pint nearby due to the ground being marooned in the middle of a less-than-lovely industrial estate. The World Turned Upside Down Harvester on Basingstoke Road is your best bet. Many away fans drink in the town centre pubs near the train station, where there's generally a very visible police presence.

The police sometimes confine away fans to The Three Guineas, which has a good choice of ales. Buses to the stadium also stop for pick-ups a short distance away. Taxis from this pub will cost about £10. Greyfriars Road has several reasonable watering holes including The Gateway.

Head down Friar Street if you don't mind drinking in chain bars like Yates's and The Pitcher and Piano. Cover your colours otherwise you may not get in. The Black Boy Inn and The George and Dragon - mentioned above - are great if you're driving and have time on your hands.

Stopping over in Reading?

Holiday Inn Reading South is located just off Junction 11 of the M4, and two miles from Reading town centre and railway station. It has an Irish bar and Traders restaurant and you might get special rates. Doubles are from £55 (0870 400 9067). To be at the heart of Reading's nightlife, check into Novotel Hotel on Friar Street. B&B is from £69 per night (0118 952 2600).

If you do one thing in Reading…

Visit The Living Rainforest at Hampstead Norreys, near Thatcham.

It's a rainforest recreated under 20,000 square feet of glass and houses a collection of tropical plants, birds and rainforest mammals (signposted from Junction 13 of the M4) - www.livingrainforest.org.

No biccies, no name

The club changed their nickname from the Biscuitmen to the Royals in 1974. The old moniker became inappropriate due to the closure of the Huntley & Palmers factory in the town.

Don't mention

Alan Pardew or Mark McGhee: leaving Reading for a club in a higher league, even if you've led them to promotion, is unforgivable in Berkshire.

Do Mention

Steve Coppell: manager who led the Royals into the top flight for the first time in the club's history. Robin Friday: immensely skilful player from the 1970s.

Travel Information

CAR
Easy to find from the M4; leave at junction 11 and head north on the A33 relief road which leads you directly to the stadium. There is a huge car park at the ground and one at the nearby greyhound track – both for around seven quid– but beware - they can fill up if you leave it late. The club also operate a park-and-ride scheme at Foster Wheeler at Shinfield Park at the cost of £3 for adults and £1.50 for children. Take the B3270 towards Earley and then follow the signs to 'Football Car Park C' – buses run from about an hour and a half before kick off.

TRAIN
It's advisable to get a number 79 bus from Reading Station to the Madejski Stadium as it's about four miles out of town; a return ticket is around three quid. It takes about fifteen minutes when the roads are clear, but can take up to half an hour the closer it gets to kick-off. If you want to walk to the stadium (which could take anything over forty minutes) head through the town centre and out of town on the A33 which leads to the stadium.

more conservative, that was until Alan Pardew's 13th-man initiative. Now they get a bit of atmosphere going inside the Madejski. Rivals: Swindon Town, Oxford United, Bristol City, Wycombe Wanderers.

Rochdale

Thumbs up for Spotland

Over the last decade, all four sides of quaintly-named Spotland Stadium have been given a facelift. The completion of the 3,650-seater Westrose Leisure Stand (Willbutts Lane) during the 2000/2001 season was the final piece in the modernisation programme.

This stand hosts travelling fans and offers good views of the pitch. Home fans find their voices in the Sandy Lane Stand, the only standing area left at Spotland.

It's a far cry from the tinpot stadium of old when the venue featured only one stand. Built in 1920, it was known as the smallest seated area for spectators anywhere in the league.

As recently as the late 90s, the ground still left a wee bit to be desired. Fans have fond memories of the toilets in the Willbutts Lane end - basically an uncovered area where men emptied their bladders against a wall. It meant you could go to the toilet and watch the game at the same time.

Nowadays, you can stuff 10,249 fans into the ground at a squeeze. But there's rarely a full house - average attendances are around 2,500. One Dale wag suggests one of the best attributes of the stadium is that "you get a whole row each whether standing or sitting". And the worst? "You have to shout bloody loud to ask the person next to you if he's got a light."

Spotland is shared with the Rochdale Hornets rugby league team, so the pitch can take a battering. But the stadium has gained favourable reviews among visiting fans and elsewhere - it featured in 'Total Football' magazine best grounds list one year. For the matchday experience, the ground is one of the best in the lower divisions.

Eating out

Away supporters can look forward to munching on "a feast of culinary delights" - well, pies, pasties and peas at any rate. Such delectable fare is available from the catering kiosk housed in the Westrose Leisure Stand. The pies are recommended - voted second in a football grounds' food awards one year. Studds Bar underneath the WMG stand welcomes both sets of supporters and serves good quality food before the game at reasonable prices. If you're after a seat, it's wise to head there early as it can get busy. Pub meals are also served in the Cemetery Hotel (see below). There's a chippy opposite the entrance for away fans and another shop on Sandy Lane.

Mine's a pint

At the ground, Studds Bar is open for pre-match pints and banter, and also has Sky Sports. Take your pick from a selection of pubs within a five-minute walk from the ground. Top of your list should be the 'official' away pub: The Church Inn on the corner of Willbutts Lane. It's always buzzing on matchday and features an outside drinking area, darts and TV. The Cemetery Hotel, a pub situated at the traffic lights on the approach to Spotland, is frequented by many Dale fans but there's a

Club Information Stadium: Spotland, Sandy Lane, Rochdale OL11 5DS Capacity: 10,249 Tel: 0870 8221907 Web: www.rochdaleafc.co.uk Train: Rochdale Colours: Blue and white Songs: Pretty much generic favourites at Spotland: 'You Are My

friendly atmosphere. Guest beers complement the usual beverages. The Merry Monk on College Road is another recommended for its real ale offering. According to one local, The Dog & Partridge on Bury Road contains "a pool table without a ripped baize, tipless cues, and real chalk like teacher used to use".

Stopping over in Rochdale?

 Manchester, with its big-city appeal, may prove tempting but if you've come on a long journey to this north-west outpost and you're intent on resting up for the night, here are a couple of budget options to meet your needs.

The Broadfield Hotel at Sparrow Hill - only minutes from the M62 and M60 motorways - is a homely place (0161 643 5140). Costing a little more is Macdonald Norton Grange Hotel & Spa on Manchester Road (0870 194 2119). It's only a couple of miles or so from the centre of Rochdale and only eight from Manchester. The venue includes a gym, an 18-metre swimming pool and a thermal suite comprising sauna and steam rooms - perhaps the perfect place to wind down after a 4-0 drubbing!

If you do one thing in Rochdale...

There's not a fantastic amount to detain you. Castleton Water Activity Centre on Manchester Road, Castleton, offers swimming, canoeing, kayaking and raft building - or how about trekking on the Rochdale Way.

Otherwise, the best ploy is to seek out your thrills in the city of the Red Devils. For more information, see our take on Manchester's attractions in the city guide.

Not so 'Rock on' Tommy

Tommy Cannon rose to prominence in the comedy duo Cannon & Ball and had a spell as club chairman in the mid-80s. But the former welder - real name Thomas Derbyshire - caused uproar in the town when the new-look board supposedly made some decisions deemed not to be in the best interests of the club and quit - leaving, according to the club's website, "a whole host of debts".

Don't mention

That Rochdale have been in the Football League's bottom division (Division Four, Division Three and League Two) since 1974: in the post Premiership and Championship league shake-ups it's even been referred to as the 'Rochdale Division' to avoid confusion.

Do mention

That Rochdale are the only team from the bottom division of the Football League to reach the League Cup Final. In 1962 they met Norwich City at Wembley.

Travel Information

CAR
At junction 20 of the M62 take the A627(M) towards Rochdale. At the end of the A627(M) turn left at the traffic lights and straight over the roundabout into Roch Valley Way, which becomes Sandy Lane at the crossroads. The ground is less than a mile further on the right. You should find street parking easily, or you can opt to park at Oulder Hill School (on the left hand side, along Sandy Lane before you reach the ground).

TRAIN
Served by trains from both Manchester and Leeds, Rochdale Station is around two miles from the ground. You may want to opt for a bus (number 436 to Sandy Lane) or a taxi, but it is walk-able in about twenty-five minutes. Exit the station into Tweedale Street and follow this to the main Manchester Road. Turn right and cross the dual carriageway using the pedestrian crossing. Turn left into Dane Street which leads into Mellor Street and then left along Spotland Road. A left into Willbutts Lane will lead you to the ground.

Rochdale', 'Give Us An R'... that type of stuff and anything anti their rivals. Rivals: Bury, Burnley, Oldham, Manchester United and Manchester City.

Rotherham United

Laughter is the best medicine

When The Chuckle Brothers asked people to join the 'Save Our Millers' campaign in 2006, fans probably didn't know whether to laugh or cry. But the likeable idiots meant it from the heart. Really. They are lifelong fans of Rotherham and, like all Millers supporters, wanted to do something to secure the club's future.

Rotherham was spending more than it was bringing in at the time - losses of more than £140,000 a month were reported - contributing to the club's growing debts. The 'Save Our Millers' campaign was launched to raise the £1million needed to stay afloat for the rest of that season.

Neighbours Sheffield United and Sheffield Wednesday helped out by holding bucket collections and whip-rounds among their players. Neil Warnock's United even lent the Millers a couple of players.

In the end, the campaign could raise only £250,000. But a consortium of local businessmen stepped in to rescue the club. Denis Coleman took over as chairman and made the Chuckle Brothers honorary presidents of the club in January 2007.

The Millers started the 2006/07 season with a 10-point deficit served by the Football League, after creditors agreed to a Company Voluntary Agreement which saved the club from liquidation.

Rotherham's half-developed stadium isn't an attractive proposition for locals when neighbouring clubs accommodate supporters in much nicer surroundings. Millers fans like to slag off fierce rivals Sheffield Wednesday. This seems to be a shared pastime on the Rotherham message boards and at 8,300-capacity Millmoor. Away fans are housed in the covered and all-seated Railway End, which holds around 2,000 supporters.

Eating out

Millmoor was the first ground in the country to sell Pukka Pies some 25 years ago. You could chow down on the usual football food at the ground, including sausage rolls, pork pies and the like. Or head to the greasy spoon across the road from the stadium. It does an all-day breakfast. Chinese and Indian takeaways are also close by. The Tesco supermarket on the way to the town centre is a cheap snack stop. The chip shop at the side of it enjoys a good reputation.

There are dozens of restaurants around Rotherham's town centre to satisfy all post-match cravings, including decent Italians such as E'Lupo's on Effingham Street and Galliano's on Bawtry Road. La Mancha Tapas Restaurant on Corporation Street has a good atmosphere and interesting menu. Nearby Sheffield, however, has a far wider choice of dining options.

Mine's a pint

There's an away supporters' bar at the Railway End. Near to the ground, The Millmoor on Masbrough Street has a lively pre-match atmosphere and serves a

Club Information Stadium: Millmoor, Millmoor Ground, Rotherham S60 1HR Capacity: 8,300 Tel: 01709 512434 Web: www.themillers.co.uk Train: Rotherham Colours: Red and white Songs: A Rotherham original is 'Miller Men', which goes:

nice pint. Hot and cold food is also available and families are welcome. The Moulders Rest, a traditional family boozer just down the road, is popular with both groups of supporters but doormen can sometimes be fussy about away fans. It has a pool table, darts and a beer garden. Away fans are welcome in most Rotherham pubs. It's a town with a friendly vibe. The Kingfisher on Mary Street is worth a visit for its range of ales and a bite to eat. It's doubtful you'll want to sample the nightlife in Rotherham when Sheffield is only six miles away but if Rotherham does hold some appeal, check out the watering holes in town and then hot foot it to Liquid & Deva or Blue Minx Gentlemen's Club on Main Street.

Stopping over in Rotherham?

 The cheapest recommended option in Rotherham is the Prince of Wales B&B just round the corner from Millmoor on Princes Street (01709 551366). The Moulders Rest does B&B with rooms from £30 (01709 560095). Ibis Rotherham on Moorhead Way is more expensive but well placed at the start of the M18 and close to J32 of the M1

(0870 752 2235).

Sheffield is another option to consider.

If you do one thing in Rotherham...

The Magna Science Adventure Centre on Sheffield Road is one of the most popular tourist destinations. Exhibits, shows and interactive features demonstrate the power and force of the four natural elements: air, water, fire and earth.

To me, to you

The Chuckle Brothers (real names Paul and Barry Elliot) first starred in the ChuckleVision television show in 1987. As of 2005, there had been 18 series and 264 episodes of the children's television show. If you look hard enough, some of these are available on DVD. Best not to ask for them though.

Don't mention

The ten-point deduction dished out by the Football League in 2006/07: it simply proved too much of an Achilles heel for the Millers and they were relegated to the league's basement division.

Do Mention

Ronnie Moore: a legend as both a player and a manager at Millmoor. In both stints he helped the club reach the second tier of the Football League.

"Miller men, Miller men; In red and white; We'll stand and fight; We're Miller men!" Rivals: Both Sheffield clubs, Barnsley and Doncaster Rovers aren't popular either.

Scunthorpe United

Hard as Iron

The north Lincolnshire outfit doesn't have much to boast about when it comes to honours. But since the club gained admission to the league in 1950 it has groomed some footballing greats.

Ray Clemence and Kevin Keegan got their breaks in the United team of the late 1960s before making their names for Liverpool and England. Ian 'Beefy' Botham famously had a spell here but chose cricket ahead of football, some might say wisely. And of course there's Peter Beagrie, the journeyman footballer better known for his acrobatic goal celebration and terrific moustache than for his nifty wing play.

Nicknamed The Iron on account of the town's development around iron-ore resources, Scunthorpe play their brand of football at the 9,088-capacity Glanford Park. They moved here from the Old Showground in 1988, becoming the first English club in more than 30 years to build a purpose-built stadium. It was built for just £2.5 million.

Glanford Park currently has three all-seater stands and one side standing, which is used to house the majority of the home fans. The Caparo Merchant Bar Stand (aka the South Stand) with a seating capacity of 1,678 is where you'll be watching the match. Some of the seats here were brought in from Aston Villa who share the same claret and blue colours. Additional seats can be made available in the Evening Telegraph Stand (south corner of the West Stand) if demand requires.

They're a friendly shower at Scunthorpe, though you'll have to exercise those vocal chords to generate some atmosphere at the ground. However, promotion to the Championship is sure to up the average gate of 5,000.

Eating out

Catering outlets inside the ground offer the expected footballing fare. There's a McDonald's, KFC, Pizza Hut and a Tesco's café within a few hundred yards of Glanford Park. The Old Farmhouse next to the stadium is away-friendly and is recommended for its good value pub grub. But you'll have to cover up club colours to gain entry. Doncaster Road not far from the ground has a number of fast food outlets.

You can also get a good post-match feed at restaurants along this street, including a number of Chinese and Cantonese eateries such as Dynasty Chinese Restaurant. Jubraj Tandoori Restaurant and Sicilian's Pizzeria are also found on this stretch.

Mine's a pint

At the ground, The Iron Bar is open only for home supporters. You'll be well looked after in The Old Farmhouse, a top choice for visitors. It has a decent drinks menu, pool table and a children's play area. The Berkeley, around the corner from the ground, is perhaps the most welcoming for away fans and there's a good pre-match atmosphere here with home and away fans swapping banter. The railway station is about two miles from Glanford Park, so if you're

---

Club Information Stadium: Glanford Park, Doncaster Rd, Scunthorpe DN15 8TD Capacity: 9,088 Tel: 0871 2211899 Web: www.scunthorpe-united.co.uk Colours: Claret and blue Train: Scunthorpe Songs: 'Any Old Iron' has been reworked to pay homage to Scunny (the Iron) and also have little dig at rivals Grimsby. Rivals: Hull

arriving by train, why not pop into The Honest Lawyer for a tipple before heading for the ground. Turn left out of the station and head towards the crossroads (facing a church) and turn right into Oswald Road where you'll find the pub and a Wetherspoons called the Blue Bell. When it comes to nightlife, Scunny (population around 72,000) is found wanting compared to its bigger neighbouring towns. There are numerous old-fashioned pubs and inns dotted around the town centre. But if you want a more diverse collection of drinking dens and fancy stepping out at a decent nightclub, travel to Hull, via the impressive Humber Bridge, or Doncaster.

Stopping over in Scunthorpe?

If you're intent on staying in Scunthorpe there's a Travelodge (and a 24hr Tesco) next to the ground, but you may be better off towards the town centre. The three-star Wortley House Hotel on Rowland Road is less than a kilometre from the centre and has comfy rooms from £55 (01724 842223). Premier Travel Inn is at Lakeside Retail Park off the A18 (08701 977226).

If you do one thing in Scunthorpe...

Scunthorpe is not an arresting sight, nor does it have an abundance of attractions. In fact, it has virtually nothing to look at.

Originally made up of five rural villages, it owes its growth to the discovery of vast iron-stone deposits found in 1860 and the subsequent development of its steel industry.

Nearby Sheffield may offer more in the way of entertainment.

Mighty Mouse leaves his mark

Joseph Kevin Keegan joined Scunthorpe as an apprentice in 1968 and made a huge impact as a midfielder. He played 120 league games before being snapped up by Liverpool boss Bill Shankly for £35,000.

Keegan was capped 63 times for England and scored 21 goals.

Don't mention

Christmas Day 1952: Scunthorpe fans weren't given much of a present, they lost 8-0 at Carlisle in a Division Three North fixture.

Do Mention

That two England captains began their football careers at Scunthorpe: Kevin Keegan and... Ian Botham; the England cricket captain played 11 times before switching back to bat and ball. Ray Clemence: he also began his career with the Iron.

Travel Information

CAR
Leave the M180 at junction 3 for the M181 to Scunthorpe. At the end of this motorway, you will see the ground on your right. Turn right at the first roundabout and right again into the large car park where you can park for a couple of quid.

TRAIN
It is about a twenty-minute walk to the ground from Scunthorpe Station – so it might be worth considering the number 7 or 8 bus which runs along Doncaster Road. Turn left out of the station and head along Station Road. At the cross roads turn right into Oswald Road and at the second set of traffic lights turn left into Doncaster Road (this is where you can hop onto the bus, it's about a pound for the fare) or you can walk the mile and a half to the ground. Whichever way you choose, head along Doncaster Road and eventually you come to Glanford Park on your left.

City, Grimsby Town, Lincoln City and Doncaster Rovers. Scunny fans also chant: "Who needs Mourinho we've got our physio" in homage to Nigel Adkins, who stepped up from physio to manager and led the club to promotion.

Sheffield United

Home of the greasy chip butty song

Originally a cricket ground, Bramall Lane is one of the oldest football grounds in the country, having hosted its first game in 1862. Crown green bowling, lacrosse and baseball were also staged at the Lane down the years.

But it's football that makes the Steel City tick. And the Blades have outshone the Owls in the past decade. In September 2001, United celebrated the 2,000th league match to be held at the ground. The Blades retained bragging rights over rivals Sheffield Wednesday when they returned to the Premiership for the 2006/07 campaign after 12 years of waiting – although now the playing field has levelled again.

Investment in stadium expansion has reflected the team's improvement on the pitch and the club's increased popularity. In 2005, the ground's 150th anniversary, wooden seats were removed from the South Stand and a year later the new 2,000-seat corner stand between Cherry Street and Bramall Lane opened, raising capacity to 32,609. Plans are afoot to boost capacity further, but it will probably depend on whether the club can ever put back-to-back Premiership seasons together.

Away fans are seated in the lower tier of the Bramall Lane end (Halliwells Stand), where 2,557 tickets are available. A further 2,696 seats can be allocated in the upper tier should demand dictate.

You'll be surrounded by Blades fans cheering and chastising their team, and hurling some choice language in your general direction. It all adds up to a cracking atmosphere, especially when the Blades faithful bawl their rendition of United's unofficial-but-legendary anthem, The Greasy Chip Butty Song, to the tune of Annie's Song by John Denver.

Eating out

If you're not eating at the ground, there's no end of eating places nearby. Adjacent London Road is full of culinary wonders, from greasy fast food to noodle shops, Turkish, Thai, Greek, Chinese and Mexican restaurants. Kebabish is voted one of the best kebab joints in Sheffield. At Bohan's Irish Kitchen, there's quality homemade food. The city centre offers the usual fast food haunts. The Moor Fisheries on Cumberland Street is arguably the best chippy in these parts. Also recommended on this road is El Paso. Try somewhere like Munchies on Chapel Walk, the place to grab a hot sandwich. Cambridge Street's bars are good for food. They include RSVP, The Cutler and The Sportsman Inn. East Ocean Café on Matilda Street is great for an evening meal with its tasty selection of Chinese, Thai and Japanese food. Café Guru, Westfield Terrace, is singled out as the best curry house. *www.sheffieldrestaurant.co.uk* the most comprehensive guide to Sheffield restaurants, is a fantastic resource for visitors.

Mine's a pint

Seek your liquid refreshments outside the ground for the best pre-match atmosphere. Blades pubs to avoid near the ground include The Railway, The Cricketers and Sheaf House Hotel. One which does admit visiting support is The Golden Lion on Alderson Road just up the street from the Sheaf. If you're coming by train, The Howard opposite the station is the main pub for away fans and also offers decent food. The Royal Standard, en route from the station to the ground, welcomes away fans depending on the fixture. The Broadfield on Abbeydale Road does a nice line in real ales. City centre pubs and bars are about one mile (10 minutes' walk) from Bramall Lane. The Red Lion on Charles Street is a great boozer with a fine range of hand-pulled beers and friendly bar staff. If you're staying, try the venues on Cambridge Street and West Street. The Fat Cat and Kelham Island Tavern – both close together, in Alma Street and Russell Street respectively – are also worth a look.

Stopping over in Sheffield?

Novotel at Arundel Gate makes a good city centre base (0114 278 1781): only five minutes' walk from the station and shops with restaurants, pubs and clubs nearby. Rooms from £55 per night. Grosvenor House hotel on Charter Square in the heart of the city offers rooms at about £50 (0114 272 0041).

If you want to stay in an unpretentious, friendly boutique hotel in the cultural, retail and commercial centre, book a room (around £45) at The Cutlers Hotel on George Street (0114 273 9939). Sheffield's only independently-owned boutique hotel is just minutes away from all the city's transport links and attractions.

If you do one thing in Sheffield...

Weekend hedonists can make good use of their time and money at Sheffield Ski Village located on Vale Road (0114 276 9459). Take a ski or snow-boarding lesson or just tank it down what is one of Europe's largest outdoor artificial ski slopes. There's also Adventure Mountain and a host of other kids' activities if you have the family in tow.

No more leather on willow

League and county cricket was played at Bramall Lane until 1973, the last county clash taking place between rivals Yorkshire and Lancashire.

Don't mention

The 1993 FA Cup Semi Final: the Blades lost to city rivals Wednesday in the second semi-final to be played at Wembley. Last minute relegations: Don Givens missed a penalty in the last minute of the 1980/81 season, which, had he scored, would have saved United from relegation to Division Three. In 1993/94 they went down again thanks to a last-minute goal, they lost 3-2 at Chelsea; a draw would have ensured survival.

Do Mention

Brian Deane: a Bramall Lane legend. Over three separate spells with the Blades Deane smashed in over 100 goals.

Travel Information

CAR
From the north: Exit the M1 at J36 and follow the A61 into Sheffield and negotiate the ring road around the city centre and at the third roundabout take the A621 Bramall Lane. From the south: Exit the M1 at junction 33 and take the A630 (which becomes the A57) towards Sheffield and the city centre. On reaching the inner ring road follow signs for the A621 towards Bakewell, which eventually leads into Bramall Lane. Alternatively you can exit the M1 at junction 31 and take the A57 into the city centre – or you can exit at junction 29 and go via Chesterfield on the A617 and A61. Remain on the A61 until you reach the outskirts of the city; then pick up the A621 Bramall Lane – the ground will be on the right. Parking is limited to street parking, unless you park in one of the city centre car parks, which will be about a fifteen-minute walk.

TRAIN
It's about a ten-minute walk from Sheffield Station to the ground. Turn left out of the station and walk along Shear Street and into Shoreham Street. Cross St Mary's Road and you'll eventually come to the ground by turning right down John Street or Cherry Street.

other clubs have copied, but the United original is by far and away the best. Rivals: Sheffield Wednesday (they call each other the Pigs) are the main rivals – but Barnsley, Rotherham United and Leeds aren't the most welcome visitors.

Sheffield Wednesday

Hear the Owls a hootin'

Almost 20 years on from the Hillsborough tragedy that led to the development of all-seater stadia in the top tiers of British football, the Owls' home is regarded as one of the best-equipped outside the Premiership.

Attendances hover around the 24,000 mark, so you're sure to get an electric atmosphere here. The Steel City derby featuring arch foes Sheffield United is one hell of an occasion and it's back for 2007/08.

Witness what happened when the derby transferred to London for the 1993 FA Cup semi-final at Wembley. More than 75,000 Blades and Owls fans packed the famous Twin Towers for a match in which Chris Waddle and Mark Bright shone to send the blue-and-white army into ecstasy. Wednesday lost both domestic finals to Arsenal that year by the same 2-1 scoreline.

Owls' fans have been starved of success since, although the 39,814 capacity Hillsborough went on to stage several games at Euro '96 to cement its reputation as a world-class venue.

The terracing of the West Stand (or Leppings Lane end as it is known) was closed for two years following the stadium disaster. It emerged as an all-seater section.

Away support is normally restricted to the upper tier (4,194 seats), apart from bigger games when the 2,464-seat lower tier is opened.

The North West terrace, the only corner of the ground to be filled, is all-seated but uncovered and only comes into use when the West Stand is completely full. This is a rare occurrence but can happen for local derbies and cup ties, increasing the away allocation to 8,000.

Eating out

Hillsborough offers chip butties and more of the same. If you plan on eating in the city, don't underestimate the time it will take to travel to the ground three miles north of the centre. But you'll find plenty of places to eat in between and around the ground. If you want a good pork sarnie, head to Beres Pork Shop on Halifax Road. Four Lanes chippy opposite the away end on Leppings Lane is convenient for a greasy snack.

Penistone Road North (A61), bordering the other end of the ground, is home to McDonald's, KFC and Pizza Hut. It also contains one of the best Chinese takeaways in Sheffield. Hoong Too offers large, meaty, inexpensive portions, according to locals who've been there. You can wash down a hot pie with a pint or two at The Horse and Jockey on Wadsley Lane, which leads uphill from the Leppings Lane end. The New Barrack Inn on Penistone Road North is an old-fashioned real ale pub which does good grub.

Mine's a pint

No alcohol is served to visiting supporters at the ground but you'll have no problem finding a liquid lunch nearby. Away-friendly pubs are plentiful. The Horse and Jockey on Wadsley Lane, close to the Park Hotel, is one of

---

Club Information Stadium: Hillsborough, Sheffield S6 1SW Capacity: 39,814 (all seated) Tel: 0870 9991867 Web: www.swfc.co.uk Colours: Blue and white Train: Sheffield Songs: 'Honolulu Wednesday' and anything which is popular with

the favourites and only 10 minutes' walk from Hillsborough. A wide range of lagers and bitters are on tap. On the A61, the main pubs for away fans are the Norfolk Arms and The Red Lion in Grenoside. The Pheasant is just off Halifax Road before the railway bridge and the New Bridge Inn a bit further on. No-go zones for away fans on the A61 nearer the ground are The Park, The Gate and The Travellers. They're for home fans only. As are several at Hillsborough Corner, including The Ball, The Shaky and Legends. Real ale fans will enjoy The New Barrack Tavern - it's a CAMRA pub with fine beers. The Fat Cat and Kelham Island Tavern –both close together, in Alma Street and Russell Street respectively – are also worth a look.

Stopping over in Sheffield?

 Novotel at Arundel Gate makes a good city centre base (0114 278 1781). It's only five minutes' walk from the train station, and shops, restaurants, pubs and clubs are nearby. Rooms from £55 per night. Grosvenor House hotel on Charter Square is also located at the heart of the city and offers rooms at about £50 (0114 272 0041). For an unpretentious, friendly boutique hotel in the cultural, retail and commercial centre, book a room (around £45) at The Cutlers Hotel on George Street (0114 273 9939).

Sheffield's only independently-owned boutique hotel is minutes away from all the city's transport links and diverse attractions. Doubles from £65.

If you do one thing in Sheffield...

Head to the Magna Science Adventure Centre. Celebrating the power and force of earth, air, fire and water, you can walk on air, feel the heat of a fire tornado, blast water cannons, see 'The Big Melt' or try the indoor bungee jump.

What's in a name?

The name originates from Wednesday Cricket Club whose players were craftsmen who took a half day off every Wednesday. The football club was known as "The Wednesday" until 1929 when it was officially rebadged Sheffield Wednesday. The Owls get their nickname from the suburb of Sheffield that used to be known as Owlerton.

Don't mention

That Sheffield Wednesday were originally nicknamed 'The Blades' and played at Bramall Lane: it probably won't go down well with fans of either team in the city.

Do Mention

The Boxing Day Massacre: a famous match on 26th December 1979, when Wednesday beat city rivals United 4-0 in a Third Division fixture. The 1991 League Cup win.

Travel Information

CAR
Exit the M1 at Junction 36 and take the A61 towards Sheffield. After eight miles or so you will come to Hillsborough Stadium on your right. There is limited street parking for early birds, otherwise head to one of the car parks along the A61, where you'll be able to park for about three quid, or opt to park at the ground for a fiver.

TRAIN
Sheffield Station is more than two miles from the ground – so you may want to opt for a taxi or the short walk to the bus station (the number 53, 77 or 80 will get you to the ground in around twenty-five minutes). The best option is the tram: get a blue tram and change to a yellow one in the city centre and head for Leppings Lane.

Wednesdayites Rivals: Mainly Sheffield United (they call each other the Pigs), but also Leeds United, Rotherham United, Barnsley, Chesterfield and Doncaster Rovers.

Shrewsbury Town

The grass is greener at the New Meadow

Excitement is building in this Shropshire market town as the Shrews prepare to kick off the 2007/08 season in their new £15 million home. The 10,000-seat New Meadow at Oteley Road, near Meole Brace, is a replacement for the old but picturesque Gay Meadow which was situated on the banks of the River Severn.

A charming little stadium it may have been, but locals say the ground suffered from a lack of maintenance after the club announced plans to relocate. So Shrews' fans are wasting no time in bragging about their shiny new nest to anyone who cares to listen. Dave Matthias of the 'Blue and Amber' fanzine told a local newspaper: "Other clubs and other towns are going to be very jealous."

Away fans will surely have plenty to say about that. Nice ground, chaps, shame about the footballing product, for instance... or something a little snappier. See, there's not been much for rival fans to get jealous about in recent years as Shrewsbury Town have flattered to deceive on the pitch. A brief spell playing Conference football in 2003/04 will never be forgotten.

For travelling supporters, the main benefit of the new stadium is that the pitch will not be waterlogged as frequently as the Gay Meadow, which flooded when the Severn swelled. It wasn't uncommon for several games a season to be postponed due to a soggy playing surface.

The away end is the North Stand on Oteley Road. Concourse facilities are housed under the north, south and west stands.

74. SHREWSBURY TOWN

Eating out

Various food and beverages are available at outlets around the ground. If you're in town you'll find satisfying dishes at any number of drinking establishments. The Dun Cow on Abbey Foregate prides itself on its range of steaks and also offers a long list of 'classic meals' as well as Desperate Dan Pies. Three Fishes on Fish Street is another good inn where you can get home-made food. Fast food and takeaways are easy to find in the small town centre. For something more refined, try Chambers Restaurant and bar on Church Street (varied menu) or The Cornhouse on Wyle Cop, where you can get individually-cooked dishes using fresh produce. La Trattoria on Fish Street serves up authentic Italian cuisine.

Mine's a pint

Shrewsbury has a fine cast of wonderful pubs. Pop into many of them and you'll get a hearty welcome from the locals. Among the recommended pubs for away fans is The Crown on Abbey Foregate. It has a comfy bar and lounge and shows Sky Sports on matchdays. The Crown Inn, backing onto the river at Longden Coleham, is worth a visit. It's cosy inside but always a good atmosphere and there's a big beer garden to accommodate drinkers during fine weather. The Nags

---

Club Information Stadium: New Meadow, Oteley Road, Shrewsbury SY2 6QQ Capacity: 10,000 (all seated) Tel: 01743 360111 Web: www.shrewsburytown.com Train: Shrewsbury Colours: Blue, amber & white

Head on Wyle Cop is popular with home and away fans. However, The Dun Cow is the pick of the pubs. Set in a Tudor building complete with all its period features, this is the place to spend a few hours. An open fire and oversized sofas are added bonuses when the real ale is this good. Guest beers are available throughout the year and the venue regularly hosts live music.

Stopping over in Shrewsbury?

 Located in glorious countryside near to the Welsh borders, Shrewsbury is one of England's finest medieval market towns. It's worth staying, if you don't fancy traipsing back home after the football. The 164 Bed & Breakfast is cheap and central - at Abbey Foregate - perfect for exploring the town and a pub crawl (01743 367750). Charnwood Guesthouse on the outskirts on London Road is an alternative which won't break the bank (01743 359196). Others include The Sleep Inn hotel, just two miles from the centre from the A5. It offers large bedrooms - from around £50 - and good facilities, plus a restaurant and bar with plasma screen showing Sky Sports (01743 276020). The Lion Hotel, a 17th century Coach Inn in the heart of Shrewsbury (Wyle Cop) enjoys a reputation for friendly hospitality (bookings on 0870 609 6167).

If you do one thing in Shrewsbury...

Shrewsbury's town centre is full of character (600 listed buildings) and won't take long to explore if you're here for the day. Anyone staying for longer can visit to The Ironbridge Gorge Museums near the world's first iron bridge spanning the River Severn. For a family day out, The Severn Valley Railway is recommended as it's one of Shropshire's biggest attractions. The steam railway runs for 16 miles through countryside and restored stations. Catch the train at Bridgnorth station, south-east of Shrewsbury.

Nice Smalls

Shrewsbury's 1980s blue-and-amber shirt was worn by Harry Shearer's bass-playing Derek Smalls in cult film This Is Spinal Tap, starring members of the fictional heavy-metal rock band Spinal Tap.

Don't mention

That Shrewsbury went from heroes to zeroes in less than six months in the 2002/03 season: they knocked Everton out of the FA Cup in one of the most famous cup giant killings of all-time in January, but in May were relegated out of the Football League.

Do mention

Arthur Rowley: Shrews' all-time leading goalscorer and the Town record holder for most goals in a single season - 38.

Travel Information

CAR
Take the M54 onto the A5. Ignore the signs for the town centre at the junction with the A49. Instead take the A5112 to Shrewsbury at the next roundabout. At the next roundabout take the fourth exit onto the B4380. The stadium is on the right. There is limited parking at the stadium and the local area has restrictions; however the club do operate a park and ride scheme.

TRAIN
Shrewsbury Station is served by trains from Birmingham New Street & Crewe; it is two miles away from the stadium, so you may want to consider a taxi or bus from the bus station in the town centre. If you want to walk it: head left out of the station and into Castle Street and on into St Mary's Street. At the end of the road take a left and left again, you should find yourself on Wyle Cop. Once you cross the river turn right into Coleman Head, which becomes Belle Vue Road and then Hereford Road. After about a mile you'll reach a roundabout, where you take the second exit into Oteley Road for the stadium.

Songs: The team run out to 'Catch Us If You Can' – they've been doing it on and off for 23 years. Rivals: Wrexham, Hereford and Walsall.

Southampton

Saints alive

Like many of the new-builds, St Mary's Stadium is compact and stunning in its design – and a great place to watch football, either as a home fan or visiting supporter.

Southampton moved from The Dell to the new £32 million stadium in 2001, ending their years at the old ground on a high when Matt Le Tissier slotted home a last-gasp winner to seal a 3-2 victory over Arsenal.

The new venue was something of a return to the club's roots. The Saints were formed in 1885 as Southampton St Mary's before they upped sticks to the then newly-constructed £10,000 Dell. With a capacity of 32,689, St Mary's is more than double the size of the Saints' former pad. It includes first-class concourse amenities with televisions, catering bars and decent toilet facilities to enhance the quality of your visit. There are also two external toilet blocks situated by the main ticket office and the Saints Megastore.

You'll be sitting in the Northam Stand with anything up to 3,200 away fans. The views are excellent and the stewards friendly. Two 34 square metre big screens - one above each goal - add to the entertainment spectacle.

The Saints' most memorable day came in 1976 when the club - a second division side managed by Lawrie McMenemy - won the FA Cup for the first time, beating hot favourites Manchester United 1-0.

Eating out

Hollands Pies and cheeseburgers are tasty delights on offer at St Mary's. As the ground is in an industrial area, there's nothing to recommend in the way of cafés and takeaways in the immediate locale. Best to grab a quick snack in the town centre, a 15-minute walk away. Check out the Bargate Shopping Centre for cheap eats. The area of Above Bar includes KFC and Subway. Oxford Street close to the marinas is best for café bars and restaurants serving contemporary British and continental cuisine. Olive Tree Restaurant is Mediterranean. Bedford Place boasts some good places including Langley's Bistro where you choose from an à la carte menu or try one of their fresh fish specials. Other top-rated eateries include the classy Café Soleil on High Street, which offers brunch specials on the weekend. Check the huge menu at City Beijing on the same street. Ennio's Al Porto on Town Quay Road is highly regarded for its pastas and fresh seafood. Ocean Village marina has a wealth of restaurants and bars, including a harbour-side Pitcher & Piano.

Mine's a pint

Glug down a few jars on the concourses at St Mary's or settle in a local watering hole for a couple of hours. Options are limited near the stadium, but The Chapel Inn on Marine

Parade isn't too far away. Make sure to miss out St Mary's Street's Saints-only pubs such as The OddFellows Arms or the Plume Of Feathers. Northam Social Club on Northam Road is a hive of footy fans on matchdays with visiting supporters made welcome and some food laid on. The Prince Of Wales and the Old Farmhouse nearby are traditional boozers with real ales on tap and food menus. Both are walkable from the ground. As is The Court Jester on Terminus Terrace, which serves reasonably priced food. Away-friendly bars are also found at Shamrock Quay, a little further away. In town, The Victory opposite the station remains enduringly popular among the away contingent. The beer garden is a bonus in warm weather. The usual chain bars are dotted around the centre and most are okay but avoid The Toad In The Park, a haven for youthful Saints fans. Ikon and Diva in Leisure World is on West Quay Road, billed as the largest nightclub in the south.

Stopping over in Southampton?

A night or weekend stay in Southampton holds plenty of promise with many waterfront attractions. Budget accommodation includes Premier Travel Inn due to its handy location to St Mary's and the city centre (0870 238 3308) and Holiday Inn on Herbert Walker Avenue (0870 400 9073).The Southampton Park Hotel on Cumberland Place is convenient for the Bedford Place nightlife while not more than 15 minutes to the ground (0808 144 9494). Rooms cost around £60. The Dolphin Hotel (023 8033 9955) and Star Hotel (023 8033 9939) are options with similar rates on High Street.

If you do one thing in Southampton...

This major port town is best explored on foot and the city's vibrant waterfront should be top of your list. Ocean Village marina is popular for its mixture of shops, restaurants, cinemas and bars. The waterfront also hosts the annual Southampton Boat Show and provides the setting for Cowes Week.

The hitman and Le God

Mick Channon, a prolific marksman for Saints in the 1970s and early 80s, is Southampton's leading goalscorer (185). Matt Le Tissier notched up 161 in his 16-year stint at the club.

Don't mention

Harry Redknapp: he came to Saints from arch rivals Pompey, the team were relegated out of the Premiership and he then went back to Pompey.

Do mention

Matt Le Tissier: a legend to supporters of the club, he turned down moves to better teams, like Spurs, and stayed at the club for all of his career.

Travel Information

CAR
From the M3 take the A33 into Southampton. Continue on the A33 until you reach the junction with the A3024 Northam Road and turn left onto this road towards Northam. A right onto the B3038 Britannia Road leads to the stadium. You can pre-book parking at the stadium for around a fiver, or opt to park in the city centre and walk. Otherwise there is a park and ride option at junction 8 of the M27.

TRAIN
It's about a twenty-minute walk from Southampton Central Station. Exit the right along Blechynden Terrace and then turn right into Havelock Road and left into Civic Centre Road. Stay on this road, which becomes New Road. At the end of New Road turn right then left into Northam Road and right into Britannia Road. There is also a shuttle bus in operation taking fans from the station to the ground. This operates from the Blechynden Terrace bus stop outside the station.

Central Colours: Red, white & black Songs: Classically, 'When The Saints Go Marching In'. Rivals: Portsmouth.

Southend United

Leaving their Roots

The Shrimpers could soon be welcoming away fans to a new home. Impressive plans for their new 22,000-seater stadium at Fossetts Farm got the go-ahead from Southend and Rochford councillors in January 2007. However, the plans were later called in by the government and a public enquiry is due to start in the autumn. Designed by HOK Sport, the global architecture firm behind Arsenal's Emirates Stadium, the stadium scheme incorporates training facilities, retail space, a 114-bed hotel, conference venue and flats.

Club chiefs are hoping the stadium, costing upwards of £25 million, will be up and running in time for the 2009/10 season, although this seems a little optimistic. Finance for the scheme would come from the enabling development, the sale of Roots Hall and development of the training ground into a retail park.

Like all smaller clubs playing at this level of football, Southend sees a 24/7 multi-purpose facility as the Holy Grail - a revenue-generator with the potential to significantly boost stadium income and fund quality additions to the squad.

It seems the 12,392-capacity Roots Hall, Southend's home since 1955, will be no sad loss to anyone. Roots Hall is a crumbling infrastructure, admits Blues chairman Ron Martin. "This would give us significant funding above the revenue streams that ordinarily operate from a football club, because we will have property and leisure incomes included within this development," he says.

Certainly, away supporters, currently housed in the covered all-seated North Stand, are unlikely to mourn its passing. The stand is a converted terrace with seats bolted on when the stadium was made all-seater. The seating isn't that comfy with minimal legroom, you get restricted views of the pitch and the toilet facilities leave a lot to be desired. Fossetts Farm - bring it on.

Eating out

Refreshments within the away area are served from a 'Transport Café' type establishment, complete with tables and chairs. For a couple of quid you can get a bacon roll, hot dog or cheeseburgers. The Fish House across the road from Roots Hall is described as a brilliant chippy and it's become a favourite with all fans. It has a restaurant area for those wanting a gut-busting plate of food. Super Pizza, located behind the North Bank on Victoria Avenue, is one of the nearest takeaways. If you're hungry, try the cafe on Button Road which does a big breakfast. Stroll into Southend and you'll find pretty much all you need on High Street or London Road, crammed with fast food outlets and restaurants. Fleur de Provence is a top-rated French restaurant on Alexandra Street. Food is good and the staff are welcoming.

Mine's a pint

The Golden Lion on Victoria Avenue is the premier venue for visiting supporters as it's so close to the away turnstiles. A range of real ales is available and it has a big screen, pool tables and serves sandwiches on matchdays. There's a beer garden at the rear for warm weather. It's only yards from The Spread Eagle, which is similarly equipped and known for its

Club Information Stadium: Roots Hall, Victoria Avenue, Southend-On-Sea SS2 6NQ Capacity: 12,392 (all seated) Tel: 01702 304050 Web: www.southendunited.co.uk Train: Prittlewell Colours: Blue Songs: 'We ain't

variety of ales. Some away fans congregate in The Blue Boar, also on this stretch of road, mingling with home fans in a rather cosy environment. The Railway on East Street is mainly a 'home' pub and it can get a bit hostile if away fans make their presence felt with some attitude. But it does have table football! North Road pub The Nelson is a better port of call - it's a traditional away-friendly ale house and only a short walk to the ground. A secluded, lawned beer-garden with ample seating makes it a popular place in the spring and summer months. Eastern Esplanade and Marine Parade are the recommended areas for night-time revelry.

Stopping over in Southend?

 The seafront is littered with B&Bs and guesthouses. You could turn up unannounced and find somewhere fairly quickly. The Tower Hotel is a small friendly family-run hotel on Alexandra Road, which does B&B with doubles from £55 (01702 348635). It's close to all the town's amenities. You know what you'll get at the Travelodge on Chichester Road. It's near the main train station and well placed for the football and town centre activities (01702 612694). Southend's Premier Travel Inn is located on the A127 at the intersection with the B1013, adjacent to Tesco supermarket (08701 977 235).

If you do one thing in Southend...

Enjoy a bracing walk along Southend Pier - the longest pleasure pier in the world. Built in 1830, it stretches 1.33 miles into the Thames Estuary. Visit the museum at the shore end, RNLI Lifeboat Station at the Pier Head, or splash the cash in the amusements. Adventure Island on Marine Parade & Western Esplanade provides over 40 great rides and attractions suitable for all.

Why the Shrimpers?

Fishermen caught shrimps in the Thames until the 1950s, giving the club their nickname. But club chiefs still seem to prefer the Blues tag, perhaps because it makes United sound less parochial. Many years ago, former chairman Vic Jobson dropped the shrimp from the club's badge to improve the club's image but a campaign by fans brought it back... a victory for tradition.

Don't mention

Back-to-back relegations in the 1990s: Southend were in all sorts of bother both on and off the pitch. The downward slide only ended once they'd slid into the Football League's basement.

Do mention

Freddy Eastwood: one of United's best players in recent times, he helped the club win two promotions and was called up to the Welsh international squad.

cockneys we're Southenders tra la la la la...' and any song to aggravate Colchester. Rivals: Colchester, Leyton Orient and West Ham.

Stockport County

Fancy a sing-song?

Whatever your mode of transport, Edgeley Park is easily accessible. County share the ground with Sale Sharks, the Guinness Premiership rugby union outfit. As all-seater stadia go, the 11,000-capacity venue doesn't rank among the best in the division for away support - there's no roof on the stand dedicated to visiting fans.

But Hatters' fans - a nickname referencing Stockport's history as the centre of the hat-making industry, though they prefer the 'County' label - are a passionate shower.

The Sharks may enjoy bigger gates but the County faithful lay claim to all the best tunes - they even like to pretend The Cheadle End is louder than Liverpool's Kop. They published a booklet of 100 County favourites from four decades called 'A Swaying Mass of Humanity' and released 'Songs of the Cheadle End', an album of 46 of the best Hatters' hits. It includes such priceless lyrical masterpieces as, erm, 'The Can-Can' and 'All Around My Hat'. Enough said.

The old Cheadle End was a simple timber and corrugated tin structure. During the 1960s, 3,000 County fanatics regularly packed into the stand and lent their vocal backing to an appreciative team. Its modern replacement is the 5,000-seat Robinson's Brewery Stand built in the mid-1990s.

Edgeley Park can accommodate up to 2,500 visitors, mostly housed in The Vernon Stand, which is split between home and away support. The Railway End is also allocated to opposition fans if needed. There have been ongoing talks between the club and local council about redeveloping the stand, in the mould of the Robinson's Brewery Stand, but no firm plans have surfaced.

Best not to argue with the overzealous stewards, according to County fans. They have a fearsome reputation and won't tolerate any backchat... or people standing up in their seats.

Eating out

Try the stadium's Edgeley Burger if you dare, basically a burger topped with lardy doner meat. Other food kiosks dotted around the ground offer more wholesome snacks. Fast-food joints, takeaways and cafes are found in the shopping area along nearby Castle Street. Various pubs along this road also do food. Or you could book a sit-down meal in the Robinson's Brewery Stand's 500-capacity restaurant. The club offers a £25 package for away supporters, which includes a three-course carvery meal, programme and pre-match entertainment. A selection of restaurants - including Indians, Italians and Chinese diners - are just a 10-minute walk from the ground.

Mine's a pint

Castle Street's watering holes are the most convenient for a game. The Sir Robert Peel is a Greenalls pub with a games room. The Royal Oak, Prince Albert and The Grapes Hotel are bustling locals. Three minutes from the ground, you'll find The Armoury at Shaw Heath, a pub retaining much of its 1920s' charm. For the

Club Information Stadium: Edgeley Park, Hardcastle Road, Stockport SK3 9DD Capacity: 11,000 (all seated) Tel: 01612 868900 Web: www.stockportcounty.com Train: Stockport Colours: Blue & white Songs: Plenty of generic offering with a

town's best choice of real ale, including some micro-brews, dive into The Crown Inn on Heaton Lane. The Nelson, opposite the town hall on Wellington Road South/Greek Street, also does a tasty line of guest beers. Other good taverns are scattered along the A6 and include The George and The Unity.

Stopping over in Stockport?

 Manchester, just eight miles up the road, has better options. But if you don't want to journey there, you'll find some cheap, well-run B&Bs and hotels in and around Stockport.

The Wycliffe Hotel in Edgeley is recommended for its "superb food" (0161 477 5395). You're also guaranteed a pleasant stay at its sister hotel/B&B on Buxton Road, The Alma Lodge, a 30-minute walk from the ground (0161 483 4431). The Premier Lodge on Churchgate in the town centre meets all basic requirements and is good for Stockport's nightlife (0870 700 1484).

Full leisure facilities are available at The Britannia Hotel on Dialstone Lane (0161 930 1000).

More upmarket is the four-star Eleven Didsbury Park, a Victorian town house set in the fashionable Manchester suburb of Didsbury (0161 448 7711).

If you only do one thing in Stockport...

You could easily kill a few hours at Stockport's Grand Central shopping and leisure complex. It has a cinema, swimming pool and bowling alley, department stores and many eateries. Manchester isn't far away either and for more information on the sights and sounds, see our city guide.

In safe hands

In summer 2005, ownership of the club transferred to County's supporters' trust in a bid to revive its financial fortunes. The move has paid dividends. Stockport's now one of only a few supporter-owned clubs in the country.

Don't mention

Carlton Palmer: he had a disastrous spell as manager which ended in relegation at the end of the 2001/02 season.

Do mention

1996/97: County won promotion to the second tier of English football and reached the semi-final of the League Cup – claiming three Premiership scalps along the way!

Travel Information

CAR
Exit the M6 at junction 19 onto the A556 towards Manchester. Join the M56 towards Manchester Airport and then the M60 towards Stockport. Leave the M60 at junction 1 towards Stockport. At the second set of traffic lights go right onto the A560 towards Cheadle, then left into Edgeley Road for the ground.

TRAIN
Stockport Station is served by trains from Manchester Piccadilly and it's only a very short walk to and from the ground. Exit left out of the station and up Station Road. Go straight over the roundabout and turn left into Caroline Street for the ground.

favourite being 'You are my County, my only County, you make me happy when skies are grey...' Rivals: Manchester City, Crewe Alexandra and Oldham.

Stoke City

Sleeping giant... number 24

It's now 10 years since the great Sir Stanley Matthews opened Britannia Stadium. The unveiling marked the beginning of a new chapter for the Potters, following their move from the Victoria Ground where they spent the previous 119 years.

But the honeymoon period was short-lived. Stoke City's fortunes on the pitch nosedived and they were relegated in their first season at The Brit. The horror show included a 7-0 drubbing at the hands of Birmingham and a clutch of other painful thrashings.

Such performances initially failed to endear Potters' fans to the ground but they now feel a greater attachment to the stadium and the team's revival continues apace. The club's takeover by local businessman Peter Coates in May 2006 was a stabilising factor. His dreams of a Premiership berth is the stuff of fantasy football until a team is built to challenge for promotion - and the omens aren't good even if they do go up.

Making it into the top-flight is one thing; staying there is quite another. Potters fans know this only too well. The last time they entertained the big guns of English football was in 1984/85, but they swiftly departed the old First Division, bagging only three wins and 17 points from 42 games. In fact, Stoke's only major success to date is the 1972 League Cup.

At least the 28,383-capacity stadium is on a par with some of the Premier League's mid-table roosts. The South Stand holding 4,800 visiting spectators affords good views of the action and features more than adequate refreshment and toilet facilities. Passions run high among Stoke City fans, so you can expect a boisterous reception.

Eating out

The visitors' stand includes snack bars selling the usual matchday fare. The Harvester pub/restaurant next to the ground is good for cheap meals and welcomes away fans. But you are likely to be in for a long wait. Visiting support can also grab a bite to eat at the Power League Centre adjacent to the stadium. Nearby Campbell Road has two sandwich shops.

There's an abundance of greasy takeaways and cafés in Stoke town centre and plenty of places to pick up oatcakes and Wrights pies, the local specialities in the Potteries. Burslem – a few miles away and in Vale territory - has a number of decent places to eat. If you're after some classy British cuisine, head for Denrys, a restaurant over two levels in an old Victorian building on St. Johns Square. The neighbouring suburb of Hanley offers plenty of dining options. Roberto's on Pall Mall is an Italian with a good reputation. Good Indians include Bombay Club, on Hartshill Road in Stoke, and Jalsa on George Street in Newcastle-under-Lyme.

Mine's a pint

You might want to grab a beer at the stadium - Stoke's ground is not great for an away day booze-up due to its location on the site of a former colliery. There's a dearth of traditional taverns

---

Club Information Stadium: Britannia Stadium, Stanley Matthews Way, Stoke On Trent ST4 4EG Capacity: 28,383 (all seated) Tel: 01782 592221 Web: www.stokecityfc.com Colours: Red & white Songs: They have their own rendition of

nearby. Alternatively, seek liquid refreshment at The Harvester pub or The Power League Centre where you can expect a lively pre-match atmosphere. Do not go into any town centre pubs. There's really no telling what kind of reaction you might receive. Other pubs frequented by visiting support include The Plough Motel on Campbell Road, closer to the site of the old Victoria Ground, and The Gardener's Retreat across the way on Sideway Road. If you've travelled by train, turn right out of the station and head for the Roebuck or the Fawn & Firkin pub. But you'll need to get a taxi or bus to the ground. Hanley and Newcastle-under-Lyme offer a diverse collection of pubs and bars for a top night out.

Stopping over in Stoke?

 Express by Holiday Inn on Sir Stanley Matthews Way next to the ground is value for money and just three miles from Hanley for shopping, leisure and nightlife (01782 377000). The Borough Arms Hotel on Kings Street, Newcastle-under-Lyme, is recommended for a cheap night (01782 629421). The independently-owned hotel is in the style of a traditional English town centre coaching inn. Another option is the four-star Best Western Moat House on Festival Way, Stoke, a short drive from either junctions 15 or 16 of the M6 (01782 609988). Also recommended

is Manor House Hotel, a converted farmhouse in Alsager on the Cheshire-Staffordshire border (01270 884000). It's eight miles from Stoke-on-Trent but a pleasant place to stay. Rooms from £50.

If you do one thing in Stoke...

Waterworld at Stoke's Festival Park boosts the first-ever indoor water rollercoaster ride. Other options include nearby Alton Towers and the Tamworth Snowdome – which has real snow all year round. If that doesn't turn you on, you could always spend a few hours at the nearby Jodrell Bank Observatory. The centre is home to the Lovell Radio Telescope and has interactive exhibitions devoted to the thrill of space and space travel.

Turner off

Former Blue Peter presenter Anthea Turner was born in Stoke. She came 15th in Channel 4's 2003 survey of the '100 Worst Britons We Love to Hate'.

Don't mention

The Icelandic revolution: Icelandic owners took over Stoke in 1999 and promised so much, but in reality delivered little – except for a number of Icelandic players and management staff.

Do mention

Ex-players like Sir Geoff Hurst, Sir Stanley Matthews and Peter Shilton to name a few.

Travel Information

CAR
Exit the M6 at junction 15 and take the A500 towards Stoke. You will see the stadium on your right, go past it, turning right onto the A50 towards Uttoxeter and turn around at the next junction. Tickets for the stadium car parks in advance for under a fiver.

TRAIN
Stoke Station is over three miles away and a very long walk, including some dual carriageways so it's recommended to take a taxi or bus. You can catch a bus from Glebe Street in Stoke to the Britannia Stadium and back. For Glebe Street turn right from the station and head down Station Road. At the traffic lights at the bottom of the road turn right to go along Leek Road and across the A500 dual carriageway into Glebe Street. A return ticket is around three pounds for adults, with concessions for children and senior citizens.

'Delilah' by Tom Jones and sing songs generally aimed at abusing Port Vale, their local rivals. Rivals: Port Vale and Crewe Alexandra.

Sunderland

Away fans' favourite

Sunderland's magnificent 49,000-seat Stadium of Light is the spiritual home for Geordie-bashing locals – never more so than now they're back in the Premiership.

The Black Cats moved to the Stadium of Light in 1997 after 99 years at Roker Park. On the banks of the Wear, the site of the old Monkwearmouth Colliery, it is a proud landmark for Wearside.

A cauldron famous for producing an intense atmosphere, the stadium is widely regarded amongst football followers of all colours as one of the best in the UK for the matchday experience and spectator comfort.

The four-Star UEFA venue - in 2006/07 the biggest stadium outside the Premiership - was voted 'Best Away Ground' in the 2007 Football League Awards by BBC Five Live listeners.

Proud Sunderland supporters have turned the Stadium of Light into something a bit special, as SAFC chief executive Peter Walker noted after the club collected the award: "It is more than just bricks and mortar, it's about the people and the fans who create a great atmosphere."

It helps that the Black Cats are again attracting crowds of 40,000-plus. The atmosphere reaches fever pitch when Prokofiev's stirring 'Dance of the Knights' segues into U2's 'Elevation' as the teams run onto the pitch.

The buzz of a Sunderland away game and the hospitality of locals (if you're not from Newcastle or Middlesbrough) make this among the most enjoyable fixtures on the footballing calendar.

Away fans are allocated a maximum of 3,000 seats in the two-tiered Metro FM Stand, which offers decent views of the action.

Eating out

Special offers on club grub at the snack bars include pizza & pint deals. Burger vans around the ground are perfect for something to soak up a few lagers. If you're walking from the city centre - only five minutes from the stadium - you could nip into one of Greggs baker's shops for a sarnie or pasty. Or pick up some fast food from a takeaway on Bridge Street en route to the ground. There are plenty of chippies around town. For a good sit-down meal, try the Chinese or Indian restaurants on Bridge Street – although real curry connoisseurs should head to Ocean Road in South Shields, the north-east's equivalent of the curry mile. The best post-match restaurants are in the centre - and there's plenty to choose from. Angelos on West Sunniside is a recommended Italian. Thai Manor on Foyle Street offers good value. Hollathans café-bar on John Street is a swanky pad that aims to provide that little bit extra on the food and drink front. Stone-baked pizzas, tasty burgers and sizzling steaks dot the menu.

Mine's a pint

Opposite the stadium away fans mix well with home supporters in the Colliery Tavern. The other away pub of choice is Old Orleans on Wessington Way, about 10 minutes' walk from the ground: American-

---

Club Information Stadium: Stadium Of Light, Sunderland SR5 1SU Capacity: 49,000 (all seated) Tel: 01915 515000 Web: www.safc.com Train: Sunderland Metro: St Peters Station or Stadium of Light Colours: Red & white Songs:

style food with everything reasonably priced - good offers on food sometimes available. The efficient park-and-ride to the stadium picks up from outside. Sunderland is a friendly place which opens its arms to visitors on matchdays. Most hostelries around the stadium and downtown are considered away-friendly. Try The Kings Arms in Beach Street for great ales and brilliant free post-match soup on cold days. The Halfway House on Southwick Road and The Fort on Roker Avenue are said to be okay. Head to The Harbour View or Queen Vic on the waterfront if you want a few real ales in a lively environment. City centre highlights include Fitzgeralds on Green Terrace, ranked by locals as one of the finest real ale pubs in the city centre.

Stopping over in Sunderland?

 Plenty of B&Bs on St. Georges Terrace and Roker Terrace near the seafront. The Balmoral Guest House on Roker Terrace is one budget option with sea views (0191 565 9217) or try the Tavistock Roker Hotel on the same road. This sizeable Victorian hotel retains many period features and is close to the city centre with rooms at reasonable rates (0191 567 1786). Travelodge in the city centre is on Low Row in easy reach of the city centre (0870 191 1550). The Marriott Hotel on Queens Parade is more expensive (0191 5292041).

If you do one thing in Sunderland...

The largest city between Leeds and Edinburgh has a proud industrial heritage in glass-making - the National Glass Centre is near the stadium - shipbuilding and coal-mining. It's a city on the up but top tourist attractions are to be found elsewhere - a 30-minute Metro ride away in Gateshead. Go to a concert at the architectural wonder that is The Sage Gateshead or to the Baltic Centre for Contemporary Art on the River Tyne, with a dynamic, diverse and international programme of art.

It's a steal

The Stadium of Light originally cost about £23 million to build. Almost double the size, the new Wembley Stadium opened in March 2007 with a £757 million price tag.

Don't mention

That Sunderland hold the record for the lowest points total in the Premiership: they amassed just 15 points in 2005/06, beating their own previous record of just 19 a few seasons earlier.

Do mention

Roy Keane: he's pretty popular after taking them from bottom of the Championship on nil points after six games to champions of the league and gaining automatic promotion to the Premiership. Peter Reid: he also led Sunderland into the Premiership.

Travel Information

CAR
Exit the A1 at junction 62 and take the A690 towards Sunderland. After about eight miles turn onto the A19 and then take the second slip road towards Sunderland. Take the bridge crossing over the River Wear and turn right onto the A1231 to Sunderland. After four roundabouts and then two sets of traffic lights you will see the stadium car park on your right. There is limited parking at the ground and surrounding streets, so you may choose to park in the city centre and walk to the ground.

TRAIN/METRO
It is about fifteen minutes' walk from Sunderland Station to the stadium. Exit the train station left down High Street West. Turn left into Fawcett Street and over the Wear Bridge. Turn left into Millennium Way. The Metro stations Stadium of Light and St Peters both serve the stadium. Both are incredibly close to the stadium, and away supporters should alight at St Peters Station as it is closer to the away end.

'Sunderland till I die...' and songs that most clubs sing just with their own club names in. Rivals: Newcastle and Middlesbrough.

Swansea City

Swansea and its elephants

Liberty Stadium, better known as Morfa or White Rock by home fans, is an impressive change of scenery for the Swans. City's move from the Vetch Field after 93 years has given the club a new lease of life and fans turn up in their droves these days. Few tears were shed when Swansea left their knackered former home.

The purpose-built 20,500-seat replacement - shared with Ospreys regional rugby club - is the premier conference and events venue in south-west Wales and forms part of a mixed-use retail and leisure development. It markets itself as an ideal place to hold a wedding ceremony.

People in the stadium construction industry like to astound with useless facts about their state-of-the-art sporting palaces with the weight of double-decker buses or elephants often used as handy comparisons. And so it is with Liberty Stadium. The upper floors and roof structure are supported by 2,500 tonnes of structural steelwork. Fact. Which is reportedly equal to the weight of "300 average-sized African elephants or 1,400 Ford Focus cars". Which begs the question - exactly how much do these floppy-eared beasts weigh and when does a moderately-sized elephant become an obese one?

The North Stand accommodates up to 3,000 away supporters. It's a comfortable spot affording fantastic views of the game. The wide and well-equipped concourse facilities for visiting fans take some beating. One downside is the very jobsworthy stewards, according to some locals.

The most important thing to remember when planning a trip to Swansea City is that you must buy tickets in advance from your club's ticket office as there's no cash admission here on matchdays.

Eating out

Concourse outlets provide food and drinks, albeit a bit on the expensive side. The Morfa retail park has a KFC and Pizza Hut and there's Rossi's chippy across the road. Vesuvio Pizzeria is directly opposite, too. Morrisons supermarket at the park is a useful port of call for snacks and cheap eats. Frankie & Benny's, the 1950s New York-style diner which serves authentic American and Italian dishes, is right on the stadium's doorstep.

You'll find a variety of places down town - Wind Street and Kingsway are the best areas. Restaurants specialise in everything from Spanish and French to Thai, Vietnamese and Indonesian cuisine. If you have an appetite for fruits of the sea, sample Swansea's fresh sea food. Hanson's on Trawler Road at the marina is recommended for its innovative fish menu. Gallini's at the marina is famed for its traditional Italian and fish meals. Miah's bar, café and restaurant on St. Helens Road has a good reputation for its Indian cuisine. In Mumbles, you'll get classy British cuisine at Patricks on Mumbles Road.

Mine's a pint

You can buy beers on the stadium concourse. There are no real away pubs near the ground. However, several are frequented by visitors, including Frankie &

Club Information Stadium: Liberty Stadium Morfa, Swansea SA1 2FA Capacity: 20,500 (all seated) Tel: 01792 616600 Web: www.swanseacity.net Train: Swansea High Street Station Colours: White and black Songs: 'Lee Trundle My Lord' is a

Benny's and the Brewer's Fayre next door. The Coopers Arms on Neath Road is a large pub with plenty of drinks on draught and an extensive, good value food menu, while The Station Inn on Hamilton Street is a cosy place and people spill out into the beer garden during the summer. Or you can prop up the bar at The Globe on Mysydd Road with a fine real ale in hand. Bar meals are available.

Don't set foot in The Railway on Siloh Road - the fact that it's adorned with Swans memorabilia speaks volumes. For post-match revelling, head for Wind Street and Kingsway down town, packed with an array of pubs, bars and clubs. Stay in Mumbles if you want to try the Mumbles Mile pub crawl.

Stopping over in Swansea?

Plenty of good, cheap B&Bs on Mumbles seafront. Sea Haven, a B&B, is recommended (01792 653131). Premier Travel Inn on Wind Street is conveniently located for the nightlife (0870 990 6562). Ramada Jarvis Hotel on Phoenix Way is a short drive from the ground and within easy reach of picturesque beaches and attractions such as Swansea's marina and the hills of the Brecon Beacons (01792 310330). Rooms are priced at about £70. A tad more expensive is family-owned Towers Hotel at Jersey Marine on the outskirts of Swansea

(01792 814155). The Morgans Hotel at Somerset Place is the upmarket option (01792 484848) just yards away from the city centre.

If you do one thing in Swansea...

Take a trip to Mumbles and the scenic Gower Peninsula, the first place in Britain to be designated as an 'Area of Outstanding Natural Beauty'. The Gower is a great place to spend a few hours during a weekend break taking in the football. Its sandy beaches are some of the best in Britain.

The green, green artificial grass of home

The pitch is a hybrid of natural grass and artificial fibres, a system designed to maintain the quality of the surface year-round. About 20 million artificial grass fibres are sewn into the Desso pitch, 20 millimetres apart and looped to a depth of 20 centimetres. This enables the plant roots to entwine and develop around the fibre, guaranteeing maximum stability.

Don't mention

Leon Knight: scored some goals to help Swansea into the play-offs in 2004/05, but attitude led to a one-way ticket out of Swansea.

Do mention

Lee Trundle: a firm favourite with the fans due to his impressive skills and goalscoring. Cyril The Swan: City's legendary mascot.

Travel Information

CAR
Leave the M4 at Junction 45 and take the A4067 into the City centre. After about two miles or so you will reach the stadium on your left. Car parking at the stadium is for permit holders only and most of the immediate residential areas around the stadium now have 'residents only' parking schemes in place. Away supporters are encouraged to use the park and ride at Swansea Vale. It is signposted off the A4067, shortly after leaving the M4. It costs a fiver and there are separate buses for away fans; they will wait outside the away stand at the end.

TRAIN
Swansea High Street Station is on the main line route from London Paddington. It's about half-an-hour's walk to the Liberty Stadium: exit the station and turn right up the High Street, then turn right onto Bridge Street, which leads into Neath Road and right to the stadium. There are also local bus services, while a taxi will cost under a fiver.

popular ode to their striker; they also like anything which has anti-Cardiff or anti-English connotations. Rivals: Cardiff City.

Swindon Town

Saving the Robins' nest

Not content with having one of the larger grounds in this corner of the Football League (15,728), Swindon Town want to take the club to the next level with a stadium redevelopment. The aim is to emulate the success of local rivals Reading who have reaped financial rewards from their move to the Madejski Stadium.

The supporters' trust has unveiled plans to transform the County Ground into a 20,000-capacity venue with affordable flats and a hotel. Additional leisure facilities for the community also feature. Town chiefs are currently in negotiations with the local borough council over the redevelopment of the stadium, their home for over 100 years.

Robins fans have busied themselves with various campaigns in recent years. There's been the 'Save Our Home' and 'Keep Town in Swindon' campaigns. It's a coalition of the official supporters' club, the supporters' trust and the fans behind the 'Loud and Proud' initiative.

What's this 'Loud and Proud' campaign? Depression and disillusionment in the 2005/06 season when Town were bottom of League One, led a group of fans to form Red Army Loud & Proud. And their aims? "To be the 12th man at every match" and "to have fun on match days". Admirable stuff. Has such behaviour improved the mood of the Swindon faithful and inspired the team to new heights? Just look around the ground for any cheerful Robins fans - the proof is in the tweating!

Away fans are accommodated in the Arkells Stand at the north end (1,200 covered seats) and an overflow area in the Stratton Bank End if necessary. This section is exposed to the elements so come prepared if the weather's bad.

Eating out

Food kiosks at the County Ground will meet most people's dietary needs. There is a Burger King on Queens Drive, just two minutes from the ground, and a McDonald's one mile away at Greenbridge Retail Park where you'll also find a KFC. There's not much else near the ground, bar a few takeaways and locals which do food, such as The Malt & Hops on Drove Road. You'll have better luck hunting down pre-match snacks and meals in the town centre. Further afield but worth the drive for the cut-above-the-rest nosh is The Blunsdon Arms on Thamesdown Drive in the north of Swindon with main meals or burgers, lighter bites and sandwiches. Food is fresh and service is said to be quick. The pub's leather sofas, pieces of art and nooks & crannies give it a bit of character and make it a good port of call before or after a game.

Mine's a pint

Home and away fans mingle happily in The Malt & Hops, only five minutes from the ground. The Grove is a few strides further down Drove Road and recommended for travelling supporters. Whatever you do, however, don't make the mistake of

---

Club Information Stadium: County Ground, County Road, Swindon SN1 2ED
Capacity: 15,728 (all seated) Tel: 08704 431969 Web: www.swindontownfc.co.uk
Train: Swindon Colours: Red and white Songs: A version of 'All Things Bright And

strolling into The County Ground Hotel on County Road - this is strictly for home fans. Enter at your peril. The Glue Pot on Emlyn Square and Steam Railway on Newport Street are among only a handful of real ale pubs in Swindon listed in CAMRA's 2007 Good Beer Guide.

Stopping over in Swindon?

Doubtful you'll want to hang around for much longer than an afternoon. Bristol's not far away and has better options. However, if you're really determined to stay in Swindon, here are a few tips. The large Goddard Arms Hotel on High Street in the old part of town has rooms from about £55 (01793 692313). Just off junction 16 of the M4 is Express By Holiday Inn. Similarly priced, it's close to various commercial parks and ideally located for travel to Bath, Bristol and the Cotswolds (01793 818800). Or check out The Lodge at The Wiltshire Golf & Country Club, Vastern, Wootton Bassett. This modern hotel with an 18-hole golf course and full leisure facilities is only a short distance from the M4 (01793 849999).

If you do one thing in Swindon...

If a look around the Old Town doesn't float your boat, or you're not up to a wander around the rolling Wiltshire countryside, there's only one thing for it - get dizzy driving the multi-mini roundabout dubbed 'Magic Roundabout'.

Really, you'd be fool to miss out on Swindon's greatest eyesore-cum-attraction. Devised to handle traffic converging at a point from five directions, it even inspired a pop song: 'English Roundabout' by Swindon's very own XTC.

The short of the town

Swindon chairman Willie Carson, the squeaky-voiced five-times British Champion Jockey and BBC racing expert, had a total of 3,828 wins to his name in UK racing. One of the funniest sights at Royal Ascot (or any televised race requiring its presenters to don smart clobber) is always 7st 10lb Carson in a top hat.

Don't mention

Their one and only season in the Premiership: 1993/94 saw them record just five wins and let in 100 goals.

Do mention

Former players Harry Morris and Maurice Owen: Morris scored an astonishing 229 goals in just 279 games and Owen made 601 appearances.

Travel Information

CAR
The ground is well signposted. Exit the M4 at junction 15 and follow the A345 Queens Drive to Drake's roundabout. Turn left towards the Magic Roundabout, and you will see the County Ground on the corner of this roundabout. There is parking at the ground for under a fiver, plus plenty of street parking.

TRAIN
Swindon Station is served by trains from London, Reading and Bristol and it's about ten minutes' walk to the ground. Leave the station, cross the road into Wellington Street and turn left into Manchester Road, following it to the end, which will lead you to County Road and the County Ground.

Tottenham Hotspur

Raising their game

Where the Lilywhites' future home lies remains unclear. Club chiefs are keen to improve the capacity for home support but no concrete plans have surfaced on whether this will involve redevelopment of the 36,257-seater White Hart Lane or a move to a new stadium.

Tottenham chairman Daniel Levy has stated for some time that the focus is on improving the team and construction of a new academy facility before any redevelopment or move to a new stadium.

In order to compete in the same revenue league as the Premiership's big guns, and in Europe, something must be done - and soon. The message from Spurs fans, who don't have to look far to glimpse the 60,000-seat Emirates Stadium, is clear enough: "We're being left behind and we need to sort something out now."

Improving the notoriously poor transport infrastructure under any ground expansion presents a major challenge and may force the club to relocate. But Spurs fans stand divided on the prospect of moving to a purpose-built stadium in the mould of their north London rivals - history and tradition are held dear by some.

Normally 2,900 away fans can be seated in the corner between the South and West Stands (maximum of 4,000). The closeness of Spurs fans always allows for some colourful exchanges. Don't let your passions boil over - the police control centre is up above you.

White Hart Lane mainline station is five minutes walk from the stadium, which joins the Victoria Line tube service via Seven Sisters. The stadium is also accessible via a bus service from Seven Sisters. The M25 is 20 minutes' drive from the stadium, once the rush has passed.

Eating out

Pre-match tucker is available in and around the ground. There's an abundance of places to pick up a snack or have a meal on Tottenham High Road. From chippies, cafés and sandwich shops to curry houses and restaurants of many types, you'll soon find something you fancy. Sainsbury's is a stone's throw away, if you prefer supermarket offerings. Tottenham Biegel Bakery comes highly recommended. There's also a Greek place called Taste Of The Med and the Caribbean restaurant Ekubanz Paradise. More cafés, takeaways and eating joints are found heading south to Seven Sisters. You could eat like a king at Van Langs on High Road, Wood Green, where the à la carte dishes cover cuisine from China, Malaysia, Thailand and Vietnam. It does a reasonably-priced lunch buffet.

For similarly classy dining, try The Lock Dining Bar at Hale Wharf in Tottenham Hale, a top-notch place to eat before or after a match and within walking distance. It serves a modern international menu, including a good Sunday lunch. Otherwise, dine out in Islington or Camden Town, if you don't want to journey into the city.

Club Information Stadium: White Hart Lane, Bill Nicholson Way, 748 High Rd, Tottenham, London N17 0AP Capacity: 36,257 (all seated) Tel: 08704 205000 Web: www.tottenham hotspur.com Colours: White and navy Train: White Hart Lane Tube: Seven

Mine's a pint

If you plan to drink in some of the pubs around the ground, either don't wear colours at all or cover your jerseys. The Park next to Northumberland Park Station admits visiting supporters and is only a short walk from the away end. Northumberland Arms nearby is a decent boozer with a lively pre-match atmosphere. Gilpins Bell is a large Wetherspoons, left on to High Road if you're coming out of White Hart Lane Station, which gets busy with both sets of supporters on matchdays and has a variety of ales.

The Bootlaces across the road is a sports bar and, like many pubs in this neighbourhood, is decorated with Spurs memorabilia. The drinks are nothing special but it has plenty of TVs tuned to Sky and a large beer garden.

Avoid partisan pubs close to the ground such as The Cockerel, The Corner Pin and The Bell and Hare.

Stopping over in Tottenham?

Stay on the north side of London by all means, but head for a more attractive location. Spring Park Hotel on Seven Sisters Road overlooks Finsbury Park and is ideally situated for public transport into central London. A one-minute walk takes you to Manor House Underground station on the Piccadilly line, which has direct access to the west end and city. Five minutes away is Finsbury Park station. Doubles are from £40 (020 8800 6030).

B&B at the Majestic Hotel on the same road is similarly priced (020 8800 2022). Aber Hotel on Crouch Hill, Finsbury Park, offers high standards at reasonable rates (020 8340 2847).

Crouch End has a plethora of restaurants, bars and shops.

If you do one thing in north London...

Visit Camden Town's open-air and indoor markets, each with their own distinctive feel. Get to Camden by tube on the Northern line or alight at Chalk Farm.

Trophy wins

Spurs have won the FA Cup eight times. Their last major trophy was the 1998-99 League Cup.

Don't mention

Christian Gross: he had a terrible spell in charge at White Hart Lane.

Do mention

Bill Nicholson: legendary manager who led Spurs to the double in 1960/61.

Travel Information

CAR
At junction 25 of the M25 take the A10 towards Enfield. At the roundabout with the A406 North Circular, take a left turn onto the A406 and then take a right onto the A1010 which becomes Tottenham High Road and you will come to the ground on your left. There are plenty of unofficial car parks (expect to pay a fiver), plus limited street parking north of the ground.

TRAIN
The nearest tube station is Seven Sisters which is on the Victoria Line – but the ground is at least a twenty minute walk straight up Tottenham High Road – exit left out of the station. You may want to opt for one of the many buses running up Tottenham High Road to the ground. Another option is to take the overland train either from Liverpool Street Station or you can change from the tube to train at Seven Sisters. White Hart Lane Station is a few minutes' walk away. Come out of the station and turn right along White Hart Lane and right into the High Road for the stadium.

Sisters Songs: 'Glory Glory Tottenham Hotspur' is a White Hart Lane original. Rivals: Arsenal and to a much lesser extent Chelsea.

Tranmere Rovers

Viking heritage

Prenton Park became an all-seater ground in 1995 since when only piecemeal improvements have been made. The 16,587-capacity venue is a friendly place to visit and even the smallest number of away fans can make a racket in the Cowshed Stand, which holds about 2,500.

Over the years, Tranmere have toiled away in the shadow of Merseyside's Liverpool and Everton, struggling to attract a loyal following in the face of competition from the two footballing giants. But the club - in Birkenhead on the Wirral Peninsula - have successfully carved out their own identity, making an asset of their location across the Mersey. Friday night matches at Prenton Park have become a regular feature as part of efforts to entice casual fans who would normally head to Anfield or Goodison on a Saturday.

Club chiefs believe Friday night kick-offs can be a huge advantage in a title run-in, allowing Rovers to put pressure on the sides playing on Saturdays - providing they bag three points the night before.

Rovers are the only team in English football with a Viking name. Tranmere, meaning 'cranebird sandbank' in Old Norse, was named by the Norwegian Vikings who settled in Wirral in the 10th century.

Rovers youngster Craig Curran ended last season in some style. In his first appearance at Prenton Park on Easter Monday, he netted within 30 seconds of coming off the bench to help defeat Brighton 2-1. The final game of the season saw the 17-year-old bag a 31-minute hat-trick in his first start in attack as Tranmere beat Brentford 3-1. Curran will be one to watch in 2007/08.

Eating out

Fast food kiosks and a licensed bar for away fans are available in the Cowshed Stand. Food sold at the ground is a bit hit and miss but the hot dogs are said to be superb. Cheaper and better takeaway grub is on offer at the Eastern Delight chip shop on Borough Road, while you'll see other takeaways and restaurants close to the ground.

The Villa Venezia Italian restaurant right next to the ground is highly recommended. The Ruhi Balti House on Woodchurch Lane serves a great Indian. Locals say Heswall, West Kirby, is the best area for top-notch restaurants. What's Cookin on Telegraph Road in Heswall is a lively and friendly family restaurant worth checking out. And, of course, there's a wealth of dining options across the water in Liverpool.

Mine's a pint

The Mersey Clipper by the stadium car park is the away fans' favourite. Visitors and Rovers fans mix in here quite happily, there's good-natured banter with decent beer and food to boot. The Prenton Park on Borough Road is fine, but generally bustling with the Tranmere faithful. Others within walking distance of the ground are The Halfway House, The Sportsman and

---

Club Information Stadium: Prenton Park, Prenton Road West, Birkenhead CH42 9PY
Capacity: 16,587 (all seated) Tel: 08704 603333 Web: www.tranmererovers.co.uk

The Swan. For a night out on the Wirral, there are some good bars in Hoylake and West Kirby. In Liverpool, Concert Square and Matthews Street offer a diverse collection of drinking venues and are said to be the liveliest parts of town. Heebie Jeebies is an intimate live music venue on Seel Street and recommended for late drinking. According to one in the know: "You can wear your trainers and nobody is orange-coloured".

Stopping over in Tranmere?

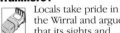Locals take pride in the Wirral and argue that its sights and nightlife compare favourably with the attractions in Liverpool just a few miles away. If you're eager to explore the Wirral Peninsula or north Wales, one accommodation option is The Villa Venezia opposite the ground (0151 608 9212). The Village Leisure Hotel Wirral, Bromborough, is a good base and has rooms from £59 (0151 643 1616). It has gym, restaurant and bar facilities. Liverpool, however, is only 10 minutes' train ride from Prenton Park and has so much more to offer.

If you do one thing in Tranmere...

Locals rave about the promenades in New Brighton, West Kirby and Hoylake. And there's Spaceport, the space-themed attraction at Seacombe Ferry Terminal, Wirral. You can become a virtual astronaut in the 360 degree Space Dome show and explore the solar system through exciting interactives and audio visual exhibits. The Mersey Ferry to Liverpool is an experience and the city itself has cultural attractions in spades. It's not the European Capital of Culture 2008 for nothing, you know. For more information on Liverpool, see our city guide.

The legendary John Aldridge

The former Liverpool hitman made an immediate impact at Rovers when he arrived in 1991 following a spell at Real Sociedad. An inspirational figure in the team, he was appointed player-manager in 1996. Aldo netted 170 goals for Tranmere before hanging up his boots at the age of 40 to concentrate on team affairs. He quit in 2001 and hasn't managed anywhere since.

Don't mention

Phil Neal: the former Bolton manager is incredibly unpopular with Rovers fans after comments made prior to the 1990/91 play-offs, saying Tranmere didn't deserve to go up.

Do mention

Mark Palios: the former FA chief played 286 games for Rovers and scored 33 goals before moving to Crewe.

Travel Information

CAR
From the M6/M56 join the M53 until junction 4. Take the B5151 Mount Road from the fourth exit of the roundabout. After two-and-a-half miles, as Mount Road becomes Storeton Road, turn right into Prenton Road West for the ground.

TRAIN
The closest railway stations are Rock Ferry and Birkenhead Central. Both are served by Liverpool Lime Street, and it's about a twenty minute walk from either to and from the ground. From Rock Ferry exit right out of the station along Bedford Road and on into Bedford Avenue until you reach the roundabout. Turn right into Bebington Road and then left down Everest Road for the ground. It's best to get off at Rock Ferry if you're walking, but from Birkenhead Central there is a Soccerbus which leaves every 15 minutes from just outside the station. It's free if you have a match ticket, otherwise it's 50p.

Train: Rock Ferry Colours: White Songs: Songs poking fun at Bolton Wanderers are popular. Rivals: Bolton, Liverpool, Everton, Chester

Walsall

Cinderella of the West Midlands?

The Saddlers moved from Fellows Park to the newly-erected Bescot Stadium in 1990. Crowds at the 11,300-seat venue rarely exceed 6,000, making Walsall the smallest of the Black Country clubs plying their trade in the Football League.

Visitor allocation in the William Sharp Stand is 1,900 but more space is available in the Banks's and H. L. Fellows stands if the size of the away following demands it (up to 3,000 in total). It's a bit cramped and there are restricted views due to the stand's supporting pillars. However, there are future plans to redevelop the 'away' end, and it may be modelled on the two-tier cantilever Purple Stand.

Not all Saddlers' fans are content with the stadium either. Asked how it could be improved for all fans, one local puts it bluntly enough: "Invent a time machine, go back about 18 years and do it all differently."

Referred to unkindly by some as the 'Cinderella' club of the West Midlands, Walsall's record down the years is a patchy one. They've yo-yoed between the divisions in the last decade, failing to consolidate - after being promoted to the second tier - on several occasions.

With little to cheer about in recent times, Saddlers' fans love to reminisce about any win over a fierce local rival - however long ago. The opening day hammering of West Bromwich Albion on the first day of the 2003/04 season always gets a mention. As does the presence of the talismanic Paul Merson in the side that year. Sweet dreams were made of these memories. Obviously, the Walsall faithful would have liked to avoid relegation. But who cares about the drop when you can dine out on a 4-1 victory over the Baggies?

Eating out

Chicken balti pies and Bovril go well together don't they? Fine fare for footy folk on a damp day. Two catering kiosks for away supporters stock these with a variety of other hot food, drinks and snacks. Fact: Walsall FC were the first league club to sell these pies. Other crusty delicacies include Cornish pasties and the cheese & onion variety. You can also try the Saddlers Club at the Bescot Crescent end of the ground which has a large function room, lounge, games and family room and is very welcoming. There's a McDonald's on a retail park near the stadium and a decent chippy called Oyster's in town, where you can enjoy a slap-up sit-down meal. In town, try Sofias for Italian nosh or Pucci for a pizza. The Arbor Lights pub on Lichfield Street does some cracking cheap food. Ikea in Wednesbury offers some cheap eats, if you can stand the crowds. There's a greater variety of restaurants to be found in Birmingham.

Mine's a pint

Sink a pint at The Saddlers Club but get there early as it fills up quickly

Club Information Stadium: Bank's Stadium, Bescot Crescent, Walsall, W Midlands WS1 4SA (Formerly the Bescot Stadium) Capacity: 11,300 (all seated) Tel: 08704 420442 Web: www.saddlers.co.uk Train: Bescot Colours: Red and white Songs: "Stand up if you

on matchdays. A small admission fee is charged, by the way.

Bescot Stadium is not well served by local pubs.

The nearest and best away pub is The King George V on Wallows Lane - it's 10 minutes' walk from the ground, opposite Morrisons supermarket.

One to avoid at all costs if you're sporting rival colours is The Fullbrook on West Bromwich Road.

Those with a taste for real ale will enjoy The Royal Oak on Lord Street.

Stopping over in Walsall?

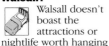 Walsall doesn't boast the attractions or nightlife worth hanging around for.

There's nothing stopping you from bedding down here, but Birmingham is just down the road with much more to offer, especially if you're planning a shopping spree and/or night out on the sauce.

Still, the Ramada Encore on Bescot Crescent is an option, with rooms from £45 (01922 639100).

It's helpfully adjacent to Bescot railway station, which offers direct twenty minute links to Birmingham New Street station.

If you only do one thing in Walsall...

Not far away is Dudley Zoo and Castle, if you like ogling endangered species.

Or you can get your thrills at Drayton Manor Theme Park, near Tamworth, Staffordshire.

However, nearby Birmingham has the pick of the sights and attractions. For more information, see our city guide.

Famous scalps

Walsall's legendary 2-0 FA Cup win over Arsenal in 1933 is mentioned during a game of pool in the film Fever Pitch. The Saddlers also notched famous FA Cup wins against Manchester United and Newcastle United in 1975.

Don't mention

That Walsall are considered the smallest of all the West Midlands teams: it won't go down well with their loyal bunch of followers, who have laudibly shunned the attractions of the area's selection of Premiership and Championship sides.

Do mention

Gilbert Alsop: he scored over one hundred goals for the club and helped Walsall famously defeat Arsenal 2-0 in the FA Cup in the 1930s.

Travel Information

CAR
The Bescot Stadium is next to the M6. From the south exit the M6 at Junction 7 and take the A34 towards Walsall. At the end of the dual carriageway turn left into Walstead Road.
If you're coming from the north leave at junction 9 and take the A461 towards Walsall. Bear right on to the A4148 and take a right at the second set of traffic lights.
There's ample parking at the ground, for a few quid per car; alternatively there's street parking.

TRAIN
Bescot Stadium has its own station situated right next to the ground. It's on a local line from Birmingham New Street and the journey time is about twenty minutes.

hate the Wolves" and also a song aimed at the other West Midlands teams which starts: "We are the pride of the Midlands..." Rivals: Wolves, plus West Brom, Birmingham, Villa & Shrewsbury.

Watford

Rebuilding the Hornets' nest

The Hornets were granted planning permission for the first phase of a £32.5 million revamp of Vicarage Road in April 2007. This scheme mainly centres on a housing development at the Rookery end to accommodate key workers from neighbouring Watford General Hospital.

Construction of a new East Stand will eventually follow, replacing the part-condemned and very ramshackle construction on Occupation Road. This will boost capacity to 24,000. Housing association Origin is jointly funding both phases.

Home fans using the Rookery Stand are benefiting from the large concourse extension undertaken in the first quarter of 2007, with additional bar and catering facilities a big bonus.

Part of the Vicarage Road Stand - formerly open terracing until a refurb in 1993/94 - is allocated to away fans, but the whole stand can be given over to larger away followings if necessary. So the allotment of tickets can vary between 2,250 and 4,500 although for Watford's recent Premiership campaign, away fans were given no more than the lower figure. There are unimpeded sightlines from anywhere in this stand and the seating is decent enough with adequate legroom.

The Hornets have called Vicarage Road home since 1922. It is also shared with Saracens, the Guinness Premiership rugby union club which has played here as a tenant since 1997.

Watford were forced to sell their ground in 2003 due to financial problems. But they bought it back two years later for £7.6 million. In 2005, a concert by honorary life president Sir Elton John at Vicarage Road attracted 23,000 mainly Hornets fans and raised £1.3 million, which was later used to repay loans secured against the repurchasing of the stadium's freehold.

Eating out

Vicarage Road supplies the usual club grub but you can easily satisfy your appetite elsewhere. Fry Days next to the ground gets busy but the fish & chips are good value. Ten minutes from the ground is the The Harlequin shopping centre opposite McDonald's, with a variety of fast food outlets, cafés and restaurants including a Burger King, John Lewis eaterie and Pizza Express. Domenic's Snack Bar on Merton Road offers reasonably priced lighter bites. Sarnies on Clarendon Road offers home-made butties to meet all needs. If you're after a hearty sit-down meal, head to The Parade for a selection of restaurants. At The Counting House you can wash down a cheap steak dish with modestly-priced wine, beer or a cocktail. Hanako up the road is a Japanese held in high regard by locals: a bit soulless but the food is described as exceptional and it's cooked fresh to order. Yummy is a recommended Chinese on Charter Place. Nearby Rickmansworth has a number of fine eating establishments. Among them is Robertos on Money Hill - popular for its fish, pasta and meat menu.

Mine's a pint

Avoid the Red Lion opposite the ground - it's a real Hornets'

Club Information Stadium: Vicarage Road, Watford WD18 0ER Capacity: 19,900 (all seated) Tel: 08701 111881 Web: www.watfordfc.com Train: Watford Junction Colours: Yellow and red Songs: Favourites include 'Hornets', 'Yellows'

nest, but Macs Bar round the corner in Addiscombe Road is usually more away fan-friendly. Best though before the match to go to one of the town centre pubs within easy distance of Vicarage Road. The Moon Under Water on the High Street is one of the main away haunts and gets chocca, so get there early if you want to get served quickly. It's a typical Wetherspoons with cheap nosh and drinks but has few other redeeming features, according to local reviewers. If you don't like the sound of this, try the Hogs Head, Rose and Crown or the One Bell on High Street. Mangans on Market Street may just be the best choice for a pre-match snifter. It shows sport on several screens in a more relaxed atmosphere than your traditional footy pub. Doesn't get too packed either. If you arrive at Watford Junction by train, drop into the Flag and Firkin for a quick one to quench your thirst. There are few good real ale pubs in this neck of the woods - Nascot Arms on Stamford Road is probably the best. This Greene King hostelry serves a good range of well-kept beers.

Stopping over in Watford?

 Stay in the Hilton on Elton Way or in the centrally located Premier Travel Inn on Water Lane. You may prefer to stay in and around London if you want to make a weekend of your jaunt to Watford. For more on London guesthouses and hotels, turn to the city guide.

If you do one thing in Watford...

Fantasy Island on Watford Road, Wembley, is the nearest attraction in the locality: a theme park with slides and interactive laser tag games.

Legendary Luther

Luther Blissett is the club's all-time record appearance-maker and goalscorer - he scored 186 times in 503 matches in a Hornets jersey. Blissett hit a hat-trick on his England debut against Luxembourg in 1982.

Don't mention

Gianluca Vialli: the former Chelsea boss got off to a bad start by sacking popular backroom staff members Kenny Jackett and Luther Blissett; he then wasted millions on mediocre signings and Watford plummeted into a financial crisis; with things not much better on the pitch, he refused to resign, so Watford sacked him.

Do mention

Graham Taylor: the former England manager had two spells as boss at Watford and was massively successful in both, winning promotions a-plenty.

Travel Information

CAR
Leave the M1 at junction 5 and take the A4008 into Watford, which will lead right to the stadium. There is no parking at the ground, but there is street parking available and some unofficial car parks for around a fiver.

TRAIN
Leave Watford Junction station and go straight down Clarendon Road all the way to the bottom and turn left into the High Street. Take a right into Market Street and at the end turn left into Whippendell Road. Vicarage Road is on the right.

and "Watford wherever you may be, we are the boys from the Rookery" – and anything abusive towards Luton. Rivals: Luton Town.

West Bromwich Albion

Don't mention the Wolves

The Hawthorns has been home to the Baggies for more than 100 years and is in great shape as a football venue. The last areas of terracing were replaced by two new stands and an all-seater venue was unveiled in 1995.

Since this time, the ground has undergone further modernisation with completion of the £7.5 million East Stand in 2002 making the ground fully enclosed. Demolition of The Woodman pub in 2004 has opened up the possibility of the 28,000-seater being expanded to over 30,000.

Away fans are housed in the Smethwick End, opened in 1994, which accommodates 5,816 and offers good views. Visitors are allocated 3,000 seats for one half of the stand, although the whole stand is given over to larger away support. The Hawthorns has the dubious honour of being the highest ground in English football. It's 551ft above sea level, you know. Which isn't to say you'll be starved of oxygen when you visit. But you might struggle for a breath of fresh air in the concourse behind the away stand as it gets fairly congested for major clashes.

Baggies' fans enjoy rewinding the clock back to 2001/02 and prattling on about the way Albion overcame an 11-point deficit on arch rivals Wolves to pinch the second automatic promotion spot and end the club's 16-year wait for top-flight football.

Albion and Wolves fans really hate each other with a passion. It's one of the most intense rivalries in English football... and it yields some comical chants on derby days such as "Always **** on the gold and black" to the tune of Python's "Always look on the bright side of life". Actually, that's the sum total of lyrics and it doesn't even work that well.

Eating out

Catering at the ground is pretty good, although you won't get much change out of three quid for a burger or hot dog. Hot drinks include Bovril and soup. The Albion restaurant at the ground is quite popular among away fans seeking a bit of comfort and a good feed on matchdays. There's a dearth of cafés and takeaways around the ground due to its location - it's about one mile from West Bromwich town centre. High Street has it all, from McDonald's and KFC to sandwich shops, healthier eateries and numerous Indian and Chinese restaurants. The Park Inn Hotel, just off the M5 junction and only half a mile from The Hawthorns, is recommended for its meals in the traditional carvery and à la carte in Rafferty's Restaurant. You could park here, eat and walk to the ground.

Mine's a pint

Alcohol is available at the ground and many away fans end up drinking here because there are no pubs nearby. The Royal Oak on the A41 is about 10 minutes' walk away and sure to be bustling with a large contingent of away fans. Good-natured banter is the order of the day - the beer's not bad and it offers Asian food. Further into town is The Desi Junction, which has won over some away fans with its friendly atmosphere, Balti

---

Club Information Stadium: The Hawthorns, Halfords Lane, West Bromwich, West Midlands, B71 4LF Capacity: 28,003 (all seated) Tel: 08700 668888 Web: www.wba.co.uk Train: Smethick Rolfe Street Metro: The Hawthorns Colours: Navy and

buffets and curries. Albion fans and the away brigade mix well in The Vine on Roebuck Street. It's family-friendly and specialises in Indian fast food. The Park Inn Hotel is also away-friendly. Places to avoid because they're designated Baggies' pubs are The Waggon & Horses on Halfords Lane and The Island Inn by Trinity Way. You probably won't get a great reception in the pubs near West Bromwich bus station, particularly The Rising Sun in Barton Street, billed as "the best pub with Albion attitude". West Bromwich is packed with many other traditional boozers and you can make merry here on a night out. High Street is one popular area. The Odd Fellows Arms, The Wheatsheaf and The Old Hop Pole are recommended for real ale quaffers.

Stopping over in West Bromwich?

 The Park Inn Hotel on Birmingham Road, mentioned previously, has rooms from about £60 per night. The Village Hotel & Leisure Club at Castlegate Park, Birmingham Road, Dudley, is also recommended and offers accommodation at similar rates (01384 216600). It's just a short walk to Dudley Zoo and within easy reach of Birmingham city centre and the rest of the Black Country. Birmingham may be a better choice of location for a weekend break or stopover.

It's only a 10-minute ride on the metro from The Hawthorns train station.

If you do one thing in West Bromwich...

Most of the attractions nearby are in Birmingham, which is easy to get to via public transport. Dudley Zoo is good for a few hours of exotic animal gazing, especially if you have kids in tow. It's well signposted from the city.

The legend lives on

The Jeff Astle Memorial Gates were erected in 2003 to commemorate the late Albion striker, who scored the extra-time winner to earn the Baggies their fifth FA Cup win in 1968. He spent 10 years at the club and scored 174 goals in 361 appearances. After his retirement, he popped up on Fantasy Football League, fronted by David Baddiel and Baggies' nut Frank Skinner.

Don't mention

West Brom: locals prefer to give the team them their full title of West Bromwich Albion, although you don't need the Football Club suffix.

Do mention

Legendary former players such as Ronnie Allen, Astle, Willie Johnstone, Bryan Robson. The afro-Caribbean trio of Brendon Batson, Cyrille Regis and Laurie Cunningham: nicknamed 'The Three Degrees' these three were real trailblazers for other black footballers in the UK.

Travel Information

CAR
Leave the M5 at junction 1 taking the A41 towards Birmingham, and you will see the ground on your right. Beware the speed cameras dotted along the A41 at regular intervals. You'll find street parking around the ground, a few matchday car parks in the industrial units around the ground, or at The Hawthorns Station for under a fiver.

TRAIN/METRO
The closest railway station is The Hawthorns which as the name suggests is a short walk (down Halfords Lane) to the ground. It is served by a Metro service from Birmingham Snow Hill Station. Train tickets are not valid on the Metro - a separate return ticket will cost less than a couple of quid. Smethwick Rolfe Street is served by local trains from Birmingham New Street, but about fifteen minutes' walk: come out of the station and up North Western Road and bear right into Brasshouse Lane; where the road splits, bear left down Halford Lane for the stadium.

white Songs: The number one anthem at the Hawthorns is: "Boing Boing, Baggies Baggies, Boing Boing..." Rivals: Mainly Wolves (the Dingles, after the dippy family in Emmerdale), Birmingham and Villa.

West Ham United

Nice shorts Malcolm

The Boleyn Ground, commonly known as Upton Park, has been West Ham's home since 1904 and is likely to remain so for a while yet.

Club chairman Eggert Magnusson signalled his ambition for the faltering Hammers when he engaged in talks with London 2012 organisers about moving to the Olympic Stadium after the games. But the plan was abandoned when it was revealed that the 80,000-seat stadium would be downsized to an even smaller capacity than the present 35,647 seats.

Having touted the idea of expansion on many occasions to lift capacity over 40,000, West Ham are now examining the possibility of building a new stadium with the London Development Agency.

Upton Park was subject to major redevelopment during the 1990s, the last building effort resulting in the two-tier Dr Martens Stand.

Away fans are seated in the lower tier of the Centenary Stand, which can hold up to 3,600. Views are best in seats nearest the home fans but you can get unlucky if you're in the corner block that isn't in line with the pitch - you'll have to twist your body to the right the whole game.

The Hammers did not live up to their reputation for entertaining, attacking football last season. But the club's principles and progressive philosophy are very much part of the fabric of a club which has picked up the FA Cup three times.

Managers and players over the years have embodied these values. Influential skipper Malcolm Allison was so entranced by the wonderful Hungary side of the late 50s that he encouraged West Ham to adopt continental ideas and thinking. Among other things, it resulted in the Hammers being the first team in English football to be kitted out in that rather fetching style of smaller, tighter shorts.

Eating out

Upton Park is one option on matchday. Club legends like Malcolm Allison and John Bond used to congregate at Cassetari's Café after training to plan tactics over food. This place on Barking Road is still going and good for an all-day breakfast. There is no shortage of fast-food outlets near the ground - it's pie & liquor territory so get stuck in. Everything you need is located on Green Street.

The Green Street Café opposite the ground is reportedly a fine venue for plates of fried food and butties. This road is also home to a Dixy Fried Chicken, Greggs bakers, KFC and a Kebabish. Queen's Fish Bar next to Upton Park Station is the pick of the chip shops. Brick Lane offers the best selection of Indian restaurants in London. There are also plenty of down-to-earth eateries on Roman Road, stretching from Mile End to Bow.

Mine's a pint

The Boleyn next to the ground will be packed to the rafters with claret and blue types. The very wise thing to do is to go elsewhere. If you're arriving by tube, duck into The Queens on Green Street, on the way from the station to the ground. It's popular among away fans and you won't find any

Club Information Stadium: Upton Park, Boleyn Ground, Green Street London E13 9AZ Capacity: 35,647 (all seated) Tel: 0208 5482748 Web: www.whufc.com Tube: Upton Park Colours: Claret and blue Songs: West Ham United has a catalogue of songs (you can purchase a CD in the club shop) with the famous 'I'm Forever

bother drinking here. Followers of the club's London rivals or Manchester United should sup somewhere else or keep colours covered. Another pub within walking distance of Upton Park and okay for away fans is The Duke of Edinburgh (turn left out of the tube station to find it). Millers Well on Barking Road, East Ham, is a typical Wetherspoons.

Visiting supporters are welcome in The Central, a spit-and-sawdust pub also found on this road. The Victoria Tavern is a friendly pub near Plaistow Station and a fine boozer for a pre-match jar. Other options for beer quaffing include the bars and pubs at the Royal Docks, which are located just two miles east of Canary Wharf on the north side of the River Thames.

Stopping over in West Ham?

 The hotels at Canary Wharf make a good London base for the football and city attractions. Tube links from these hotels are good but rooms may be a little pricey. For a budget bed, try The Central pub/hotel on Barking Road with rooms from £35 (020 8470 6686).

Custom House Hotel on Victoria Dock Road is good value for money at about £50 a night (020 7474 0011). Situated in the heart of London Docklands, the hotel is a 25-minute drive from Junction 30 of the M25. There are a couple of Express by Holiday Inn hotels offering reasonably priced accommodation - one on Silvertown Way, Canning Town, the other on High Street in Stratford (0870 400 9670).

If you do one thing in east London...

Head west from West Ham on the District Line tube to visit the colourful, vibrant Brick Lane, otherwise known as Banglatown. It's home to the capital's finest curry houses and also a great Sunday market, a mad mixture of treasures and trash.

Brick Lane market, which stretches into Cheshire and Sclater Streets, is open early on Sunday until about 2pm (*www.visitbricklane.com*).

Boss men

West Ham have employed only 11 managers, including Alan Curbishley, since 1902.

Don't mention

That you think West Ham should have been relegated because of the Carlos Tevez affair: it won't go down well.

Do mention

Geoff Hurst, Bobby Moore, Martin Peters: three of England's World Cup winners in 1966, who were in the employ of West Ham United.

Travel Information

CAR
The park-and-tube option is worth considering, with the Upminster Underground Station a good bet – it's just outside the M25. You can park all day for a pound and it's a short distance from junction 29, taking the A127 east. If you want to drive the distance exit the M25 at junction 27 for the M11 southbound and join the North Circular following signs for the City. Leave the A406 at the Barking junction and take the third exit towards East Ham, west along A124 Barking Road and, after several sets of traffic lights, you will eventually reach the ground on your right. If you're coming from the south east, exit the M25 J31 and take the A13 to Barking, picking up the A124 as above. With little street parking, the best option is the pay-and-display car park at Newham Hospital: use the directions as above, but instead of turning right into Green Street, carry straight on for about five hundred metres and turn left into Prince Regent's Lane.

TRAIN
The nearest tube station is Upton Park which is on the District, plus the Hammersmith & City Lines. It is a short walk along Green Street to the ground.

Blowing Bubbles' and 'Bow Bells Are Ringing (For The Claret And Blue)' at the top of the list. Rivals: The oldest rivalry is with Millwall – but Arsenal, Tottenham, Chelsea, Charlton and Manchester United are pretty unpopular at Upton Park.

Wigan Athletic

Reach for the pies

The JJB Stadium has been a fairly happy stomping ground for the Latics in recent seasons but the club still struggles to fill three-quarters of its 25,000 capacity. Nevertheless, the stadium design allows away day trippers to make a proper racket. That's if they're not suffering indigestion from Wigan's famous culinary treats - calling local fans pie-eaters means no disrespect in this part of Greater Manchester.

Pooles, the undisputed king of pie retailing in the town, produces thousands of the stodgy meat delicacies to line the stomachs of those supporting the Latics and rugby league's Wigan Warriors, who also play at the JJB.

Dave Whelan, owner of both teams and the stadium, has his finger in many pies - in fact he owns the pie giant, which produces about 250,000 a day and reportedly shifts some 8,000 at every Latics and Warriors game. Chunky steak and peppery meat are the most popular, if you're asking, and there's no excess of pastry here.

Whelan has pumped a fortune into the club and was behind the development of the JJB, built at a cost of £30 million and opened in 1999. Latics diehards have sung their guts out to inspire 'Plucky Wigan' ever since - their rollercoaster ride in the Premiership continues to defy expectations, something of a fairytale for a club who only entered the Football League in 1978.

Going to Wigan is a good day out, such is the fervent Latics support and the friendly local reception. Seats for away fans in the North Stand, where over 5,000 can be accommodated, have average leg room but provide quality views.

Eating out

Join the pie-munchers. Pooles pies sold at the ground are the best in the Premiership. Meat and potato, cheese and onion, and chunky steak are usually available. Expect a bit of a scrum to reach the food counters. Best to grab something before the match or make haste at the half-time whistle. Alternatively, grab something lardy from one of the burger and pie vans outside the ground or try Rigaletto's housed in the stadium – although you'll need to pre-book via the club. Asda (next door) and Morrisons in town stock a wide range of Poole's pies. A word of warning: you'll get funny looks if you go asking for a Pimblett's pie - they're big business in the St Helens area but the firm is a long-standing rival of Pooles. In the neighbouring Robin Park retail complex you'll find a number of restaurants including Frankie & Bennys, Pizza Hut and Burger King. The Red Robin is a family pub/restaurant a few minutes from the ground. It's more a haven for home fans but if you cover colours and behave you'll be okay.

Le Frog Bistro is a recommended restaurant in town on Upper Dicconson Street with a wide selection of modern English and Mediterranean dishes. Papa Luigi's on Wigan Lane has earned a fine reputation for its pizza and pasta.

Club Information Stadium: The JJB Stadium, Robin Park, Newtown, Wigan WN5 0UZ Capacity: 25,000 (all seated) Tel: 01942 774000 Train: Wallgate/Wigan North Western Web: www.wiganathletic.tv Colours: Blue and white Songs: The rather

Mine's a pint

Sometimes the club erects a beer marquee under the away stand, which is great for pre-match bevvies. The Red Robin down the road serves a range of real ales, while Champions Bar located in the Robin Park sports centre welcomes away fans. The Swan & Railway in the town centre is a rowdy hangout best avoided by away fans. The Orwell on the canalside at the heart of Wigan Pier is perfectly placed for a few scoops on the way from the train station to the JJB, a 10-minute stroll along the canal bank. It has a varied and reasonably-priced hot and cold food menu. The Brocket is a nearby Wetherspoons on Mesnes Road. Last Orders on Wallgate is also handy for the train station. The Anvil on Dorning Street, a pub run by Allgates Brewery, has a superb choice of ales and was named Premiership Pub of the Year by the Football & Real Ale Guide in 2006.

Stopping over in Wigan?

Wigan isn't the kind of north-west outpost to stay a night when the sights and nights out in Liverpool and Manchester beckon. But in case you do, perhaps if you've had one too many fizzy beverages for the road, here are a couple of suggestions. The Bel Air Hotel on Wigan Lane is close to the town centre and less than a mile (ie: a walk) from the JJB (01942 241410). It includes a restaurant and lounge bar. Doubles are priced £45, which includes full English breakfast. The Bellingham Hotel, also on Wigan Lane, offers similarly priced accommodation (01942 243893).

If you do one thing in Wigan...

If you've a few spare hours to kill, why not visit Wigan Pier on the banks of the Leeds-Liverpool Canal. Witness the Trencherfield Mill Engine in action - the world's largest original working mill steam engine - and take a waterbus trip along the canal.

Mighty Trotters

The Latics' local rivals are Bolton Wanderers, who have finished higher in the league than Wigan in every season since 1987/88.

Don't mention

Low attendances: Wigan have always been up against the more traditional sport in the town of Rugby League, with Wigan Warriors a huge success, but football crowds are steadily rising. That Wigan's a rugby-supporting town: that's changing thanks to Whelan.

Do mention

Dave Whelan: the Latics chairman who oversaw a remarkable transformation of Wigan Athletic, from a basement outfit at the dilapidated Springfield Park to the Premiership, with the fabulous JJB.

Travel Information

CAR
If you're coming from the south exit the M6 at junction 25 for the A49 to Wigan. After about two miles you come to a large roundabout with traffic lights. Take the first exit off the roundabout into Robin Park Road for the stadium. If you're coming from north of Wigan, leave the M6 at junction 26 and take the A577 towards Wigan and you'll come onto the A49. As above, exit the traffic-light-controlled roundabout into Robin Park Road.

TRAIN
Wigan's central stations are Wallgate Station and Wigan North Western Station, both within 100 metres of each other and together well served by trains from London, Birmingham, Manchester and Edinburgh. From either station it's a twenty-minute walk to the ground. Whichever you come out of go under the railway bridge. Keeping to the right follow the A49; as you pass under a second railway bridge the JJB Stadium will come into sight. Turn down Robin Park Road and you are there.

bizarre but effective: 'We come from Wigan and we live in mud huts; Ooh, aah, ooh ooh aah; Ooh to be a Wiganah!'
Rivals: Man City, Preston North End, Bolton and Burnley.

Wolverhampton Wanderers

Can anyone wake the sleeping giant?

"Perennial underachievers" and "sleeping giant" are two labels attached to Wolves virtually every year. And with good reason.

The gold-and-black army feel their team deserves to be contesting the Premiership title every year rather than tussling with the makeweights of the Championship. Fair dos. Doesn't every football fan suffer such seasonal affective disorder? True. But Wolves diehards suffer it real bad... the pre-season promotion chat reaches fever pitch. Shame, then, that Wolves frequently fail to deliver. Recent years have seen a succession of big-name managers fail to guide them out of the second tier – although Mick McCarthy came closer than most in 2006/07.

The last time Wolves graced the Premiership was in 2003 - a brief taster after 19 years out of the top flight. But they couldn't keep up and slipped back into Division One the following season.

Wolves' seasonal delusions have something to do with Molineux, a football ground steeped in a rich history dating back to 1889. The Golden Palace has witnessed some gripping football and seen stars emerge in its time, not least striking sensation Steve Bull who hit 50 goals in successive seasons in the late 80s.

Sir Jack Hayward's millions transformed the decaying Molineux in the early 90s. Today, it provides unobstructed views for 28,500 seated supporters. If the club ever manages to establish itself in the Premiership, the corners could be filled and extra tiers added to boost capacity.

Away fans watch from a section of the Jack Harris Stand, which accommodates 2,000. For larger followings, space is also allocated in the lower tier of the Steve Bull Stand.

Eating out

Catering at Molineux is said to be pretty good with chicken balti pies among the offerings. Numerous burger vans around the ground offer reasonably priced nosh, including roast pork rolls and bacon grills. There's an Asda next to the ground, which is handy for a cheap sarnie, snack or all-day breakfast in its café. Fast food joints are found in the main shopping area of Wolverhampton, a 10-minute walk from the ground. You'll discover a variety of kebab houses and takeaways en route. Some town centre shops and takeaways sell roast meat sandwiches. Cleveland Street and Queen Street are dotted with cafés, Indian and Chinese restaurants, amongst others.

Mine's a pint

Most pubs around the ground such as The Wanderer and The Feathers are gold-and-black venues. You may be admitted into The Goal Post behind the Stan Cullis Stand but exercise caution by covering colours otherwise you'll get some stick from rowdy Wolves fans. The same applies for town centre hostelries - cover up or expect abuse

---

Club Information Stadium: Molineux Stadium, Waterloo Road, Wolverhampton WV1 4QR Capacity: 28,500 (all seated) Tel: 08704 420123 Web: www.wolves.co.uk Train: Wolverhampton Colours: Old gold and black Songs: 'Those Were The Days' and 'I Was

or bouncers blocking the route to the bar. The Great Western, behind Wolverhampton train station, is recommended for its range of beer, including guest ales, and food. It can get rammed on matchdays but it's worth it for the service, drinks and pub grub. Like all Wetherspoons pubs, The Moon Under Water on Lichfield Street attracts a mixed crowd but it excels in cheap food and beer. The Litten Tree on Victoria Street is okay for away fans with a DJ kicking out tunes on the weekend. The Varsity and Hogshead on Stafford Street both boast a decent range of beer.

Stopping over in Wolverhampton?

 The best accommodation options in Wolverhampton include the Novotel on Union Street, which offers good value for money (01902 871100). Or try The Connaught Hotel on Tettenhall Road (0870 7522235). It's not far from the town centre or railway station. Rooms are priced upwards of £55. Nearby Birmingham also offers a wide range of hotels.

If you do one thing in Wolverhampton...

If you fancy a flutter on the gee gees at Dunstall Park,

go to Britain's first floodlit all-weather racecourse (0870 220 2442). Saturday evening meetings are themed to ramp up the excitement. Holiday Inn Garden Court Hotel is also on site should you wish to make a night of it. Wolverhampton Racecourse is less than two miles from the city centre and within easy reach of the motorway network. Also check out our city guide for nearby Birmingham.

The agony... and the Sherpa Van Trophy

Wolves lost the 1972 UEFA Cup final 3-2 on aggregate to Tottenham Hotspur. But they made up for it when they beat mighty Burnley to win the Sherpa Van Trophy 16 years later.

Don't mention

The early-to-mid 1980s: Wolves suffered three successive relegations in 1984, 1985 and 1986.

Do mention

Steve Bull: England striker who stuck with the club, despite their Second Division status and scored over three hundred goals. Sir Jack Hayward: very popular chairman who ploughed millions into the club to help redevelop the stadium and build a side which eventually won promotion to the Premiership.

Travel Information

CAR
From the south: Exit the M6 at junction 10 onto the A454 towards Wolverhampton. Turn right at the ring road onto the A4150 and at the second set of lights you will see the ground to the right.
From the north: Exit the M6 at junction 12 and take the A5 towards Telford and then the A449 towards Wolverhampton. At the sixth roundabout, called the Five Ways roundabout, take the fourth exit for Waterloo Road for the ground. You'll find 'football parking' is signposted, plus there is the option of the city centre car pay-and-display car parks which are only a short walk away.

TRAIN
The ground is about fifteen minutes' walk from Wolverhampton Station, which is on the West Coast Mainline and well served by trains from London, Birmingham and Manchester amongst others. To get to the ground leave the station and walk towards the town centre and as you reach the inner ring road turn right. Just follow the ring road as it continues in a circular pattern around to the left. Eventually you will come to Waterloo Road on your right.

Born Under A Wanderers Scarf' to the tune of 'Wandering Star'. Rivals: West Brom (who they claim wear Tesco carrier bags as shirts) are very unpopular, but also Birmingham and Aston Villa.

Wrexham

Trouble and strife in north Wales

Wrexham have played at the Racecourse Ground ever since their formation in 1872. The latest improvements were the construction of the 3,500-seat Mold Road stand and upgrading of other areas in the late 90s.

In recent years, Wrexham have been hit by a series of off-field problems that threatened their very existence. In 2004, the Red Dragons survived an attempt by former chairman Alex Hamilton to evict the club from their stadium so that he could sell it off for redevelopment. Shortly afterwards, they went into administration with huge debts - a move that landed Wrexham with a 10-point deduction under rules governing administration drawn up by the footballing authorities. To add to their woes, they were relegated to the league's bottom tier in 2005.

But there was a change in fortunes a year later - faced with expulsion from the league, a consortium led by local car dealer Neville Dickens bought the club and secured its future.

The away end is the fully-covered Eric Roberts (Builders) Stand, seating 3,800 spectators. The top tier contains just over 2,000 seats and a further 1,000 are available below if demand requires it. Bar the odd pillar, the stand offers brilliant views of the action. If the travelling contingent exceeds capacity of this stand, space is allocated in The Pryce Griffiths Stand and the Sainsbury's Lower Stand.

Wrexham Supporters' Trust, which raised thousands of pounds to help save the club, is now backing plans for the 15,500-capacity ground's redevelopment, which includes replacement of The Kop with an all-seater stand.

Eating out

Refreshments are available from the concession booths at the away end. Pub meals and bar snacks are served at the Plas Coch and Wetherspoons pubs in the vicinity of the stadium as well as town centre venues. Not far from the ground is the Frankie & Benny's Italian diner at Plas Coch Retail Park. Wrexham town centre has numerous dining options, the usual high street fast-food joints (McDonald's and Burger King are on the road into town) and restaurants offering food styles from modern British and Italian to Chinese and Thai are easy to find. Curry Mongul on Bridge Street and Pebble Fish Restaurant on Argyle Street are among them.

Mine's a pint

You're spoilt for choice around the Racecourse Ground. The away fans' favourite is the Banks's Plas Coch at the retail park. There's a relaxed atmosphere and spacious beer garden. But be warned: the pub shuts for some derby games. Probably best to avoid The Turf. Within easy walking distance of the stadium is The Walnut. Walk down Crispin Lane running alongside The Kop, take a right at the junction leading under the railway bridge and follow it up a hill to find it. Take a left at the junction for The Railway Inn. Wrexham town centre is rammed with pubs, bars and

Club Information Stadium: The Racecourse Ground, Mold Road, Wrexham LL11 2AH
Capacity: 15,500 (10,500 seated) Tel: 01978 262129 Web: www.wrexhamfc.co.uk
Train: Wrexham General Colours: Red and white Songs: To the tune of Bread Of Heaven,

nightclubs and is only a 10 minute walk from the visiting supporters' turnstiles. The Wrexham Lager Club is the first pub you'll encounter. Elihu Yale is a Wetherspoons on Regent Street which attracts its fair share of football followers. For real ale enthusiasts, The Horse & Jockey on Hope Street sells guest beers and the Albion Hotel at the top of Town Hill sells Lees beers.

Stopping over in Wrexham?

 Ramada Plaza Wrexham on Ellice Way offers four-star accommodation with decent amenities and services including restaurant and bar (01978 291400). The Lemon Tree hotel, set in a neo-Gothic style building on Rhosddu Road, is a comfortable place located in the town centre. Rooms are priced from £55 and it also features an Italian restaurant where you can get good home-cooked food (01978 261211). Also think about nearby Chester as a destination for a short stay. The Llwyn Onn Hall Hotel is something a bit snazzier with rooms costing about £64. A converted 17th-century manor house on the outskirts of Wrexham, it's ideally situated for visiting Snowdonia, Chester and Bangor-on-Dee (01978 261225).

If you do one thing in Wrexham...

You might not be able to pronounce Pontcysyllte Aqueduct but, impressive as it is, you may want to invest a little time in seeing this civil engineering marvel. The longest and highest navigable cast iron aqueduct in the world carries the Shropshire Union Canal across the River Dee. Alternatively, you can easily pass the time in the quality indoor markets and bustling streets of north Wales's biggest town. If it doesn't conflict with your footballing plans, a good family day out can be had at Bangor-on-Dee Races.

Red Dragons in good voice

You'll hear the roar from Red Dragons fans down at The Kop end - with standing room for 4,000 it's one of the largest and noisiest terraces in the league. Bend an ear to cries of 'Wrexham lager, Wrexham lager... feed me till I want no more. Want no more!' sung to the tune of 'Bread of Heaven'.

Don't mention

Alex Hamilton: former chairman who bought Wrexham with the purpose of evicting the club from the ground and selling the land for development.

Do mention

Micky Thomas: he was a bit of a legend in Wrexham before helping the fourth division club knock champions Arsenal out of the FA Cup in 1991. And his stock fell only slightly when he was nicked for counterfeiting.

Travel Information

CAR
From the north: Follow the A483 towards Wrexham turning off at the junction with the A541 Mold Road, following the signs for Wrexham town centre, and you'll soon see the ground.
From the south: At the end of the M54 join the A5 towards Shrewsbury. After passing the turnings for Shrewsbury and Oswestry, join the A483 towards Wrexham and take the directions as above.
You should find ample street parking in the area around the ground.

TRAIN
Wrexham General Station is located right next to the ground. It is served by trains from Birmingham, Liverpool and London.

fans are heard singing: "Wrexham lager, Wrexham lager, Feed me till I want no more, Feed me till I want no more." Rivals: Chester, Cardiff, Swansea, Tranmere, Crewe and Shrewsbury.

Wycombe Wanderers

More of a Wasps' nest

Opened in 1990, Adams Park has witnessed a series of ground refurbishments which have improved the comfort factor no end. It's a far cry from their previous non-league home, Loakes Park, which reportedly had an 11ft slope from one side to the other.

Adams Park - briefly sponsored and called the Causeway Stadium in recent seasons - is not the easiest place to find, nor is it situated in the most salubrious location. Chairboys' fans have had to get used to traipsing to the end of an industrial estate to see their beloved team play.

Not that you'll see that many marching the two miles from the town centre to the stadium - average attendances are often a shade less than half the 10,000 capacity. A pre-season friendly against Chelsea in July 2005 saw the ground full to bursting for a football match for the first time.

Wasps Rugby Club, who share the Buckinghamshire venue, attract a much larger following, regularly packing out Adams Park. The Guinness Premiership outfit want to see a new access route built and capacity lifted to 15,000. They could seek a move to another location to cash in on their popularity if plans are not progressed.

The Dreams Stand holds 2,000 visitors and there are no restricted views. Matchday food and beverage facilities could be added under the stand as part of a future renovation.

Eating out

Tea bars are at either end of The Dreams Stand. Food and drink wagons are located in the main car park outside the ground on matchdays. For the 2006/07 season, a curry wagon made a successful debut with its spicy fare. As the ground is so far out of town, there's not much else in the way of food and beverage facilities near the ground. Your nearest chippie is 15 minutes or so down the road (the corner of Mill End Road and Dashwood Avenue) travelling in the opposite direction to The Hour Glass pub. High Wycombe is where your hunger will be satisfied - take your pick from a variety of fast food outlets or restaurants. The Spicy Cuisine in Frogmore includes an interesting mix of takeaways. And there are a number of Indian and Italian restaurants dotted around.

Mine's a pint

Nearest pub to the stadium is The Hour Glass on Hillbottom Road. It's a good 10-minute walk. Away fans are admitted but only in small groups. Food is served and there are pool tables and sport showing on the box. The Half Moon on Dashwood Avenue is just over a mile from Adams Park and has a small beer garden. West Wycombe Road has a few hostelries. Bird in Hand

---

Club Information Stadium: Adams Park, Hillbottom Road, Sands, High Wycombe HP12 4HJ Capacity: 10,000 Tel: 01494 472100 Web: www.wycombewanderers.co.uk Train: Wycombe Colours: Navy and light blue Songs: Mostly generic offering reworked to pay

is the pick of these - it sells tasty ales and good food. Closer to the town centre you'll find The Hobgoblin, High Street (Hobgoblin Brewery), serving snacks and with a beer garden. The Falcon on the same street delivers the Wetherspoons experience. Hop in the car to Stokenchurch if you prefer socialising in the cosy confines of a country pub. The Fleur De Lys is highly regarded for its real ales and grub (about five miles from Adams Park). The Clayton Arms and The Osborne Arms, comfy pubs in Lane End, just three miles from Stokenchurch, serve similar.

Stopping over in High Wycombe?

 High Wycombe is about 30 miles west of London and, with good rail links into the capital, it's become a commuter belt.

You could of course stay in London. Alternatively, search for a vacant sign on the B&Bs along West Wycombe Road (20 minutes walk to Adams Park) or hole up at the Holiday Inn, found just off junction 4 of the M40 (0870 400 9042). It's close to the park-and-ride, so you can dump your car and head uptown for a few pre-match sherbets.

If you do one thing in High Wycombe...

There's Wycombe Air Park, just south of the centre, featuring a museum containing a collection of historic flying machines. Otherwise, there's very little to recommend about this town, once known as 'the furniture capital of England'.

It's not famous for anything now, though, unless you count the Chairboys and Wasps.

Well, there is the annual 'weighing-in' ceremony, thought to date from medieval times. Each May, the incoming and outgoing mayors are weighed at a public ceremony to determine if they have grown fat at the ratepayers' expense. Bring some ripe tomatoes!

Record crowd

Wanderers played before 41,591 fans in their 4-0 loss to Chelsea in the semi-final second leg of the 2006/07 League Cup at Stamford Bridge - the biggest crowd they've performed in front of at an opponent's ground in the 120-year history of the club.

Don't mention

Tony Adams: Mr Adams wasn't the most popular man at Adams Park, after an unsuccessful stint as boss which ended in relegation.

Do mention

Martin O'Neill: the genial Northern Irishman led Wycombe into the Football League in 1993 and to an instant promotion the following season.

Travel Information

CAR
Exit the M40 at junction 4 taking the A4010 towards Aylesbury. At the fourth roundabout take a left into Lane End Road, after crossing another roundabout you'll find yourself in Hillbottom Road. There is a car park at the ground for less than a fiver and unofficial car parks around the same price. It can take until next week to get out of them.

TRAIN
Wycombe Station is served by trains from London and Birmingham. On arrival it's worth considering getting the football special bus (number 501) which runs from the station to the ground on match days. Otherwise it's about a two-mile or twenty-five-minute walk: turn left out the station and right along West Wycombe Way. Eventually you'll need to take a left into Chapel Lane and right down Lane End Road for the ground.

homage to Wycombe or poke fun at Oxford United. Rivals: Oxford and Colchester United – which dates back to a 1980s FA Cup tie in which then-non-league Wycombe beat their league rivals.

Yeovil Town

What happened to the famous sloping pitch?

Like the brilliantly-named Yeovil Casuals - the team's earliest incarnation - the pitch with the gradient was scrapped in favour of something more modern. Huish Park replaced the old ground in 1990. The Glovers' previous home is now a Tesco supermarket.

Plans are afoot to modernise and expand the 9,614-capacity stadium to match the club's Championship football ambitions. Average gates of 5,500 to 6,000 don't seem to warrant such a move, but crowds swell when the Glovers entertain local rivals Bristol City or Swansea City, indicative of the numbers that might regularly frequent Somerset's only league ground.

The Glovers have gone from strength to strength since gaining promotion to the Football League for the first time in 2003, after years toiling away as a non-league club specialising in FA Cup giant-killings. They advanced to the first round proper on more than 40 occasions.

Away fans are accommodated in the Yeovil College Stand and the Copse Road Terrace. This uncovered terrace holds 1,500.

Cider lovers will smack their lips about the prospects of a trip to this corner of Somerset. But don't be fooled, it's not all apple orchards and ruddy-cheeked farmers wielding hoes and shouting obscenities in a west country burr. No, the reality is far worse. You'll be watching football in a stadium next to a trading estate in a rather dismal local suburb. Rolling out the cider barrels will have to wait.

Eating out

Catering kiosks sell pasties along with the usual mix of food and drink common to football stadia up and down the land. A three-course meal is available at the stadium's Glovers Restaurant, but don't forget to pre-book. If it's cafés or takeways you're after, don't expect to find any near the ground. Its out of town location means that Asda 10 minutes away is the nearest snack stop. Towards the centre of town there's a Morrisons supermarket for similar fare and a McDonald's. Palmers chippy is next to Brewsters pub en route to the ground.

It's a bit of a hike into Yeovil, so grab a taxi or bus if you're not driving. The award-winning Tamburino Pizza and Pasta Ristorante on South Western Terrace is one of the best restaurants in town, offering the finest authentic Italian dining experience around these parts.

Mine's a pint

Don't bother with the hospitality marquee for your alcohol fix as it doesn't welcome away fans. However, you can seek liquid refreshments at three decent watering holes nearby - The Bell, The Arrow and Brewsters. These are considered okay for visiting supporters. In town, there's plenty to choose from including a Chicago Rock Café on Stars Lane and The

---

Club Information Stadium: Huish Park, Lufton Way, Yeovil, Somerset BA22 8YF
Capacity: 9,614 (5,374 seated) Tel: 01935 423662 Web: www.ytfc.net Train: Pen
Mill Colours: Green and white Songs: Various odes to Yeovil and Somerset, plus the

William Dampier, a Wetherspoons, on Middle Street. The Armoury Inn on The Park is a no-frills boozer and one of many locals with a decent real ale range.

Stopping over in Yeovil?

Greystones Court Guest House at Hendford Hill prides itself on upholding the best traditions of Somerset B&B hospitality (01935 426124). It's little more than a mile from the town centre. Good value accommodation is also available at Globetrotters Lodge on South Street (01935 423328). Prices start from £32. The Alex Lodge opposite the Yeovale leisure complex on South Western Terrace and close to Huish Park is another safe bet for those on a budget (0870 444 1357).

The Yeovil Court Hotel on the outskirts of the market town is more stylish and features a restaurant serving modern British cuisine (01935 863746). It's only a short drive from the so-called Jurassic Coastline and wildlife parks. Alternatively, base yourself in the county town of Taunton about 20 miles away where you can bed down at the Travelodge or Holiday Inn.

If you do one thing in Yeovil...

Drink some cider. And if you're not partial to a drop, hell just give it a chance. Pop into one of the many cider producers scattered around the Somerset countryside,

learn about the production process and slug back a scrumpy or two. You won't regret it.

Probably. If cider is a turn-off, the Fleet Air Museum is the best day out in Yeovil. Check the website - *www.fleetairarm.com* - for regular events and exhibitions galore.

The museum also houses a restaurant, picnic area and children's adventure playground. It is located on the B3151 just off the A303 and A37.

The gloves are off

The town's history of glove-making gave the team the Glovers nickname. It has latterly built its reputation as a centre of the aircraft and defence industries.

Yeovil has spawned a few famous people over the years, including rock singer PJ Harvey and actress Sarah Parish, star of TV shows such as Cutting It and Blackpool.

Don't mention

The famous sloping pitch at Yeovil: that was at their old ground, they moved into the rather nice purpose-built Huish Park in 1990.

Do mention

Gary Johnson: he led the club from the non-league to the heady heights of League One. Giant-killers: the fact that prior to winning League status Yeovil were regarded as the most famous of giant killers in the FA Cup.

Travel Information

CAR
Exit the A303 at the Cartgate roundabout and take the A3088 towards Yeovil. After eight or so miles you will reach the Westlands Airfield roundabout, on the outskirts of Yeovil. At this roundabout turn left up Burnford Lane. After crossing three roundabouts turn left into Corpse Lane for the ground. You can park at the ground for a couple of quid, or there is plenty of street parking in the area around the ground.

TRAIN
Yeovil has two railway stations: Yeovil Junction and Pen Mill. Both are out of town, on the wrong side of Yeovil to the west; the ground is out of town to the east. It's a hefty trek of two to three miles from the ground. So you are strongly advised to get a taxi to the stadium – or if you arrive at Yeovil Junction, then catch the 'Hopper' minibus to the bus station in the town centre and a bus from there out to the stadium.

'Drink Up Your Cider (And Be Merry)' song. Rivals: Weymouth from non-league days; Bournemouth and both Bristol clubs (City and Rovers).

PITCH PUBLISHING WOULD LOVE TO HEAR FROM YOU!

Send us your feedback and in return we might send you a <u>free</u> 2008/09

FOOTBALL FANS GUIDE

Mail us your comments on our existing guide, and/or your own reviews and recommendations for next season. The best will feature in next season's guide, and the contributors will receive a free copy of the new edition. Write to us at our head office address (which can be found in the front of the book) or send us an email by logging onto the 'contact us' section of our website, which can be found at <u>www.pitchpublishing.co.uk.</u>